D0426935

WITHDRAWI

The Ends of the Earth

STUDIES IN ENVIRONMENT AND HISTORY

Editors
Donald Worster   *Brandeis University*
Alfred Crosby   *University of Texas at Austin*

Advisory Board
Reid Bryson   *Institute for Environmental Studies, University of Wisconsin*
Raymond Dasmann   *College Eight, University of California, Santa Cruz*
E. Le Roy Ladurie   *Collège de France*
William McNeill   *Department of History, University of Chicago*
Carolyn Merchant   *College of Natural Resources, University of California, Berkeley*
Thad Tate   *Institute of Early American History and Culture, College of William and Mary*

Other Books in the Series
Donald Worster   *Nature's Economy: A History of Ecological Ideas*
Kenneth F. Kiple   *The Caribbean Slave: A Biological History*
Alfred W. Crosby   *Ecological Imperialism: The Biological Expansion of Europe, 900–1900*
Arthur F. McEvoy   *The Fisherman's Problem: Ecology and Law in the California Fisheries, 1850–1890*
Robert Harms   *Games Against Nature: An Eco-Cultural History of the Nunu of Equatorial Africa*
Warren Dean   *Brazil and the Struggle for Rubber: A Study in Environmental History*
Samuel P. Hays   *Beauty, Health, and Permanence: Environmental Politics in the United States, 1955–1985*
Michael Williams   *Americans and Their Forests: A Historical Geography*

304.209
W898

The Ends of the Earth

Perspectives on Modern Environmental History

Edited by

DONALD WORSTER

Brandeis University

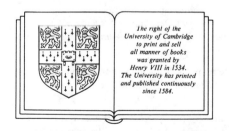

The right of the
University of Cambridge
to print and sell
all manner of books
was granted by
Henry VIII in 1534.
The University has printed
and published continuously
since 1584.

CAMBRIDGE UNIVERSITY PRESS

CAMBRIDGE

NEW YORK NEW ROCHELLE MELBOURNE SYDNEY

LIBRARY ST. MARY'S COLLEGE
176767

Published by the Press Syndicate of the University of Cambridge
The Pitt Building, Trumpington Street, Cambridge CB2 IRP
32 East 57th Street, New York, NY 10022, USA
10 Stamford Road, Oakleigh, Melbourne 3166, Australia

© Cambridge University Press 1988

First published 1988

Printed in the United States of America

Library of Congress Cataloging-in-Publication Data
The Ends of the earth : perspectives on modern environmental history /
edited by Donald Worster.
p.   cm. – (Studies in environment and history)
Bibliography: p.
Includes index.
ISBN 0-521-34365-8. ISBN 0-521-34846-3 (pbk.)
1. Human ecology – History.   2. Nature conservation – History.
3. Environmental policy – History.   I. Worster, Donald, 1941–
II. Series.
GF13.E52   1988
304.2'09 – dc19   88-15293
                                                             CIP

British Library Cataloguing in Publication Data
The ends of the earth : perspectives on
modern environmental history. – (Studies
in environment and history).
1. Man. Ecology to 1988
I. Worster, Donald, 1941 –
304.2'09

ISBN 0 521 34365 8 hard covers
ISBN 0 521 34846 3 paperback

Four chapters are reprinted here, by permission, as follows:

Chapter 2, "Environment, Population, and Technology in Primitive
Societies" (by Ester Boserup) from *Population and Development Review* 2
(March 1976): 21–36. [The original French essay appeared in *Annales* 29 (May–June
1974).]

Chapter 3, "Climatic Fluctuations and Population Problems in Early Modern
History" (by Gustaf Utterström) from *The Scandinavian Economic History
Review* 3 (1955): 3–47.

Chapter 4, "The English Industrial Revolution" (by Richard G. Wilkinson)
from Richard G. Wilkinson, *Poverty and Progress: An Ecological Perspective on
Economic Development* (New York: Praeger Publishers, 1973), chap. 6.

Chapter 5, "Ecological Imperialism: The Overseas Migration of Western Europeans as a
Biological Phenomenon" (by Alfred W. Crosby) from *The Texas Quarterly* 21
(Spring 1978): 10–22.

$12.95 ℋₑₗₗ 10-2-89 (L.L.)

LIBRARY ST. MARY'S

Contents

v

Contents

Preface

THE PURPOSE OF THIS BOOK of essays is to introduce readers to the new and rapidly growing field of environmental history. Every so often comes the question with blunt, honest simplicity, "What is this field all about?" It is easy enough to respond that the field deals with all the interactions people have had with nature in past times. Or to illustrate its themes with an example or two showing how ecological transformations have shaped the course of history. Or to put the case that conventional history has been too anthropocentric in outlook, sundering the seamless unity of humankind and the rest of nature; that in contrast this new history insists humans are and always have been creatures of nature dwelling in a natural world. But, as is usual with such ready formulaic answers, they do not begin to capture the variety and complexity of the field, nor reflect the disagreements among its practitioners, nor exemplify the richness of ideas and perspectives animating the work. So, it is hoped, this book may provide a more thoroughly enlightening answer to the question "What is it?"

A few of the selections included here are reprinted from other sources, and their authors may never have thought of themselves as environmental historians. But in their own time and way they dealt with the substance of the field even before it had a name – with climate, food, resources, population, and the like – and thus deserve recognition as forerunners or predecessors. I have reintroduced a few essays of this genre that deserve to be remembered yet are rather inaccessible to the public today. The large majority of essays, however, are new to print and have been commissioned from scholars presently active in the field; their efforts may be taken as representative of the current state of the art. Included are scientists, geographers, and anthropologists as well as historians. And there are many others whose work equally deserves attention but could not be included here. The ambitious reader who wants to pursue the study further can find their names and publications listed in the Bibliography.

The chronological scope of these essays covers the modern era, that is, roughly the past five hundred years. Of course, modern history is so involved and complex a phenomenon that we cannot in any way pretend to be comprehensive. We are not trying to present a full-blown new synthesis covering all of the events and forces active in this era; rather, our aim is to give readers a sample of what environmental historians do that is different, as well as to demonstrate how they approach such familiar subjects as colonialism or the capitalist revolution or the rise of industrial society.

The large divisions of the book should be self-evident in content, and the individual essays are so clearly written that no summary or interpretation is required in advance. Readers can discover for themselves where they agree or disagree, succeed or fail. But I have tried in the Introduction and the Appendix to lay out, by way of an overview, some of the general, underlying themes and methods of analysis that connect these varied essays.

Environmental history has a great potential for changing the way we conceive of the past. It can help us explain more satisfactorily how we got to be what and where we are today. Like the new social history that has of late revolutionized the study of history, environmental history has both the strength of enormous ambition and the weakness of too much diffuseness. It enters, not offering a single overarching theory to which all past experience must be reduced, but organizing a constellation of interests, insights, questions, and convictions, some old, some new, about what is important and what we ought to pay attention to. Above all, it speaks to our present and future situations. Surely the most significant issue facing the human species in the late twentieth century, and beyond into the twenty-first, is our ecological predicament: How can we survive as a species without undermining or degrading the planet Earth and its fabric of life, the very means of our survival? This predicament gathers force year by year. As these essays demonstrate, historians are beginning to add their voices to its resolution.

A list identifying the contributors may be found near the end of the book. One name does not appear there and deserves acknowledgment: Frank Smith, history editor at Cambridge University Press. He has had as much as or more to do with the book's preparation than any of its authors. It was he who first suggested the idea of such a collection, and it was he who broached the idea of the Cambridge series in which the book appears, "Studies in Environment and History." We owe him warm thanks for the careful, insightful work he has done on these pages. Even more, we applaud him for his deep personal commitment to expanding the boundaries of history and enriching its discourse.

INTRODUCTION

I   The Vulnerable Earth:
Toward a Planetary History

Donald Worster

> It is man's earth now. One wonders what obligations may
> accompany this infinite possession.
> —Fairfield Osborn, *Our Plundered Planet* (1948)

IN THE EARLY DAYS of October 1492, great flocks of birds, migrating southward along the eastern flyway of North America, following an ancient course over open water far from sight of land, fly over three small Spanish caravels. The ships' crews and their captain, Christopher Columbus, have come from Europe across more than two thousand miles of open ocean. They have no idea of how many more miles they have yet to go to reach land, and many of them are tired and fearful. So far they have been following abstract theory, not instinct. But now, abandoning all their logical calculations, the men follow in the wake of the birds. They are on a direct line to the nearest landfall. On 12 October a lookout discerns a whitish cliff in the moonlight and sings out, "Tierra, tierra!" By noon of that day Captain Columbus is ashore on a tiny green island in the Bahamas, bearing the cross of Christendom and kneeling in joy and relief that his voyage has been a success. He is nowhere near his goal, Japan and the Indies, he will soon realize. Instead, with the help of the migrating birds he has arrived at a new and altogether unsuspected world.

If modern history has a single, fabled point of beginning, it is here with Columbus's finding of the Americas. They had not been lost, they simply had not existed heretofore in the European mind. Now suddenly there they loomed, all shining with hope and invitation for the new people of power: an array of islands, continents, vast tropical jungles, a promise of gold and spices and who knew what else, a place inhabited by a race that seemed, in the words of court historian Peter Martyr, "to live in that golden world of which the old writers speak so much, wherein men lived simply and innocently without enforcement of laws, without quarreling, judges and libels,

3

content only to satisfy nature."¹ That momentous discovery would be followed by many explorations into faraway corners of the earth, including Ferdinand Magellan's crossing of the Pacific Ocean less than thirty years later, in 1520 and 1521. There would follow too the most extraordinary period of economic and demographic expansion in history, one that would radically alter the human condition. Food and other resources from the New World would provide much of the raw material for that expansion. And Columbus's discovery would also open a long era of global destruction, when native peoples everywhere would fall before the European onslaught, before an aggression that was at once biological, political, and cultural, when the entire planet's fabric of life would be torn asunder in a frenzy of greed, lust, noble ambition, and high-minded idealism.

We are now approaching a grand ritualistic climax in this story, the five hundredth anniversary of Columbus's arrival in the New World. On such an occasion, it is irresistible to ask whether we are passing from one era into another, from what we have called "modern history" into something different and altogether unpredictable. No one can know for sure the answer to that question, but there is some reason to think that we may be. In recent decades two nations, the Soviet Union and the United States, have launched new ships, new voyagers, into the unknown, the uncharted space lying beyond the earth, and landed them on the moon. As surely as Columbus's report from the Bahamas opened wide the imaginations of European men and women, so these recent events are impelling us all, Westerners and non-Westerners alike, into new realms of thought and perception. The intuition of Columbus and his age that the world was a sphere has now become a photograph. It has appeared on the covers of news magazines, on posters, and in corporate advertising. What that photograph says to us is elusive and contradictory. For some it seems to say that, at last, the earth is ours – we own it all, we dominate it, and it is our launching pad for further quests of power into outer space. For others, however, it says we live on a very small and vulnerable ball, the blue and green planet of life, floating alone and unique in the solar system, drifting in all its minuscule fragility among billions of other planets and suns and galaxies. Whatever the message in the photograph, we may not be the same after seeing it. Such a revelation of where we live may bring with it, slowly, at first almost imperceptibly, a revolution in thinking.

Grant the possibility that these two dramatic events of human exploration, the beaching in the West Indies and the landing on the moon, may indeed mark off a distinct phase of history. During its course our species, though to a widely varying degree among us, has extended its sense of a

¹ Martyr, cited in Samuel Eliot Morison, *The Great Explorers: The European Discovery of America* (New York, 1978), p. 403.

4

home place beyond any single parish or country to encompass the entire globe. Today we are vividly aware that we share this globe with many other races, cultures, and ideologies, that though other people may live completely out of our sight, may dwell on the far side of the globe, what we do here can affect them there. Quite simply, we have been acquiring over the past half millennium a sense of global interdependence. The fact is so familiar, so commented on, that it has begun to lose its simple, riveting force. At the same time the immense implications in this mental revolution for our understanding of history have scarcely been realized.

Similarly, we have been drastically altering our understanding of the earth itself. In Columbus's time and before, people felt themselves wholly at the mercy of natural forces. At sea they went where the wind would take them, trusting it would bring them back home again. They realized that nature had terrific power over them, but could not anticipate in this life the reverse occurring. Columbus, for example, had no inkling of the impact his voyage would have on the ecological order of the New World. He expected the natives would be converted to Christianity, but the organization of nature would remain, he assumed, inviolable as decreed by God, safely immune from human impact.[2] How extraordinary has been the change in that way of thinking! Today we are made aware, by almost every newspaper issued, of some destruction that humans have worked in nature. We read daily about pollutants spewing across national borders, even across oceans, to poison trees and sterilize lakes. We have learned that our burning of fossil fuels may be changing the carbon dioxide level in the atmosphere, with frightening implications for world climate patterns, for agriculture, for coastal settlements that may be flooded by a melting ice cap. We have had to confront the fact that when we in the United States manufacture a pesticide like DDT and sell it around the world, it can eventually turn up in the bodies of penguins living innocently at the South Pole. We may not want to accept responsibility for those outcomes – and many of us do not – but we cannot be unaware of them.

It was just such facts of environmental damage on a global scale that led, in 1971, to the United Nations Conference on the Human Environment in Stockholm, Sweden, and the subsequent founding of the United Nations Environment Programme. The official report of the Stockholm conference bore the title *Only One Earth*. Its authors, the British economist Barbara Ward and the American scientist Rene Dubos, articulated as well as anyone the change in consciousness that has occurred in the modern era. "As we

---

2 The European impact is authoritatively discussed in Alfred Crosby's *The Columbian Exchange: Biological and Cultural Consequences of 1492* (Westport, Conn., 1972) and his *Ecological Imperialism: The Biological Expansion of Europe, 900–1900* (New York, 1986).

enter the global phase of human evolution," they wrote, "it becomes obvious that each man has two countries, his own and the planet Earth."[3]

If each of us now has two countries to care about, we also have two histories to write, that of our own country and that of "planet Earth." And it is high time we began asking what that second history has been, began pursuing not merely the history of this people or that living in isolation from all others – glorifying their achievements or tracing their follies – but the history of all peoples colliding and cooperating with one another on a shrinking island in space.

When that larger planetary history gets fully written, it will surely have at its core the evolving relationship between humans and the natural world. Planetary history has been fundamentally environmental history. It has been the story of a long shifting away from direct and local interaction with the earth, as the defining context of daily life, to dealing with it more indirectly and globally, through the impersonal mediation of powerful centralized political institutions, elaborate technologies, and complicated economic structures. Some will insist that there have been significant gains in that shift and strong, compelling reasons for making it. True enough, but all the same the transformation did not come without costs, ecological as well as social, and a large part of the new planetary history must entail calculating those costs and determining who or what paid them and why.

Planetary history has itself a history: a cycle of getting invented, being endlessly refined, of going through radical revisions. To locate the very earliest gropings in this direction one would have to go back to Genesis, to Clio, the Muse of history, to thousands of anonymous creation myths and stories.[4] But in terms of modern consciousness, secularized and scientized as it is, one could locate the origins of planetary history in a small book published in 1779, *Des epochs de la nature*. Its author was the French naturalist Georges-Louis Leclerc, the Compte de Buffon, who was one of the most influential minds of his day. Beginning back at the point of creation, Buffon argued, there have been seven grand epochs in the history of the earth. The first six follow closely the biblical story of creation, including the appearance of humans and their long bondage under the authority of nature. Then comes the seventh and last epoch, commencing with the invention of agriculture, when the tables begin to turn and humans

---

3 Ward and Dubos, *Only One Earth: The Care and Maintenance of a Small Planet* (New York, 1972), p. xviii.

4 The earliest and most common of these "histories" had humans emerging, as in an actual birth, from their Mother Earth. When people stopped believing that account, turning on their mother with exploitation in mind, it can be said that the modern era began. See Carolyn Merchant, *The Death of Nature: Women, Ecology, and the Scientific Revolution* (San Francisco, 1980), esp. chap. 1.

assume more and more command, destined in modern times to become lords of the earth. By the eighteenth century, Buffon believed, that final age of human dominance had arrived in full glory. "The state in which we see nature today," he writes, "is as much our work as it is hers. We have learned to temper her, to modify her, to fit her to our needs and desires. We have made, cultivated, fertilized the earth; its appearance, as we see it today, is thus quite different than it was in the times prior to the inventions of the arts."5

Buffon's book, so neatly rational and schematic, appeared almost three hundred years after Columbus's first voyage of discovery, but it could not have been conceived without that event. It was part of the new empire of European reason, asserted in this case over the past. In reports from the New World, telling how other Europeans had followed in the wake of Columbus and altered the landscape, Buffon believed he could see recapitulated the entire seventh epoch of history: First, there was a state of wilderness; then savages cleared the land by fire and ax; finally, the savages were supplanted by civilized people who gave polish and embellishment, creating a work of art out of rudeness. "Uncultivated nature is hideous and languishing," the first human declares; "It is I alone who can render it agreeable and vivacious." But the European, nor the feeble savage, feels that ambition most intensely; and eventually, by draining marshes, cutting away forests, confining rivers, exterminating all weeds and vermin, he makes the New World over into "a place of perfect repose, a delightful habitation, where man, destined to aid the intentions of Nature, presides over every other being."6

The Count died in 1788, never having had the opportunity to see firsthand, in action, his program of New World conquest. Nor did he apprehend how soon the triumphant epoch of man would begin to go sour. Within another seventy or eighty years that souring had begun. A radically different view of the human transformation of the earth was emerging, one in which humans appeared, not as the earth's redeemer, but as its destroyer.

The first writer to so portray and systematically document the latest epoch was an extraordinary American polymath, George Perkins Marsh, born on the primitive frontier of Vermont but destined to an international career in diplomacy and conservation. In 1864 he brought out the first edition of his book *Man and Nature,* which would start many people thinking about the darker consequences of emerging human power. Marsh's object was to indicate the character and

5 Buffon, cited in Clarence Glacken, *Traces on the Rhodian Shore: Nature and Culture in Western Thought from Ancient Times to the End of the Eighteenth Century* (Berkeley and Los Angeles, 1967), p. 666.

6 Buffon, *Natural History, General and Particular,* trans. William Smellie, 2d ed. (Edinburgh, 1785), vol. 6, pp. 257–9.

the extent of changes produced by human action in the physical conditions of the globe we inhabit; to point out the dangers of imprudence and the necessity of caution in all operations which, on a large scale, interfere with the spontaneous arrangements of the organic or the inorganic world; to suggest the possibility and the importance of the restoration of disturbed harmonies and the material improvement of waste and exhausted regions; and, incidentally, to illustrate the doctrine, that man is, in both kind and degree, a power of a higher order than any of the other forms of animated life, which, like him, are nourished at the table of bounteous nature.

Beneath those rotund Victorian phrases lay a feeling of revulsion toward many of the environmental changes going on, changes Buffon had seen as improvements. Marsh had grown up in the New World as it was undergoing invasion and conquest, and what he saw was not a nobler design emerging out of chaos but a violent ravaging of natural harmonies. Something irreplaceable was being shattered, and the destroyers were in the end sure to be losers. "The earth," Marsh wrote, "is fast becoming an unfit home for its noblest inhabitant."[7]

Both Buffon and Marsh would have agreed that nature is no longer in a position to set all the terms of human life. They alike celebrated the modern age as a time of liberation for the species, a time of its coming to power. Neither man regretted that revolution or wanted to return to some more vulnerable, fearful dependency on nature. Why then did Marsh find so much cause to be alarmed? What had happened in the short interval between his own and Buffon's lifetime to produce so critical an appraisal?

There were two major forces that appeared full-blown in that interval, and each force would continue to reverberate down to our lives today. Marsh identified neither of them, probably because he was not yet in a position to connect them clearly with the damage going on. But the two forces are clear enough to us in retrospect. We can see how, working together, they began to put the earth and its processes of life in an unprecedented state of vulnerability.

The first of those forces was an explosive increase in the European population, followed by a wave of out-migration to new lands all over the globe. That increase had gotten underway much earlier, though for a long time it was not easy to perceive. In Buffon's time one group of savants were actually convinced that the world had fewer people living in their day than in ancient times. Buffon was not one of them, believing as he did, and quite accurately, that the demographic trend was upward, not downward. Indeed, that belief was one of the reasons for his optimism: More people meant more hands to rearrange the earth into a civilized state. But if Buffon saw the trend rightly,

---

7 Marsh, *Man and Nature, Or, Physical Geography as Modified by Human Action* (Cambridge, Mass., 1965), p. 3. See also David Lowenthal's biography *George Perkins Marsh: Versatile Vermonter* (New York, 1958).

he did not appreciate the full momentum of that increase or anticipate where it would lead or what problems it would entail.[8]

Go back to the year 1500, when the European population stood somewhere around 80 million. It had been on a slow rebound from the hideous losses brought by the black death, the epidemic of bubonic plague that had swept the continent in the mid-fourteenth century, when between a quarter and a third of the people had died. By the sixteenth century the European numbers had been restored to what they had been at their medieval peak – and thereafter they would soar and soar and soar. Plagues, wars, and famines would continue to occur, but they would have only a minor moderating impact. By 1750 the number of people in Europe had climbed to an estimated 140 million. The largest agglomerations were found, in descending order, in Russia, France, Germany, and Italy. And the numbers were far from leveling off. Over the next hundred years they rose to 266 million, at a rate of increase that was more than twice the previous record set back in the twelfth century. Now the fastest growing region was the British Isles, increasing threefold from 9.25 million in 1750 to 28 million in 1850, and that despite the massive potato famine that struck Ireland late in the period. These were the most spectacular rates in world experience. Outside Europe, only China came close to matching them.[9]

More people meant more crowded conditions and fewer opportunities to make a living: the iron law of human ecology. Consequently, surplus population began leaving the Old World for the New, leaving in droves and hordes, leaving by boats and ships of every dimension. The overwhelming majority headed for lands lying in the temperate latitudes, wherever the natives were few in number or were dying from introduced diseases or were militarily weak. The invaders entered North America, Argentina, Australia, South Africa – but not densely populated China or Japan or the tropics. Wherever they did not settle in large numbers, Europeans tried to take command through winning and defending their colonial empires. By the time George Perkins Marsh wrote, evidence was accumulating from all over the earth on the ecological impact of this outflow of numbers and power. Marsh, however, was struck not only by that impact overseas. In Europe, he realized, extensive environmental changes had been going on. For instance, in France, which Buffon had once held up as a model of environmental improvement, there had been widespread degradation; from 1750 to 1860,

---

8 Glacken, *Traces on the Rhodian Shore*, pp. 625–32, 678.
9 These statistics are taken from Colin McEvedy and Richard Jones, *Atlas of World Population History* (Harmondsworth, Engl., 1978), pp. 19–119. See also, among the large number of titles in historical demography, William Langer, "Europe's Initial Population Explosion," *American Historical Review* 69 (October 1963): 1–17. Langer argues that a major reason for the increase may have been the introduction of the potato from the Americas, which gave two to four times the food value of grain per acre.

the country had cut down no less than half its forest acreage, leaving people exposed to floods, soil erosion, and timber shortages.[10]

But it would be completely unsatisfactory to ascribe all those environmental changes to the crude, blunt agency of population increase. Such an explanation would not tell us precisely which groups, or which economic classes, in European society were experiencing most of the increase and why. It would not inform us that, within nations, some regions were gaining while others were losing population. Nor would it reveal the full complexity of the out-migration going on: which people left and why, which villages and cities furnished the largest numbers, whether the migrants were rich or poor, and so forth.[11] Finally, it would not acknowledge the fact that eventually, with rising levels of food and affluence, Europe would begin to see its birth rates fall, would even experience in some places by the twentieth century a negative growth rate. This so-called demographic transition, in which fertility responded to improving economic conditions, suggests that population has not always been a steady, unrelenting force of change, that it waxes and wanes in intensity, that one day it might even disappear altogether as an important agent of environmental vulnerability.[12] Explaining the modern degradation of nature requires us, in other words, to look beyond these broad demographic trends.

We come thus to the second force that was making Marsh's world seem quite different from that of the eighteenth century: the rise of the modern capitalist economy, its evolution into industrialism, and its diffusion to the rest of the globe. Here again, the origins of this agency go back well before the modern era; markets and trade had existed in premodern times, indeed could be found through most of the world and most of history. Nonetheless, they were nowhere rigorously made the center of economic life and social organization before 1500. The market had not yet become the key economic institution, nor the values associated with it the basis of a new social philosophy. A preliminary stage in the transformation occurred in what Immanuel Wallerstein has called "the long 16th century," the period running from 1450 to 1640, during which a capitalist world-economy began to take shape out of a concatenation of the northern cities of Italy and the old Hanseatic League of Germany.[13] But the market did not really remake the

10 Marsh, *Man and Nature*, p. 253.

11 Bernard Bailyn's *Voyagers to the West: A Passage in the Peopling of America on the Eve of the Revolution* (New York, 1986), esp. chap. 1.

12 On the demographic transition, see William Peterson, *Population*, 3d ed. (New York, 1975), pp. 8–15. One must always remember that such a transition is not a law but only a pattern observed, with no assurance of universal validity.

13 Wallerstein, *The Modern World-System: Capitalist Agriculture and the Origins of the European World-Economy in the Sixteenth Century* (New York, 1974), esp. chap. 4. For a more comprehensive treatment of the origins of market society, see Fernand Braudel, *The Wheels of Commerce*, vol. 2 of *Civilization and Capitalism, 15th–18th Century*, trans. Sîan

lives of most Europeans until much later, until the eighteenth and even nineteenth centuries. It had first to pass through several more stages, from the organized trading of goods produced in traditional ways to industrial capitalism, which was a radical new mode of producing those very goods, using wage labor in factories owned by a new class of capitalists. Moreover, on the level of culture and ideas, the full emergence was slow in coming, and not until 1776 did it reach a kind of culmination, with the publication of Adam Smith's masterly blueprint *The Wealth of Nations*. That work provided, at last, a sophisticated rationale for the emerging economic system, showed it had achieved a high level of self-awareness, and finally put into clear, compelling words a new way of regarding nature.

The capitalists and their theoreticians promised that through the technological domination of the earth, they could deliver a more fair, rational, efficient, and productive life for everyone, themselves above all. Their method was simply to free individual enterprise from the bonds of traditional hierarchy and community, whether the bondage derived from other humans or the earth. That meant teaching everyone to treat the earth, as well as each other, with a frank, energetic self-assertiveness, unembarrassed by too many moral or aesthetic sentiments. To behave otherwise must be tantamount to failure as a human being. People must begin to work and produce not for the purpose of meeting their own family and community needs directly, but for selling to others, more often than not to strangers, and then must buy whatever was needed at home. Above all, they must learn to pursue relentlessly their own private accumulation of wealth. They must think constantly in terms of making money. They must regard everything around them – the land, its natural resources, their own labor – as potential commodities that might fetch a profit in the market. They must demand the right to produce, buy, and sell those commodities without outside regulation or interference.[14] Such a way of thinking was supposed to be superior to any that preceded it because it was more logical and scientific, more "natural" to humans. As Adam Smith put it, capitalism rested on a "certain propensity in human nature . . . to truck, barter, and exchange one thing for another."[15] Natural it might have been, but neither he nor any other promoter of this new ethos expected it to be accepted without plenty of persuading. It would take a dedicated effort on their part to transform what traditionally had been regarded as vices, the dark energies of greed and envy, into virtues and blessings to the race.

Reynolds (New York, 1982); and the succeeding volume, *The Perspective of the World* (New York, 1984).

14 Karl Polanyi's *The Great Transformation* (New York, 1980) still offers the best account of this moral attitude. See esp. chaps. 11 and 15.

15 Smith, *The Wealth of Nations* (New York, 1937), p. 13.

Still the most magisterial and remorseless analysis of this industrial capitalist order is that of its German critics Karl Marx and Friedrich Engels. With devastating penetration they ripped away its rational, benign mask of prosperity to reveal an ugly reality of sundered social relations, where one class brutalized another. The Marxist exposure of the ugly face of society is well known. Less familiar is its companion argument that the everyday dealings of people with nature were radically altered too, that ecological relations, deriving as they did from human social relations, also became more destructive as they grew more distant. Just as the capitalists organized the new underclass of workers into instruments of profit, so they organized the earth as the raw material for that labor to exploit. Eventually, the capitalists would spread over the entire globe in search of resources to turn into profit. As Marx and Engels observed,

In place of the old wants, satisfied by the productions of the country, we find new wants, requiring for their satisfaction the products of distant lands and climes. In place of the old local and national seclusion and self-sufficiency we have intercourse in every direction, universal interdependence of nations.[16]

As wants multiplied, as markets grew more and more far-flung, the bond between humans and the rest of nature was reduced to the barest instrumentalism.

Two global forces emerged then, both of them appearing in the wake of the discovery of America and the other new lands, both undoubtedly responding to that distant glimmer of riches, both stirring up a fear of impending resource scarcity in Europe, both becoming powerful engines of change as the nineteenth century opened, both destined to remake nature with geological effectiveness. It could hardly have been mere coincidence that they emerged at roughly the same time and place. Surely they were related, though whether one was cause and the other effect, whether each was at once cause and effect, is not to be easily decided. Some have argued that the Europeans invented the market economy to feed their growing numbers. Others, including many Marxists, have insisted on an equally rigid, linear causality, but with the lines of force running the other way, from capitalism to population growth. Each position has a certain plausibility, a way of making sense of human-nature interactions.

Supporters of the first position insist that industrial capitalism appeared as a remedy for the failure of feudal land systems to furnish, in the face of swelling populations, an adequate living. It is true that revolutionary changes first began to occur in agriculture, involving commercializing the land, letting its ownership and revenue become concentrated in fewer and fewer hands, long before any factories were built. Hungry people, the argument would go,

---

16 "Manifesto of the Communist Party" (1848), *Basic Writings on Politics and Philosophy: Karl Marx and Friedrich Engels*, ed. Lewis Feuer (Garden City, N.Y., 1959), p. 11.

were induced to accept those changes in the hope of securing more food for themselves. They turned to the leadership of a group of rural innovators, who promised to force up the production of food and other organic materials. The cost for success was high: The surplus population had to leave the land for the cities. But no matter that they were now dispossessed and uprooted; they found, some insist, a better life in towns and cities. Capitalist innovators there, counterparts to those in the countryside, imported food and created work for them in new textile factories, powered by water and the fossil fuels. And then, as human demand continued to swell, the same capitalists found still more supplies overseas. Cotton began to enter the British Isles from the countryside of India, Egypt, and the American South, as by and by did lumber from Sweden, fur from Canada, wheat from California, tea from Ceylon, sugar from the West Indies, mutton and wool from New Zealand, and beef from the Argentine. The sheer, unrelenting pressure of population growth drove that economic development forward.[17]

Perhaps indeed it was so, but there is some contradictory evidence suggesting that capitalism came first and then began promoting the increase of European, and later non-European, population for its own insatiable ends. Those who owned the means of production and had something to sell wanted buyers, and lots of them. They wanted to buy labor too, and lots of it and at the cheapest price possible. In a culture based on the endless pursuit of money, there was every reason to promote the most spectacular rates of population growth. Any local surplus might be sent abroad, where it would reproduce the entire society of market producers and consumers, thereby further augmenting the sources of wealth. Certainly it was the case that the economic revolution brought with it a glorious promise, a great utopian ambition, that was pronatalist to the core.[18] The industrialists offered to make not only the existing population of the world infinitely rich, but also *any conceivable increase* in that population. They would fill the world to the brim with well-fed, happy, affluent humans. There were, to be sure, some pessimistic economists around, men like Thomas Malthus and John Stuart

---

17 Though no apologist for capitalism, Victor Skipp has identified population increase as the force lying behind some of these changes in *Crisis and Development: An Ecological Case Study of the Forest of Arden, 1570–1674* (Cambridge, 1978). See also Richard Wilkinson, "The English Industrial Revolution," in this volume; and Marvin Harris, *Cannibals and Kings: The Origins of Cultures* (New York, 1977), chap. 14. For an alternative view, emphasizing the role of surplus accumulation rather than resource scarcity, see Eric L. Jones, *Agriculture and the Industrial Revolution* (New York, 1974); and *The European Miracle: Environments, Economics, and Geopolitics in the History of Europe and Asia* (Cambridge, 1981), esp. chaps. 4–5.
18 An illuminating account of how reproduction came to be manipulated for the purposes of economic expansion is Claude Meillassoux's *Maidens, Meal and Money: Capitalism and the Domestic Community*, trans. from French (Cambridge, 1981).

Mill, who objected that the earth could not be made to produce fast enough to keep up with the rising population, that poverty would be much harder to get rid of than anyone thought; but their gloominess was not the spirit that dominated the new industrial culture, certainly not in the long run, and certainly never in that most avid nation of technology believers, the United States. Far from being Malthusian, the prevailing spirit was utopian in the extreme. The epoch of man was to be the epoch of universal and unlimited wealth.[19]

Neither of these historical explanations will altogether do, for causality in history is seldom a matter of a straight line running from A to B; more often, it is a matter of A and B complexly reacting to each other. In any case, the combined effect of these two forces on the natural environment was both stupendous and completely unappreciated by anyone for a long time. At home or abroad Europeans assumed that God had made the world for them and, in his wisdom and benevolence, had so designed it that nothing they did could interfere with its order; whatever happened to nature was furthering God's work of creating and managing it for the greatest good of his noblest species. Even had they been more humble in their sense of self, Europeans would still not have found it easy to visualize the damage potential in their demands. The market economy had the peculiar tendency of hiding much of it from them. For one thing, it put increasing numbers of them in urban areas, removing them from any sense of the limits of the land, leaving them completely unaware of how their food and other commodities were produced. On the other hand, those who did the producing no longer, in many cases, owned the means of production—the land or the tools used to work it – and, naturally enough, took little responsibility for them. Those who owned the means, and it mattered not whether they were single or collective owners, were under pressure from themselves and their society to squeeze a higher return from the land, distribute it to a wider market, and earn a bigger profit. Worst yet, the extension of their resource base globally left virtually everyone in Europe uninformed and unconcerned about the ecological disturbances they caused abroad. They had successfully transcended their own immediate limits, they were pleased to note, and the wide world would now provide for them. Not until Marsh took up the question in the 1860s did anyone manage to gain a comprehensive view of the environmental upheaval worked by the economic and demographic revolutions.

Over the 120-odd years that have followed Marsh's book the combined

---

19 That early utopianism is by no means dead; see, for example, the work of recent exponent Julian Simon, *The Ultimate Resource* (Princeton, 1981); and, with Herman Kahn, editor of *The Resourceful Earth: A Response to Global 2000* (Oxford, 1984). Somewhat more restrained is Walt W. Rostow, *The World Economy: History and Prospect* (Austin, 1978), pp. 571–624.

forces of human population increase and industrial capitalism have spread that vulnerability into the remotest corners, into thousands of ecosystems. That happened through the medium of a vast new arsenal of technologies in transportation, crop production, and the like. For instance, the Europeans and their offspring threw a railroad across the United States in 1869 and finished digging the Suez Canal in the same year.[20] One year later India began exporting its wheat to England via the canal, sending food that once had been stored against times of scarcity and hunger. In the severe famine years of 1876–7, India exported record quantities of its precious food grains. To facilitate this commerce, the Europeans put coal to work carrying cargoes across all the oceans, and under the water they laid down a network of telegraph cables to communicate instantly and globally any news of supply and demand. They mass-produced steel plows and steam-driven threshers, gasoline tractors and bulldozers, logging mills and chain saws. Every one of those inventions, it should be noted, occurred within the industrial capitalist order and under its imperatives, though often with state aid. In fact, over the past century or two every fundamental modern innovation, every important machine, every new system of transportation, has derived mainly from the needs of that economic culture. Only in a secondary sense, therefore, can we speak of technology as the agency that was changing the land. The controlling, directing hands behind those changes were generally those of capitalists and their political allies.

For a long while the most dramatic environmental alterations came from the massive conversion of natural ecosystems into arable, that is, into croplands. Historian John Richards has calculated that, from 1860 to 1920, 432 million hectares (or about 1,067 million acres, a hectare being equivalent to 2.471 acres) of land were converted worldwide to regular cropping. Of that total, 164 million hectares were converted in North America, 88 million in Russia, 84 million in Asia, and the rest were scattered across the remaining continents. Then, in the period from 1920 to 1978, he calculates, another 419 million net hectares were added to world croplands. That is nearly one billion hectares put to work raising food and fiber since the publication of Marsh's book. One billion hectares of forests and grasslands that had been teeming with biological complexity, much of which was lost in the simplifications of commercial agriculture.[21]

---

20 Between 1870 and 1890 the United States alone built 110,000 miles of railway, and with those facilities increased wheat exports from 39 million bushels to 226 million in roughly the same period. See Lee Benson, *Turner and Beard: American Historical Writing Reconsidered* (New York, 1960), pp. 47–52. Also, Daniel R. Headrick, *The Tools of Empire: Technology and European Imperialism in the Nineteenth Century* (New York, 1981), esp. part 3.

21 Richards, "Global Patterns of Land Conversion," *Environment* 26 (November 1984): 6–13, 34–8.

There is more to human impact than the conversion to arable – the slaughter of bison, for example, or the pollution of streams – but that will do to indicate something of its scale. And to suggest some of the grounds on which observers, from Marsh on and in nation after nation, began to talk about the new vulnerability of the earth and the implications it had for human welfare.

What Marsh began in the way of criticism and protest, others have carried on year by year, until today the literature on the vulnerable earth is immense. A brief sampling of twentieth-century titles in that literature might start with the geographer Alexander Woeikof's essay of 1901, "De l'influence de l'homme sur la terre," move on to Ernst Friedrich's 1904 article, "Wesen und geographische Verbreitung der Raubwirtschaft," and follow with selections from the American conservationists John Muir, Gifford Pinchot, and Theodore Roosevelt.[22] In the 1930s there were such books and essays as Paul Sears's *Deserts on the March*, Graham Jacks and R. O. Whyte's *The Rape of the Earth*, and Carl Sauer's "Destructive Exploitation in Modern Colonial Expansion."[23] Then came the postwar period, when the number of titles accelerated as the anxiety deepened. One could cite Fairfield Osborn's *Our Plundered Planet* and William Vogt's *Road to Survival*, both published in 1948; the Princeton conference report, *Man's Role in Changing the Face of the Earth* (1956); Rachel Carson's *Silent Spring* (1962); Jean Dorst's *Avant que nature meure* (1965); Paul Ehrlich's *The Population Bomb* (1968); Dennis and Donella Meadows's *The Limits to Growth* (1972); Robert Heilbroner's *An Inquiry into the Human Prospect* (1974); and the *Global 2000 Report to the President* (1980).[24] That long string of writings came from men and women in many fields – science, geography, economics, politics, and conservation – and though heavily American in recent years, was written in many languages and published in even more. It was truly a global genre. For historians, it offered full documentation of how far the damage to the environment had

---

22 On Woeikof and Friedrich, see Jussi Raumolin, "L'homme et la destruction des ressources naturelles: La *Raubwirtschaft* au tournant du siècle," *Annales: Economies, Sociétés, Civilisations* 39 (July–August 1984): 798–819; and J. R. Whitaker, "World View of Destruction and Conservation of Natural Resources," *Annals of the Association of American Geographers* 30 (September 1940): 143–62. Muir, Pinchot, and Roosevelt were mainly worried about forest destruction; see Samuel P. Hays, *Conservation and the Gospel of Efficiency: The Progressive Conservation Movement, 1890–1920* (Cambridge, Mass., 1959), chap. 3.

23 The Sears book appeared in 1935, the Jacks and Whyte volume in 1939. Sauer's essay was published in International Geographical Congress, *Proceedings, 1938* (Leiden, 1938), vol. 2, sec. 3c, pp. 494–9.

24 In response to these titles came, predictably, quite a few debunking works, including John Maddox, *The Doomsday Syndrome* (New York, 1972).

gone and plenty of suggestions on how that damage had itself become an historical force, threatening to bring down political regimes, disrupt social patterns, and force fundamental economic and technological change that could ramify throughout the planet. The history of nature and that of civilization became more inseparably linked than ever.

Increasingly, the industrial capitalist nations of the West had the illusory satisfaction of watching their values become sovereign almost everywhere. In distant corners of the globe a growing production and consumption of commodities became, as it was in the developed nations, the most frequently consulted measure of success. As economist Herman Daly has written:

Economic growth is the most universally accepted goal in the world. Capitalists, communists, fascists, and socialists all want economic growth and strive to maximize it. The system that grows fastest is considered best. The appeals of growth are that it is the basis of national power and that it is an alternative to sharing as a means of combating poverty. It offers the prospect of more for all with sacrifice for none.[25]

However clumsy and inefficient they were in the drive to turn the earth into a factory, however much they claimed to put justice above profit, the disciples of Karl Marx had joined in what was becoming a specieswide, transideological crusade for domination. Overthrowing the capitalistic world economy, therefore, would not bring an end to the planet's vulnerability.

More commodities for all must mean, no matter how inexact the translation, more pollution, more crowding, more depletion, and more extinction. The human mind was not yet, and perhaps never would be, capable of avoiding such costs. By 1971, one study calculated, the ecological impact of humans on the earth was increasing at the rate of 5 percent a year, which would mean a doubling every fourteen years.[26] As their habitats disappeared into the maw of commodification, species of plants and animals began to vanish at an alarming rate. First it was one species every year, then one every day, soon it would be one every hour, one every half hour, one every fifteen minutes. By the mid-1980s somewhere between five hundred thousand and one million species were under threat of extinction, all victims of rising human demand. "Never in the 500 million years of terrestrial evolution," wrote two biologists, "has this mantle we call the biosphere been under such savage attack."[27]

25 Daly, *Steady-State Economics: The Economics of Biophysical Equilibrium and Moral Growth* (San Francisco, 1977), p. 8.
26 Report on the Study of Critical Environmental Problems, *Man's Impact on the Global Environment* (Cambridge, Mass., 1970), p. 22.
27 Paul Ehrlich and Ann Ehrlich, *Extinction: The Causes and Consequences of the Disappearance of Species* (New York, 1981), p. 8; Norman Myers, *Gaia: An Atlas of Planet*

As the very process of evolution itself was suspended and even reversed, there appeared a third force of human-induced environmental change, one that would prove even more difficult to contain than either population or capitalism, economic growth or industrialism. Its name was Knowledge, alias Science. Its aim was power, whatever its applications. Industrialism was only one of its manifestations. More and more, that power was accumulated, not merely for individual consumer satisfaction, but in the interests of the state and its military strength.

One side of science told people that nature was a thing of beauty and integrity, a set of laws that must be obeyed, an order that must be respected and protected. From that teaching derived, in large measure, the movement from George Perkins Marsh on to protect nature against human violation. It was a movement for nature conservation and preservation. On the other hand, science also told laymen about a nature that was power inchoate, power latent and potential, power waiting for human ingenuity to develop it, power that should not be left dormant. Nature so understood became, as Jean Baudrillard has written, "the concept of a dominated essence and nothing more."[28] It became merely the means to whatever end men had in mind, whether it be wealth or war, pleasure or security, bondage or freedom. In that way of regarding nature as an instrument of power, it did not matter what the ends were, so far as the vulnerability of the earth was concerned. Jonathan Schell has acutely noted this fact:

> Though from the point of view of the human actor, there might be a clear difference between the "constructive" economic applications of technology and the "destructive" military ones, nature makes no such distinction: both are beachheads of human mastery in a defense-less natural world.[29]

Between these two radically opposed views of nature, these two teachings of science, the modern world has swung back and forth, though undoubtedly it is the second one that has had the more decisive impact. Otherwise, we would not be living today on the brink of nuclear annihilation.

The most awesome manifestation of this science-based power came with the creation of the atomic bomb. First detonated on 16 July 1945, on the desert sands outside Alamagordo, New Mexico, the bomb testified to a capacity and a will to destroy that went far beyond either human fertility or greed. It also went beyond the capacity of any ordinary group of people to express unaided, requiring as it did the trained intelligence of some of the brightest scientists in the world. One among them, physicist and project

Footnote 27 *(continued)*
> *Management* (Garden City, 1984), p. 154; Michael Soulé and Bruce Wilcox, *Conservation Biology: An Evolutionary-Ecological Perspective* (Sunderland, Mass., 1980), p. 7.
28 Baudrillard, *The Mirror of Production*, trans. Mark Poster (St. Louis, 1975), p. 55.
29 Schell, *The Fate of the Earth* (New York, 1982), p. 110.

leader at Alamagordo, J. Robert Oppenheimer, exulted with his colleagues over their ability to unleash the hidden, blinding energy of the atom. Then from the Hindu scripture Oppenheimer recalled the ominous sentence "I am become Death, the shatterer of worlds." For the first time in two million years of human history, he began to realize, there existed a force capable of destroying the entire fabric of life on the planet.[30]

Once again, it was European civilization and its offshoots that had spawned destruction, though soon the bomb would come into the hands of non-Western people too. Once more, there were roots going back deep into history: to an archaic human thirst for power that had animated magicians and empire builders long before the modern era. But the organized, systematic pursuit of research and development was a distinctive, characteristic part of modernity. It was not common in earlier times and places. There had been a foreshadowing of it in the sponsored voyages of Columbus and the other discoverers, and the Scientific Revolution of the seventeenth century came speaking the language of conquest as much as understanding. Since then that effort would augment quietly, steadily, until by the present century it had become by far the greatest source of power around: a power to do good, of course, but also, as many scientists themselves began to realize, a power to do profound evil.

The pursuit of disciplined reason as the basis of national power could take the form of machines, assembly lines, automobiles, nuclear weapons, industrialism, or militarism. It animated communist nations as well as noncommunist. Unless societies imposed on themselves the most stringent controls over research, such power would continue to accumulate, ever ready for some work of domination. In short, the threat to the earth now came from a source far broader and more diffuse than any economic or social or political system. It lay in that complex and ambitious brain of *Homo sapiens*, in our unmatched capacity to experiment and explain, in our tendency to let reason outrun the constraints of love and stewardship, and in our modern, nearly universal drive to achieve infinite power over our surroundings.

Approximately five centuries ago, when the present era began, the human species found itself groping toward a new position on the planet. It had managed to escape – or at least the Europeans had – the old, narrow constraints of place that had forced thousands of preceding generations to struggle constantly to control their numbers and demands. Previously, only a tiny elite had been able to live extravagantly, disregarding the limits of nature. The vast majority had no such freedom. In their valleys, hills, forests, and bays, they confronted daily the need to behave with extreme

---

30 Oppenheimer, cited in Robert Jungk, *Brighter Than a Thousand Suns* (New York, 1958), p. 201.

care. Where else, in the event of a degraded environment, could they find a living? But when the great round world opened wide, it became possible to throw off much of that old caution and let imagination run wild. We could do what we wanted with impunity, and maybe, some thought, we could even seize command for ourselves. It was in that mood of cutting loose from all earthly restraint that the English philosopher of science Francis Bacon spoke confidently of enlarging "the bounds of Human Empire, to the effecting of all things possible." By and by, anything and everything came to seem possible to a people who believed, with Bacon, that "the world is made for man, not man for the world."[31]

But at some point that mood of release and conquest must exhaust itself. No cultural drive has ever lasted forever, unchanging, unchallenged, unchastened. It may be that this one is beginning to wear off at last. We have lately seen the earth from outer space and have come to understand how quickly we could blow it up. Perhaps, as a consequence, we may be entering a new phase of history, a time when we begin to rediscover, through that other, nurturing side of science, through travel and a broadening of sympathies, through the growth of a reason framed by compassion, through the evolution of moral awareness, some long forgotten ideas: the traditional teaching that power must entail restraint and responsibility, the ancient awareness that we are interdependent with all of nature and that our sense of community must take in the whole of creation. For the first time, we can see that we have a planet on our hands to take care of.

31 *The Works of Francis Bacon*, ed. James Spedding (New York, 1872–8), vol. 1, pp. 47–8, 398.

Dynamics of Change

2 Environment, Population, and Technology in Primitive Societies

Ester Boserup

WHEN THE RATE OF INCREASE of European populations accelerated in the second half of the eighteenth century, European economists elaborated a theory of interrelationships between environment, population, and technology, which continues to be applied by many social scientists who are dealing with problems of development of primitive societies. The basic characteristic of this theory is that it deals with demographic trends as an adaptive factor: It assumes that a given environment has a certain carrying capacity for human populations, defined as the number of persons who can be accommodated in that region under the prevailing system of subsistence. Population is kept within the limit for subsistence in a particular environment by customary restraint on the number of births or by high rates of mortality, including various forms of infanticide. According to this theory, over the long run primitive societies tend to have a rate of zero population growth. The rate rises above zero if improvements in the technology of food production increase the carrying capacity of the environment, but only until the new limit is reached, after which the rate of population growth again returns to zero.

This reasoning suffers from two main weaknesses: First, the theory focuses exclusively on the technology of food production, ignoring the effects of technological changes in other areas and the effects of the environment; secondly, the theory ignores the effects of demographic change on both environment and technology.

EFFECTS OF TECHNOLOGICAL CHANGES ON POPULATION

Demographic trends in primitive populations are influenced not only by food technology but also by health, transport, and war technologies, and by the system of organization, which could be called "administrative technol-

23

ogy." Until recently, health technology was so primitive that many well-fed populations had low birth rates owing to endemic venereal disease and malaria, and high mortality rates, particularly for infants. The main technique of avoiding contamination by epidemic disease was to isolate oneself as much as possible from the source of contamination by such procedures as abandoning the old village and building a new one in another place, fleeing the town, and closing the gates of the town or the frontiers of the country. Some of these measures tended to spread the epidemics more widely rather than to contain them.

Improvements in the means of transport, which open up new regions for human contacts, are likely to raise mortality rates by giving greater sway to the spread of epidemics. It is true that improvements in transport technology might sometimes reduce mortality by facilitating the supply of food to a famine-stricken region, but since such improvements make it easier for a conqueror or an indigenous ruling class to move food away from the region where it is produced, they could also result in reduction of food available for the local population, with negative effects on demographic trends.

Improvements in military technology usually raise mortality rates, particularly when they are of a kind to benefit the aggressor more than the victim. However, the effects of a given type of technological change are often complex. For instance, building walled towns probably reduced losses in warfare but increased mortality by epidemics if sanitary and other health technology was not improved. In other words, this particular improvement in military technology caused deterioration of the (urban) environment, which might have raised mortality by more than it reduced direct war casualties.

Administrative technology is particularly important in affecting mortality rates in cases of military events and food shortages. A breakdown of the organization of society might transform a local war or harvest failure into a demographic catastrophe.

The examples above may suffice to illustrate that improvements in food technology are only one among many types of technological changes that influence demographic trends in primitive societies. Therefore, it seems unwarranted to assume that population growth was rapid in primitive societies in the past whenever the rate of growth was unhampered by an inelastic supply of food. Many primitive peoples who were not underfed and who did not fully use the subsistence capacity of their territory must have been decimated by epidemics and wars repeatedly; and I surmise that such wars were waged rarely in order to conquer empty land for a people suffering from overpopulation, but more often in order to conquer slaves or inhabited land (i.e., people who could be made to pay tribute).

Thus, the most reasonable assumption about past demographic trends seems to be that some unfortunate peoples, decimated by disease and war,

24

had negative rates of population growth and disappeared, while other more fortunate ones had positive, but fairly low, rates of growth over long periods. There seems to be little reason to assume that zero rates of population growth occurred more frequently in past history than other rates of growth, positive or negative.

In many cases, peoples with positive rates of growth may have migrated to land that became free when the previous inhabitants were reduced in numbers. But in many other cases, the effects of different rates of population growth among neighboring peoples must have been the opposite: Peoples with positive rates of population growth would use their increasing numerical advantage to force neighboring peoples with declining or less rapidly increasing numbers to become slaves or wage workers in the villages and towns of the stronger people, thus further increasing the differences in population densities within a region. I shall return to the effects of such variations in population density later.

INCREASE OF POPULATION AND CHANGE IN SUBSISTENCE TECHNOLOGY IN THE EARLY DEVELOPMENT OF EUROPE

Until fairly recently, agricultural history dealt mainly with Europe, and European agricultural history was interpreted in the light of the classical theory mentioned above. It was assumed that the primitive nature of agricultural equipment prevented the cultivation of most of the land that is under cultivation today. It was also assumed that the European population was unable to expand, except in periods when better equipment was introduced. In such periods, rates of population growth would have been positive until the new capacity limit for food production was reached, at which time the long-run rate of population growth was assumed to have returned to zero.

This theory fails to take account of the fact that much of the land that was uncultivated in prehistoric times and later, was not land that could not be used with the existing types of equipment, but rather land that was used in certain years but that in other years lay fallow under the prevailing systems of long fallow.[1] Europe's population began – like populations on other continents – as hunting-gathering communities, but as early as 4500 B.C. some populations in temperate Europe seem to have adopted a system of forest fallow similar to that still in use in some contemporary primitive communities on other continents. When this system is used, a plot cleared in the forest is cultivated for a brief period and, when weeds appear, it is left

---

[1] Evidence to this effect is presented by Ester Boserup in *Conditions of Agricultural Growth* (Chicago: Aldine, 1965).

to regrow into forest. The system requires a large area of land to feed a small group of people. The next step in the development of European agriculture was a gradual shortening of the fallow periods and lengthening of the periods of cultivation for any given piece of land, in step with the gradual increase of the European population.

During many centuries, systems of shorter and shorter fallow spread gradually over Europe, until finally annual cropping became widespread in the eighteenth and nineteenth centuries. The change was slow because the increase of population was slow and intermittent, and an increasing labor force was the precondition for a type of change under which the share of land under cultivation at any given time would increase and the share under fallow correspondingly decline. In regions of Europe that remained sparsely populated the land-using systems of long fallow continued to be used for many more centuries than in those regions of Europe where population increased more rapidly, whether by natural increase or by immigration. By ignoring the process of gradual shortening of fallow, the classical economists, and the economic historians who were influenced by their reasoning, failed to notice the link between demographic trends on the one hand and environment and technology on the other.

The gradual transition to shorter fallows changed the environment. Forests were thinned out and eventually disappeared, and natural grazing pastures and man-made fields replaced them. Also soil conditions changed as forest areas were transformed either into grassland or into drained, marled, and manured fields. In step with all these changes, the primitive digging sticks and stone axes used in the food-gathering and forest-fallow stages had to be replaced by other hand tools and later by ploughs.

The gradual shortening of fallow served to feed larger and larger populations in Europe, but the effects of this change on labor productivity in European farming seem not always to have been positive. When fallow was shortened, labor-intensive operations of land preparation, weeding, and fertilization became necessary in order to prevent a decline of crop yields and exhaustion of the soil. The negative effects of this on labor productivity tended to offset the positive effects of improved equipment.

Agricultural historians have described cases in which reduction of population after major epidemics or wars was accompanied by a reversion to systems of longer fallow.[2] This would seem to indicate that, in these cases, the previous expansion of output by shortening of fallow had been obtained at the cost of a decline in output per unit of labor. The point is important in evaluating the effects of these technological changes on the demographic trends, because these changes could be expected to accelerate

2 See, e.g., Marc Bloch, *Les caractères originaux de l'histoire rurale française*, vol. 1 (Paris: Les Belles Lettres, 1931), vol. 2 (Paris: Armand Colin, 1956); and B. H. Slicher van Bath, *The Agrarian History of Western Europe* (London: E. Arnold, 1963).

population growth only if they raised output per unit of labor. If the only positive effect of these changes were to allow a larger population to raise total food production in proportion to the increase in numbers, there would seem to be little reason to expect any acceleration of the rate of population growth as a result of the changes of methods.

Effects of Demographic Trends on Environment

The recent acceleration of rates of population growth in contemporary primitive communities on continents other than Europe provides much new information about the interrelationships between demographic growth, on the one hand, and environment and technology, on the other. Both natural and social scientists have studied the changes in environment and technology that are occurring under population pressure in contemporary primitive societies, and a number of scholars are taking this evidence as a starting point for a reinterpretation of the ancient history of primitive and other preindustrial societies.

In order to provide a framework for discussion the main primitive subsistence systems are listed below according to the difference in periods of cultivation and fallow, beginning with the most primitive systems with the longest periods of fallow and the smallest carrying capacity in terms of human populations. This framework also illuminates the preceding discussion of early European development and underlies the examination of the impact of demographic trends on technology in the sections that follow.

1. Gathering of food – no cultivation, all land "fallow land"
2. Forest fallow – one to two crops, followed by 15–25 years of fallow
3. Bush fallow – four to six crops, followed by 8–10 years of fallow
4. Short fallow – one to two crops, followed by one year of fallow
5. Annual cropping – one crop each year with a few months of fallow
6. Multicropping – two to three crops each year without any fallow

The number of persons who can live in a given area of land is, of course, higher the shorter the period of fallow. It is not possible to use all the subsistence systems in all environments, but most environments are adaptable and allow a choice between several of these systems: A semidesert can be used for herding but also for irrigated crops.

If the population using one of these subsistence systems increases (by natural growth or by immigration) to the point of exceeding the carrying capacity of the land under that system, the environment is likely to deteriorate. If the subsistence system is food gathering, edible plants and animals may gradually disappear. If the subsistence system is forest fallow, the forest may gradually disappear and become replaced by bush or

27

grassland. In other cases, grassland may become overgrazed, and the cultivation of steep hillsides may result in erosion and barrenness. In such cases, the population may have to move to another region, leaving a useless desert behind. This seems to have happened, for instance, in some parts of southwestern Asia during ten millennia of agricultural exploitation of the environment.[3]

But sustained demographic growth among primitive peoples does not always result in deterioration of the environment, because the possibility exists that the population, when it outgrows the carrying capacity of the land with the existing subsistence technology, may change to another subsistence system with a higher carrying capacity. Sometimes this change is even facilitated by the transformation of the environment, for instance, by the replacement of forest by bush or grassland, which forces the population to shift to bush fallow or grass fallow instead of forest fallow and to introduce types of tools that can cope with grassy weeds.

CHANGES IN SUBSISTENCE SYSTEMS UNDER POPULATION PRESSURE

Studies of changes in subsistence systems in contemporary primitive societies have been undertaken by many anthropologists, geographers, and agricultural experts. These studies are usually limited to a single change within a particular community or region, for instance, from food gathering to agriculture, or from forest to bush fallow, or from short fallow to annual cropping. Likewise, economic historians and archaeologists have taken an interest in changes in primitive subsistence systems that have occurred in the history of the peoples they are studying. Most of these studies are also limited to a single change, but by linking a number of studies made by different scholars, it is sometimes possible to follow the whole process of gradual change from land-using to land-saving systems in step with demographic growth within a major region. I mentioned above the changes that have taken place in the course of European history; similar changes from land-using to land-saving systems have taken place in other parts of the world. For ancient Mesopotamia, evidence from many studies has been combined to show a gradual change from the food gathering on mountain slopes before 8000 B.C. to intensive agriculture based on large-scale irrigation and plough cultivation in the southern plains four thousand to five thousand years later.[4]

3 Frank Hole, "Evidence of Social Organization from Western Iran 8000–4000 B.C.," in *New Perspectives in Archeology*, Lewis R. Binford and Sally R. Binford, ed. (Chicago: Aldine, 1968).

4 A more detailed discussion of agricultural growth in Mesopotamia is provided in Philip E. L. Smith and T. Cuyler Young, Jr., "The Evolution of Early Agriculture and Culture in

It is apparent from the few examples mentioned above that the change from the food-gathering stage to intensive preindustrial agriculture has been a very slow process. It apparently took ancient Mesopotamia over four thousand years to pass from the beginning of food production to intensive, irrigated agriculture, and it took Europe still longer to pass from the introduction of forest fallow to the beginning of annual cropping a few hundred years ago. Moreover, the geographic diffusion of land-saving systems was also very slow and, in some cases, it failed altogether to take place. Even today, some food-gathering peoples are left, and primitive long-fallow systems continue to be the basic subsistence system in large areas of Africa and Latin America and in parts of south and Southeast Asia.[5]

The subsistence systems mentioned above are distinguished not only by differences in periods of cultivation and fallow but also by differences in types of equipment used. Food-gathering peoples use little or no equipment – they may use sticks to dig up edible roots and fire to enlarge hunting or grazing areas. Forest fallow cultivators also use digging sticks and fire, but bush fallow cultivators usually use hoes or machetes. Most short-fallow cultivators, annual croppers, and multicroppers use ploughs and keep draught animals, and many annual croppers and most multicroppers use various types of irrigation equipment. Thus, the equipment used for the more land-saving systems of subsistence is much more complicated than that used for the more land-using systems.

It is pertinent, therefore, to ask whether primitive peoples are likely to invent new tools and new subsistence systems when their population size comes to exceed the carrying capacity of their environment with the existing system. The answer is, of course, that it is not necessary to "invent" either a new system or the tools needed for operating it in order to change the subsistence system and to introduce new types of equipment. Both in contemporary and in past primitive communities, technological innovation

Greater Mesopotamia," in *Population Growth: Anthropological Implications,* ed. Brian J. Spooner (Cambridge, Mass.: MIT Press, 1972).

5 There are studies of people on all continents who apply land-using subsistence systems and do not utilize the full subsistence capacity of their territory with the prevailing system. See, e.g., W. Allan, *The African Husbandman* (London: Oliver and Boyd, 1965); Robert L. Carneiro, "Slash-and-burn Agriculture: A Closer Look at Its Implications for Settlement Patterns," in *Men and Cultures* (Papers of the Fifth International Congress of Anthropological and Ethnological Sciences, 1956); Robert B. Ekvall, "Demographic Aspects of Tibetan Nomadic Pastoralism," in Spooner, *Population Growth;* M. B. Gleave and H. P. White, "Population Density and Agricultural Systems in West Africa," in *Environment and Land Use in Africa,* ed. Michael F. Thomas and G. W. Whittington (London: Methuen, 1969); and Richard B. Lee, "Work Effort, Group Structure and Land Use in Contemporary Hunter-gatherers" (Paper for research seminar on archeology and related subjects, University of London, 1970).

was rarely the result of invention but rather the result of diffusion of technology from one community to another. A growing population that is beginning to outgrow the carrying capacity of its subsistence system is likely to be receptive to the idea of borrowing technology from other communities with higher population densities and with less land-using subsistence systems.[6]

When we observe that even today some peoples use primitive land-using subsistence systems and primitive transport systems that were abandoned by other peoples many millennia ago, we should not ask why these peoples never invented the plough and the wheel, but why the diffusion of these technologies seems to have happened fairly rapidly in some cases and not at all in other cases. In other words, why did small groups of people who live in regions of very low population density and use primitive land-using subsistence systems never adopt the better technologies that were used by other peoples with whom they have been in contact?

LABOR PRODUCTIVITY OF
LAND-USING AND LAND-SAVING
SUBSISTENCE SYSTEMS

The main answer to the question posed above seems to be that the primitive land-using subsistence systems, that is, food-gathering and long-fallow agriculture, have a higher output per unit of labor input than usually assumed and, therefore, the primitive peoples who use them have little incentive to change to more land-saving subsistence systems, as long as they are few enough to obtain the necessary food by use of the land-using systems. But the advantage of the land-using systems has been overlooked, partly because of lack of proper information about labor input and partly because many of the peasants who use land-saving systems produce large surpluses that they deliver to landlords or sell to merchants, while the primitive peoples who employ land-using systems rarely produce any surpluses beyond the immediate needs of their families. It seems, however, that the surpluses produced in preindustrial peasant communities, which have been taken as proof of the relatively high labor productivity of the land-saving agricultural systems used in such communities, are partly yields on labor investments and partly the result of a larger input of labor in the cultivation of crops than that customary in primitive communities where land-using systems are used.[7] In other words, it seems that the peoples who

6 The relationship between population growth and the diffusion of technology is discussed in D. E. Dumond, "Population Growth and Cultural Change," *Southwestern Journal of Anthropology* 21 (1965).
7 Boserup, *Conditions of Agricultural Growth*; "Present and Potential Food Production in Developing Countries," in *Geography and a Crowding World*, ed. Wilbur Zelinski, Leszek

employ land-using systems would also be able to produce surpluses if they were to make labor investments and work longer hours. We shall see below why such peoples usually fail to produce any surpluses.

A number of anthropological studies show that present-day hunting-and-food-gathering communities obtain the necessary food without working very hard, even when they live in inhospitable environments. A study by Lee of the Bushmen living in the Kalahari Desert reveals that the women who do the food gathering use only two to three days a week to provide the necessary food. Lee's studies of the Bushmen show the alternatives available to a food-gathering people when their group size increases and the ways in which they adapt to increasing group size.[8] He measured the distances that the women must walk in search of food and the burden they have to carry under varying assumptions about group size and the average number of young children per woman. With increasing group size, a woman must walk longer and longer distances in search of the necessary food, and the choice is between spacing the children more (children born alive and allowed to live) and splitting into separate smaller groups. The latter solution would of course be excluded if the number of Bushmen in the whole territory were to become so large that there would be no free space for new groups. In that case, women would have a strong incentive to produce some crops instead of gathering all the food. It is tempting to ask if the connection found by Lee between the need to carry children around and the increasing burden of food gathering with increasing group size can help to explain the fact that it is the women who usually cultivate crops in the most primitive systems of long-fallow agriculture that follow the stage of food gathering.

Many hunting-gathering peoples produce some crops as a supplement to their diet, and it seems that when their territory becomes more densely populated and their hunting-and-food-gathering activities therefore become less productive, they come to rely increasingly on their crops and on domestic birds and animals. In other words, as population pressure in groups of food gatherers and hunters gradually makes the environment in which they live less productive, they may react by adopting an alternative technology, which was already known but had hitherto been little used. This new technology will increase the carrying capacity of the environment but will probably lower labor productivity. Therefore, the new technology is unlikely to be transferred from one people to another as long as the population size permits the

Kosinski, and R. Mansell Prothero (London: Oxford University Press, 1970); and *Women's Role in Economic Development* (London: St. Martin, 1970).

8 For a fuller discussion of this topic, see Lee, "Work Effort, Group Structure and Land Use." See also Lee, "Population Growth and the Beginning of Sedentary Life," in Spooner, *Population Growth*.

continued use of the old technology.[9] The neolithic revolution – the change from food gathering to agriculture – is not a sweeping revolutionary change but a process of gradual evolution.[10]

Turning from anthropological to archaeological evidence, we have an example of gradual change from food gathering to food production in Flannery's diggings in Mesopotamian village sites from the period 7500–5500 B.C. In a site that contained remnants from this very long period, he found striking changes in the composition of vegetable foods, with a gradual decline in the use of wild legumes, the major staple food at the beginning of the period, and a gradual increase in grains of cultivated cereals, weeds, and plants typical of fallowed agricultural land. Flannery rejects the idea that early agriculture caused any drastic improvement in people's diet or provided a more stable food supply. He assumes that the slow change from wild food to produced food was a means to increase the carrying capacity of the environment in response to population growth, and he points out that the anthropological studies by Lee and others also suggest that population pressure was the factor that made prehistoric hunting-gathering peoples turn to agriculture.[11]

The sequence of gradual change from more land-using to increasingly land-saving types of agriculture in step with population growth in ancient Mesopotamia has been traced by Smith and Young by means of the archaeological finds of equipment. The plough was in use in the southern plains from the fourth millennium B.C., but hoes for short-fallow cultivation were found in much older sites in mountain villages in the area. It is more difficult to trace digging sticks by archaeological excavation because they are made of wood, but Smith and Young have suggested that holed stones found in the oldest of village sites may be weights for digging sticks and that the lack of hoes in other very old sites may be "evidence from silence" for the use of wooden digging sticks for long-fallow cultivation. The excavations seem also to indicate that a considerable increase of population took place during the period when primitive tools were gradually replaced by better equipment.[12]

Sanders has traced the development of subsistence systems in the Mesoamerican region from ancient times to the Spanish conquest and compared them to the apparent demographic trends in various parts of the region, taking account of the special environmental and other factors. He con-

---

9 Lewis R. Binford, "Post Pleistocene Adaptations," in Binford and Binford, *New Perspectives in Archeology.*

10 G. R. Galy, "Pour une géographie de la France préhistorique," *Annales* 24 (1969).

11 Kent V. Flannery, "Origins and Ecological Effects of Early Domestication in Iran and the Near East," in *The Domestication and Exploitation of Plants and Animals,* ed. Peter J. Ucko and G. W. Dimbleby (Chicago: Aldine, 1969).

12 See Smith and Young in Spooner, *Population Growth.*

cluded that the most productive direction for research in the evolution of civilization is to study the history of population growth and its relationship to increasingly intensive agriculture.[13]

The low labor input needed for subsistence under long-fallow agriculture has been brought out by a large number of studies from many parts of the world. Carneiro concluded from a study in the Amazon Basin that the easiness of the long-fallow system was one of the factors that induced primitive cultivators to split up their local communities and disperse over the territory when their numbers were growing, instead of changing to more land-saving systems. He suggested that because of the centrifugal effects of land-using systems with growing populations, old civilizations based on land-saving, labor-intensive agricultural systems are found in what he calls "circumscribed areas," that is, regions where growing populations were confined in a restricted area surrounded by inhospitable mountains, deserts, or oceans and thus had no other choice than to adopt the land-saving systems in spite of the lower labor productivity.[14]

In comparing the labor needed to obtain food for a family by means of either land-using or land-saving systems, it is necessary to take account not only of the labor needed for actual food gathering or crop growing but also of inputs of labor that are in the nature of investments and that are prerequisites for the use of more land-saving systems of production. While no such labor investment is needed for food gathering and very little for forest fallow if the clearing of land is done mainly by fire, the land saving systems usually cannot be applied without some preliminary labor-intensive land improvements. These labor investments range from clearing roots and stones from land before it can be ploughed for the first time to building wells, ponds, dams, terraces, bunds, and so on, for irrigation. Once such labor investments have been made, it may be possible to obtain higher output per man-hour from the cultivation of permanent fields than from long-fallow agriculture on similar land, but for a primitive population that must choose between undertaking the labor investments and starting long-fallow cultivation in a new place, it is a labor-saving operation to split up the group and continue with long-fallow agriculture in two different places. The yields of the labor investments – if properly maintained – may last forever, but the planning horizon of peoples who subsist by food gathering or long-fallow agriculture is a few years at most.

---

13 William T. Sanders, "Population, Agricultural History and Societal Evolution in Meso-america," in Spooner, *Population Growth*.
14 Robert I. Carneiro, "Slash-and-burn Cultivation among the Kuikuru and Its Implications for Cultural Development in the Amazon Basin," in *The Evolution of Horticultural Systems in Native South America*, ed. Johannes Wilbert (Caracas, 1961).

33

Ester Boserup

DEMOGRAPHIC TRENDS AND
NONAGRICULTURAL TECHNOLOGY

For obvious reasons, the more land-using subsistence systems can be pursued only as long as the population in the region remains below a certain size. There are many other types of technology, however, that require the density of population to be above a minimum level.

It is well known, since Adam Smith's famous dictum, that the division of labor is limited by the extent of the market. This applies not only to modern industrial technology but equally to specialized products of traditional crafts and provision of services. Full-time specialized craftsmen could not possibly exist in villages of long-fallow producers in the Amazon region with populations of 50–150 persons. Craftsmen and other specialists can find enough customers for full-time specialization only in large villages or in small villages in regions that are so densely populated that the distances between villages are small enough to allow one craftsman or other specialist to serve several villages. Thus, very small, isolated groups of persons who practice the land-using primitive subsistence systems cannot afford such specialized activities. Their inhabitants must remain jacks-of-all-trades, which means that their relatively high labor productivity in the provision of food is partly offset by a low labor productivity in the provision of other necessities of life. Such communities are caught in a trap because the maximum density consistent with their subsistence system is below the minimum density needed for development in fields other than food supply. They are not likely to escape from the trap until population density in the region becomes so high (by natural growth or by immigration) that they are forced to adopt a land-saving system of subsistence.

Also much transport technology – modern as well as primitive – can only be applied where there is a certain minimum population. Even a footpath through tropical forest can exist only if used regularly by a certain number of people (or animals). Transport by cart or wagon can develop only where the local population is large enough to build and maintain a network of roads, and the canalization of rivers also requires a large labor force. Thus, small groups living in regions without naturally navigable waterways cannot develop urban centers because the necessary transport of food to such centers cannot be organized. Most ancient civilizations were situated on navigable rivers, and until fairly recently the towns in the interior of Africa were in fact large villages drawing their food supplies from surrounding fields.

With growing population density in a region, it becomes possible to construct and maintain a good network of roads linking the town or towns to food-producing areas or it becomes possible to dig canals or to canalize rivers for transport purposes. At this stage of development, it is no longer

34

necessary that specialized craftsmen and persons performing specialized services for society at large live scattered in villages or move frequently from place to place living off the land, as did the European kings and their courts until population density in their kingdoms increased and the transport system improved. When population density increases, and the land-using subsistence systems are replaced by land-saving systems, both rulers and craftsmen can settle permanently in towns with the additional advantages of still more specialization, better organization, and more specialized equipment.

We may define a town as a major population center, the inhabitants of which do not themselves produce the food they consume. This definition brings into focus the fact that urbanization in primitive societies requires either a high density of rural population or particularly favorable opportunities for the transport of food, for instance, by boat.

It is thus inaccurate to say that the appearance of towns depends upon a high level of labor productivity in agriculture or upon a high degree of exploitation of peasants by a social hierarchy. What is needed is a large food surplus in an absolute sense but not necessarily a large food surplus per agricultural producer. Urbanization in Europe made rapid strides in the eleventh and twelfth centuries; we know that population was increasing considerably in this period, but we have no reliable information about any major improvements in agricultural equipment and in the productivity of agricultural labor at that time.[15] However, a large town may be supplied by small marketable surpluses produced by a large number of producers, if settlement patterns and the available means of transport permit the transportation of food surpluses.

Thus, as far as production is concerned, there may be nothing to prevent long-fallow agriculture from making available the surpluses needed for the supply of towns, but the producers fail to do so because transport to towns is uneconomical with this type of agriculture and because the dispersion of populations using long-fallow systems usually prevents them from reaching the stage of specialization and social organization needed for the development of urban centers. Orans has stressed that long-fallow producers have potential surpluses of food that are not actually produced because there is no need for more than what is customarily consumed in their local communities.[16] But food is not the only article of consumption, and it could as well be said that such peoples have potential surpluses of specialized crafts and services that do not materialize because the local market is too small to permit specialization of labor.

Many of the ancient urban centers obtained their food supply from

15 Bernard Wailes, "Plough and Population in Temperate Europe," in Spooner, *Population Growth.*
16 Martin Orans, "Surplus," *Human Organization* 25 (1966).

intensive irrigated agriculture in the region where they were located, and it is usually suggested that this is because labor productivity is particularly high with irrigated agriculture. It seems more relevant to point out that this type of primitive subsistence system has a particularly high output per unit of land, since crop yields are high and more than one crop may be obtained per year. The high demand for labor per unit of land and the high output per unit of land make it necessary and possible for a large number of families to live within a small area. Therefore, even if the surplus per family is small, the total surplus available within a fairly small distance from the town will be large. In addition, the irrigation canals, or the river used for irrigation, can be used for boat transport of food to the town.

It takes a large labor force, however, to construct and maintain a major irrigation system and to cultivate irrigated crops with primitive technology. Therefore, a major town can be provided with food from this type of agriculture only if the region where it is situated is densely populated or if the military strength of the town forces the outlying population to settle around the town and construct and operate the irrigation system. In any case, it is the total labor force at the disposal of the society that matters and not the size of the surplus that can be extracted per agricultural family. As long as the ancient civilizations had small populations, they used small-scale irrigation; the systems of major irrigation seem to have been created after these societies had grown populous by natural population growth and by immigration of either slaves or free labor from other areas.[17]

EFFECTS OF UNEQUAL DEMOGRAPHIC GROWTH ON SOCIAL ORGANIZATION

There seems to be a fairly close correlation between population size and density, on one hand, and the degree of stratification and complexity of the social system, on the other.[18] Hunting-gathering groups are usually small and scattered, and they have a simple social organization. Long-fallow cultivators usually live in somewhat larger groups and in regions of somewhat higher population density, and they may reach the stage of tribal organization and chiefdoms. But only larger groups, with higher population densities and more land-saving agricultural systems, are likely to reach the next stage, that of preindustrial peasant community with a certain degree of urbanization. Thus when the size and density of population are increasing

---

17 Robert M. Adams, "Early Civilizations, Subsistence and Environment," in *Man in Adaptation*, ed. Yehudi A. Cohen (Chicago: Aldine, 1968).

18 Relevant studies of this correlation have been made by William T. Sanders and Barbara J. Price, *Mesoamerica: The Evolution of a Civilization* (New York: Random House, 1968); and Michel J. Harner, "Population Pressure and the Social Evolution of Agriculturalists," *Southeastern Journal of Anthropology* 26 (1970).

in a primitive society, the social organization of this society becomes increasingly complex through the interplay of several factors, all of which seem to be related to population density. One of these factors is the gradual development of hierarchical systems of land tenure, in step with the change to more land-saving systems of subsistence. Another is an increasing tendency toward tension and hostility both within each local group and between neighboring groups, when the numbers in each group become larger and the distances between the local groups smaller. This may create or enhance social differentiation and a more centralized organization of society either through warfare or through the appearance of a ritually sanctified social ranking.[19]

Egypt and some "circumscribed areas" in Asia reached fairly high population densities many centuries before the Western Hemisphere or Africa (as far as we know), and this may help to explain why we have found the oldest urban civilizations in the Near East and Asia. Robert Adams has shown that ancient Mesopotamia and Mesoamerica at the time of the Spanish conquest reached strikingly similar stages of civilization. But both the Old World during the height of Mesopotamian culture and America before Columbus seem to have had such small populations that only a few peoples in each continent reached the minimum population density required for urban civilization. The few existing urban civilizations were like small islands in a sea of "barbarian" communities, primitive tribes practicing one of the land-using subsistence systems.

To build an urban civilization with the technology available to the population in such a center required a large labor force occupied in labor-intensive investment work, and, as a rule, the peoples who managed to build such civilizations seem to have used all the means at their disposal to obtain foreign labor from the surrounding barbarian groups. But if the urban civilizations skimmed off the population increase of the surrounding barbarian peoples or even decimated their numbers, the remaining barbarian population was prevented from reaching the minimum density for urbanization. The barbarians continued their land-using subsistence systems, caught in the trap of low population density described above. More recently, the American slave raids in Africa seem to have had similar effects.

Such developments entailed a growing technological and cultural gap

19 A number of writers have reviewed specific factors in the relationship of complexity of society to density. Thus, Boserup in *Conditions of Agricultural Growth* reviews changing patterns of land ownership. Carneiro, in Wilbert, *Evolution of Horticultural Systems,* and in "A Theory of the Origin of the State," *Science* 169 (1970), relates inter- and intra-group hostility to group density. Robert McC. Netting in "Sacred Power and Centralization: Some Notes on Political Adaptation in Africa," in Spooner, *Population Growth,* discusses ritualistic stratification of society. And Robert M. Adams, in *The Evolution of Urban Society: Early Mesopotamia and Prehispanic Mexico* (Chicago: Aldine, 1965), discusses such stratification as it is brought about by warfare.

between the centers and the surrounding peoples. The high-level technology used in the centers was inapplicable in the sparsely populated regions that separated the centers from each other, and this also hindered the diffusion of technology from one center to another.

ENVIRONMENT AND
POPULATION GROWTH

While war casualties and forced migration no doubt helped to keep rates of population growth below or close to zero in many primitive societies, environmental differences also are often important in explaining divergent demographic trends. However, we should avoid the common fallacy of thinking of environment exclusively in terms of potential for gathering and producing food. We must also take account of other factors, especially the different incidence of disease in different environments.

It is well known that most contemporary primitive peoples live in the wet tropics – an environment in which both temperature and humidity allow abundant plant growth in all seasons, but one that also provides particularly good conditions for the growth of bacteria and other parasites that decimate primitive populations. As a consequence, mortality due to disease is likely to be much lower in dry and temperate climates. This positive environmental factor in the latter climates may be more important for rates of population growth than the negative environmental factor: the greater difficulty of providing food because of the interruption of plant growth in the dry or cold seasons. In view of the foregoing discussion of the far-reaching impact of population growth on technological change, the implied demographic differential may help to explain why it was the dry and temperate climates that gave rise to most of the early civilizations.

3 Climatic Fluctuations and Population Problems in Early Modern History

Gustaf Utterström

I

EVER SINCE MALTHUS AND RICARDO, all discussions of the pressure on food supplies have started from the assumption that population is the active factor and nature the fixed. This interpretation, however, can hardly be reconciled with modern scientific thought, especially if the problem is viewed in the long term. It is not necessary to go to other geological periods in order to discover great changes in nature. Two changes have occurred in Sweden in the course of the last few thousand years which have radically altered the living conditions of human beings: the great land-elevation which followed the melting of the inland ice, and the climatic fluctuations which have occurred continually. The former was a gradual change and is still proceeding; the latter have made themselves felt at irregular intervals and with varying intensity.

I have suggested in an earlier article that the development of population in Scandinavia and the Baltic regions during the first half of the eighteenth century, far from supporting the Malthusian theory of population, can only be explained by exogenous factors, in particular by the fact that a period of unusually mild climate occurred in the early decades of the century until it was brought to a close about 1740 by a return to more extreme conditions. Even the later surges of population growth seem to have been made possible above all by a mild climate.[1] This prompts the question whether earlier climatic fluctuations might not also have played a decisive part in the development of population – perhaps not only in Scandinavia but in central and western Europe as well. For example, is a partial explanation of the great advance in European economic life from the ninth century to the end of the thirteenth, as well as of the subsequent secular depression during the fourteenth and early fifteenth centuries, to be found in changes in the

[1] G. Utterström, 'Some Population Problems in Pre-Industrial Sweden', *Scandinavian Economic History Review* 2 (1954):108ff.

climate? It now seems probable that both the rise and the subsequent decline were closely linked with agricultural and demographic developments.[2]

I have no intention of suggesting that climate is a universal explanation of all these complex relations. On the other hand the possible influence of climatic fluctuations seems to have received very scant notice from historians outside Scandinavia, a fact which in itself is reason enough to draw attention to the discussion which has been going on in the northern countries. The role which climate played in developments in north Scandinavia, Iceland, and Greenland during the later Middle Ages has been a matter of lively debate among Scandinavian historians for a very long time.[3] Now that the general European depression of the fourteenth and fifteenth centuries has come under the scrutiny of historical research, the subject has acquired added interest.

A few preliminary observations have to be made before we turn to the climate itself. It is reasonable to suppose that in large parts of medieval Europe the general economic and monetary factors, which are of decisive importance in the modern world, were of very little significance compared with agriculture. Agriculture obviously always depends to a

---

2 M. Postan, 'Some Economic Evidences of Declining Population in the Later Middle Ages', *Economic History Review* (1950), pp. 221–46; Postan, 'The Trade of Medieval Europe: The North', in vol. 2 of the *Cambridge Economic History of Europe* (1952), pp. 213 ff.; Postan, 'Die wirtschaftlichen Grundlagen der mittelalterlichen Gesellschaft', *Jahrbücher für Nationalökonomie und Statistik* 166 (1954):180–205. See also R. S. Lopez, 'The Trade of Medieval Europe: The South', in vol. 2 of the *Cambridge Economic History of Europe*, pp. 293 ff. Without expressing a definite opinion on the controversy between Professor Postan and Professor Schreiner (see J. Schreiner's article *Scandinavian Economic History Review* 2 [1954]:61–73), I think that Professor Schreiner's argument is partly weakened by the fact that he has chosen the years 1310–19 as the basis of his tables of wheat prices, since this period includes the two years of what was probably the worst famine recorded in the Middle Ages. As early as 1866 Thorold Rogers observed on the famine years 1315 and 1316: 'Nor will any parallel, it may be asserted confidently, be discovered for these two years. We shall find, indeed, that the years 1321 and 1369 approach the famine which prevailed in the two years before us, but at a considerable distance, whether we consider the rate at which corn was purchased or the universality of the dearth. The highest prices which have ever prevailed since the annual corn returns of 1582, are, when we consider the proportion which the rates of 1315–16 bear to the average price and the value of money, indicative on comparison of almost a trivial increase. The highest quotation of wheat in modern English history is that of December 1800, when it is returned at £6 13 s. 4d. This, however, was not much more than double the ordinary price, while the scarcity of 1315 represents a quintuple rise in many places, and that of 1316 almost a quadruple of the general average.' (*A History of Agriculture and Prices in England*, 1:198). The years 1315–16 marked the peak but wheat prices were unusually high also in other years of the period.
3 The account given here is based mainly on S. Thorarinsson, 'Tefrokronologiska studier på Island', *Geografiska Annaler* (1944):1–217. For further references to the relevant literature see also O. A. Johnsen, *Norwegische Wirtschaftsgeschichte* (1939):132 ff.

considerable extent upon the weather, but how sensitive it is varies greatly according to the standards of husbandry and agricultural technique. The primitive agriculture of the Middle Ages must have been much more dependent on favourable weather than is modern agriculture with its high technical standards. Of weather factors, both temperature and rainfall are of decisive significance for vegetation. Too much or too little of either can easily cause a serious crop failure. In southern Europe the greatest danger usually lies in too little rain during the period of growth; in Great Britain the danger is that the rainfall will be too great. In Scandinavia, especially in the north and in the upland regions of the south as well as in other parts of northern Europe, the outcome of the harvest is determined above all by temperature and by the length of the period of growth. For that reason a continental climate with long and severe winters followed by cold and dry springs may have devastating effects. Such conditions easily arise when the circulation of air from the west is weak.

Norwegian historians, especially Professor Edvard Bull (1881–1932), have for some considerable time been discussing the question whether the country's political decline during the late Middle Ages might not have been connected with an economic decline caused by a deterioration in the climate. They have pointed out that two facts might indicate that this was so: the extinction of the Nordic population in Greenland, and the cessation of corn growing in Iceland. This theory gained scientific support with the publication of *Climatic Variations in Historic and Prehistoric Time* by the Swedish oceanographer Otto Pettersson, which first appeared in Swedish in 1913, in English in 1914.[4] According to Pettersson, the forces which govern the tides are subject to periodic changes which conform to certain laws determined by the periodic variations in the position of the moon and the sun in relation to the earth. These forces are at their strongest at the time of a constellation which occurs at intervals of about eighteen hundred years.

Changes in the tide-governing forces give rise to periodic changes in the tides themselves and in oceanic circulation. When the forces are at their maximum, the ice of the Arctic Ocean is more extensively broken up and in consequence the East Greenland and Labrador Currents carry unusually large quantities of drift-ice at those times, causing the climates of Iceland and Greenland to deteriorate. According to calculations by other scientists, the constellation which brings maximal oceanic circulation occurred about 350 B.C. and about A.D. 1430 while the constellation bringing minimal oceanic circulation, minimal drift-ice, and a favourable climate in Iceland and Greenland occurred about A.D. 500 or 600. This would mean that, according to

4 The Swedish version was published in *Kungliga Svenska Vetenskapsakademiens. Handlingar* 51:2 (1913), the English version in *Svenska Hydrogr.-Biolog. Kommitténs Skrifter 5* (1914).

Professor Pettersson, there was a relatively favourable climate in both Iceland and Greenland during the Viking Age and until the middle of the twelfth century. Conditions then deteriorated uninterruptedly until the middle of the fifteenth century. This climatic fluctuation made itself felt even in the south of the European continent. In support of his theory Professor Pettersson produced data concerning ice conditions both in Scandinavian waters and in rivers on the continent and concerning the state of drift-ice off Greenland and Iceland during those centuries, as well as information about the presence of shoals of herring off the coast of Skåne and the cessation of corn (wheat) growing in Iceland.

Professor Pettersson's tide theory is a bold one, perhaps too bold, but many leading oceanographers and meteorologists have subscribed to it, and even now it has not been abandoned.[5] Let us therefore turn to see what other types of empirical research have contributed.

Scholars in widely different fields of science have taken part in the debate which arose out of the publication of Professor Pettersson's work: meteorologists, glaciologists, geologists, archaeologists, and historians. Two lines of thought soon emerged from the discussions: One accepted the theory that climate deteriorated in the Middle Ages, the other rejected the evidential value of the arguments and facts put forward. Some of the latter, though not contested, were considered not to need a theory of climate to explain them. It is, however, quite certain that among scientists the opposition to Pettersson's theory nowadays is much less than in the decades immediately after 1913, and it can be accepted as a fact beyond discussion that a considerable deterioration in climate did take place in Europe in the middle of the first millennium B.C.

Conditions in Iceland may be used to illustrate the problem. The economic life of Iceland began to change radically during the first half of the fourteenth century. The economic centre of gravity moved away from the interior of the island to the coast where fishing was the main occupation. The change was reflected early in the fourteenth century in a considerable decline in the export of homespun (*vadmal*). In its place fish products became the most important articles of export. Corn growing became less and less important and the import of grain increased. These events are easily explained by the climate theory. But they can also be regarded as having originated in the contemporaneous changes in trade and commerce. The Hanseatic League took over Bergen's fish trade in the first half of the fourteenth century, and the changes in Iceland may have been connected with the activities of the Hanseatic merchants.[6]

5 See, eg, Rachel Carson, *The Sea around Us* (1951), chap. 12; C. E. P. Brooks, *Climate through the Ages* (1949), chap. 22.
6 Thorarinsson, 'Tefrokronologiska studier', pp. 72 f.

Conditions in Iceland in the Middle Ages and early modern times have been thoroughly investigated by Dr. Sigurdur Thorarinsson, a scientist whose research has been conducted in association with Professor Hans W:son Ahlmann, the Swedish geographer and glaciologist. Thorarinsson does not contest the fact that changed conditions of trade and commerce may have been an important cause of the changes in Iceland's economic structure, but he considers it highly probable that changes in climatic and physico-geographic conditions were also determinant factors. The eruptions of Hekla in 1300 and eruptions of other volcanoes later in the century made farming difficult, or for a time impossible, over extensive areas. Conditions for cattle raising deteriorated. It is beyond dispute that in Iceland the epoch 1270–1390 was a period of unusually numerous bad years climatically. This seems to have been a universal phenomenon; 'even though we (i.e., the Icelanders) have experienced similar periods later, especially in the seventeenth and eighteenth centuries, there is no record that we ever had one in our earlier history, and it is that which is decisive in this connection'.[7]

Dr. Thorarinsson considers that the expansion and subsequent decline of corn growing which he has investigated for different parts of the island can hardly be explained by alterations in trade and commerce alone. He concludes that climatic conditions probably played a considerable part. But the data on corn growing are too scanty to make it possible to determine exactly the period of its swiftest decline. It is evident, however, that corn growing declined in the fourteenth and fifteenth centuries, and probably very considerably, though it did not cease altogether until towards the end of the sixteenth century. The fact that corn-growing has been successfully resumed in recent times he regards as an argument not against, but for the theory that climate deteriorated in the late Middle Ages and was unfavourable in the sixteenth and seventeenth centuries. The fluctuation in climate now taking place has in this view restored favourable conditions for corn growing.

The weightiest of Dr. Thorarinsson's arguments, however, seem to be those which concern changes in the glaciers. Both opponents and supporters of the climate theory seem to be agreed that the glaciers of Iceland were considerably smaller in extent during the island's period as a free state (870–1262) than they were later. The opponents prefer the explanation that this was due to the effects of subglacial volcanic action; Thorarinsson's view is that volcanic action merely affects the glaciers' substance. In the long run it cannot result in an increase in the extent of the glaciers. The activities of the Icelandic subglacial volcanoes increased in the periods after the free state, and the glaciers might therefore be expected to have declined in

7 Ibid., pp. 147–61. As to climatic conditions in Europe, Thorarinsson refers to E. Huntington and S. S. Visher, *Climatic Changes, Their Nature and Causes* (1922), chap. 6.

43

extent. But instead they increased, and they did so 'not *because of* but *in spite of* volcanic action, and their increase provides a minimum measure of the increase occasioned by [deterioration in] climate'.[8]

It is difficult to say exactly when the glaciers started to advance. Thorarinsson considers, however, that the main extension occurred after 1200. They were still advancing in the sixteenth century and reached their maximum about the middle of the eighteenth century; some glaciers, however, had almost attained their maximum as early as the middle of the seventeenth century. The retreat began about 1850 and has been very marked since about 1890. The connection with the climatic fluctuation now in progress is obvious. Professor Ahlmann's demonstration of the relationships between glacier behaviour and the temperature of the ablation season has made it possible to relate the small fluctuations of climate during the past 250 years to the advances and retreats of Icelandic and north European glaciers; with these also the climatic fluctuations in England and Holland appear to be accordant. Active glacier advance has taken place notably during those periods in which the average temperature of spring and summer was unusually low. These cold climatic spells, for example, 1739–48, 1799–1820, and 1836–45, are probably related to variations in the vigour of the atmospheric circulation over the North Atlantic and/or variations in the extent of the Arctic sea-ice.[9]

Professor Ahlmann has expressed complete agreement with Thorarinsson's interpretation. He observes that the excavations at Herjólfsnes in Greenland (the present Ikigait near the southern point), which in the Middle Ages was the Norsemen's most important commercial centre in Österbygden, confirm the conclusions reached concerning Iceland. The bodies at Herjólfsnes must have been buried in soft earth which later froze and remained frozen until the present. The well-preserved clothes and hats found there are of the same kind as Dante and Petrarch wore.

We must, however, consider additional causes of the destruction of the Norsemen's colony. Professor Ahlmann summarizes present opinion as follows: 'There were certainly several causes of the ruin of the Norsemen's settlements in West Greenland. Isolation and the burden of steadily increasing poverty in all probability played their part. The skeletons found at Herjólfsnes show that the women were so deformed that they were obviously incapable of bearing children. It is also probable that there was a plague of insects which destroyed the grass. Attacks by the Eskimoes and defeat at their hands also contributed to the destruction of the Väster- and Österbygd. But these raids confirm the idea of a deterioration in climate. The Eskimoes had

8 Ibid., pp. 158 f.
9 H. W:son Ahlmann, 'The Present Climatic Fluctuation', *Geographic Journal* (1948): 165–95. Cf. G. Manley, 'Variations in the Mean Temperature of Britain since Glacial Times', *Geologische Rundschau* (1952):125–7.

lived in those parts prior to the arrival of the Norsemen, but had obviously withdrawn to the north. They were entirely dependent for their livelihood on the seal and hence on the drift-ice, and it is thus logical to assume that, during the period in the 12th and 13th centuries when the Norsemen's colonies flourished, the favourable climate reduced the ice to such an extent that the Eskimoes were compelled to move further north. With the deterioration in climate which occurred later, both the drift-ice and the Eskimoes returned and thus, during the 14th and 15th centuries, the latter came into conflict with the Norsemen who fought and defended themselves in external conditions which were steadily deteriorating.[10]

The problem of corn growing in Iceland has a parallel in England. I refer to the cultivation of the English vineyards. Thus, Professor George Kimble contends that at the time of the Domesday Survey and as late as the second half of the thirteenth century vine growing in England was at its height. Later it deteriorated and by the end of the fourteenth century it disappeared almost completely. William of Malmesbury, writing about A.D. 1150, highly praises the abundance and quality of the vine in the vale of Gloucester, whereas Polydore Virgil, writing about the English in the early sixteenth century has quite another opinion: 'They plant vine in their gardens rather for a covert and commodity of shadow than for the fruit, for the grapes seldom commit to ripen, except a hot summer ensue'. Professor Kimble concludes:

It would seem then, that the English summers were distinctly warmer during the 12th and 13th centuries than they normally are today. Although we have no means of telling precisely what the difference was, we can obtain a satisfactory first approximation by comparing the present summer temperatures of the southern half of England with those prevailing along the northern limit of the commercial grape-growing belt in France. The mean temperature for the three summer months of June, July and August in the London area (the hottest part of England) now lies between 61° and 62°F., whereas the corresponding temperature for the Paris-Nantes region (north of which towns very little wine is produced) lies between 64° and 65°F. It seems probable, then, that when the English grape husbandry was at its best, the summer temperatures averaged between three and four degrees higher than they have done in recent times.

It should be noted, however, that in the seventeenth century a number of

---

10 The excavations at Herjólfsnes were conducted by the Danish historian and archeologist P. Nörlund; see his paper 'Buried Norsemen at Herjólfsnes', *Meddelelserom Grönland Svenska Hydrografisk-Biologiska Kommissionens Skrifter* 67 (1924). Cf. also his article 'Kirkegaarden paa Herjolfsnaes. Et Bridrag til Diskussionen om Klimateorien' (Norwegian), *Historisk Tidsskrift,* 5th ser., 6 (1927):385–401 (with an English Summary', pp. 401 f.). See also W. Hovgaard, 'The Norsemen in Greenland. Recent Discoveries at Herjólfsnes', *Geographical Review'* 15 (1925), and J. Marcus, 'The Greenland Trade-Route', *Economic History Review* (1954):77 ff. Ahlmann's survey, 'Europas erövring av jorden', *Nordisk Tidskrift,* 30 (1954):71.

English writers, commenting on the disappearance of the vine, argued that this was due to the lowered standard of fruit cultivation rather than to a change in the climate. One author, while admitting that vine was no longer grown in Gloucester, said that 'no doubt many parts would yeald at this day, but that the inhabitants forbeare to plant vines, as well they are served plentifully, and at a good rate, with French wines, as for that the hills most fit to beare Grapes, yeelde more commoditie by feeding of sheepe and cattel'.[11]

It is not self-evident, however, that the contentions of the seventeenth-century writers must be preferred to the explanation given by Professor Kimble. It may well be that a deterioration in the essential requirements for grape growing prepared the way for the import of French wine, although other factors also may have contributed to the decline of the English grape husbandry.

The contribution by a historian to the debate on Norway's decline during and after the fourteenth century which has attracted the most attention in recent years has been Professor Johan Schreiner's *Pest og Prisfall i Senmiddelalderen (Plague and Falling Prices in the Late Middle Ages* [Oslo, 1948]). Also in Norway the problem is a complicated one, and we must suppose that there were several contributory causes. Professor Schreiner examines European conditions in general as a background to the Norwegian problem. The main task he set himself was to discover why Norway did not recover from the black death of the fourteenth century as quickly as did her Scandinavian neighbours.

According to Professor Schreiner, Sweden, and especially Denmark, recovered from the reduction of their populations in the course of two or three generations, but Norway did not recover until the sixteenth or early seventeenth century. He considers that this cannot be satisfactorily explained either by epidemics of plague or by the climate theory, if only because the stagnation of the Norwegian population was not confined to the mountain districts which were most sensitive to a lowering of the temperature (though the decline certainly was greatest there) but also affected the plains in the southeastern part of the country. 'It is difficult to believe, if not completely out of the question, that for generation after generation the weather [in Norway] can have been much worse than in Denmark and even parts of Sweden which had essentially the same geographic conditions. This could only have been possible if the temperature followed the national frontiers.'[12] Professor Schreiner puts forward the alternative hypothesis that the higher prices of butter and its increased

---

11 G. Kimble, *The Weather* (Penguin Books, 1951), pp. 232 f; *An Historical Geography of England, A.D. 1000–1250*, ed. H. C. Darby (1948), pp. 196, 408.
12 J. Schreiner, *Pest og Prisfall i Senmiddelalderen* (1948), p. 9.

export from Norway to Lübeck after the great reduction in population induced the Hanseatic merchants to encourage and maintain the shift which subsequently occurred in agricultural production away from corn growing and towards a relative increase in cattle raising.

It is legitimate to enquire what means the Hanseatic merchants could conceivably have used in a land of peasant proprietors like Norway to prevent a return to corn growing, if the climate and the development of the population had been favourable. In a country like England with a large class of landed proprietors it might be expected that changes in the relative prices of wool and corn would have had considerable influence on the use to which land was put. Arable land might have been turned over to pasture causing the farmer, who did not own the land himself, to have to leave. But the Norwegian peasants generally owned the land they farmed. It is true that they too might have considered it advantageous to use their land for pasture instead of tilling it if it paid them to sell butter and buy grain. But it is difficult to understand how relatively high butter and low corn prices can have been responsible for preventing the country's recovery.

Professor Schreiner seems to have followed another line of thought. His view is that the Hanseatic merchants exploited the fact that Norway depended on them for grain in order to fetter the Norwegian system of production. But this at once raises new questions. A peasant population normally does everything possible to avoid what it considers to be unnecessary expenditure, in other words to preserve the highest possible degree of self-sufficiency. How did it come about then that in the fourteenth century the Hanseatic merchants could have established such a dominance over Norway's supplies of bread? It is difficult to understand why the Hanseatic merchants did not exploit their power by forcing down the price of Norwegian butter. If the Norwegians were completely dependent upon their grain, the Hanseatic merchants can scarcely have feared that the quantity of butter offered would be reduced.

As we have said, Professor Schreiner does not dispute the fact that a deterioration in the climate may have played some part in Norway's decline. The question is therefore to estimate how much importance can be attached to the factor of climate. It is obvious that the deterioration of climate was not confined within the country's political frontiers. But what evidence is there to show that districts in Sweden with similar climatic conditions as the Norwegian did in fact recover more swiftly than the Norwegian districts? If the decline followed the frontier, the reasons must have been political rather than economic. Comparisons with Denmark and, more particularly, with England[13] are quite irrelevant, since the geographical positions of those

---

13 Schreiner, 'Bemerkungen zum Hanse-Norwegen-Problem', *Hansische Geschichtsblätter* 72(1954):69.

countries are quite different. As can be seen from my earlier article, population developments in the 1740s[14] show that a change in climate may have had quite different effects in England and in Scandinavia.

It is worth noting that Professor Schreiner admits that the decline in Norway was greatest in regions where the climatic conditions were most unfavourable for corn growing, but does not attach any great importance to this fact. The climate theory seems to be quite compatible with one of the many theories advanced in Germany to explain the great number of *Wüstungen* [deserted lands], the *Fehlsiedlungstheorie*. In recent years German investigators have also tried to demonstrate that part of the *Wüstungen* in central Germany during the fourteenth and fifteenth centuries owed their occurrence to fluctuations in climate. These *Wüstungen* are supposed to have come about mainly during two periods with different climates: *Wüstungen* on dry, sandy soil especially during a warm, dry period in 1360–1430, and *Wüstungen* on heavy soil during a cold, wet period in the decades immediately after 1430.[15]

It is important to enquire at this stage how a fluctuation of climate in the direction of a continental climate affects vegetation. The effects in fact vary greatly between different regions and different kinds of plants, according to whether temperature or rainfall is the decisive factor for the crop, in accordance with Liebig's law of the decisive minimum. Phenology has taught us that the period of ripening is considerably shortened within continental areas, that dry warmth accelerates the phases of flowering and fruition, that sharp changes in temperature cause the buds to open earlier, and finally that extremes of temperature are of special significance in the vegetable world.

The corn harvest may, therefore, be excellent when a fluctuation of climate occurs towards the continental type, provided that temperature and rainfall do not fall below the minimum requirements of the kind of grain in question. On the other hand, the growth of grass will deteriorate considerably since it depends first and foremost on moisture. Thus it was reported from Austria in 1951 that the increasingly continental climate in recent years has led in certain districts to a disastrous shortage of hay.[16] The same phenomenon was evident in Sweden in the 1740s and 1780s for example.[17] In northern and central Europe there is the additional factor that cold winters prolong the period during which cattle have to be stall-fed and may also mean that the corn's minimum requirement of warmth is not attained

14 Utterström, 'Population Problems', pp. 131 ff.
15 G. Richter, 'Klimaschwankungen und Wüstungsvorgänge im Mittelalter', *Petermanns geographische Mitteilungen* 96 (1952):249 ff. and the literature cited there.
16 F. Rosenkranz, 'Klimacharakter, Natur und Wirtschaft', *Wetter und Leben*, 3 (1951):4.
17 There is much information on this in the accounts of crops made by the county governors in their annual reports or in their special seasonal reports about the harvests.

and that the period of vegetation is far too short. In the Mediterranean area the greatest danger lies in the possibility that the plants' requirements of moisture in the decisive months will not be met. Thus the north and the south of Europe are liable to suffer more from an increasingly continental climate than are the centrally situated areas.

The climate theory, therefore, can explain certain economic phenomena of the fourteenth and fifteenth centuries which other theories leave unexplained: violently fluctuating harvests and grain prices, not only from year to year but from one period to another, considerable increases in the prices of animal products, especially butter, relative to corn prices, and perhaps also partly the decline of wool production in England and the shift of the cloth industry to the western parts of the country where the rainfall was greatest. In this last example it is, of course, obvious that changes in technique were of great importance.[18] It is, however, evident that in any attempt to explain changes in the relative prices of grain and butter partly in terms of climatic factors both the production and the demand side must be examined. Here the shrinkage of population and scarcity of labour in relation to other productive factors, especially land, come into the picture. I do not propose to go into this question any further, but the influence of climate on production must be borne in mind when the economic conditions in Europe around 1600 are considered.

Other bioclimatic questions are worth mentioning. It is known that phases of continental climate in the past were often accompanied by the appearance of certain pests, especially locusts. As late as 1864 there was an invasion of locusts even in England. After their destruction the bodies might be found lying an inch thick on the ground. The locusts are merely one example of how the plant and animal worlds reflect in their individual manifestations of vitality the influence of the transition to a more continental type of climate.[19]

The plague almost completely disappeared from most parts of Europe more than two centuries ago. Many reasons have been suggested for this: House rats ceased to infect houses occupied by human beings after the black rat was eliminated by the brown and after the standard of dwellings and hygiene improved. Epidemiologists also say that the dangerous rat flea (*Xenopsylla cheopis*), which has an especial predilection for the black rat, multiplies most rapidly in a subtropical climate, and in Europe during hot summers.[20] Hot summers are of course characteristic of a continental climate. It may be possible to infer that during the centuries in which the

18 E. M. Carus-Wilson, 'The Woollen Industry', in vol. 2 of *Cambridge Economic History of Europe*, pp. 411 f. Postan, 'Die wirtschaftlichen Grundlagen', pp. 192, 199.
19 F. Rosenkranz, 'Klimacharakter', p. 4.
20 L. F. Hirst, *The Conquest of Plague* (1953), pp. 260 ff.

plague ravaged northern Europe, the climate was more continental than it is at present.[21]

The data which scientists have accumulated from glacier research, from the excavations in Greenland, from the study (by the application of pollen analysis) of the peat bogs in central Sweden, and from other experiments and observations, must be considered to give strong support to the theory that a general change of climate took place during the Middle Ages. Many questions still remain unresolved, however. An archaeologist who has studied the Swedish peat bogs writes: 'It is not yet known when the change set in; it may already have started in the later decades of Norseman times. Possibly it took the form of a lower annual temperature but certainly there was less precipitation, mostly to the detriment of grazing areas'.[22]

Professor Gordon Manley, the meteorologist, who has devoted special attention to climatic fluctuations, emphasizes that the data on climate are very meagre until the fourteenth century. He says that it is nevertheless evident that a long period of severe drought occurred about A.D. 1275 both in Europe and in the western parts of the United States. 'Later the frequency of reports of climatic catastrophes of one sort or another becomes so marked as to suggest that the fourteenth and early fifteenth centuries were a period of great variability. The number of extremely severe winters was very great. We have, for example, reliable accounts showing that the Baltic was completely icebound in the years 1296, 1306, 1323, 1408, 1423, 1426 and 1460'.[23] On the other hand climatic conditions later in the fifteenth century appear to have been somewhat milder.[24]

The meteorologist Dr. Hermann Flohn has arrived at similar conclusions concerning Germany by comparing the data available in chronicles and similar sources about extremely cold winters. According to him it is possible to distinguish a number of shorter periods. The years 1365–98 and 1420–28 apparently were times when the climate was comparatively mild. From a maximum warmth about 1400 there was a progressive transition to a minimum around 1450; the period 1429–45 especially was marked by severe winters and cool summers. According to Dr. Flohn, there then

21 Cf. H. Faust, 'Wetter und Klima als gestaltende Fäktoren in der Geschichte der Menschheit', *Universitas* 9 (1954):1002.
22 A. Roussel, *Farms and Churches* (cited in Thorarinsson, 'Tefrokronologiska studier', p. 153).
23 G. Manley, *Climate and the British Scene* (1952), pp. 236 ff.; C. Easton, *Les hivers dans l'Europe occidentale* (1928); A. Norlind, 'Einige Bemerkungen über das Klima der historischen Zeit nebst einem Verzeichnis mittelalterlicher Witterungserscheinungen', *Lunds Universitets Årsskrift*, N.F., Avd. 1, 10:1 (1914):3–20; C. J. Ostman and H. Henrikson, 'Om köld och is i nyare och äldre tid', *Ymer* 62 (1942):35 f.
24 See notes 58–62 below.

followed a further period of warmer climate after the middle of the fifteenth century, a very conspicuous rise in temperature occurring in the first half of the sixteenth century.[25]

Dr. Flohn's results agree closely with those reached by Professor K. Müller through his study of the German grape harvests.[26] The good grape years occurred as a rule at the same time in all the German wine districts. A good grape harvest requires a hot, sunny and predominantly dry summer. There were good wine years in 1372–7, 1386–90, 1894–7, and 1420–6, but otherwise only in occasional years in the fourteenth century and in the first half of the fifteenth. If these data are compared with what is known of the grain harvests in western Europe, it appears that warm summers and good harvests generally coincided, as did cool summers and poor harvests.[27]

These facts are surely enough to indicate that the question of a possible connection between climate and the general European depression during the fourteenth and the first half of the fifteenth centuries is one which is worth taking up for examination. We have long ago left behind the time when scholars like Jevons and Moore sought to explain the duration and periodicity of the modern trade cycle in terms of sun spots; but empirical meteorological research has nevertheless shown that, at irregular intervals during the last few centuries, wide variations in temperature have occurred in Europe simultaneously affecting places as far apart as London, Berlin, and Stockholm, though with varying degrees of intensity.[28] It is significant, too, that the crop failures which Lord Beveridge recorded in 'Weather and Harvest Cycles'[29] as having occurred in modern times in western and central Europe, almost all appear in the Swedish material as well.

There is reason to believe that a change in climate which strongly affected northern Europe cannot have failed to leave some mark on more southernly parts.[30] Shortages of fodder occurred in many areas of southern Europe when the cattle could not be kept out on the pastures.[31] There too the poor suffered badly in severe winters, as can be seen from the havoc wrought in

---

25 H. Flohn, 'Klimaschwankungen im Mittelalter und ihre historisch-geographische Bedeutung'. *Berichte zur deutschen Landeskunde* 7 (1949/50). Summary in Richter, 'Klimaschwankungen', pp. 249 ff.

26 K. Müller, 'Weinjahre und Klimaschwankungen der letzten 1000 Jahre', *Der Weinbau. Wissenschaftliches Beiheft* 1 (1947). Summary in Richter, 'Klimaschwankungen', pp. 249 ff.

27 Cf. data about harvests in Postan, 'Trade of Medieval Europe', p. 198.

28 D. Brunt, 'Climatic Cycles', *Geographic Journal* (1937):214–38.

29 *Economic Journal* 31 (1921):429–52.

30 Cf. conclusions about weather and harvests in J. H. Kremp, *Über den Einfluss des Ernteausfalles auf die Getreidepreise während der Jahre 1846–1875* in den hauptsächlichsten, Ländern Europas (1879), pp. 157 ff.

31 K. F. Helleiner, 'Introduction' to *Readings in European History* (1946), p. 9.

France by *le grand hiver* of 1709, as well as by previous and subsequent cold winters.[32] The influence of the winter was not confined to the direct effects of cold and of high corn prices; most important of all was the fact that in countries with a temperate climate employment was considerably lower during the winter than in the more clement seasons.[33]

It is of course true that crop failures had often occurred before the fourteenth century. Boissonnade counted, for example, sixty years of famine in France between 970 and 1100.[34] But we know very little of their intensity. If the climate had deteriorated periodically and at short intervals in such a way that the number of extremely cold winters and/or cold wet summers increased, the effects may have been quite different and more radical. H. S. Lucas's paper on the great European famine of 1315, 1316, and 1317 has interesting points to add in this connection. More interesting still are the statements we have about the advances and retreats of the glaciers, although their reliability must be regarded as somewhat dubious. According to some scientists the glaciers of the western Alps were at a minimum in the centuries preceding A.D. 1300. During the following century there was a readvance, followed by a retreat to their minimum extent in the fifteenth century.[35]

In his comprehensive study of the economic foundations of medieval European society Professor Postan discusses the possible influence of climate on economic change.[36] He accepts it as obvious that agricultural depression in England, France and Germany in the fourteenth century was ushered in by a series of crop failures caused by torrential rains and floods in 1309–23. Conditions in Sweden appear to have been similar during those years.[37] But Professor Postan is not inclined to attach great significance to

---

32 M. R. Reinhard, *Histoire de la population mondiale de 1700 à 1948* (1949), pp. 74 f.; J. Meuvret, 'Les crises de subsistences et la démographie de la France d'ancien régime', *Population* (1946):643–50.

33 Cf. the statistics of the monthly distribution of deaths in various European countries 1906–10 given in F. Prinzing, *Handbuch der medizinischen Statistik* 2 (1931), pp. 529 ff.

34 Quoted by Helleiner, *Readings*, p. 9.

35 Brooks, *Climate*, p. 301.

36 Postan, 'Die wirtschaftlichen Grundlagen', pp. 190 f.

37 The Chronicler Ericus Olai (d. 1486; see his biography by E. Nygren in *Svenskt biografiskt lexikon* 14 [1951]) wrote in Sweden of the year 1314: '*Hoc anno Visby combusta est, tunc etiam fames nimia Sueciam oppressit*' (*Scriptores Rerum Suecicarum Medii Aevi* 2:1 [1828], p. 92). The editor has added this note: '*De 'karistia temporis' pluries hujus anni diplomata mentionem faciunt*', Ericus Olai's statement must be supposed to have been derived from some annals which are now lost. A. O. Rhyzelius, *Brontologia theologico-historica, thet är enfaldig lära och sanferdig berettelse om åskedunder, blixt och skott* (1721), states (p. 61) quoting the vicar of Veckholm, Jacobus Gisloni's *Chronologia* (printed 1592), p. 88, for the year 1315: '*Pluvia et tonitrua horrenda per totam aestatem; fames et pestis secutae, quibus tertia pars viventium absumta est.*' The source of this information, in all probability some lost annals, is unknown. Rhyzelius adds: 'At this time

climate as a cause of the secular depression. He has four main objections to doing so: (1) The crop failures of two decades cannot explain a depression lasting one and a half centuries; (2) even if it could be shown that the east coast of England did recede during this period and that hydrologic conditions in England were fundamentally altered, it still remains difficult to understand how these climatic conditions, if sufficiently lasting to keep England's agriculture in a state of depression right up to the last quarter of the fifteenth century, could nevertheless permit it to flourish in the sixteenth century; (3) it is equally difficult to understand why the so-called wet cycle also caused a depression in areas with a dry climate, like southern and southeastern Europe as well as in countries with a moist climate like England; (4) there is still no proof that, during the early Middle Ages, western Norway and Iceland were self-sufficient in grain, or that the decline of agriculture there should not be attributed to such purely economic causes as the import of cheap corn from the Baltic countries.

Professor Postan's objections are hardly convincing. (1) If the glaciers in northern and central Europe did expand and the climate of Europe became more continental, then the unfavourable weather conditions of 1309–23 can be interpreted as a temporary intensification of a secular deterioration of climate which had already begun; in other words, it would be an exact parallel to the crop failures around 1600 which will be discussed in more detail below. (2) The end of the depression towards the close of the fifteenth century and the revival of agriculture in the sixteenth century can be explained as partly the result of an improvement in climate. (3) The famous Austrian meteorologist Eduard Brückner concluded that 'wet cycles' and 'dry cycles' occurred of about thirty-five years' duration, but the existence of these cycles is not unchallenged. Meteorologists reckon nowadays with a number of different cycles varying very greatly in length.[38] The particular consequences of increased precipitation in southern and southeastern Europe in the latter half of the sixteenth century – dealt with below – should also be taken into consideration. The question of precipitation, however, calls for more detailed discussion. (4) Dr. Thorarinsson's research into the history of corn growing in Iceland provides strong grounds for not accepting the import of grain as the one and only explanation of the decline of corn growing. In general, even those Norwegian historians who have sought explanations other than climatic for the country's decline in the later

there was great hardship throughout our dear fatherland which lasted many years.' The work is based on annals and chronicles as well as on other sources. Among those who contributed by giving information, Rhyzelius thanks Elias Palmskiöld, employed in the Royal Archives and known for his great collection of manuscripts.

38 H. C. Willett, 'Long-Period Fluctuations of the General Circulation of the Atmosphere', *Journal of Meteorology* 6 (1949):34–50; Kimble, *Weather*, pp. 147 ff.

Middle Ages have admitted that Norway had earlier been mainly self-sufficient in foodstuffs, especially corn.

In the discussions of climatic conditions during the Middle Ages German scientists have emphasized that there were two distinct types of climates distinguishable in central Europe: one characterized by mild winters and warm summers, the other by cold winters and cool summers. The former type of climate presupposes an especially strong formation of subtropical anticyclones. In the winter, mild westerly maritime winds flow along the northern flank of the high pressure system; in the summer the anticyclone itself moves in over central Europe. These conditions result in prolonged warm and dry weather. With the second type, cold continental air in the winter spreads across central Europe from the Euro-Asiatic mainland. In the summer the same areas come under the influence of cool maritime air masses which stream in over the warmer mainland.[39]

Precipitation cannot simply be disposed of by making a division into 'wet cycles' and 'dry cycles'. Attention must also be paid to the movements of cyclones and of the so-called weather fronts.

Brückner, and after him the American geographer and meteorologist Huntington, both emphasized the great importance of the part played by the wandering paths of the cyclones in the fluctuations of climate which have taken place in Europe in historic times.[40] When the climate in northern and central Europe was continental in character (i.e., with cold winters), the tracks of the cyclones should have followed a southerly route. Thus, during the cold winters of the eighteenth century northerly anticyclones were over long periods predominant in eastern England.[41] Maritime winters with mild damp climate should presuppose the existence of cyclones moving in more northerly latitudes. The southerly displacement of the cyclones may have varied in intensity at different periods. Huntington, for example, has tried to explain the flourishing of the ancient civilizations of Greece and Rome and their subsequent decline according to changes in the tracks of the cyclones. As long as the depressions followed southerly tracks the climate is supposed to have been favourable, especially so far as rainfall was concerned, but when the cyclones were later displaced towards the north the climate deteriorated. Conversely, the climate of northern Europe now improved, although there the winters had been arctic ever since the deterioration of climate in the middle of the first millennium B.C.[42] It must be stressed, however, that this hypothesis lacks a firm scientific foundation. The recent

39 Richter, 'Klimaschwankungen', pp. 249 ff.
40 E. Brückner, *Klimaschwankungen seit 1700* (1890); Huntington and Visher, *Climatic Changes*.
41 Brooks, *Climate*, pp. 313 f.; 'Winds in London during the Early Nineteenth Century', *Meteorological Magazine* 66 (1931):56–62.
42 Brooks, *Climate*, pp. 314 ff.

improvement in climate in northern latitudes has been shown to be linked in all probability with a diminution of precipitation in more southerly latitudes, for example, in Africa, Australia, Brazil and the United States.[43]

It is by no means impossible that crop failures in England caused by increased cyclonic activity, that is, cyclonic rain, might coincide with crop failures in south and southwest Europe resulting from severe drought. But it cannot at all be considered certain that crop failures brought about by severe torrential rain and floods in Great Britain and central Europe have a necessary connection with a maritime type of climate. On the contrary, the climate can be presumed to have been continental during the grievous years of 1309–23.

An intensive condensation into rain can result from the ascension of warm air above the boundary zones in the air, the so-called fronts, with their acute slopes. Thus, for example, a mainly stationary high pressure or anticyclone with cold air can force the mild, moisture-saturated air masses of the westerly cyclones upwards, usually with frontal or cyclonic precipitation as a result. Anticyclones can force wedges of cold air underneath the warm air, driving the warm air upwards and releasing rain akin to a cloudburst. Rain of this description can also have other causes. It is not altogether unusual for prolonged heat and drought to be followed by violent heavy rain.[44] An example occurred in 1771 at the time of the extremely serious crop failure in large parts of Europe.

In the first half of the fourteenth century the rainfall seems to have been considerable not only in western and central Europe, but also well to the east; during this period the water in the Caspian Sea was unusually high.[45]

Professor Postan suggests that the climate theory as an explanation of the depression in the late Middle Ages is mainly upheld by some Scandinavian scholars. This may be true as far as historians are concerned. But these are nowadays in company with probably all prominent meteorologists in Great Britain and the United States as well as in Scandinavia. Scandinavian historians have, in the main, only considered north European conditions; the meteorologists regard the deterioration of the climate during the Middle Ages as a main cause of the all-European depression. The opinion of the scientists is well expressed by one of the leading American meteorologists, Professor H. C. Willett:

Beginning early in the eleventh century the world climate began to return toward a more glacial pattern. This severe climate reached its peak during the 13th and 14th centuries, when Europe was swept by record storms, blizzards and cold weather, far exceeding anything which has occurred since. . . . In the Alps, glaciers closed

43 Kimble, *Weather*, pp. 235 f.
44 T. Bergeron, 'Nyare rön om nederbördens uppkomst och fördelning', *Ymer* 69 (1949): 161–88.
45 Brooks, *Climate*, pp. 321 ff.

permanently passes which during the previous mild centuries had been routes of commerce.[46]

The great depression of the Middle Ages cannot be explained by climate alone and its precise significance is not easily determined. When the effects of climatic changes in later ages are considered, however, it may well be that the factor of climate in the Middle Ages also will appear to merit more careful consideration by economic historians than it has hitherto been accorded.

II

Professor Eli F. Heckscher described the reign of Gustav I (1523–60), especially the latter part of it, as a golden age in Sweden from the material point of view. His account of the period shows that people were able to enjoy an almost barbarous abundance of food and drink. A marked lowering of the standard of living appears to have taken place during the seventeenth century, this being especially pronounced in the consumption of animal products. It is true that some doubts have been expressed concerning the reliability of Heckscher's sources as a means of estimating the general standard of living. It has recently been shown that the changes were less pronounced than Professor Heckscher supposed, even for the population groups to which the material applies. But on the whole the trends indicated by Heckscher appear probable.

Professor Heckscher found a reasonable explanation of what he regarded as the unexpected prosperity of the sixteenth century in the fact that Gustav I, by putting an end to continual internal strife and by building up an efficient administrative machinery, must have made it more possible for the people to apply themselves to the work of supplying their material needs with less interference than before. The recession during the seventeenth century is then explained as resulting partly from a large increase in population during the previous century, partly, perhaps mainly, from the great pressure exerted on the population by the many wars.[47]

The peaceful conditions created by the rule of Gustav I and the order introduced into the administration were certainly important prerequisites for the country's material prosperity. There are, however, reasons for asking whether there were not other contributory causes as well. Professor B. Boëthius has particularly emphasized the importance of the land elevation

46 Willett, pp. 49 f. Cf. Huntington and Visher, *Climatic Changes*, chap. 6, 'The Climatic Stress of the Fourteenth Century', pp. 98–109.
47 Heckscher, *Sveriges ekonomiska historia från Gustav Vasa* 1:1, pp. 84–100, 263 ff., 1:2, pp. 420 ff. (hereafter cited as *Sv. ekon. hist.*). Cf. K.-G. Hildebrand, 'Salt and Cloth in Swedish Economic History', *Scandinavian Economic History Review* 2(1954):77ff.

in determining the secular trend towards decreased animal and increased vegetable consumption.[48] It is possible that climatic changes also played a part.

It is a striking fact that in the whole of the great series of Gustav I's letters (published in twenty-nine volumes for the years 1521–60)[49], comments suggesting the occurrence of crop failures of any gravity are few and far between. The harvests were apparently poor in the late 1520s, but nothing suggests that there were serious crop failures. The king's many lamentations about 'the dear times' in the middle of the 1540s appear less significant when it is remembered that the rise in prices was largely due to his own monetary policy.[50] Nevertheless it is apparent from several sources that the supply situation was disquieting. During the severe winter of 1544 the king expressed apprehensions 'that a large part of the cattle [in central Sweden] will starve to death, if this winter does not soon grow milder'. The farmers are also said to have suffered from a shortage of seed corn that year.[51] In 1545 there was apparently a great shortage of grain in central Sweden as well as in Denmark.[52] A royal manifesto of 1546 concerning the dear times can scarcely have had its sole cause in the results of monetary policy. The winter of 1546 was in fact extremely severe,[53] and also 1551 was evidently a bad year.[54] On the other hand, the international crop failure of 1556 does not appear to have extended to Sweden.[55] Owing to Sweden's northerly situation the country suffered relatively few severe crop failures caused by excessive heat and drought. Nor is there anything to indicate that the years in question were comparable with the years of famine which were to follow at the end of the sixteenth century and on several occasions during the seventeenth century. Is any explanation to be found in a change in the type of climate?

Suspicions in this direction have already been raised, though for other reasons, by Professor Gerd Enequist. During her investigations of agrarian conditions in the lower part of the valley of the River Lule in the province

48 B. Boëthius, 'New Light on Eighteenth-Century Sweden', *Scandinavian Economic History Review* 1(1953):159 f.
49 'Konung Gustaf I:s registratur', 1–29, *Handlingar rör. Sveriges historia*, 1st ser. (1861–1916), (hereafter sited as GVR).
50 GVR, 4:414; 5:18, 81, 84; 7:131, 180, 184, 290, 304; Heckscher, *Sv. ekon. hist.*, 1:1, p. 210.
51 GVR, 16:124.
52 GVR, 18:106, 168–76.
53 GVR, 18:30–59; Ostman and Henrikson, 'Om köld och is', p. 36. Changes in price relations for different goods, especially the rise in the price of butter, must also be seen against the background of the severe winters (cf. Heckscher, *Sv. ekon. hist.*, 1:1, pp. 214 f.).
54 GVR, 22:2 f., 185, 399.
55 On the crisis of 1556 see Astrid Friis, *Scandinavian Economic Review* 1(1953):200 ff.

of Norrbotten in the extreme north of Sweden, she found that the yield of the grain harvests declined between 1559 and 1640, even if crop failures are disregarded. Professor Enequist could not discover an explanation for this phenomenon but suggested the possibility that 'some general change in climatic conditions' had occurred.[56] When Dr. J. Westin investigated the history of the province of Ångermanland, he discovered that the period around 1560 marked the highest level of economic life and the most extensive colonization in the province for almost two whole centuries. In Dr. Westin's view the decline took place in two stages, 1561–71 and 1600–15.[57]

Numerous signs indicate that climatic conditions affecting plant and animal life – as well as human beings – changed about this time. The number of severe winters, large during the fourteenth and early fifteenth centuries, was very low for a considerable time after 1460. In 1460 it appears that the whole Baltic remained icebound right until the end of March. The winter lasted into May. After 1460 the southwestern part of the Baltic was not again completely frozen over until 1546. During the second half of the sixteenth century and the first half of the seventeenth century, on the other hand, there was a very large number of extremely cold winters.[58]

The hundred years from the mid-fifteenth to the mid-sixteenth century were mild also in England: 'among other things the cultivation of the cherry spread northward, and it seems to have been known in county Durham in the sixteenth century, even at 800 feet. There is, too, a long break in the reports of the freezing of the Thames at London – from 1434 to 1540. In Elizabethan days, however, the climate as a whole appears to have turned a little cooler'.[59]

Dr. Flohn, who had no knowledge of the results of this Swedish and English research, drew similar conclusions concerning the climate in Germany. His most significant finding is that, following a long period of mild weather, a prolonged and pronounced deterioration of climate began in the middle of the sixteenth century and in all probability continued until the nineteenth century.[60] This three-hundred-year period, interrupted by a short but marked heat maximum around 1720, must now be considered an important fact in the history of climate.

As far as can be judged, the climate throughout almost the entire temperate zone during the latter half of the sixteenth century was continental, dry and cold. Evidence to this effect is found in the number of cold

---

56 Gerd Enequist, 'Nedre Luledalens byar', *Geographica. Skrifter från Upsala univ. geografiska institution* (1937), pp. 64 f.
57 J. Westin, *Ångermanlands historia under Gustav Vasa och hans söners tid* (1944), p. 73.
58 Ostman and Henrikson, 'Om köld och is', pp. 36 f.
59 Manley, *Climate and the British Scene*, p. 238.
60 Richter, 'Klimaschwankungen', pp. 249 f.

winters indicated by Tycho Brahe's notes of wind conditions as well as by other similar sources. In northern and western Europe the prevailing winds appear to have been easterly, that is, cold in winter. Precipitation was then mostly in the form of snow. The glaciers advanced rapidly at the end of the sixteenth century or during the first years of the seventeenth century. The advance was so remarkable that the subsequent period has at times been called the 'Little Ice Age'. Both in the Alps and in Iceland the glaciers reached their first maximum in the middle of the seventeenth century. In these two areas their advance exceeded all corresponding advances in any period since the postglacial age. A retreat followed during the first half of the eighteenth century.[61] Other evidence that the climate grew colder around 1600 has come to light by examinations which have been made of the annual rings of trees, German investigators having succeeded in drawing up a chronology of more than seven hundred years for the larch trees in the district round Berchtesgaden. It appears from this that the annual growth in thickness of larch trees was twice as great during the period before about 1600 as in the following centuries. From his investigations of the annual rings of trees in northern Scandinavia D. J. Schove has concluded that a number of shorter warm and cold climatic spells are discernible. According to Schove, during the latter half of the sixteenth and during the seventeenth centuries the following clusters of cold and warm summers can be inferred:

1547–1554 cold	1614–1620 cold
1563–1581 warm	1635–1645 cold
1587–1601 cold	1657–1668 warm
1604–1610 warm	1684–1694 warm

He adds, however, that the true temperature curves may have varied somewhat from this pattern; as, for example, Manley pointed out, there is evidence from various parts of Europe for a cool climatic spell about 1691–1702.[62]

What were the consequences for human beings and for their economic life of these climatic changes which scientists have established as having taken place? The problem is one which has generally been ignored by historians – a consequence of the isolation between the various branches of science caused by extensive specialization. When the results have been

61 Brooks, *Climate*, pp. 301 ff., 312 ff.
62 K. Brehme, 'Jahrringchronologische und -klimatologische Untersuchungen an Hochge-birgslärchen des Berchtesgadener Landes', *Zeitschrift für Weltforstwirtschaft* 14 (1951): 73; D. J. Schove, 'Tree Rings and Summer Temperature A.D. 1501–1930; *The Scottish Geographical Magazine* (June 1950):40; G. Manley, 'Variations in Mean Temperature', pp. 125 ff.

observed, the causes have remained hidden and the relationship has thus been wrongly interpreted.

The severe winters of the 1540s and the general crop failure in central Europe of 1556, affecting Denmark as well, were a presage of what was to come. There is a plethora of reports of natural catastrophes, crop failures and famine in Scandinavia during the 1590s and persisting for the next hundred years. The crop failures which occurred in Sweden in 1596–1603, 1649–52, 1675–7, and several years in the 1690s, especially 1695–7, were nothing short of catastrophic.[63] The harvests were very poor in many other years as well, such as the late 1620s and the early 1630s, several years in the 1640s and around the middle of the 1660s.

The probable reason why the crop failures of the 1590s in Sweden have escaped the notice of many investigators, even of Professor Heckscher, is that they were mainly confined to western and southern Sweden, though their effect there was disastrous; only the crop failures of 1601–3 extended also to the central and northern parts of the country.[64] In the 1590s crop failures obviously occurred in various parts of Europe including England.[65] In Norway the year 1591 has been described as 'the black year in which the grass did not turn green at all north of the Dovre throughout the summer'. Floods caused by rainstorms ravaged western Denmark on no less than four occasions in the course of little more than one year, from October 1592 to Christmas 1593. They caused very serious destruction and many people were killed.[66]

The parish register of Örslösa in the district of Kålland in western Sweden contains an entry for the grievous year of 1695 reproducing a document on the famine of one hundred years before.[67] The document is in the form of

---

63 Cf. Heckscher, *Sv. ekon. hist.*, 1:2, pp. 403 ff.
64 For the crop failures of 1601–3 Heckscher has used the same source as S. Sundquist in *Sveriges folkmängd på Gustaf II Adolfs tid* (1938), p. 33, i.e., a parish register from Vallentuna in the vicinity of Stockholm. Westin, *Ångermanlands historia*, pp. 91 f., also mentions crop failures for the years 1601–3 only. The repercussions of the earlier crop failures, however, extended to central Sweden. Crop failures and not political conditions explain the high grain prices at the end of the 1590s. Cf. Heckscher, *Sv. ekon. hist.*, 1:1, pp. 221 f. In the *tiondelängd* (tithe records) for Västerbotten for 1602 all the corn was said to be ruined and frozen everywhere in the country (Sundquist, p. 43 n). Johannes Bureaus has recorded for 1602 'Bark-year all over the land'. ('Anteckningar af Johannes Agrivillensia Buraeus', ed. G. E. Klemming, *Samlaren*, 4 [1883], p. 22.)
65 C. Walford, 'The Famines of the World, Past and Present', *Journal of the Royal Statistical Society* 41 (1878):434 ff.; Rogers, *History of Agriculture and Prices*, vol. 5 (1887), pp. 179 ff.
66 T. Troels-Lund, *Danmarks og Norges Historie i Sluttningen af det 16de Aarhundrede* 1 (1879):44; D. J. Schove, 'Summer Temperatures and Tree Rings in North Scandinavia A.D. 1461–1950', *Geografiska Annaler* (1954):65 f.
67 Published in Rhyzelius, *Brontologia theologico-historica*, pp. 70 ff., and in C. J. Ljungström, *Kinnefjerdings och Kållands härader samt staden Lidköping* (1871), pp. 19 ff.

an official affidavit, sealed with the parish seal, drawn up by the vicar of the parish and certain named persons, and addressed to one Lars Persson in Söderby. For horrifying detail and the graphic description of the possible effects of natural catastrophes, the document probably has no equal in Sweden. The following is a condensation of the text:

In 1596 at midsummer-tide the land was abundantly covered with splendid grass and much corn, so that everybody thought that there would be sufficient corn in the country. But at the time of the annual meeting of the clergy (i.e. the beginning of July), when the people were at Skara market, there came so much rain and flood that all the bridges floated away and people had great difficulty and anxiety how they were going to get home. And with that same flood began the punishment for our sins, for the water went over the fields and pastures, so that the corn and the grass were ruined, and thus there was little of both grain and hay. In the autumn thereafter the cold was so great that no fish came near the land. Because of our sins the weather deprived us of God's gifts both on land and in the water. The clothes rotted on the backs of the poor. In the winter the cattle fell ill from the rotten hay and straw which was taken out of the water, so that he who had a hundred goats and sheep could not keep two, in fact not one of them. It went the same way with the cows and calves, and the dogs which ate their dead bodies also died. The soil was sick for three years, so that it could bear no harvest. After these inflictions it happened that even those who had good farms turned their young people away, and many even their own children, because they were not able to watch the misery of them starving to death in the homes of their fathers and mothers. Afterwards the parents left their house and home going whither they were able, till they lay dead of hunger and starvation, for times were so dear that an ox which cost six *riksdaler* was given for a barrel of corn and a cow for half a barrel. Those who gave silver, gave first one *lod* (half an ounce) for the bushel and straightaway afterwards, two *lod*. People ground and chopped many unsuitable things into bread; such as mash, chaff, bark, buds, nettles, leaves, hay, straw, peatmoss, nut-shells, pea-stalks, etc. This made people so weak and their bodies so swollen that innumerable people died. Many widows, too, were found dead on the ground with red hummock grass, seeds which grew in the fields, and other kinds of grass in their mouths. People were found dead in the houses, under barns, in the ovens of bath-houses and wherever they had been able to squeeze in, so that, God knows, there was enough to do getting them to the graveyard, though the dogs ate many of the corpses. Children starved to death at their mothers' breasts, for they had nothing to give them to suck. Many people, men and women, young and old, were compelled in their hunger to take to stealing, so that none could keep his belongings, whether under lock and key or not. Gallows were built in our district and hung full. Women were flogged and had their hair and ears cut off at the gallows. Wives went sighing and weeping and bewailing that they must in such great misery sunder their marriage and never more see their husbands (*totus horresce dum haec scribo*). At times these and other inflictions came and also the bloody flux (dysentery) which put people in such a plight that countless died of it. Our vicar, Dominus Bengt Petri, was without a cow and had to resort to oat-cake; many went to him and received the sacrament knowing that they would die of hunger within a few days. The vicar exhorted them that they should diligently come to God's table,

Gustaf Utterström

while they still could, but the following Sunday many were dead, some of hunger and some of the bloody flux. Those who stayed at home and in their hand-mills ground chaff, bark and other things, were found there lying dead. You can say that over the land and people lay part of the plagues of Egypt and something of the fall of Jerusalem.

From the diocese of Stavanger, especially the region of Agder, in south-western Norway in about the same latitude as Kålland we have information of severe famines in the same years (1596–8), and of people eating bark and grinding hay, straw and chaff into bread. The winters there are said to have been very cold and the snow so abundant that on even ground it measured ten to twelve feet in depth.[68]

Conditions in southeastern Sweden appear to have been similar. During the years 1596–1608 Petrus Magni, the vicar of the parish of Ålem on Kalmar Sound, made detailed notes of the weather, natural phenomena and harvests.[69] In view of the support they give to the thesis being upheld here, they will be examined in detail.

In 1596 the rain was so violent in the realm (which to the writer meant Småland and Östergötland, two provinces in southeastern Sweden) that the hay in the meadows floated away and the fields were flooded with water. On 6 August the floods were such that the idle (a carp-like fish) swam up into the meadows and fields and there hid in the corn so that they could not be caught either by net or fish spear. The corn was lost, cattle perished in great numbers and many households were left altogether without livestock. The result was 'a deplorable famine and dear time.'

On 12 May 1597 came 'a horribly cold and strong north-wind' bringing with it rain like a cloudburst. All the newly sown seed floated away and the fields were like lakes. The cold weather and north wind lasted almost the entire spring. Masses of livestock froze or starved to death. On 17 June came another day and night of torrential rain; the water rose higher than the rye and the new sown barley floated away. In the same year there was 'so dreadful a hunger that the greater part of the people had to take to bark-bread and made bread of peatmoss'. Beggars roamed the countryside in hordes. People who were strong and in good fettle, both farmhands and girls, offered to work for their keep alone. Many were heard to say that they wished for death.

No weather details of interest are given for 1598; during that year the vicar only noted political events. From the following year (1599) it is

68 P. Claussøn Friis, *Samlede skrifter*, ed. G. Storm (1881), p. 57. Cf. J. Bromé, *Jämtlands och Härjedalens historia* 2 (1945):171.
69 Ålems kyrkoräkenskaper (parish accounts) (L I a: 1, pp. 379–93), Vadstena landsaarkiv. A short abstract previously published in M. Hofrén, *Ålems socken. Historia och beskrivning* (1949), p. 174. Further details of the famine years in G. V. Sylvander, *Kalmar slotts och stads historia*, 2:3 (1872), pp. 388 ff.

62

mentioned that in June and July the heat was very great and that extensive forest fires raged. The spring of 1600 was cold. On Easter Day, 23 March, the bells of sleigh horses could be heard on marsh and lakes. Even on Whitsunday neither leaves nor grass were to be seen. All that was said of the summer which followed was that the supply of beech mast [beech nuts] in the beech woods was unusually rich. The winter came suddenly with severe cold and with snow two feet deep while the pigs were still out in the beech woods; great numbers of pigs were discovered dead of cold and hunger.

The next year (1601) was 'a quite amazing year'. The winter which had begun at Martinmas (11 November 1600) was severe and long. Snow came in such quantities that in many places it stood level with the roofs of the houses. It was said that on Öland almost no houses were visible. In many places there people burned down their houses, or at least all the inside woodwork, in order to get warmth. 'And great and horrible damage was done among the cattle both on Öland, as well as here in Småland elsewhere'. Along the line of the skerries and in certain other places snowdrifts towered up to a height of twenty feet. The warmth of spring suddenly arrived in April and melted the snow. The spring floods were the worst in living memory. They took with them all the bridges and almost all the water mills. Large mounds of ice could still be seen on the rocks and skerries in Kalmar Sound at the end of May. From the melting of the snow to the Feast of St. James (25 July) there was a persistent drought accompanied by night frosts, severely retarding the growth of both corn and grass. As a result the harvest was very meagre. In addition, in eastern Småland the roots of the corn were attacked by insects, so that the corn looked as 'though it had been cut through with a sickle'. The corn was mainly harvested unripe, damaged by the damp of the autumn rains with the result that it either heated [spoiled] or rotted in the barns. Meteorological interest attaches to the information that the corn had not ripened because 'in that year the sun did not have its right natural shine or heat, but in a clear sky shone as though through smoke until nine or ten in the day and in mid-evening [midday?] lost its shine again'. This suggests that the cold air was not dissipated even during the summer creating cloud formation through which the sun appeared as if seen through opaque glass.

In the autumn of 1601 the catch of *strömming* (small herring) was so abundant that 'such catches have not been had in living memory'.

The winter of 1601–2 in Ålem was so mild after Christmas that the vicar sowed spring rye on 8 March. In Norrland, on the other hand, he informs us, the winter was severe, with a great deal of snow, and lasted until Whitsuntide. The poor harvest of 1601 resulted in very great distress also in Småland. A fresh impetus was given to the roamings of the beggars, numbers of whom were found dead of hunger in the fields. Severe epidemics began to rage in the spring, including dysentery. On 8 July the plague also

LIBRARY ST. MARY'S COLLEGE

appeared in the parish and caused great ravages until 19 November, claiming 427 victims altogether or roughly 25 percent of the population. In the spring and summer of 1603, it spread to Uppland and the northern provinces of the realm.[70]

In 1602, we are informed, more than half the fields in Ålem were left unsown. Those who had any seed, however, harvested quite good crops. The 1603 harvest was poor, partly because of a serious spring drought and night frosts.

The years 1596–1603 show how severe the effects of a phase of continental climate may be at its height. Nevertheless, a continental climate did not necessarily lead to serious crop failures even in Sweden, as the harvests of the subsequent years prove.

Of 1604 the vicar wrote: 'This has been a splendidly prolific year, so that it may well be called a golden year'. The grain harvests were so heavy that their like had not been seen for twenty years. In 1605 the corn was 'most excellent and heavy in the head', although the hay was very thin and without succulence. The next year (1606) was even better: 'In this summer the crops of the earth have been so prolific with all sorts of good and heavy-headed grain in all parts of the country here in Sweden, that never has such a thing been in living memory, so that this year may rightly be called a truly golden year'. Nor did that exhaust his superlatives. In 1607 he had to have recourse to the Sixty-fifth Psalm, 'because no more fruitful year with such splendid and heavy grain and other crops has there been in living memory'.

The weather suddenly changed and the winters became unusually mild. In 1605 vessels were able to put out from Kalmar for harbours in Germany and for other Swedish ports as early as Candlemas (2 February). In 1606 sledging was never once possible for as much as a week at a time. Winter rye was sown at the New Year and at Candlemas. The same happened in 1607, when wild chervil and other herbs stood green together, 'as had also happened Anno 1602, when the pestilence raged immediately afterwards in the summer'. On 2 February 1607, ants and various summer birds such as pigeons and starlings were observed. But on Maundy Thursday, Good Friday and Easter night the cold was intense and ice formed far out among the skerries. The 'Christmas-summer' thus turned into an 'Easter-winter'. Nevertheless almost all the deciduous trees were in leaf by May Day.

Whether the winter was severe or mild, the summers as a rule were warm

---

70 Estimate by M. Hofrén, *Ålems socken*, p. 174. According to Hofrén the population in Ålem was considerably greater in 1571 than in 1618. The decrease was due not only to crop failures and epidemics but also to the war between Sweden and Denmark, 1611–13. Mortality was in all probability considerably higher in the towns than in the countryside, cf. G. G. Molin, 'Pesten vid Uppsala Universitet under 1600-talet', *Lychnos* (1953):144. The plague seems to have started at Uppsala on 10 May 1603.

and dry. The summer of 1605 was no doubt an extreme example, yet it was typical of the prevailing type of climate. From the time the snow melted in 1605 until snow and rain fell in March and April of 1606, the ground was not once properly soaked, 'and its veins have mostly all been so dried up that wells which were 40 or 50 feet deep, marshes and streams', dried up completely, which had never happened in living memory'. Still more remarkable is the description of the Baltic Sea. The level of the water was so low from Michaelmas (29 September) until nearly Christmas that shoals were revealed which people had never seen before. The explanation of this must be sought in the conditions of atmospheric pressure and wind.

Thus, during a phase of climate such as that described above, it has to be expected that in Scandinavia and the northerly parts of the European continent there will have been periods of alternate very good and very poor corn harvests, with hay harvests as a rule meagre. Corn prices from different parts of the continent indicate that in many countries crop failures during the 1580s and 1590s were followed by a succession of good harvests after the turn of the century. This phenomenon must presumably to a great extent be explained by climatic conditions similar to those of Sweden. The extremes are likely to have been much more pronounced in northern Europe and on the Continent than in the British Isles. It would appear from the sporadic details of prices which have been preserved from the Middle Ages that this was so also during the preceding period.[71] Can the only reason for such price discrepancies have been the existing confusion in monetary systems?

The peculiar weather conditions around 1600 suggest that the Icelandic cyclones were relatively weak during these years. The character of the winters was determined by anticyclones coming alternately from arctic and subtropical areas. In central Europe and in Sweden vegetation largely depends on the amount of rainfall during the summer. Thunderstorms very often provide most of the rainfall required. Consequently, even after the dry heat of a prolonged anticyclone, drought seldom causes as much damage there as in southern Europe.

The years of famine around 1600 engraved themselves on the minds of those who survived and were long remembered. A vicar in Vårmland named Petrus Magni Gyllenius (1622–75), the son of a peasant from Ölme in that province, gives in his memoirs a detailed account of the distress and of the experiences of his parents and relatives during those years:

The dreadful dearness and hard times lasted for seven years. And during those years in many places people were without seed and in others had very little. Sometimes the

---

71 G. Wiebe, 'Zur Geschichte der Preisrevolution des XVI und XVII Jahrhunderts', *Staats und socialwissenschaftliche Beiträge*, ed. A. v. Miaskowski, 2:2 (1895), tabs. 234–5, 238–9, 469–71; J. D. Gould, 'The Trade Depression of the early 1620s', *Economic Historic Review* (1954):86, 88. Cf. Postan, 'Trade of Medieval Europe', pp. 206 f.

crops were destroyed by too much damp and sometimes by an unnatural drought. One year frost ruined all the crops over the whole realm of Sweden. In those dear times many starved to death and they lay on the roads and elsewhere in heaps, having died of hunger. May God avert such grievous years and punish us not with them. Immediately after that dear time came the battle of Stångebro (1598) and also a violent *pestilentia* over the entire country.[72]

This has the usual weakness of hearsay evidence and the chronology is somewhat uncertain. But there is no reason to doubt the reality of the facts contained in it.

The crop failures in the middle of the seventeenth century, when the glaciers in Europe are supposed to have reached their maximum extent, were caused, as they obviously were also at the turn of the century (1600), either by violent cloudbursts, as in 1649, or by prolonged drought, as in 1652, a year long afterwards remembered as 'the year of the great drought'.[73] I do not propose to list the crop failures and famine years of the seventeenth century. The details so far given have been intended to verify and illustrate the argument, that is, to show that fluctuations of climate have been an important factor in the economic and social history of Sweden and that they may be supposed to have exerted a very strong influence on demographic changes in agrarian society.

The reign of Gustav I appears to have been free from serious crop failures. The people seem to have been spared even the worst ravages of the plague. The first bad outbreak of plague in Sweden in the sixteenth century probably occurred in 1565 during the war between Sweden and Denmark – Norway, Poland, and some of the Hanse towns, 1563–70.[74] The court records (*dombok*) of Uppvidinge *härad* (Småland) for 1612 also mention the 'great pestilence of some 46 years ago'.[75] The plague returned to Sweden several times during the sixteenth and seventeenth centuries. The epidemic of 1602–3 was one of the worst. It is recorded as having raged in both Denmark and Norway in the immediately preceding years. It is supposed to have come to Kalmar from Denmark and to have spread thence

72 *Diarium Gyllenianum*, ed. R. Hausen (1882), p. 4.
73 Ibid., pp. 143, 158 f., 173, 199. Gyllenius gave many details about the weather in the course of the years.
74 A list of the outbreaks of plague in Sweden is given in *Svenska archivum*, ed. S. Loenbom (1776), vol. 1, p. 113. It is true that this list indicates that plague occurred in several years during the reign of Gustav I. It is very uncertain, however, if the bubonic plague is meant. The Swedish word "pest" used to serve for a number of different epidemics. (See O. T. Hult, *Pesten i Sverige* 1710 [1916], pp. 7 ff.) Years of severe outbreaks of the plague during the fifteenth and sixteenth centuries are stated to have been 1451, 1485, 1495, 1565, 1579 and 1588.
75 P. G. Vejde, 'Om pesten i Småland 1710–11; *Hyltén Cavallius-föreningens årsbok* (1938), p. 161.

in different directions.[76] Dr. P. G. Vejde's discoveries during his investigations of the plague in Småland 1710–11 are remarkable. Even at that time, apparently the last occasion when an outbreak of bubonic plague occurred in Sweden, the memory of what had happened at the beginning of the seventeenth century was still alive. The court records for 1712 of southern Allbo *härad* relate about Virestad parish that '112 years ago, when the great pestilence was here in the parish, the churchyard was quite full and corpse was laid upon corpse'. The court records of Norrvidinge *härad* and Kinnevalds *härad* also mention 'the great sickness' at the beginning of the seventeenth century,[77] even though the plague had raged on many occasions in the realm since then.

It has recently been emphasized that scarcely any century of European history since the thirteenth and fourteenth can show such a large number of devastating epidemics as the seventeenth.[78] Is this a mere coincidence, or perhaps a result of the great wars and of people's diminished powers of resistance after the bad crop failures? The leading expert on the history of plague in Sweden, Professor O. T. Hult, states that epidemiologists hold a different view. 'The idea people had in the past, one which runs like a red thread through the history of the epidemics, that there is an intimate connection between upheavals in nature, mass deaths among rats and other smaller animals, and a subsequent epidemic of plague, has been given a thoroughly satisfactory explanation through modern epidemiological research. Rats at times migrate in mass, either as a result of crop failures, floods, large fires or other similar catastrophes, or for other unknown reasons. When this happens and the various rat communities, infected and uninfected, intermingle, the infection can spread rapidly and a mass epizootic occur'.

The English microbiologist Dr. L. F. Hirst, one of the leading specialists on plague, is of the same opinion. The main reason why the rats migrate, according to him, is hunger. Epidemics of the plague among rats cause the rat fleas to seek other hosts, preferably rats, but also people. In the countries which are the home of the plague this fact is so well known in certain places that as soon as the natives notice that rats are dying in large numbers they at once leave their homes.[79] The great plague epidemics of the fourteenth, fifteenth and seventeenth centuries are therefore likely to be connected with upheavals in the world of nature which obviously occurred at the same time. The plague is, however, not necessarily spread by rats. The rat fleas, even when they have left their hosts, may continue to live in granaries, as rats do, and they can easily be spread to other districts with consignments of grain.[80]

76 Hult, *Pesten*, p. 10; Sylvander, *Kalmar plotts*, 3:3, pp. 386 f.
77 Vejde, 'Om pesten i Smaland', pp. 161 ff.
78 E. Hobsbawm, 'The Crisis of the Seventeenth Century', *Past and Present* (1954): 5, 35.
79 Hult, *Pesten*, pp. 92 f.; Hirst, *Conquest of Plague*, pp. 213, 303 ff.
80 Hirst, *Conquest of Plague*, pp. 121 ff. passim.

The picture which so far has been given here of Sweden's agricultural conditions during the seventeenth century is a rather gloomy one. There were, however, some brighter periods of considerable length, for example, about twenty years after 1604 (although war was raging in the southern and western parts of the country and the plague paid yet another visit in 1620–3), the greater part of the 1660s, the first half of the 1670s and the 1680s. The famous Swedish statistician Gustav Sundbärg maintained that it is possible to calculate from the age distribution at the middle of the eighteenth century the relative size of the annual birthrate ever since the 1660s. He reached the conclusion that the number of children born and surviving during the period 1661–90 was very large, especially when compared with the period 1691–1720. One of the causes of this presumably was that there was no serious outbreak of plague during the former period.[81] It is also probable that, despite war and crop failures, the population of the Sweden proper of those days (that is, not including Finland and the former Danish-Norwegian provinces in the south and west) increased from between 850,000 and 900,000 in the 1620s to 1,120,000 in 1720, although the estimate for the 1620s is very uncertain.[82] However, even if there was an increase in population – and the settlement of new areas confirms that there was – the general impression derived from a study of agricultural conditions is that the increase of population in the seventeenth century was not only considerably slower than during the eighteenth century, but slow even in comparison with the sixteenth century. This view was advanced even before Heckscher by Major S. Sundquist who has investigated population conditions in seventeenth-century Sweden more thoroughly than anyone else. He estimated that the increase was very slight in the period 1560–1630 and that in 1695–1720 there was no increase at all. From 1630 to 1695 he reckoned that the increase in population amounted to about 25 percent.[83]

If the regional distribution of this increase is examined, it seems to have

81 G. Sundbärg, *Bevölkerungsstatistik Schwedens* (1907), p. 11; Molin, 'Pesten vid Uppsala universitet', p. 153.
82 Sundquist, *Sveriges folkmängd*, pp. 264, 278. Cf. Heckscher's review in *Sv. ekon. hist.*, 1:2, pp. 383 f. The only possibility of obtaining reliable information about the development of population during the sixteenth and seventeenth centuries would seem to be thorough local study. In Sweden geographers have given the lead in this respect. An account of such local investigations is given in the list of sources and the introduction to N. Friberg, 'Dalarnes befolkning på 1600-talet', *Geografiska Annaler* (1953). It only needs to be mentioned here that Westin in *Ångermanlands historia* (p. 73) reached quite different conclusions to those of Sundquist (pp. 232 ff.). Westin considers that there was a decline in population after 1560 which was very protracted. It can certainly not be regarded as impossible that this was also true of other parts of the country.
83 Sundquist, *Sveriges folkmängd*, pp. 278 f.; Heckscher (*Sv. ekon. hist.*, 1:2, pp. 383 ff.) is inclined to assume a somewhat larger increase of 31 to 32 percent. All the figures, of course, are purely hypothetical.

been most conspicuous in the mining districts of central Sweden, in western Värmland and in Southern Norrland. The increase in the mining districts was obviously linked with the rapid advance of the iron industry; in the other two areas it was connected with the settlement of fresh land. In the essentially agricultural regions as well as in districts such as Småland and Upper Norrland the increase in population, if any, was only very slight.[84]

Thus, during the seventeenth century, not only wars but also physical conditions exerted a strong pressure on the population. The efforts of which the population showed itself capable during the Thirty Years War and later thereby appear all the more remarkable. At the same time this shows how cautious one has to be in historical analysis in deducing a country's economic situation from its relative political strength. The strength of a state does not depend on economic factors alone, however important these may be, but also on the imponderable forces of idealism, individual exertions, leadership and organization.

At this point it must be emphasized more strongly than has been done so far that the years of famine and plague at the turn of the sixteenth and seventeenth centuries must be considered to mark an important turning point in the development of the Swedish population. As far as can be judged, the population must have been greater in 1590 than in 1620, even admitted that the high death rate of 1597–1603 probably led to an increased marriage frequency among the survivors and to the birth of numerous children. To be properly understood, however, the development of population in Sweden must be seen against the general European background.

III

In his great work *La Méditerranée et le monde méditerranéen à l'époque de Philippe II* (1949), Professor Fernand Braudel gives a graphic picture of the great increase in the population of the Mediterranean countries during the period 1450–1600. He describes how this found expression in a regular migration from mountain districts to the plains and to the cities near and far, how new towns grew up and old ones expanded, and how this occurred all over the Mediterranean area. The population was still increasing in the period 1550–1600. During the next half century, however, there was a noticeable reaction; signs of the coming change could already be perceived in the latter decades of the sixteenth century.[85]

This reversal of the population trend cannot satisfactorily be explained as having been the result of changes in the supply of precious metal and associated price movements, even though these may have had great significance in influencing the fluctuations in economic life and thereby in employment.

84 Sundquist, *Sveriges folkmängd*, passim.
85 Fernand Braudel, *La Méditerranée et le monde méditerranéen à l'époque de Philippe II* (1949), pp. 347–59, 459.

The outstanding features of the new situation were the deterioration in the supplies of food and the stagnation of the population. The crop failures did not increase so much in frequency as in intensity since they had always been common. It is a significant fact that during the last two or three decades of the sixteenth century the great granaries of the Mediterranean basin no longer had any surplus grain to sell although they had been exporting large quantities around 1560. This was equally true of the grain centres of the Turkish Empire (Egypt, the Balkan plains) and of Sicily and Spain. The deterioration was considerable even in France.[86]

The 1570s seem to mark the boundary between two epochs. After 1573 the Near East was no longer able to satisfy the large need for grain of the western Mediterranean countries, since it was suffering from serious crop failures. Professor Earl J. Hamilton has shown that in Spain the price of grain followed the general increase in prices quite normally until 1570, but that after that it rose very much more quickly. The curve of grain prices shows a number of peaks over a very few years.[87] There was a devastating famine in Sicily in 1591; a similar famine occurred in France in 1587, caused by torrential rain;[88] numerous revolts and disturbances are recorded as having taken place between 1590 and 1600 in the Turkish Empire and elsewhere in southern Europe, occasioned presumably by the prevailing distress.[89] The Mediterranean economy could no longer work efficiently. The stage was set for the mass import of grain from the Baltic to the Mediterranean which began in the 1590s at the initiative of the Hanseatic merchants and, particularly, of the Dutch.[90]

The second feature was the stagnation in population. This also was a general phenomenon but was the most conspicuous in Spain. According to Professor Hamilton, the population of the cities in Castile had doubled between 1530 and 1594, while for Spain as a whole the population increased by 15 percent. The setback did not begin until the turn of the century – to be exact, not until the epidemic of the plague of 1599–1600. It has been maintained that during the period 1594–1694 the population of the industrial towns of Spain fell by one half, while the whole of Spain lost roughly 25 percent of its total population. The decline was most evident in the interior of the peninsula, least evident in the coastal areas.[91]

How does Professor Braudel explain this development? The change in the

---

86 Ibid., pp. 463 ff.
87 E. J. Hamilton, 'American Treasure and the Price Revolution in Spain, 1501–1650', *Harvard Economic Studies* 43 (1934), pp. 240 ff.
88 Braudel, *La Méditerranée*, pp. 466 ff.
89 Ibid., pp. 644 f.
90 Ibid., pp. 469 ff., 494 ff.
91 E. J. Hamilton, 'The Decline of Spain', *Economic History Review* 81 (1938): 169 ff.; Braudel, *La Méditerranée*, p. 356.

grain situation between 1560 and 1600 was evidently a puzzle to him: '*On lit et on relit des documents avant d'y croire. Et pourtant*' ['One reads and rereads the documents before believing them. And there it is nonetheless']. He discusses two possibilities: one a change in climate, the other an increase in population which had absorbed the grain surplus both in the Near East and in the western Mediterranean countries. The crop failures were not necessarily extremely severe merely because their effects were so grave. While leaving the first possibility open, he regards the second explanation as being more plausible; the question of climate he regards as one which needs to be solved by experts other than historians.[92]

Professor Braudel is prepared to admit the extraordinary importance of climate to the Mediterranean area, and he especially emphasizes what devastating effects a drought could have.[93] A number of facts on which he bases his arguments made it impossible for him to avoid the question of a fluctuation of climate. At least three circumstances apparently prevented him from attaching decisive significance to climate: the common tendency among historians to try to explain social phenomena exclusively in terms of political and economic causes;[94] the notion that a strong population pressure existed as a result of the great increase of population in the sixteenth century; and an incomplete knowledge of the modern literature on the history of climate.[95]

To regard population pressure as the decisive factor does not provide satisfactory explanation of these economic developments. The fact that population increased in the way it did merely raises a question which has not so far been asked: why did the population increase? As has already been shown by the investigations of Professor Karl Julius Beloch, the problem must be viewed in a general European context. It was noted earlier that during the sixteenth century, as far as can be judged, there was an unusually large increase of population in Sweden; the same was probably true of the rest of Scandinavia. Professor Wilhelm Abel has stated that, according to available information regarding internal colonization and agrarian conditions in central Europe and in Germany in particular, a large increase in

---

92 Braudel, *La Méditerranée*, pp. 230 ff., 460 ff. and passim.
93 Ibid., pp. 196–235.
94 Cf. ibid., pp. 231, 233. Hobsbawm, 'Crisis', also avoids looking for the main cause of the depression in the agrarian sector of the economy. There are, however, the most palpable facts.
95 Several German investigations of the glaciers of the Alps agree with the results in U. Monterin, *Il clima sulle Alpi ha mutato in eta storica* (1937), concerning the general advance of the glaciers during the latter part of the sixteenth century and the first decades of the seventeenth; see Brehme, 'Jahrringschronologische', p. 75. There should be no doubts about the connection between the climatic changes in different parts of Europe, or about the scientific foundation of the climatic facts. Thus it would obviously be unwise to disregard climate because the crisis can be satisfactorily explained merely by demographic and monetary factors. Cf. Braudel, *La Méditerranée*, pp. 233 f.

population occurred in those regions during the latter half of the fifteenth century and during the sixteenth century. Abel argues further that the same tendency is observable in France and England.[96] According to him, plague epidemics were on the decline during the latter half of the fifteenth century.[97]

The great increase in population was thus presumably general throughout Europe. In northern and central Europe it got well under way during the period when the climate was unusually mild. This can scarcely be a chance coincidence: there must be a causal connection. In the Mediterranean area there was always sufficient warmth. A climatic change towards the continental type would be dangerous in that region since the resultant drought and erosion would seriously threaten the crops. The many reports of heavy cloudbursts can be misleading; a serious drought might still have occurred during the period of vegetation. A statement on conditions in Aix in 1599–1600 which Braudel quotes is particularly interesting: *'le froid et le neige se firent sentir jusqu'à la fin de juin (1599), il ne plut pas depuis ce mois jusqu'en décembre. Les pluies vinrent alors en si grande abondance que la terre semblait noyée'* ['The cold weather and snow lasted until the end of June, and it did not rain between that month and December. The rains came then in such abundance that the land seemed drowned']. Alternate violent downpours and severe drought were also characteristic of the new type of Scandinavian climate. It is well known from other countries and epochs that heavy rainfall and drought are apt to alternate.[98]

It is probable, however, that rainfall on the whole increased much more in southern than in northern Europe, since in a phase of continental climate the tracks of the cyclones must be expected to have been deflected to the south. During the winter the greatest snowfall occurs in the northerly segment of a depression and consequently this was a period of heavy snowfall in the Alps, the Pyrenees and in Iceland.[99] The great number of

---

96 K. J. Beloch, 'Die Bevölkerung Europas zur Zeit der Renaissance', *Zeitschrift für Sozialwissenschaft* 3 (1900):765–86; W. Abel, 'Wachstumsschwankungen mitteleuropäischer Völker seit dem Mittelalter', *Jahrbücher für Nationalökonomie und Statistik* 142 (1935): 682 ff. See also H. Sée, *Histoire économique de la France*, vol. 1 (1939), pp. 56 ff., 80 ff. Sée explains the fluctuation in population as resulting from the alternations between war and peace. That conditions of war and peace were of great significance is obvious, but it must be doubted that they could have been the only influence upon population, especially since developments in central Europe clearly followed parallel lines to those in other countries. Cf. also K. B. Mayer, *The Population of Switzerland* (1952), p. 14; J. Clapham, *A Concise Economic History of Britain* (1949), pp. 77 f., 186.

97 Abel, 'Wachstumsschwankungen', p. 677; on the increase of population in Norway in the sixteenth and seventeenth centuries, see A. Holmsen, *Norges historia, i* (Oslo 1949), pp. 516 f.

98 Braudel, p. 234; Huntington and Visher, *Climatic Changes*, p. 102.

99 Brooks, *Climate*, p. 374.

floods in the Rhône basin should also be viewed in the light of these circumstances. The fact that the latter part of the sixteenth century was rainy in southeastern Europe fits into this picture perfectly.[100] The increased rainfall must not, however, be interpreted as meaning that the climate had improved; on the contrary, the large numbers of floods, indicating a lower temperature, point to the conclusion that it grew more severe. Some improvement may have occurred more to the south – somewhere in Africa. As to southern and southeastern Europe, the decisive point is not so much the annual total of rainfall as its distribution over the months of the year.

The prevailing type of climate and climatic fluctuations may thus be supposed to have been of decisive importance for the development of population in all parts of Europe. This fact appears all the more obvious when it is noticed that the development of population took a new turn at the same period in Scandinavia as well as in the Mediterranean area. The famine in Sweden, 1596–1603, and the great epidemic of plague there in 1600–3 have already been mentioned; they coincided with similar disasters in Constantinople: In the spring of 1597 that city suffered from a severe famine; in 1600 its inhabitants were again without bread, obviously as the result of a crop failure in Moldau-Walachia; in February 1601 the food situation was still grave, and, in addition, the plague was raging; in June 1601 torrential rain created an alarming threat to the harvest. The normal consequence of crop failures in the Balkans was that the exports of grain to Italy dropped to insignificance. In the late 1590s there were severe floods in various parts of Italy. In Provence the cold *mistral* destroyed much of the olive plantations (1599–1603).[101] The great epidemic of the plague in Spain in 1599–1600 marked a turning point in that country's demographic history. In 1603 there was a severe epidemic of the plague in England.[102] The coincidence in time of these disasters in different parts of Europe is most certainly not fortuitous. They are all – with the possible exception of the plague – part effects of the climatic fluctuation which meteorologists consider can be pinned down to the period 1560–1600,[103] and of which the advance of the glaciers around the turn of the century is evidence.

The far-reaching effects of the repeated serious crop failures in the Mediterranean area should therefore not be attributed primarily to the great increase in population of the sixteenth century. Whether or not an area is overpopulated depends on what is understood by the concept of overpopulation. Had the standard of living of the masses already declined before the fluctuation in climate began to make itself felt? If that was not the case,

100 Braudel, *La Méditerranée*, p. 234; Brooks, *Climate*, p. 374.
101 Braudel, *La Méditerranée*, pp. 233 ff., 464.
102 Hirst, *Conquest of Plague*, pp. 260, 311; E. J. Hamilton, 'American Treasure', pp. 271 ff.
103 See Ahlmann, 'Present Climatic Fluctuation'. Cf. G. Manley, 'Climatic Fluctuations, A Review', *Geographical Review* (1951), pp. 656–60.

overpopulation can only have come into existence in relation to the changed prospects of production. Even if the population had been considerably less, those natural catastrophes must have had far-reaching effects. The migrations may indicate that men and women had difficulty in obtaining a satisfactory livelihood in their home districts but they may also just indicate that more attractive opportunities for work were still to be found elsewhere. According to the descriptions of them, there is no question of these being beggars' wanderings. The stagnation of the population in the seventeenth century and the flourishing of banditry, on the other hand, obviously went together.[104] The increase in population in the sixteenth century must have contributed to making living conditions more difficult when the agricultural situation deteriorated, but it can scarcely have been the cause of the worsened supply position.

When in some regions the climate became more continental, this probably led to a decrease in rainfall during the period of vegetation which led in turn to a serious decline in the crops harvested. In other regions the main cause of poor harvests obviously was torrential rains. Drought and rainfall could in fact combine to bring about severe crop failures. The consequences of a decrease in rainfall during the growing season must have been especially disastrous in those districts where the minimum requirement of plants for moisture had only just been satisfied in the previous 'normal' conditions, such as in the interior parts of the Pyrenean Peninsula. Erosion, helped on by sheep rearing and especially by the methods used, may also have been hastened by drought and torrential rain.

The great reduction in the numbers of sheep in Spain after 1560 and especially after 1600 was probably due largely to a change in climate. That also applies to the decline of agriculture and of the agricultural population in Castile,[105] though Professor Hamilton has shown clearly that many other highly significant factors also contributed.

The effects of the change in climate extended all the way from Scandinavia to North Africa. The south probably suffered severely. On the other hand, the grain harvests may have improved across a belt of Europe reaching from the Baltic and Poland in the east to England in the west, though this obviously does not apply to extreme years such as 1556 and 1596. The situation in central and western Europe was no doubt complicated. Valuable information may, however, be gathered from Professor Aksel E. Christensen's calculations of the exports of grain through the Sound in 1583–1684. The index figures are reproduced in Table 3.1.

Professor Christensen points out that it is difficult to make comparisons in view of the fact that there is only one reference year, 1583, from the

104 Cf. Braudel, *La Méditerranée*, pp. 357 f., 643 ff.
105 E. J. Hamilton, 'Decline of Spain', pp. 170, 176.

Table 3.1. *The Exports of Corn from Danzig, as Compared with the Corn Transit in the Sound 1583–1684 (Index 1649 = 100)*

| Years | Total exports from Danzig | Corn exported through the Sound | | |
		Total	Of this from Danzig	Of this in Dutch ships
1583	63	26	34	23
1608	87	73	71	75
1618	116	88	97	100
1619	103	80	92	93
1649	100	100	100	100
1662	36	28	33	34
1670	50	48	45	57
1684	65	71	63	83

Source: A. E. Christensen, *Dutch Trade to the Baltic about 1600* (1941), pp. 415 f.

sixteenth century. Judging by this single figure, the change must have been great. The share of the Dutch vessels in carrying corn through the Sound in 1583 was only two-thirds [sic] of the total against from three-quarters to four-fifths in the seventeenth century. At the same time, the Sound Customs books show that not even half the Danzig grain exports passed through the Sound compared with over three-quarters shortly after the turn of the century. Without knowing the facts which Professor Braudel's investigations brought to light, Christensen considered it impossible that Danzig's exports of grain could have been reorganized as completely as the figures indicate, since that would have involved the disappearance of a large part of the Baltic market in favour of a purely west European one. Long before 1583 Danzig was already selling the major part of its corn to buyers outside the Baltic; Christensen therefore thought it more probable that the chief reason for the change lay in more efficient Customs control.[106] It is possible that this was so, but it can no longer be considered as likely as it used to appear. It is certain at any rate, as the figures also indicate, that the export of grain through the Sound increased greatly between the 1580s and the beginning of the seventeenth century.

It seems very likely that England did not suffer from this change of climate but, on the contrary, benefited from it. Dr. W. G. Hoskins has shown that the appearance of the English countryside changed completely during the period 1575–1625 owing to extensive new house construction which resulted in a general improvement of the standard of dwellings. At the same time there was obviously a considerable increase in population. He

106 A. E. Christensen, *Dutch Trade to the Baltic about 1600* (1941), p. 416.

answers the problem of how this building activity was financed by drawing attention to the widened gap between the farmers' and peasants' fixed costs and their growing incomes resulting from the rise in price of agricultural products, a consequence of the price revolution.[107] It is also possible that both farmers and peasants had more to sell than previously. The connection in England between good harvests and a more continental type of climate is clearly illustrated for the 1740s in the letters of the botanist Peter Collinson, while Manley has emphasized its importance throughout the whole of the eighteenth century.[108] Exceptions occurred in extreme years, but these were probably less frequent than on the Continent.

As far as Sweden is concerned, it is obvious that there is strong support for Professor Heckscher's contention that animal consumption was greatly reduced. It is probable that summer rainfall decreased and that the hay harvests deteriorated in consequence. At all events the greater number of extremely cold winters must have made dairy farming more difficult and encouraged the change to increased corn growing, even though the crops ran great risks in certain years. The decrease in animal consumption would thus be the result primarily of a deterioration of the conditions influencing production. Among these must be included the effects of the land-elevation and, in the eighteenth century, the severe epidemics among livestock. Heckscher was particularly impressed by the great decline in the consumption of fish shown by the food budgets for male and female domestic servants. This development appeared very difficult to account for. Part of the explanation may have lain in the cold winters. Meteorologists have written of the year 1635: 'Many rivers and lakes in Sweden were frozen solid and it is not difficult to imagine what happened to the fish'.[109] The winter of that year was certainly severe but by no means unique.

Throughout the seventeenth and eighteenth centuries Swedish grain production was insufficient for the country's needs. Nevertheless, the imports of grain which began in the seventeenth century were no larger than could be accounted for by the growth of Stockholm and the rapid expansion of the iron industry. These imports must, however, have been stimulated by the occurrence of crop failures in quick succession, at the same time as they were facilitated by Sweden's political influence in the Baltic provinces and Pomerania.

The food situation in the Mediterranean area would in all probability have been much more serious if the flow of precious metals from America had not provided means of payment for the large purchases of grain. Thus the climate

107 W. G. Hoskins, 'The Rebuilding of Rural England', *Past and Present* (1953), pp. 4, 44–59.
108 Tooke and Newmarch, *History of Prices*, 1:44 f.; Manley, *Climate and the British Scene*, p. 246.
109 Ostman and Henrikson, 'Om köld och is', p. 36.

fluctuation became one of the factors which helped to spread the effects of the influx of precious metals all over Europe. The expansion of commerce and shipping which had been going on since the middle of the fifteenth century must also have helped to mitigate the effects of the crop failures. Nevertheless, the climatic changes did a great deal to weaken the Mediterranean countries in relation to the rising nations on the Atlantic and North Sea. To quote Professor Braudel: *'Une ère nouvelle se marquait avec l'arrivée de ce blé que des envois d'or devaient compenser'* ['A new era began with the arrival of that wheat which must be paid for in gold shipments'].[110]

IV

In my opinion the events of the years around 1600 may also cast a ray of light on the causes of the great depression of the Middle Ages. It seems to be highly probable that one of its most important causes – perhaps the most important – was a fluctuation of climate similar to that which occurred three hundred years later. It has been said with good reason that although the depression of the Middle Ages manifested itself in different ways in different regions, it must nevertheless have had some general cause. 'World-wide difficulties also must have formed the background of the social revolts which agitated all Europe from London to Salonika and from Majorca to Flanders in the second half of the fourteenth century, although if we observe any one of these revolts too closely we discern only local causes and local peculiarities'. The development of commerce had already created a sensitive world market which quickly reacted to crises in distant countries.[111]

The downfall of the Norse settlements in Greenland, the transformation of Iceland's economy, the decline of Norway, the position of the Hanseatic merchants in Europe's grain trade, the great plague epidemics, the famines, the decrease in population, the stagnation in economic life, the fall of some of the Italian merchant bankers, and various other phenomena may all have had as one of their main causes a factor of which economists and historians usually take little account: the changeableness of nature.

Many of the phenomena mentioned here are most simply explained in that way. The great increase of population from 1450 to 1600 had an obvious counterpart in the increase which occurred between the tenth and the fourteenth century. In the former instance, the increase was presumably interrupted or retarded by a fluctuation in climate. Does not what has been said above suggest that something similar happened in the fourteenth century? If one agrees that it may have, this does not make it necessary to exclude other factors although these must be withdrawn further into the background than has usually been the case.

110 Braudel, *La Méditerranée*, p. 470.
111 Postan, 'Trade of Medieval Europe', p. 204 f.; Lopez, 'Trade', p. 342.

It has already been maintained here that the development of population during the Middle Ages and sixteenth and seventeenth centuries appears on the whole to have followed the same lines, although the increase or the decline may have been greater in some countries than in others. The unique population statistics for Scandinavia, especially for Sweden-Finland, show two great climatically conditioned waves of population growth, 1720–35 and 1750–65. It would surely be reasonable to conclude that the phenomenon was not confined to the Scandinavian states. The contention is supported by sporadic population figures from north Germany and by the corn prices in France and in Great Britain, although in England it is possible that the development was at least partly different. On the other hand, it seems very probable that the population statistics for Sweden-Finland give an important clue to the problem of the increase of population in much of Europe during the eighteenth century.

From the scientific point of view meteorologists and historians are two distinct species of the genus *Homo sapiens,* seldom in contact with each other. It is interesting, however, to see how they can arrive at similar results starting from entirely different points of departure. Professor Gordon Manley, the meteorologist, writes of Scandinavia during the Viking Age:

The weight of the evidence, however, favours the view that the period centred about the sixth-seventh century A.D. was again considerably drier and less stormy in N.W. Europe. The amelioration of the Scandinavian climate led to better and safer harvests and to an enterprising, vigorous and energetic population, increasing rapidly enough for many to be willing to seek their future overseas, and for others to display the splendid craftsmanship and incipient literary ability of which we have abundant evidence.[112]

Professor Sture Bolin, the historian, epitomizes some of his results thus:

Enterprises on such a scale have set out from the North at no other time before or since. To this period in the history of the North, there is neither economic nor political parallel. And these two aspects cannot be isolated. The two are closely inter-connected: the Vikings who terrorized the Western world came from a country where oriental silver was common. . . . The background is not at all that of an impoverished northern land extended to bursting point by overpopulation, but rather of the region further east which, according to the legend, had been conquered by Ruric and his men.[113]

The two show palpable differences in their conception of the determinant forces, but the similarities in the total picture are striking. Lord Keynes in

---

112 Manley, *Climate and the British Scene,* pp. 235 f.
113 S. Bolin, 'Mohammed, Charlemagne and Ruric', *Scandinavian Economic History Review* 1(1953):38 f.

one of his essays, half playfully, half-seriously, made one or two observations about technique and climate which are worth pondering:

> At some epoch before the dawn of history – perhaps even in one of the comfortable intervals before the last ice age – there must be an era of progress and invention comparable to that in which we live today. But through the greater part of recorded history there was nothing of the kind.[114]

This is too harsh a view of the labours of past generations; yet there is a good deal of truth in Lord Keynes's words, if the notion of the ice age is not taken too literally. Most people certainly do not know that the greatest advances made by the glaciers in postglacial times have occurred in the last four hundred years; they culminated at the middle of the seventeenth, eighteenth and nineteenth centuries. Not even when analysing the economic difficulties, the stagnation of the population, and the social unrest of the 1840s and, in Scandinavia especially of the 1860s, must the historian let the monetary and general economic factors blind him to the factor of nature. Thanks to industrialism, thanks not least to technical progress, man in our own day is less exposed to the whims of nature than he was in previous centuries. But how often is it considered that another factor is that we are living in an age in which the climate, especially in northern Europe, is unusually mild? During the last thousand years, the era during which our present Western civilization has grown up and matured, the periods of prosperity in human affairs have on the whole, though with important exceptions, occurred during the warm intervals between the great glaciations. It is in these same intervals that both economic life and the size of the populations have made the greatest advances.

114 *Economic Possibilities for our Grandchildren* (1930), reprinted in *Essays in Persuasion* (1931), pp. 358–73.

4 The English Industrial Revolution

Richard G. Wilkinson

Poverte is hateful good, and, as I gesse,
A ful greet bryngere out of bisynesse.
Chaucer, *The Wife of Bath's Tale*

THE ECOLOGICAL ROOTS of the English industrial revolution are not difficult to find. The initial stimulus to change came directly from resource shortages and other ecological effects of an economic system expanding to meet the needs of a population growing within a limited area. As the traditional resources became scarce, new ones were substituted which usually involved more processing, used more productive labour and frequently resulted in what was regarded as an inferior product. As these initial changes made themselves felt in the economic system, the preexisting technical consistency was disturbed and various secondary changes set in motion.

The ecological background to the industrial revolution was an acute land shortage. In the centuries before industrialization the English population was dependent on the land for almost all its materials. The supply of food and drink depended on agricultural land, clothing came from the wool of sheep on English pasture, and large areas of land were needed for extensive forests: Almost all domestic and industrial fuel was firewood, and timber was one of the most important construction materials for houses, ships, mills, farm implements, etc. In addition, the transport system depended on horses and thus required large areas of land to be devoted to grazing and the production of feed. Even lighting used tallow candles, which depended ultimately on the land supply. Land was bound to become in increasingly short supply as population increased.

There already were signs of the growing scarcity of agricultural land during the population rise of the sixteenth and early seventeenth centuries.[1] The remaining areas of cultivable waste had been brought under the plough

---

[1] See Richard G. Wilkinson, *Poverty and Progress: An Ecological Perspective on Economic Development* (New York, 1973), chap. 4.

and much marginal land had been improved and reclaimed. Disputes over land use had become increasingly frequent, and in many areas villagers' rights to keep animals on the commons had had to be subject to rigorous stints to preserve the grazing. The growth of towns, trade and industry during the sixteenth and early seventeenth centuries are further signs of the pressure on the land and the need to find additional sources of income as traditional subsistence methods proved inadequate.

The relative stability of population from before the middle of the seventeenth century to the mid-eighteenth century temporarily eased the pressure on the land. For a time prices ceased to rise and real wages ceased their decline.[2] But when population started to increase again in the middle of the eighteenth century, the pressure on the land was renewed and the adverse movements in prices and real wages continued. It was – significantly – during the 1760s, at the beginning of the industrial revolution, that Britain changed so dramatically from being a net exporter of wheat to a net importer. (See Table 4.1.)

A land shortage puts pressure on the agricultural sector to increase the output per acre, and new manufacturing activities may be taken up as a way of supplementing incomes. In England, however, the industrial revolution was initially not so much a matter of setting up new industries as of thoroughgoing technical innovation in established industries. The stimulus here came from the limitations which the land shortage imposed on the supply of industrial raw materials. As land-based resources became scarce, it became increasingly urgent to find substitutes for them. The substitution of coal for wood is the most important case.

The shortage of firewood and timber for construction – the 'timber famine' – became acute during the population rise of the sixteenth and early seventeenth centuries. Wiebe's indices of the general price level and of prices of firewood are reproduced in Table 4.2. Although these figures are probably not always representative, they do indicate the general trend in price rises from the early sixteenth century to shortly before the middle of the seventeenth century. The index of firewood prices rises during the same period but much faster. By the 1630s wood had become about two and a half times as expensive in relation to other prices as it had been in the late fifteenth and early sixteenth centuries.

The quantities of timber imported grew but could do little to bring the price down. The 'timber famine' was a result of purely ecological forces. Population growth and the consequent extension of the economic system led to the conversion of woodland into arable land and a simultaneous expansion in the demand for wood. The growing scarcity placed both

2 See ibid., p. 71, graphs *a*, *b*, *c*.

Richard G. Wilkinson

Table 4.1. *Trade in Wheat and Wheaten Flour of Great Britain (Thousands of quarters)*

	Imports	Exports	Net
1700–4		434	⁻434
1705–9	2	614	⁻612
1710–14		608	⁻608
1715–19		480	⁻480
1720–4		751	⁻751
1725–9	115	409	⁻294
1730–4		1355	⁻1355
1735–9		1612	⁻1612
1740–4	13	1005	⁻992
1745–9		1902	⁻1902
1750–4		2701	⁻2701
1755–9	162	589	⁻427
1760–4		1958	⁻1958
1765–9	967	394	573
1770–4	374	116	258
1775–9	926	753	173
1780–4	1046	613	433
1785–9	483	682	⁻199
1790–4	1532	634	898
1795–9	2515	198	2317

Source: B. R. Mitchell and Phyllis Deane, *Abstract of British Historical Statistics* (Cambridge, 1962), p. 94.

industrial and domestic consumers in serious difficulties. Attempts to conserve forests – and particularly supplies of timber for the navy – by legislation were frequent. So also were the comments of contemporaries. In 1631 Edmund Howes wrote:

Within man's memory, it was held impossible to have any want of wood in England. But . . . such hath been the great expence of timber for navigation, with infinite increase of building houses, with great expence of wood to make household furniture, casks, and other vessels not to be numbered, and of carts, wagons and coaches, besides the extreme waste of wood in making iron, burning of bricks and tiles, that at this present, through the great consuming of wood as aforesaid, and the neglect of planting of woods, there is so great a scarcity of wood throughout the whole kingdom that not only the City of London, all haven-towns and in very many parts within the land, the inhabitants in general are constrained to make their fires of sea-coal or pit-coal, even in the chambers of honourable personages, and through necessity which is the mother of all arts, they have late years devised the making of

Table 4.2. *English Price Indices*
(1451–1500 = 100)

	General	Firewood
1501–10	95	100
1511–20	101	106
1521–30	113	97
1531–40	118	106
1541–50	151	180
1551–60	215	265
1561–70	233	332
1571–82	257	327
1583–93	297	416
1593–1602	367	451
1603–12	389	567
1613–22	398	708
1623–32	437	1049
1633–42	451	1208
1643–52	513	759
1653–62	477	1026
1663–72	502	894
1673–82	539	1052
1683–92	494	1058
1693–1702	525	1058

Source. Figures reworked from Georg Wiebe, *Zur Geschichte der Preisrevolution des 16 und 17 Jahrhunderts* (Leipzig, 1895), pp. 375–6.

iron, the making of all sorts of glass and burning of bricks with sea-coal or pit-coal.[3]

This is just one example of the ecological pressures to substitute one raw material for another which lie behind the process of technological innovation throughout the industrial revolution. But before going on to other examples we must look at the implications of the substitution of coal for wood in more detail.

For many purposes coal could be substituted for firewood without serious technical problems. Where this was true the changeover happened quite quickly, either during the price rise or soon afterwards. Smiths and lime-

3 Edmund Howes, ed., Stow's *Annals* (London, 1631), cited in W. H. G. Armytage, *A Social History of Engineering* (London, 1961) p. 1025. The reference to the use of coal in making iron is probably a reference to the technique invented in 1614 for using coal to convert brittle cast iron into malleable bar iron, unless it is based on one of the many unsuccessful seventeenth-century experiments in smelting iron with coal.

burners had used coal from very early on, and by the mid-seventeenth century it was also used in salt boiling, dyeing, brewing and soap boiling as well as in the preparation of alum, copperas, saltpetre and tallow candles.[4] Where substances were kept separate from the fuel in a vat or cauldron of some kind, it was quite easy to substitute a coal for a wood fire, but in processes such as metal smelting, where the fuel was in contact with the raw material, or in drying processes where things were hung in the fumes above the fire, the fuel could have important chemical and other effects on the product. Bakers had to change the design of their ovens to avoid contaminating their bread with the fumes from the coal, brickmakers had to experiment with different kinds of coal till they found the less gaseous ones which did not fuse the bricks together, glassmakers used covered pots and the maltsters developed the use of coke to avoid the smoky gasses and tars given off by the raw coal. The reverberatory furnace, which threw the heat downwards over the metal, was introduced to allow lead and copper to be smelted with coal.

The only important industry which had not changed over to coal firing by the end of the seventeenth century was of course iron smelting. All experiments in smelting with coal had proved unsuccessful and the output of the English iron industry was probably stationary or declining during the second half of the seventeenth century and the early eighteenth as a result. The growing demand had to be met by importing iron mainly from Sweden. It was not until Abraham Derby borrowed the solution to the maltsters' and brewers' problems and used coke for iron smelting at the end of the first decade of the eighteenth century that the iron industry could slowly begin to free itself from the constraints of inadequate supplies of raw materials.

Several points about the changeover from wood to coal burning should be emphasized. The innovations involved could not have appeared equally well at any other point in English history. They were a response to the particular problem of inadequate fuel supplies, and yielded improvements for a society facing that problem: The same innovations would not necessarily be beneficial to a society with a plentiful supply of wood. The main period of innovation and change could only have been the seventeenth century. The exact timing of specific innovations seems to have depended on the complexity of the problem – the tougher nuts took longer to crack. (Iron smelting was a later innovation because it was complicated by the chemical interactions between the new fuel and trace elements which occurred in some of the ores.)

The shortage of firewood should not be seen merely as a stimulus to overcoming a kind of irrational technical inertia. The use of wood instead of coal in the preceding centuries represented a rational choice in a situation

---

4 The best account of the substitution of coal for firewood is in J. U. Nef, *The Rise of the British Coal Industry* (London, 1932), vol. 1.

where wood was plentiful. If wood is available locally it is obviously much easier to use wood than coal. Using coal means paying very high transport costs or accepting severe limitations on location. Not only transport, but also differences in production and use suggest that wood may be the better choice. As soon as opencast coal reserves have been used, deep mines have to be sunk making coal production considerably more difficult than felling trees for firewood. Although for some purposes wood had to be processed before use to turn it into charcoal, coal had to be put through a preliminary operation to turn it into coke for these industries as well as for others in which raw wood had previously been adequate. Harmful constituents of coal also posed problems for domestic consumers. The spread of coal as a domestic fuel during the late sixteenth and early seventeenth centuries was paralleled by the spread of chimneys as the smoke forced people to abandon the traditional custom of having fires in the centre of the room with a hole in the roof.[5] Significantly, legislation to control air pollution from coal fires in towns has a long history. Wood fires were preferred to coal fires as they still are, and the rich were able to delay using coal longer than the poor. Likewise, contemporary prejudices against cooking over coal fires could be sustained longer by the rich than the poor.

As the demand for coal increased and production expanded to meet it, opencast coal deposits were soon used up and mines had to be sunk deeper and deeper. The invention of the steam engine was a direct result of the new technical problems posed by deep mines. In terms of the theoretical model used here, the steam engine was a response to the disturbance in the established technical consistency caused by an initial change in the society's resource base. The difficulties of ventilating the mines and lifting the hewn coal up the shaft increased as workings got deeper during the seventeenth century, but it was the problem of drainage which led to the development of the steam engine. Clearly if a shaft is sunk below the level of the water table it tends to fill with water. Mines on hillsides could sometimes be drained by digging a special drainage shaft from the bottom of the pit outwards to a point lower on the hillside for the water to run out. In other areas it was possible to mine close enough to a stream to have a water-powered rag-and-chain or bucket pump. Where water power was impossible a horse-whim was used to drive the pumps. These systems were all efficient enough while workings were fairly shallow, but before the end of the seventeenth century depths up to two hundred feet were common in all fields and some reached nearer four hundred feet.[6] Numbers of Cornish copper mines had already been abandoned because of flooding, and now coal mines had also

5 Ibid., p. 199.
6 Ibid., pp. 350–3.

reached depths at which existing methods of drainage became impracticable. The method using a special drainage shaft was obviously only practical while workings were still higher than the adjacent valley floor; beyond that depth pumping became necessary. On long lifts the rag-and-chain and bucket pumps ran into difficulties because too much of the available energy was used up in the mechanics of the pumping gear itself. The energy available from a mill wheel or a horse-whim may have been enough to lift an appreciable amount of water with fairly light equipment, but with the friction of the massive equipment needed for a long lift (the numbers of stuffed balls in a long rag-and-chain pump rubbing on the inside of the pipe, the greater weight of the longer chain as well as the friction of the clumsy wooden winding gear), little energy was left for lifting water after so much had been expended just on setting the equipment in motion. It became impractical to use these pumps on longer lifts. True, more power could be applied to a horse-whim by using more animals, but the equipment would have to be made correspondingly more massive and the inefficiency would still be very great. When long lifts were necessary it was more common to divide them into stages, building special chambers to operate pumps lower down.

Attempts to pump water from mines 'by fire' date back to 1631. Steam power was introduced not because it was potentially more powerful than a horse or a mill wheel, but because the power was delivered in a more appropriate form. The easiest and most direct application of steam power to pumping was to reduce the pressure above the column of water to be raised or to increase the pressure below it. The first practical steam pump – Thomas Savery's 'Miner's Friend' patented in 1698 – had no moving parts except for its valves. Steam from the boiler was piped into an oval-shaped container full of water, forcing the water up the outflow pipe. When the container was full of steam it was condensed with the help of cold water on the outside, and, with valves to prevent the return of the water just pumped out, the partial vacuum caused more water to flow in from a lower level. Two containers operated in this way alternately. It was the directness with which the expansion and contraction of steam could be applied to pumping that led to its introduction: It obviated the need for all the heavy mechanical equipment which on other pumps used for long lifts had wasted such a disproportionate amount of the available energy.

The potential application of steam power was not limited by the constraints on the supply of resources which limited other sources of power. The use of water power was limited by the number of streams with suitable sites for mills: New sites became scarce in many parts of the country during the seventeenth century. Animal power was dependent on the supply of land which could be devoted to growing fodder. As land became increasingly scarce, the relative cost of using animal power rose. In contrast, coal to fuel the steam engine was plentiful – especially at the pit head. The spread of steam power was ecologically favoured.

The design of pumping engines was of course modified. The steam no longer acted directly on the water, but operated a piston in a cylinder which was linked by a pivoted beam to drive another piston, which did the pumping. Although this development reintroduced moving parts, it allowed heat to be converted more efficiently into work by separating the hot steam from the cold water which tended to condense it.

While enough sites were available, water wheels remained the easiest and most economical way of obtaining a rotary motion for powering mills. The use of the steam engine was confined to a reciprocating pumping motion for almost a century. It was not until the late eighteenth century, when the new cotton mills began to add to the demand for rotary power and good mill sites were no longer available, that Boulton and Watt made the first steam engine harnessed to produce a rotary motion. Before that time rotary steam power had not been an economic proposition. The problem of how to convert a reciprocating motion into a rotary one was not – as so often stated – a theoretical one: The crank had been known and used in other contexts since before the spinning wheel or treadle lathe. It is true that Boulton and Watt had to change their design because of a patent on this application of the crank, but the problem was quickly overcome by Watt's design for an alternative linkage.[7] Rotary steam power appeared as late as it did not because of the difficulties of invention, but because it was not needed earlier.

The initial introduction of steam power was then a response to new problems consequent on the growing use of coal. Its advantage lay in the fact that its power was delivered in a form which made it particularly suitable for pumping. If a mill wheel or a horse could be used to create pressure differences as easily, the steam engine would not have been introduced when it was. The substitution at a later date of steam power for the rotary power of mills and horse-whims was a response to a growth in demand for rotary power at a time when the supply from traditional sources was relatively fixed. At neither stage was steam introduced to perform traditional tasks in preference to traditional methods. It was essentially part of an attempt to keep abreast of the growing difficulties of production encountered by an expanding society.

The development of transport was one of the central features of the English industrial revolution. As local populations ceased to be self-sufficient in the goods and commodities they had formerly produced themselves, they were forced to enter into increasingly important trading relationships. The expanding volume of trade put considerable strain on the

---

7 Samuel Smiles, *Lives of the Engineers: Boulton and Watt* (London, 1904), pp. 260–2.

established transport system. The growth of wheeled transport to carry this trade had imposed an increasing burden on the nation's roads, in particular on their surfaces. Packhorses, which had predominated before the wide-spread use of wheeled transport, do not rut the roads in the way that carts and wagons do, nor are they so hampered by uneven surfaces. Ruts are always a problem when wheeled transport uses unsurfaced roads and by the eighteenth century the situation had reached crisis proportions. An increasing volume of traffic was having to travel over roads reduced to worse conditions than ever before. Many roads became almost impassable because of the mud, and reports of coaches losing wheels or being overturned were frequent. Arthur Young complained of 'barbarous' and 'execrable' conditions wherever he travelled, and described 'rocky lanes full of hugeous stones as big as one's horse, and abominable holes'. On one road he claims he passed three broken-down carts and measured ruts four feet deep 'floating with mud'.[8] Frequent attempts were made to protect road surfaces by legislation controlling maximum loads and minimum widths of wheel rims over which the load was to be spread.[9] But a more effective response to the problem came in the form of the turnpike trusts, which appeared early in the eighteenth century and spread particularly rapidly from the mid-century onwards. With the creation of an institutional framework to pay for upkeep, the way was open for the surfacing innovations of Telford and McAdam later in the century.

The road surfacing problem was not the only difficulty that stimulated change in a transport system trying to serve an expanding society facing limited resources. Because coal supplies had, to use Wrigley's words, a 'scattered punctiform distribution' in contrast to the 'areal' distribution of wood, the growing use of coal created a demand for a national transport network capable of handling heavy bulk commodities.[10] The expanding trade in other bulk commodities, such as grain and metals, added to the demand for a bulk carrier, especially for supplying urban centres. Initially more rivers were made navigable and coastal shipping increased, but in 1757 and 1764 the first two canals were opened, one to link a Lancashire coalfield with the Mersey, and the other to link a neighbouring coalfield to Manchester. By the early nineteenth century the country had enough canals to provide a primary distribution network for bulk commodities.

Canals were of course an enormous improvement on wagons and packhorses for carrying commodities such as coal, but had they been built

8 As quoted in Samuel Smiles, *Lives of the Engineers: Metcalf and Telfor* (London, 1904), pp. 80–2.

9 W. T. Jackman, *The Development of Transportation in Modern England* (Cambridge, 1916), chap. 4.

10 E. A. Wrigley, 'The supply of raw materials in the Industrial Revolution', *Economic History Review* 15 (1962):1–16.

before it was necessary to transport these commodities they might well have proved unprofitable: Indeed, canals built in the relatively unchanged rural areas did tend to be unprofitable. The basic rationale for these huge new works was the impossibility of maintaining an adequate standard of living for a growing eighteenth-century population within an economic framework of local self-sufficiency.

The other element in the ecological equation which affected the transport system was the all-pervasive land shortage. The cost of road transport used to vary with the price of horse feed.[11] Announcements in local papers such as the following were not uncommon:

We the undersigned Magistrates acting for the West Riding of the County of York, have been applied to by the Carriers in the said Riding to make further Advance, upon Land Carriage, on Account of the very High Price of Hay and Corn, and it being our opinion that an Advance is reasonable and proper do hereby signify our Approbation . . . to an ADVANCE OF THREE-HALF PENCE per STONE on LAND CARRIAGE . . . and do strongly recommend it to all persons to allow the same.[12]

Estimates suggest that between four and eight acres of land under hay were needed to feed each horse.[13] Clearly as land became increasingly scarce and horse feed expensive, the incentive to economize on horses by building canals or using some other form of traction would also increase. Contemporaries were well aware of these benefits of canals and railways. An engineer writing in about 1800 on the proposed Grand Surrey Canal Navigation calculated that 'as one horse on an average consumes the produce of four acres of land, and there are 1,350,000 in this island that pay the horse-tax, of course there must be 5,400,000 acres of land occupied in providing provender for them. How desirable', he remarks, 'any improvement that will lessen the keep of horses'.[14] The Earl of Hardwick writing in favour of the Cambridge and London Junction Canal used a similar argument: 'If the canal should be the means of releasing 1000 horses from . . . employment, . . . 8000 acres of land . . . might be applied to more useful purposes, which would help to keep the labouring poor from suffering from want of bread'.[15]

The competition for food between people and horses could not be ignored, particularly during the Napoleonic Wars when restrictions on imports caused grain prices to rise to record levels. Undoubtedly one of the most important reasons for the commercial success of the canals was the high price of horse feed. Only when competition for land had forced the

---

11 William I. Albert, *The Turnpike Road System in England 1663–1840* (Cambridge, 1972), chap. 8.
12 *Loads Intelligencer*, 20 January 1800, p. 3. As quoted by Albert, *Turnpike Road System*.
13 Jackman, *Development of Transportation*, p. 405.
14 As quoted in Jackman, *Development of Transportation*, p. 406 n.
15 Ibid.

price of horse feed sufficiently high was it worth expending labour on the construction of canals which allowed larger loads to be drawn by fewer horses. The wartime prices must have added considerably to the 'mania' for canal promotions just before the turn of the century, and have led to the execution of many schemes which proved improvident when prices fell. Although the rapid expansion in the demand for transport did not permit a reduction in the overall number of horses in the country, more horses would have been needed had it not been for the canals.

Steam railways provided another way of substituting capital equipment – or indirect labour – for horses in the transport system. A report to the House of Commons on 'steam carriages' in 1833 contains the following calculation:

It has been said that in Great Britain there are above a million of horses engaged in various ways in the transport of passengers and goods, and that to support each horse requires as much land as would upon an average support eight men. If this quantity of animal power were displaced by steam-engines, and the means of transport drawn from the bowels of the earth, instead of being raised upon its surface, then, supposing the above calculation correct, as much land would become available for the support of human beings as would suffice for an additional population of eight millions; . . . The land which now supports horses for transport on turnpike roads would then support men, or produce corn for food, and the horses return to agricultural pursuits.[16]

Like the substitution of coal for firewood, the substitution of the steam locomotive for horses in the transport system represents a response to changes in relative prices caused by the land shortage. As land becomes increasingly scarce it is almost inevitable that at some point it will become worthwhile to manufacture a machine using a mineral fuel to replace horses using agricultural land. Again, the particularly high price of feed during the Napoleonic Wars made even the earliest and most inefficient locomotives economically viable in some situations. Rolt says it was these prices which 'forced (two Tyneside colliery owners) to consider more seriously the claims of an iron horse using fuel which they produced themselves'.[17] This is a particularly clear example of the way resource shortages can force a society to adopt more complicated productive procedures which may – at least initially – require additional work.

The steam locomotive and the railway track on which it runs are of course two separate innovations. The track is another response to the surfacing problem. In a number of collieries and other places where heavy goods had to be moved, rails and plateways were laid for horse-drawn

16 N. W. Cundy, *Inland Transit*, Report of a Select Committee of the House of Commons on Steam Carriages, 2d ed. (London, 1834), pp. 20–1.
17 L. T. C. Rolt, *George and Robert Stephenson* (London, 1960), pp. 43–4.

trucks long before the introduction of steam locomotion. It was the weight of the engine with its cast-iron boiler that was responsible for the link between steam locomotion and the railway track.

Although both canals and steam railways yielded enormous economies in the use of horses, the numbers in the country were not reduced until the introduction of the bicycle and the car. The horse remained the most suitable form of personal short distance transport until the late nineteenth and early twentieth centuries. Only then was the economic climate right for the sur-render of the obvious ready-made advantages of the horse in favour of manufactured substitutes.

Once again it appears that a formidable group of innovations should not be regarded as the fruits of a society's search for progress, but as the outcome of a valiant struggle of a society with its back to the ecological wall. The development of transport during this period was a response to the devel-opment of the problems caused by two secular trends: the breakdown of local self-sufficiency, particularly in heavy commodities such as fuel and grain, and the growing pressure to economize on the use of agricultural land. As these problems became increasingly severe the society was forced to adopt solu-tions it would not otherwise have done. The problems became most acute – and the pace of innovation fastest – during the population growth and price rises of the second half of the eighteenth century and the first decade or so of the nineteenth; after that the measures adopted had begun to alleviate the situation.

An industry which underwent changes linked ultimately with the shortage of timber and the development of transport already discussed was the building industry. Until coal replaced firewood as the fuel for brick kilns in the seventeenth century, more wood was used to build a house in brick than to build it in timber.[18] Apart from a few exceptional areas, brick building before the seventeenth century was a departure from local styles which only the rich could afford – and few of them preferred it to stone. In some areas buildings used timber frames with in-filling of wattle and daub, clay or stone; in others they were made of local stone throughout. With the introduction of coal firing, brick production could be expanded without any increase in unit costs. After the Great Fire of 1666, legislation to guard against a repetition of the disaster, backed by changed economic conditions, secured the rebuilding of London in brick. As it became easier to transport coal to the brick kilns, the relative advantages of building in brick increased. Timber houses ceased to be built and by the second half of the eighteenth century building in brick was general in many areas. Brickwork was usually

18 Nef, *British Coal Industry*, vol. 1, p. 196. For the consumption of coal and breeze in brickmaking see Edward Dobson, *A Rudimentary Treatise on the Manufacture of Bricks and Tiles* (London, 1850), pt. 1, pp. 91, 101; pt. 2, pp. 44, 96.

regarded as inferior to stone and in the early nineteenth century it became fashionable – under Nash and others – to cover it over with stucco marked out to look like rectangular stone blocks. Not only did building with coal-fired bricks obviate the need for a timber framework, but the wooden lintels over windows and doors were replaced by the arched row of bricks arranged vertically which can be seen in cheaper housing from the nineteenth century onwards. On larger buildings, where longer spans were needed, this method was unsuitable and iron girders became increasingly common. Whole iron frames, particularly for industrial buildings, were used from quite early on in the nineteenth century. Concrete was introduced in the same period though reinforced concrete did not appear until towards the end of the century.

This process of substitution of materials followed the familiar pattern: Scarcity drove it on in some areas while preferences or the availability of the older materials in others tended to hold it back. Clay was more easily obtained than quarried stone, particularly around many urban areas, but where stone could still be quarried easily people went on using it. Coal was more plentiful than firewood, and iron and concrete more plentiful than timber. With the introduction of artificial materials – including artificial stone in the later eighteenth century – supplied from extralocal sources, the complexity of the productive system and the demand for labour and transport were further increased.

The growth of the cotton industry, one of the dominant features of the industrial revolution in England, is a particularly good example of the process of materials substitution. The traditional clothing material was wool supplemented to some extent by linen and leather. The division of agricultural land between sheep pasture and arable land had long been a matter of contention. Conversion of arable to pasture had brought outcries against 'sheep (which) devour men' and had been a central issue in the earlier enclosure movement. The export of considerable quantities of woollen cloth no doubt made the crisis develop sooner than it would have done otherwise. Although cotton was – like wool – a land-based resource, the fact that it depended on the exploitation of land in India and America rather than in England meant that it could provide a way out of the domestic impasse. The manufacture of clothing could be expanded without threatening the production of food.

No longer having to pay woollen cloth prices inflated by the scarcity of land, the poorer domestic consumers substituted inferior – but cheaper – cotton cloth wherever possible. Describing the clothing of the working class shortly before the middle of the nineteenth century, Engels said:

Linen and wool have practically disappeared from the wardrobes of both men and women, and have been replaced by cotton. Men's shirts are made of bleached or coloured cotton cloth. Women generally wear printed cottons; woollen petticoats are seldom seen on the washing-line. Men's trousers are generally made either of fustian or some other heavy cotton cloth. Overcoats and jackets are made from the same material. Fustian has become the traditional dress of working men, who are called 'fustian jackets'. Gentlemen, on the other hand, wear suits made from woollen cloth, and the term 'broadcloth' is used to designate the middle classes. . . . The working classes . . . very seldom wear woollen clothing of any kind. Their heavy cotton clothes, though thicker, stiffer and heavier than woollen cloth, do not keep out the cold and wet to anything like the same extent as woollens.[19]

This quotation shows not only the extent to which cotton was substituted for wool, but shows also a repetition of the pattern by which scarcity forces the substitution of materials regarded, for many uses, as inferior to the traditional ones. The inferiority of cotton and the expense of importing it presumably explain why it did not begin to be used extensively until the renewed pressure of population growth during the second half of the eighteenth century. Cotton could have been used much more extensively earlier if people had desired it: It was not a material they were unfamiliar with. Raw cotton for stuffing and quilting and yarns for candlewicks had been imported for a very long time. Fustians had featured in European trade for several centuries before they were made in England and had been manufactured in Italy since medieval times.[20]

The methods and scale of the woollen industry had been precariously balanced to fit social, ecological and economic constraints. For those engaged in it, it was a source of additional family income. The spinners and weavers were often among the poorest in the community and took up their trade when their land holdings proved insufficient. The price and quantity of wool supplies were largely fixed by the land situation; markets were limited and, given the technology, highly competitive. Within this framework the comparatively inefficient machinery in use was maintained as a way of ensuring a sufficiently wide social distribution of the small rewards available. The introduction of new kinds of machinery was strenuously opposed because of the threat to employment in the industry. People resorted to machine breaking and direct action against inventors and importers of new machinery.[21] Sometimes they were even successful in giving their opposition the force of law. From manufacture to marketing the industry was closely regulated by guilds and merchant companies.

The whole of this system was however at risk as soon as the relative prices of Indian cottons and English woollens moved sufficiently to give the advantage to the Indian goods. It seems likely that this situation would first have

19 F. Engels, *The Condition of the Working Class in England* (Oxford, 1958), pp. 78–9.
20 A. P. Wadsworth and J. de L. Mann, *The Cotton Trade and Industrial Lancashire 1600–1780* (Manchester, 1931), p. 17.
21 Ibid., pp. 97–108.

occurred some time during the population growth and price rises of the late sixteenth and early seventeenth centuries. By the late seventeenth century the Indian cottons imported by the East India Company were regarded as a substantial threat to the English woollen industry. But it was not competition in the domestic market – which could be protected – that brought the downfall of the old system, but competition in overseas markets where Indian cottons were potentially just as dangerous. However, instead of accepting a reduction of markets in face of competition from cotton, the English textile industry – supported by the appropriate duties, prohibitions and bounties – took advantage of the more plentiful raw material.

The political and economic handicaps imposed on the Indian cotton industry, and the possibility which plentiful cotton supplies provided for rapid expansion into overseas markets, meant that the introduction of new laboursaving machinery was less threatening than it had been when the possibilities of industrial growth were limited by constraints on the supplies of raw materials and on the size of the market. New machinery started to appear in the textile industry from the late seventeenth century onwards as arguments about unemployment could be increasingly easily countered by appeals to the need to compete abroad.[22] The classical innovations in textile machinery in the late eighteenth century should be seen in the context of almost a century of change in an industry which had never achieved a technology stabilized on purely economic grounds. Rapid expansion necessitated the use of spinning machines with larger numbers of spindles, hence demanding the application of additional sources of power. In the absence of suitable sites for water mills, the nineteenth-century factories made use of steam power. The woollen industry adopted similar methods and with the arrival of supplies of raw wool from Australia was able to expand output rapidly once more.

The development of the chemical industry during the industrial revolution and early nineteenth century may at first glance appear to present problems for the explanation of development put forward here. The modern chemical industry had its foundations in the manufacture of soda by the Leblanc process; it appears as a new industry rather than as a traditional one in which substitutes for scarce resources were introduced. But instead of the materials used in manufacture being subject to substitution as in the other industries discussed, the product of the early chemical industry was itself a substitute material for other industries.

The use of some form of alkali was important in the processing of a wide range of commodities including glass, soap, alum and saltpetre. When the industries making these commodities had used wood for fuel, alkali was

22 Ibid., pp. 102–3.

readily available in the form of potash, but as coal burning became general, supplies became scarce. Imports of potash eased the situation though demand continued to exceed supply.

Potash could of course be made by burning almost any vegetable matter and the fact that there could be a shortage at all is an indication of how serious the pressure was on agricultural land; the severity of the land shortage is doubly underlined when we see that supplies were augmented initially by burning seaweed instead of an agricultural product. The collection, drying and burning of large quantities of kelp along the seashore provides evidence of the ecological pressures behind development; as an attempt to exploit marine resources it is paralleled only by the efforts of the later nineteenth century to expand the fishing industry by importing tens of thousands of tons of Norwegian ice each year for preserving.[23] The sea was the only source of organic matter which did not add to the pressure on the land.

The kelping industry was introduced to England in about 1730 from Scotland where it had started a few decades earlier. It was an important source of alkali for a century before synthetic supplies of soda became available from the Leblanc process. Clow, the historian of the chemical industry, summarizing that industry's early development says, 'as a subsidiary facet of the search for an alternative to wood we have the search for a substitute for natural alkali'. After the discovery of the Leblanc process 'the industries using alkali became the focus of practically the whole chemical industry, and so remained for some fifty years'.[24] The establishment of a new industry was however a high price to pay to produce a substitute for what had previously been available free on the site in the form of wood ash.

The Leblanc process involved manufacturers in the production of a number of other chemicals which proved useful elsewhere in the productive system. Sulphuric acid was needed to make soda but was also used to dissolve bones to make superphosphate fertilizer which helped to bring the much needed increases in agricultural yields. Noxious hydrogen chloride fumes, which had been allowed to escape from the factories of the soda manufacturers, were collected after legal action had been taken by local residents to prevent their release. The supplies of hydrochloric acid which resulted were used to make chlorine for bleaching.

The new bleach was particularly useful in papermaking. Under the impetus of the spread of literacy and the increased demand for paper for packaging, the papermaking industry had expanded up to the limits imposed by the available supplies of its raw materials. The scarcity of

23 Charles L. Cutting, *Fish Saving* (London, 1955), p. 235.
24 A. Clow and N. L. Clow, 'The chemical industry', in Charles Singer et al., eds., *A History of Technology*, vol. 4, p. 235.

suitable rags had caused prices to rise sharply during the late eighteenth and early nineteenth centuries.[25] Imported rags began to supplement domestic supplies but the raw material problem remained acute. Experimenters who tried vegetable substitutes such as hay, straw, nettles and thistles met with little success. In this situation the first real advances came with the discovery of an effective bleach. Instead of being confined to white rags, bleaching meant that even the best white paper could be produced from dyed and printed rags.

The possibility of using a wider range of rags eased the raw materials problem for several decades, but it is worth noting that the effects of scarcity were only overcome at the additional cost of incorporating bleaching into the papermaking process. Bleaching was however only a temporary solution. Experiments with substitutes soon continued and during the middle of the nineteenth century some paper was made from cotton waste, hay and straw, as well as rags. It was not until the 1880s that the technique for making paper from wood pulp was discovered. This discovery of course marks the beginning of the relative decline of the industry in England in favour of timber-rich areas such as the Baltic countries and North America.

One more case of substitution worth mentioning before we move on to discuss some of the general implications of this pattern of development is the substitution of gas lighting for tallow candles.

The possibility of lighting by gas was demonstrated publicly shortly before the end of the eighteenth century. The demonstration was intended as a matter of scientific curiosity rather than as a commercial venture, and it seems that gas lighting was bound to have remained a curiosity while the gas was obtained from wood rather than coal. Tallow candles, which were the traditional form of lighting, were obviously dependent on the land supply. As prices rose, increasing quantities of tallow, vegetable oil and whale oil were imported to supplement domestic supplies, but the problem was not solved. Gas lighting, in its initial stages early in the nineteenth century, was used almost exclusively in factories; the long hours worked in cotton mills, the high price of imported animal and vegetable oils, and the extraction of gas from coal all helped to make gas lighting a commercial success. The importance of relative price movements in the substitution of coal gas for tallow was emphasized in a paper of William Murdock's, read to the Royal Society in 1808, in which he compared the costs of the two forms of lighting in a cotton mill which underwent one of the earliest conversions.[26] Outside the factory gas lighting spread more slowly. The

25 D. C. Coleman, *The British Paper Industry* (Oxford, 1958), pp. 171–3.
26 William Murdock, 'An account of the application of the gas from coal to economical purposes', read before the Royal Society by Sir Joseph Banks in 1808. As quoted by A. Clow and N. L. Clow, *The Chemical Revolution* (London, 1952), p. 432.

fumes from the impure gas were so unpleasant that people preferred to go on using the older oils, and when they did use gas they sometimes went as far as mounting the lights outside the window to avoid the fumes. In 1838 Britain still needed to import over £1 million worth of vegetable and whale oil.

We have seen how English society was forced to change its established technology by a shortage of the resources which the technology was designed to exploit. Every change discussed in this chapter was either a direct response to a particular resource shortage or was a response to changes caused by resource shortages elsewhere in the economy. These initial changes were made under duress. They were notably not introduced when the traditional economic system was functioning in ecological equilibrium – when the choice could be made freely – but were instead adapted when scarcity threatened the continuation of the established system. The reasons why the technological innovations underlying the industrial revolution were not adopted earlier are clear. Just as preindustrial agricultural development involved the expenditure of increasing quantities of labour to gain an adequate subsistence, so did the new technology. Not only was the product produced by the new technology often regarded as inferior, but the productive processes became more complex and frequently involved more labour. The innovations were only improvements in the context of the crisis situation into which they were introduced; they would not have been regarded as beneficial in equilibrium conditions of several centuries earlier. Improvements – for instance in the system for transporting heavy goods – would have been merely wasteful in an economic system that had not developed the initial inefficiency of having to transport such goods. That the new technology, methods and materials were introduced because they were profitable is not at issue. However, it would be foolish to assume that they would always have been profitable: Inevitably their profitability rested on the particular ecological context. All economic relationships take place within an ecological context, and given a set of these relationships it is hardly more than a truism to say that innovations are introduced because of their profitability; the real problem with which we are concerned is to see how these relationships change historically to make one set of choices rational in one period and another in the next.

That an increasingly complex productive system was being foisted on to a society while its original choice of resources was disallowed explains why the work load during the industrial revolution was so great. The extraordinarily long hours worked by men and increasing numbers of women and children are well known. The arduous factory routine contrasted sharply with the much shorter hours and seasonal work associated with some earlier periods of English history and with many underdeveloped countries today.

97

Such long hours of work were a reflection, on one side, of the increased difficulties of production, and on the other, of the individual's response to poverty. Growing poverty and rising prices during the second half of the eighteenth century were, in turn, the direct results of population pressure and scarcity.

As the work load increased during the industrial revolution period, the productive system became unmanageable without the introduction of laboursaving equipment. Laboursaving innovations are of course almost always desirable, but they are rarely essential. The amount of work necessary to gain subsistence can – if all else fails – be allowed to increase until it begins to approach the maximum people are capable of doing. Beyond this the system is no longer viable. Undoubtedly this point was reached for a significant proportion of the English population during the industrial revolution: The work load rose to the limits of human endurance. Although this situation was caused by social inequality as well as by the technical and ecological factors under consideration, it is clear that there had been a long-term increase in the per capita work load necessary to gain subsistence as population expanded. It was this situation which made it essential to introduce laboursaving machinery. For obvious reasons it was essential for self-employed people working maximum hours; it was also essential from an employer's point of view because he could not pay less than a minimum subsistence wage for an employee and his dependents and still maintain his labour force: He had to find ways of keeping labour productivity above the level needed to produce bare subsistence on maximum hours. (The Speenhamland system of poor relief introduced during this period is a testament to the severity of this problem – particularly during the high wheat prices of the Napoleonic Wars. While it was applied, it allowed for the payment of a supplement to wages where the economic wage was below subsistence level.)

The maximum possible work load per individual cannot of course be accurately defined, but it is safe to assume that the toleration of additional hours decreases as the work load increases. As the amount of labour needed to gain subsistence increases, the labour supply becomes the effective constraint on the supply of subsistence and so demands the transformation of the technology to economize on labour.

Many of the important innovations involving changes in the resource base came, as we have seen, long before the classical industrial revolution period of the late eighteenth century. Industrial expansion was made possible by earlier changes in the resource base. The introduction of new resources owes more to the pressure created by the population rise which ceased in the early seventeenth century than it does to the rise which started in the mid-eighteenth century. Liberated from the constraints of the land supply, industrial expansion was almost an inevitable consequence of the next population rise. When the section of the economy established on the more plentiful resources became large enough to absorb a significant rate of population growth, the pressure to delay marriages and limit family size was diminished, and the preconditions for industrialization had appeared. (If the part of the economy with sufficient resources to expand is only, say, 10 percent of the whole, then it would have to expand at a rate of 20 percent per annum to absorb an overall population growth of 2 percent per annum.) No doubt the privations of the Napoleonic Wars accelerated the spread of techniques using new resources. As well as increasing the demand for some commodities still further, the wars also hampered the import of materials which had partly offset the effects of scarcity. The first response to resource shortages is often to import additional supplies. Among the materials we have discussed, Britain had imported timber, iron, raw wool, grain, tallow, rags for paper and potash, to name only a few. The war intensified the long-term crisis, but the innovations which were the keys to continued survival had appeared much earlier.

The European Invasion

5　Ecological Imperialism: The Overseas Migration of Western Europeans as a Biological Phenomenon

Alfred W. Crosby

> *Industrial man may in many respects be considered an aggressive and successful weed strangling other species and even the weaker members of its own.*
> Stafford Lightman, "The Responsibilities of Intervention in Isolated Societies," *Health and Disease in Tribal Societies*

EUROPEANS IN NORTH AMERICA, especially those with an interest in gardening and botany, are often stricken with fits of homesickness at the sight of certain plants which, like themselves, have somehow strayed thousands of miles eastward across the Atlantic. Vladimir Nabokov, the Russian exile, had such an experience on the mountain slopes of Oregon:

> Do you recognize that clover?
> Dandelions, *l'or du pauvre?*
> (Europe, nonetheless, is over.)

A century earlier the success of European weeds in America inspired Charles Darwin to goad the American botanist Asa Gray: "Does it not hurt your Yankee pride that we thrash you so confoundly? I am sure Mrs. Gray will stick up for your own weeds. Ask her whether they are not more honest, downright good sort of weeds."[1]

The common dandelion, *l'or du pauvre,* despite its ubiquity and its bright yellow flower, is not at all the most visible of the Old World immigrants in North America. Vladimir Nabokov was a prime example of the most visible kind: the *Homo sapiens* of European origin. Europeans and their descen-

---

1 Page Stegner, ed., *The Portable Nabokov* (New York: Viking, 1968), p. 527; Francis Darwin, ed., *Life and Letters of Charles Darwin* (London: Murray, 1887), vol. 2, p. 391.

dants, who comprise the majority of human beings in North America and in a number of other lands outside of Europe, are the most spectacularly successful overseas migrants of all time. How strange it is to find Englishmen, Germans, Frenchmen, Italians, and Spaniards comfortably ensconced in places with names like Wollongong (Australia), Rotorua (New Zealand), and Saskatoon (Canada), where obviously other peoples should dominate, as they must have at one time.

None of the major genetic groupings of humankind is as oddly distributed about the world as European, especially western European, whites. Almost all the peoples we call Mongoloids live in the single contiguous land mass of Asia. Black Africans are divided between three continents – their homeland and North and South America – but most of them are concentrated in their original latitudes, the tropics, facing each other across one ocean. European whites were all recently concentrated in Europe, but in the last few centuries have burst out, as energetically as if from a burning building, and have created vast settlements of their kind in the South Temperate Zone and North Temperate Zone (excepting Asia, a continent already thoroughly and irreversibly tenanted). In Canada and the United States together they amount to nearly 90 percent of the population; in Argentina and Uruguay together to over 95 percent; in Australia to 98 percent; and in New Zealand to 90 percent. The only nations in the Temperate Zones outside of Asia which do not have enormous majorities of European whites are Chile, with a population of two-thirds mixed Spanish and Indian stock, and South Africa, where blacks outnumber whites six to one. How odd that these two, so many thousands of miles from Europe, should be exceptions in *not* being predominantly pure European.[2]

Europeans have conquered Canada, the United States, Argentina, Uruguay, Australia, and New Zealand not just militarily and economically and technologically – as they did India, Nigeria, Mexico, Peru, and other tropical lands, whose native people have long since expelled or interbred with and even absorbed the invaders. In the Temperate Zone lands listed above Europeans conquered and triumphed demographically. These, for the sake of convenience, we will call the Lands of the Demographic Takeover.

There is a long tradition of emphasizing the contrasts between Europeans and Americans – a tradition honored by such names as Henry James and Frederick Jackson Turner – but the vital question is really why Americans are so European. And why the Argentinians, the Uruguayans, the Australians, and the New Zealanders are so European in the obvious genetic sense.

The reasons for the relative failure of the European demographic takeover in the tropics are clear. In tropical Africa, until recently, Europeans died in

---

2 *The World Almanac and Book of Facts 1978* (New York: Newspaper Enterprise Association, 1978), passim.

droves of the fevers; in tropical America they died almost as fast of the same diseases, plus a few native American additions. Furthermore, in neither region did European agricultural techniques, crops, and animals prosper. Europeans did try to found colonies for settlement, rather than merely exploitation, but they failed or achieved only partial success in the hot lands. The Scots left their bones as monument to their short-lived colony at Darien at the turn of the eighteenth century. The English Puritans who skipped Massachusetts Bay Colony to go to Providence Island in the Caribbean Sea did not even achieve a permanent settlement, much less a Commonwealth of God. The Portuguese who went to northeastern Brazil created viable settlements, but only by perching themselves on top of first a population of native Indian laborers and then, when these faded away, a population of laborers imported from Africa. They did achieve a demographic takeover, but only by interbreeding with their servants. The Portuguese in Angola, who helped supply those servants, never had a breath of a chance to achieve a demographic takeover.[3] There was much to repel and little to attract the mass of Europeans to the tropics, and so they stayed home or went to the lands where life was healthier, labor more rewarding, and where white immigrants, by their very number, encouraged more immigration.

In the cooler lands, the colonies of the Demographic Takeover, Europeans achieved very rapid population growth by means of immigration, by increased life span, and by maintaining very high birthrates. Rarely has population expanded more rapidly than it did in the eighteenth and nineteenth centuries in these lands. It is these lands, especially the United States, that enabled Europeans and their overseas offspring to expand from something like 18 percent of the human species in 1650 to well over 30 percent in 1900. Today 670 million Europeans live in Europe, and 250 million or so other Europeans – genetically as European as any left behind in the Old World – live in the Lands of the Demographic Takeover, an ocean or so from home.[4] What the Europeans have done with unprecedented

3 Philip D. Curtin, "Epidemiology and the Slave Trade," *Political Science Quarterly* 83 (June 1968), 190–216 passim; John Prebble, *The Darien Disaster* (New York: Holt, Rinehart & Winston, 1968), pp. 296, 300; Charles M. Andrews, *The Colonial Period of American History* (New Haven, Conn.: Yale University Press, 1934), vol. 1, n. 497; Gilberto Freyre, *The Masters and the Slaves*, trans. Samuel Putnam (New York: Knopf, 1946), passim; Donald L. Wiedner, *A History of Africa South of the Sahara* (New York: Vintage Books, 1964), 49–51; Stuart B. Schwartz, "Indian Labor and New World Plantations: European Demands and Indian Responses in Northeastern Brazil," *American Historical Review* 83 (February 1978): 43–79 passim.
4 Marcel R. Reinhard, *Histoire de la population modiale de 1700 à 1948* (n.p.: Editions Domat-Montchrestien, n.d.), pp. 339–411, 428–31; G. F. McCleary, *Peopling the British Commonwealth* (London: Farber and Farber, n.d.), pp. 83, 94, 109–10; R. R. Palmer and Joel Colton, *A History of the Modern World* (New York: Knopf, 1965), p. 560; *World Almanac 1978*, pp. 34, 439, 497, 513, 590.

success in the past few centuries can accurately be described by a term from apiculture: They have swarmed.

They swarmed to lands which were populated at the time of European arrival by peoples as physically capable of rapid increase as the Europeans, and yet who are now small minorities in their homelands and sometimes no more than relict populations. These population explosions among colonial Europeans of the past few centuries coincided with population crashes among the aborigines. If overseas Europeans have historically been less fatalistic and grim than their relatives in Europe, it is because they have viewed the histories of their nations very selectively. When he returned from his world voyage on the *Beagle* in the 1830s, Charles Darwin, as a biologist rather than a historian, wrote, "Wherever the European has trod, death seems to pursue the aboriginal."[5]

Any respectable theory which attempts to explain the Europeans' demographic triumphs has to provide explanations for at least two phenomena. The first is the decimation and demoralization of the aboriginal populations of Canada, the United States, Argentina, and others. The obliterating defeat of these populations was not simply due to European technological superiority. The Europeans who settled in temperate South Africa seemingly had the same advantages as those who settled in Virginia and New South Wales, and yet how different was their fate. The Bantu-speaking peoples, who now overwhelmingly outnumber the whites in South Africa, were superior to their American, Australian, and New Zealand counterparts in that they possessed iron weapons, but how much more inferior to a musket or a rifle is a stone-pointed spear than an iron-pointed spear? The Bantu have prospered demographically not because of their numbers at the time of first contact with whites, which were probably not greater per square mile than those of the Indians east of the Mississippi River. Rather, the Bantu have prospered because they survived military conquest, avoided the conquerors, or became their indispensable servants – and in the long run because they reproduced faster than the whites. In contrast, why did so few of the natives of the Lands of the Demographic Takeover survive?

Second, we must explain the stunning, even awesome success of European agriculture, that is, the European way of manipulating the environment in the Lands of the Demographic Takeover. The difficult progress of the European frontier in the Siberian *taiga* or the Brazilian *sertão* or the South African *veldt* contrasts sharply with its easy, almost fluid advance in North America. Of course, the pioneers of North America would never have characterized their progress as easy: Their lives were filled with danger, deprivation, and unremitting labor; but as a group they always succeeded in

---

5 Charles Darwin, *The Voyage of the Beagle* (Garden City, N.Y.: Doubleday Anchor Books, 1962), pp. 433–4.

taming whatever portion of North America they wanted within a few decades and usually a good deal less time. Many individuals among them failed – they were driven mad by blizzards and dust storms, lost their crops to locusts and their flocks to cougars and wolves, or lost their scalps to understandably inhospitable Indians – but as a group they always succeeded – and in terms of human generations, very quickly.

In attempting to explain these two phenomena, let us examine four categories of organisms deeply involved in European expansion: (1) human beings; (2) animals closely associated with human beings – both the desirable animals like horses and cattle and undesirable varmints like rats and mice; (3) pathogens or microorganisms that cause disease in humans; and (4) weeds. Is there a pattern in the histories of these groups which suggests an overall explanation for the phenomenon of the Demographic Takeover or which at least suggests fresh paths of inquiry?

Europe has exported something in excess of sixty million people in the past few hundred years. Great Britain alone exported over twenty million. The great mass of these white emigrants went to the United States, Argentina, Canada, Australia, Uruguay, and New Zealand. (Other areas to absorb comparable quantities of Europeans were Brazil and Russia east of the Urals. These would qualify as Lands of the Demographic Takeover except that large fractions of their populations are non-European.)[6]

In stark contrast, very few aborigines of the Americas, Australia, or New Zealand ever went to Europe. Those who did often died not long after arrival.[7] The fact that the flow of human migration was almost entirely from Europe to her colonies and not vice versa is not startling – or very enlightening. Europeans controlled overseas migration, and Europe needed to export, not import, labor. But this pattern of one-way migration is significant in that it reappears in other connections.

The vast expanses of forests, savannas, and steppes in the Lands of the Demographic Takeover were inundated by animals from the Old World, chiefly from Europe. Horses, cattle, sheep, goats, and pigs have for hundreds of years been among the most numerous of the quadrupeds of these lands, which were completely lacking in these species at the time of first contact with the Europeans. By 1600 enormous feral herds of horses and cattle surged over the pampas of the Rio de la Plata (today's Argentina and Uruguay) and over the plains of northern Mexico. By the beginning of the seventeenth century packs of Old World dogs gone wild were among the predators of these herds.[8]

6 William Woodruff, *Impact of Western Man* (New York: St. Martin's, 1967), 106–8.
7 Carolyn T. Foreman, *Indians Abroad* (Norman: University of Oklahoma Press, 1943), passim.
8 Alfred W. Crosby, *The Columbian Exchange* (Westport, Conn.: Greenwood, 1972), pp.

In the forested country of British North America population explosions among imported animals were also spectacular, but only by European standards, not by those of Spanish America. In 1700 in Virginia feral hogs, said one witness, "swarm like vermaine upon the Earth," and young gentlemen were entertaining themselves by hunting wild horses of the inland counties. In Carolina the herds of cattle were "incredible, being from one to two thousand head in one Man's Possession." In the eighteenth and early nineteenth centuries the advancing European frontier from New England to the Gulf of Mexico was preceded into Indian territory by an avant-garde of semiwild herds of hogs and cattle tended, now and again, by semiwild herdsmen, white and black.[9]

The first English settlers landed in Botany Bay, Australia, in January of 1788 with livestock, most of it from the Cape of Good Hope. The pigs and poultry thrived; the cattle did well enough; the sheep, the future source of the colony's good fortune, died fast. Within a few months two bulls and four cows strayed away. By 1804 the wild herds they founded numbered from three to five thousand head and were in possession of much of the best land between the settlements and the Blue Mountains. If they had ever found their way through the mountains to the grasslands beyond, the history of Australia in the first decades of the nineteenth century might have been one dominated by cattle rather than sheep. As it is, the colonial government wanted the land the wild bulls so ferociously defended, and considered the growing practice of convicts running away to live off the herds as a threat to the whole colony; so the adult cattle were shot and salted down and the calves captured and tamed. The English settlers imported woolly sheep from Europe and sought out the interior pastures for them. The animals multiplied rapidly, and when Darwin made his visit to New South Wales in 1836, there were about a million sheep there for him to see.[10]

The arrival of Old World livestock probably affected New Zealand more radically than any other of the Lands of the Demographic Takeover. Cattle, horses, goats, pigs and – in this land of few or no large predators – even the

Footnote 8 (*continued*)
82–88; Alexander Gillespie, *Gleanings and Remarks Collected during Many Months of Residence at Buenos Aires* (Leeds: B. DeWhirst, 1818), p. 136; Oscar Schmieder, "Alteration of the Argentine Pampa in the Colonial Period," *University of California Publications in Geography* 2 (27 September 1927): n. 311.

9 Robert Beverley, *The History and Present State of Virginia* (Chapel Hill: University of North Carolina Press, 1947), pp. 153, 312, 318; John Lawson, *A New Voyage to Carolina* (n. p.: Readex Microprint Corp., 1966), p. 4; Frank L. Owsley, "The Pattern of Migration and Settlement of the Southern Frontier," *Journal of Southern History* 11 (May 1945): 147–75.

10 Commonwealth of Australia, *Historical Records of Australia* (Sydney: Library Committee of the Commonwealth Parliament, 1914), ser. 1, vol. 1, p. 550; vol. 7, pp. 379–80; vol. 8, pp. 150–1; vol. 9, pp. 349, 714, 831; vol. 10, pp. 92, 280, 682; vol. 20, p. 839.

usually timid sheep went wild. In New Zealand herds of feral farm animals were practicing the ways of their remote ancestors as late as the 1940s and no doubt still run free. Most of the sheep, though, stayed under human control, and within a decade of Great Britain's annexation of New Zealand in 1840, her new acquisition was home to a quarter million sheep. In 1974 New Zealand had over fifty-five million sheep, about twenty times more sheep than people.[11]

In the Lands of the Demographic Takeover the European pioneers were accompanied and often preceded by their domesticated animals, walking sources of food, leather, fiber, power, and wealth, and these animals often adapted more rapidly to the new surroundings and reproduced much more rapidly than their masters. To a certain extent, the success of Europeans as colonists was automatic as soon as they put their tough, fast, fertile, and intelligent animals ashore. The latter were sources of capital that sought out their own sustenance, improvised their own protection against the weather, fought their own battles against predators and, if their masters were smart enough to allow calves, colts, and lambs to accumulate, could and often did show the world the amazing possibilities of compound interest.

The honey bee is the one insect of worldwide importance which human beings have domesticated, if we may use the word in a broad sense. Many species of bees and other insects produce honey, but the one which does so in greatest quantity and which is easiest to control is a native of the Mediterranean area and the Middle East, the honey bee (*Apis mellifera*). The European has probably taken this sweet and short-tempered servant to every colony he ever established, from Arctic to Antarctic Circle, and the honey bee has always been one of the first immigrants to set off on its own. Sometimes the advance of the bee frontier could be very rapid: The first hive in Tasmania swarmed sixteen times in the summer of 1832.[12]

Thomas Jefferson tells us that the Indians of North America called the honey bees "English flies," and St. John de Crèvecoeur, his contemporary, wrote that "The Indians look upon them with an evil eye, and consider their progress into the interior of the continent as an omen of the white man's approach: thus, as they discover the bees, the news of the event, passing from mouth to mouth, spreads sadness and consternation on all sides."[13]

11 Andrew H. Clark, *The Invasion of New Zealand by People, Plants, and Animals* (New Brunswick, N.J.: Rutgers University Press, 1949), p. 190; David Wallechinsky, Irving Wallace, and A. Wallace, *The Book of Lists* (New York: Bantam, 1978), pp. 129–30.

12 Remy Chauvin, *Traité de biologie de l'abeille* (Paris: Masson et Cie, 1968), vol. 1, pp. 38–9; James Backhouse, *A Narrative of a Visit to the Australian Colonies* (London: Hamilton, Adams and Co., 1834), p. 23.

13 Merrill D. Peterson, ed., *The Portable Thomas Jefferson* (New York: Viking, 1975), p. 111; Michel-Guillaume St. Jean de Crèvecoeur, *Journey into Northern Pennsylvania and the State of New York*, trans. Clarissa S. Bostelmann (Ann Arbor: University of Michigan Press, 1964), p. 166.

Domesticated creatures that traveled from the Lands of the Demographic Takeover to Europe are few. Australian aborigines and New Zealand Maoris had a few tame dogs, unimpressive by Old World standards and unwanted by the whites. Europe happily accepted the American Indians' turkeys and guinea pigs, but had no need for their dogs, llamas, and alpacas. Again the explanation is simple: Europeans, who controlled the passage of large animals across the oceans, had no need to reverse the process.

It is interesting and perhaps significant, though, that the exchange was just as one-sided for varmints, the small mammals whose migrations Europeans often tried to stop. None of the American or Australian or New Zealand equivalents of rats have become established in Europe, but Old World varmints, especially rats, have colonized right alongside the Europeans in the Temperate Zones. Rats of assorted sizes, some of them almost surely European immigrants, were tormenting Spanish Americans by at least the end of the sixteenth century. European rats established a beachhead in Jamestown, Virginia, as early as 1609, when they almost starved out the colonists by eating their food stores. In Buenos Aires the increase in rats kept pace with that of cattle, according to an early nineteenth-century witness. European rats proved as aggressive as the Europeans in New Zealand, where they completely replaced the local rats in the North Islands as early as the 1840s. Those poor creatures are probably completely extinct today or exist only in tiny relict populations.[14]

The European rabbits are not usually thought of as varmints, but where there are neither diseases nor predators to hold down their numbers they can become the worst of pests. In 1859 a few members of the species *Orytolagus cuniculus* (the scientific name for the protagonists of all the Peter Rabbits of literature) were released in southeast Australia. Despite massive efforts to stop them, they reproduced – true to their reputation – and spread rapidly all the way across Australia's southern half to the Indian Ocean. In 1950 the rabbit population of Australia was estimated at 500 million, and they were outcompeting the nation's most important domesticated animals, sheep, for the grasses and herbs. They have been brought under control, but only by means of artificially fomenting an epidemic of myxomatosis, a lethal American rabbit disease. The story of rabbits and myxomatosis in New Zealand is similar.[15]

Europe, in return for her varmints, has received muskrats and gray

---

14 Bernabé Cobo, *Obras* (Madrid: Atlas Ediciones, 1964), vol. 1, pp. 350–1; Edward Arber, ed., *Travels and Works of Captain John Smith* (New York: Burt Franklin, n. d.), vol. 2, p. xcv; K. A. Wodzicki, *Introduced Mammals of New Zealand* (Wellington: Department of Scientific and Industrial Research, 1950), pp. 89–92.

15 Frank Fenner and F. N. Ratcliffe, *Myxomatosis* (Cambridge: Cambridge University Press, 1965), pp. 9, 11, 17, 22–23; Frank Fenner, "The Rabbit Plague," *Scientific American* 190 (February 1954): 30–5; Wodzicki, *Introduced Mammals*, pp. 107–141.

squirrels and little else from America, and nothing at all of significance from Australia or New Zealand, and we might well wonder if muskrats and squirrels really qualify as varmints.[16] As with other classes of organisms, the exchange has been a one-way street.

None of Europe's emigrants were as immediately and colossally successful as its pathogens, the microorganisms that make human beings ill, cripple them, and kill them. Whenever and wherever Europeans crossed the oceans and settled, the pathogens they carried created prodigious epidemics of smallpox, measles, tuberculosis, influenza, and a number of other diseases. It was this factor, more than any other, that Darwin had in mind as he wrote of the Europeans' deadly tread.

The pathogens transmitted by the Europeans, unlike the Europeans themselves or most of their domesticated animals, did at least as well in the tropics as in the temperate Lands of the Demographic Takeover. Epidemics devastated Mexico, Peru, Brazil, Hawaii, and Tahiti soon after the Europeans made the first contact with aboriginal populations. Some of these populations were able to escape demographic defeat because their initial numbers were so large that a small fraction was still sufficient to maintain occupation of, if not title to, the land, and also because the mass of Europeans were never attracted to the tropical lands, not even if they were partially vacated. In the Lands of the Demographic Takeover the aboriginal populations were too sparse to rebound from the onslaught of disease or were inundated by European immigrants before they could recover.

The First Strike Force of the white immigrants to the Lands of the Demographic Takeover were epidemics. A few examples from scores of possible examples follow. Smallpox first arrived in the Río de la Plata region in 1558 or 1560 and killed, according to one chronicler possibly more interested in effect than accuracy, "more than a hundred thousand Indians" of the heavy riverine population there. An epidemic of plague or typhus decimated the Indians of the New England coast immediately before the founding of Plymouth. Smallpox or something similar struck the aborigines of Australia's Botany Bay in 1789, killed half, and rolled on into the interior. Some unidentified disease or diseases spread through the Maori tribes of the North Island of New Zealand in the 1790s, killing so many in a number of villages that the survivors were not able to bury the dead.[17]

16 Charles S. Elton, *The Ecology of Invasions* (Trowbridge and London: English Language Book Society, 1972), pp. 24–5, 28, 73, 123.
17 Juan López de Velasco, *Geografía y descripción universal de las Indias* (Madrid: Establecimiento Topográfico de Fortanet, 1894), p. 552; Oscar Schmieder, "The Pampa – A Natural and Culturally Induced Grassland?" *University of California, Publications in Geography* (27 September 1927): 266; Sherburne F. Cook, "The Significance of Disease in the Extinction of the New England Indians," *Human Biology* 14 (September 1975): 486–91; J. H. L. Cumpston, *The History of Smallpox in Australia, 1788–1908* (Mel-

After a series of such lethal and rapidly moving epidemics, then came the slow, unspectacular but thorough cripplers and killers like venereal disease and tuberculosis. In conjunction with the large numbers of white settlers these diseases were enough to smother aboriginal chances of recovery. First the blitzkrieg, then the mopping up.

The greatest of the killers in these lands was probably smallpox. The exception is New Zealand, the last of these lands to attract permanent European settlers. They came to New Zealand after the spread of vaccination in Europe, and so were poor carriers. As of the 1850s smallpox still had not come ashore, and by that time two-thirds of the Maori had been vaccinated.[18] The tardy arrival of smallpox in these islands may have much to do with the fact that the Maori today comprise a larger percentage (9 percent) of their country's population than that of any other aboriginal people in any European colony or former European colony in either Temperate Zone, save only South Africa.

American Indians bore the full brunt of smallpox, and its mark is on their history and folklore. The Kiowa of the southern plains of the United States have a legend in which a Kiowa man meets Smallpox on the plain, riding a horse. The man asks, "Where do you come from and what do you do and why are you here?" Smallpox answers, "I am one with the white men – they are my people as the Kiowas are yours. Sometimes I travel ahead of them and sometimes behind. But I am always their companion and you will find me in their camps and their houses." "What can you do," the Kiowa asks. "I bring death," Smallpox replies. "My breath causes children to wither like young plants in spring snow. I bring destruction. No matter how beautiful a woman is, once she has looked at me she becomes as ugly as death. And to men I bring not death alone, but the destruction of their children and the blighting of their wives. The strongest of warriors go down before me. No people who have looked on me will ever be the same."[19]

In return for the barrage of diseases that Europeans directed overseas, they received little in return. Australia and New Zealand provided no new strains of pathogens to Europe – or none that attracted attention. And of America's native diseases none had any real influence on the Old World – with the likely exception of venereal syphilis, which almost certainly existed

---

Footnote 17 (*continued*)
  bourne: Albert J. Mullet, Government Printer, 1914), pp. 147–9; Harrison M. Wright, *New Zealand, 1769–1840* (Cambridge, Mass.: Harvard University Press, 1959), p. 62. For further discussion of this topic, see Crosby, *Columbia Exchange*, chaps. 1 and 2, and Henry F. Dobyns, *Native American Historical Demography: A Critical Bibliography* (Bloomington: Indiana University Press/Newberry Library, 1976).

18 Arthur C. Thomson, *The Story of New Zealand* (London: Murray, 1859), vol. 1, p. 212.

19 Alice Marriott and Carol K. Rachlin, *American Indian Mythology* (New York: New American Library, 1968), pp. 174–5.

in the New World before 1492 and probably did not occur in its present form in the Old World.[20]

Weeds are rarely history makers, for they are not as spectacular in their effects as pathogens. But they, too, influence our lives and migrate over the world despite human wishes. As such, like varmints and germs, they are better indicators of certain realities than human beings or domesticated animals.

The term "weed" in modern botanical usage refers to any type of plant which – because of especially large numbers of seeds produced per plant, or especially effective means of distributing those seeds, or especially tough roots and rhizomes from which new plants can grow, or especially tough seeds that survive the alimentary canals of animals to be planted with their droppings – spreads rapidly and outcompetes others on disturbed, bare soil. Weeds are plants that tempt the botanist to use such anthropomorphic words as "aggressive" and "opportunistic."

Many of the most successful weeds in the well-watered regions of the Lands of the Demographic Takeover are of European or Eurasian origin. French and Dutch and English farmers brought with them to North America their worst enemies, weeds, "to exhaust the land, hinder and damnify the Crop.[21] By the last third of the seventeenth century at least twenty different types were widespread enough in New England to attract the attention of the English visitor, John Josselyn, who identified couch grass, dandelion, nettles, mallowes, knot grass, shepherd's purse, sow thistle, and clot burr and others. One of the most aggressive was plantain, which the Indians called "English-Man's Foot."[22]

European weeds rolled west with the pioneers, in some cases spreading almost explosively. As of 1823 corn chamomile and maywood had spread up to but not across the Muskingum River in Ohio. Eight years later they were over the river.[23] The most prodigiously imperialistic of the weeds in the eastern half of the United States and Canada were probably Kentucky bluegrass and white clover. They spread so fast after the entrance of Europeans into a given area that there is some suspicion that they may have been present in pre-Colombian America, although the earliest European

20 Crosby, *Columbian Exchange*, pp. 122–64, passim.
21 Jared Eliot, "The Tilling of the Land, 1760," in *Agriculture in the United States: A Documentary History*, ed. Wayne D. Rasmussen (New York: Random House, 1975), vol. I, p. 192.
22 John Josselyn, *New Englands Rarities Discovered* (London: G. Widdowes at the Green Dragon in St. Paul's Church-yard, 1672), pp. 85, 86; Edmund Berkeley and Dorothy S. Berkeley, eds., *The Reverend John Clayton* (Charlottesville: University of Virginia Press, 1965), p. 24.
23 Lewis D. de Schweinitz, "Remarks on the Plants of Europe Which Have Become Naturalized in a More or Less Degree, in the United States," *Annals Lyceum of Natural History of New York*, vol. 3 *(1832) 1828–1836*, 155.

accounts do not mention them. Probably brought to the Appalachian area
by the French, these two kinds of weeds preceded the English settlers there
and kept up with the movement westward until reaching the plains across
the Mississippi.[24]

Old World plants set up business on their own on the Pacific coast of
North America just as soon as the Spaniards and Russians did. The climate
of coastal southern California is much the same as that of the Mediterranean, and the Spaniards who came to California in the eighteenth century
brought their own Mediterranean weeds with them via Mexico: wild oats,
fennel, wild radishes. These plants, plus those brought in later by the
Forty-niners, muscled their way to dominance in the coastal grasslands.
These immigrant weeds followed Old World horses, cattle, and sheep into
California's interior prairies and took over there as well.[25]

The region of Argentina and Uruguay was almost as radically altered in
its flora as in its fauna by the coming of the Europeans. The ancient Indian
practice, taken up immediately by the whites, of burning off the old grass of
the pampa every year, as well as the trampling and cropping to the ground
of indigenous grasses and forbs by the thousands of imported quadrupeds
who also changed the nature of the soil with their droppings, opened the
whole countryside to European plants. In the 1780s Félix de Azara observed
that the pampa, already radically altered, was changing as he watched.
European weeds sprang up around every cabin, grew up along roads, and
pressed into the open steppe. Today only a quarter of the plants growing
wild in the pampa are native, and in the well-watered eastern portions, the
"natural" ground cover consists almost entirely of Old World grasses and
clovers.[26]

The invaders were not, of course, always desirable. When Darwin visited
Uruguay in 1832, he found large expanses, perhaps as much as hundreds of

24 Lyman Carrier and Katherine S. Bort, "The History of Kentucky Bluegrass and White
   Clover in the United States," *Journal of the American Society of Agronomy* 8 (1916):
   256–66; Robert W. Schery, "The Migration of a Plant: Kentucky Bluegrass Followed
   Settlers to the New World," *Natural History* 74 (December 1965): 43–4; G. W. Dunbar,
   ed., "Henry Clay on Kentucky Bluegrass," *Agricultural History* 51 (July 1977): 522.

25 Edgar Anderson, *Plants, Man, and Life* (Berkeley and Los Angeles: University of
   California Press, 1967), pp. 12–15; Elna S. Bakker, *An Island Called California* (Berk-
   eley and Los Angeles: University of California Press, 1971), pp. 150–2; R. W. Allard,
   "Genetic Systems Associated with Colonizing Ability in Predominantly Self-Pollinated
   Species," in *The Genetics of Colonizing Species,* ed. H. G. Baker and G. Ledyard Stebbins
   (New York: Academic Press, 1965), p. 50; M. W. Talbot, H. M. Biswell, and A. L.
   Hormay, "Fluctuations in the Annual Vegetation of California," *Ecology* 20 (July 1939):
   396–7.

26 Félix de Azara, *Descripción é historia del Paraguay y del Río de la Plata* (Madrid: Imprenta
   de Sanchez, 1847), vol. 1, 57–8; Schmieder, "Alteration of the Argentine Pampa," pp.
   310–11.

square miles, monopolized by the immigrant wild artichoke and transformed into a prickly wilderness fit neither for man nor his animals.[27]

The onslaught of foreign and specifically European plants on Australia began abruptly in 1778 because the first expedition that sailed from Britain to Botany Bay carried some livestock and considerable quantities of seed. By May of 1803 over two hundred foreign plants, most of them European, had been purposely introduced and planted in New South Wales, undoubtedly along with a number of weeds.[28] Even today so-called clean seed characteristically contains some weed seeds, and this was much more so two hundred years ago. By and large, Australia's north has been too tropical and her interior too hot and dry for European weeds and grasses, but much of her southern coasts and Tasmania have been hospitable indeed to Europe's willful flora.

Thus, many – often a majority – of the most aggressive plants in the temperate humid regions of North America, South America, Australia, and New Zealand are of European origin. It may be true that in every broad expanse of the world today where there are dense populations, with whites in the majority, there are also dense populations of European weeds. Thirty-five of eighty-nine weeds listed in 1953 as common in the state of New York are European. Approximately 60 percent of Canada's worst weeds are introductions from Europe. Most of New Zealand's weeds are from the same source, as are many, perhaps most, of the weeds of southern Australia's well-watered coasts. Most of the European plants that Josselyn listed as naturalized in New England in the seventeenth century are growing wild today in Argentina and Uruguay, and are among the most widespread and troublesome of all weeds in those countries.[29]

In return for this largesse of pestiferous plants, the Lands of the Demographic Takeover have provided Europe with only a few equivalents. The Canadian water weed jammed Britain's nineteenth-century waterways, and North America's horseweed and burnweed have spread in Europe's empty lots, and South America's flowered galinsoga has thrived in her gardens. But the migratory flow of a whole group of organisms between Europe and the Lands of the Demographic Takeover has been almost entirely in one direction.[30] Englishman's foot still marches in seven league jackboots across every European colony of settlement, but very few American or Australian

27 Darwin, *Voyage of the Beagle*, pp. 119–20.
28 *Historical Records of Australia*, ser. 1, vol. 4, pp. 234–41.
29 Edward Salisbury, *Weeds and Aliens* (London: Collins, 1961), p. 87; Angel Julio Cabrera, *Manual de la flora de los alrededores de Buenos Aires* (Buenos Aires: Editorial Acme S. A., 1953), passim.
30 Elton, *Ecology of Invasions*, p. 115; Hugo Ilitis, "The Story of Wild Garlic," *Scientific Monthly* 68 (February 1949): 122–4.

or New Zealand invaders stride the waste lands and unkempt backyards of Europe.

European and Old World human beings, domesticated animals, varmints, pathogens, and weeds all accomplished demographic takeovers of their own in the temperate, well-watered regions of North and South America, Australia, and New Zealand. They crossed oceans and Europeanized vast territories, often in informal cooperation with each other – the farmer and his animals destroying native plant cover, making way for imported grasses and forbs, many of which proved more nourishing to domesticated animals than the native equivalents; Old World pathogens, sometimes carried by Old World varmints, wiping out vast numbers of aborigines, opening the way for the advance of the European frontier, exposing more and more native peoples to more and more pathogens. The classic example of symbiosis between European colonists, their animals, and plants comes from New Zealand. Red clover, a good forage for sheep, could not seed itself and did not spread without being annually sown until the Europeans imported the bumblebee. Then the plant and insect spread widely, the first providing the second with food, the second carrying pollen from blossom to blossom for the first, and the sheep eating the clover and compensating the human beings for their effort with mutton and wool.[31]

There have been few such stories of the success in Europe of organisms from the Lands of the Demographic Takeover, despite the obvious fact that for every ship that went from Europe to those lands, another traveled in the opposite direction.

The demographic triumph of Europeans in the temperate colonies is one part of a biological and ecological takeover which could not have been accomplished by human beings alone, gunpowder notwithstanding. We must at least try to analyze the impact and success of all the immigrant organisms together – the European portmanteau of often mutually supportive plants, animals, and microlife which in its entirety can be accurately described as aggressive and opportunistic, an ecosystem simplified by ocean crossings and honed by thousands of years of competition in the unique environment created by the Old World Neolithic Revolution.

The human invaders and their descendants have consulted their egos, rather than ecologists, for explanations of their triumphs. But the human victims, the aborigines of the Lands of the Demographic Takeover, knew better, knew they were only one of many species being displaced and replaced; knew they were victims of something more irresistible and awesome than the spread of capitalism or Christianity. One Maori, at the nadir of the history of his race, knew these things when he said, "As the

---

31 Otto E. Plath, *Bumblebees and Their Ways* (New York: Macmillan, 1934), p. 115.

clover killed off the fern, and the European dog the Maori dog – as the Maori rat was destroyed by the Pakeha (European) rat – so our people, also, will be gradually supplanted and exterminated by the Europeans.[32] The future was not quite so grim as he prophesied, but we must admire his grasp of the complexity and magnitude of the threat looming over his people and over the ecosystem of which they were part.

32 James Bonwick, *The Last of the Tasmanians* (New York: Johnson Reprint Co., 1970), p. 380.

6 The Depletion of India's Forests under British Imperialism: Planters, Foresters, and Peasants in Assam and Kerala

Richard P. Tucker

IN THE CENTURIES AFTER COLUMBUS reached the Caribbean islands and da Gama arrived on the coast of India, Europe's economic and strategic expansion, one fledgling nation-state rivaling another, was the driving force in domesticating the natural world. In its fundamental legacy, colonialism helped shape a globe whose once vast wildlands are now almost entirely managed to one degree or another. Even the great river-basin civilizations of India and China, home to dense populations before the European era, had extensive wild hinterlands of mountain, jungle, and desert until the past century. But the joint efforts of indigenous people and Western interlopers have now nearly completed the transformation.[1] Forests and grasslands have retreated massively before the expansion of settled agriculture, and nowhere more dramatically than in India, where step-by-step between the 1770s and 1850s, Britain established its raj, or imperial regime. From this perspective British rule in India, like other Western empires elsewhere in the developing world, must be seen as an elaborate system of resource extraction and allocation, determining not only who was to have access to nature's wealth but what pattern the biotic systems themselves would ultimately take by the time India gained independence in 1947.

This system of natural resources management was by no means monolithic or unchanging, nor did the British entirely control it. Throughout the imperial era the British administered two-thirds of the Indian subcontinent directly but left the remaining third under the autonomous rule of over five

---

1 Alfred W. Crosby, *Ecological Imperialism: The Biological Expansion of Europe, 900–1900* (Cambridge: Cambridge University Press, 1986).

hundred indigenous aristocratic houses, the "Native Princes." Within this framework an intricate system of administration and economic change evolved, so varied that almost any generalization about India as a whole in that era is nearly foolhardy. But one theme stands out in the subcontinent's history: the steady expansion of land under the plow, at the expense of forest and grassland.[2] A recent study which covers most of the subcontinent shows that over the years between 1890 and 1970, more than thirty million hectares of land were transformed from forest and grassland into areas of crop production and settlement; the amount of land being cultivated rose by over 45 percent. In the same years the population of the same area grew by 147 percent. Hence arable, grassland, and forest resources all shrank severely for each person in what is now Pakistan, India, and Bangladesh.[3]

During these decades the agricultural produce of the subcontinent increased dramatically, though probably not enough to keep pace with the expanding population. More alarming was the loss of the resources of nonarable lands, but until recently few people seriously weighed these costs against the gains in arable acreage. On the one hand, revenue and agriculture administrators measured their success on the basis of the taxation which derived from crop production. On the other hand, the rural populace had to be fed. In India's monsoon climate, with its extremes of wet and dry seasons, the relief or prevention of famine was a major challenge to the imperial rulers.

Until the end of the colonial era India followed a strategy of expanding acreage under hoe and plow, at the expense of grassland and forest, rather than intensifying production on existing acreage. The villagers of forested regions struggled to maintain their traditional subsistence uses of the forest against the incursions of the market economy, but they were more successful in expanding agriculture than in maintaining their forest resources. Only among the founders of the Indian Forest Service, set up in the 1860s to administer the exploitation of government forests, did a few voices warn that a more stable balance among forest, grassland, and tilled land must ultimately be achieved.

It was not until after India achieved independence in 1947 that its new leaders turned seriously to intensifying agricultural production on existing arable lands and thereby somewhat stabilizing a balance between forest and arable acreage. When they did, they had the advantage over their foreign

---

2 In this, India has typified global trends. See Richard P. Tucker and J. F. Richards, eds., *Global Deforestation and the Nineteenth-Century World Economy* (Durham, N.C.: Duke University Press, 1983); and J. F. Richards and Richard P. Tucker, eds., *World Forests and the Global Economy in the Twentieth Century* (Durham, N.C.: Duke University Press, forthcoming).

3 John F. Richards, Edward S. Haynes, and James R. Hagen, "Changes in the Land and Human Productivity in Northern India, 1870–1970," *Agricultural History* 59, no. 4 (October 1985): 523–48.

colonial predecessors of having new agricultural technologies which had been developed in the Western world especially after World War I,[4] and they faced the sober reality that India was nearing the end of its reserves of potentially arable land: The luxury of moving beyond existing agricultural frontiers onto new lands was no longer theirs.[5]

By 1947, India's forests were depleted not only by expanding crop production but also by both commercial timber operations and plantation cropping for European markets. Foresters and planters were two of the most significant exotic species introduced into India from Europe. Like imported botanical species competing with indigenous flora, these two human groups became competitors with villagers for access to the land. Many elements of the history of forest reduction in modern India can be understood from a survey of the work of foresters and planters. Both were major actors in the drama of the British Empire as a system of resource management and exploitation.

The landscape of India had been shaped by highly developed political and economic systems for many centuries before the first Europeans appeared there. Nonetheless, in the early nineteenth century many of its forests remained virtually untouched, especially in mountain areas. Early British travelers lyrically praised the grandeur of its landscapes under the monsoon climate (their contemporaries in North America believed that their forests would provide abundant resources for many centuries to come). The towering Himalayan mountains on the north supported almost impenetrably remote forests of conifers as well as tropical forest on the northeast fringes in Assam. And at the opposite end of India, on the jagged hills or Western Ghats of the Kerala coast, other travelers occasionally struggled through steaming jungles which seemed similarly limitless. Two British engineers who penetrated the ghats to survey the region's natural wealth in 1817–19 were captivated by the wanton beauty of the hills.

The larger portion of this desolate region is covered with lofty and luxuriant green forests in every direction. . . . The whole scene is truly sublime; a large portion of this wild tract has not been explored from the want of guides, and the difficulty of penetrating such wild extensive regions.[6]

Yet by 1947 few of those forests remained unmeasured and undisciplined. Where tea and coffee planters could work and foresters could plan, a more restricted and ordered patchwork of forests remained at the end of British

4 G. B. Masefield, *A Short History of Agriculture in the British Colonies* (Oxford: Clarendon, 1950).
5 Benjamin Farmer, *Agricultural Colonization in India since Independence* (New York: Oxford University Press, 1974).
6 Benjamin S. Ward and P. E. Connor, *Geographical and Statistical Memoir of the Survey of the Travancore and Cochin States* (Travancore, 1863), pp. 205–6.

rule. In other hill areas of the Indian subcontinent, the depletion of forests was affected in similar ways by the expansion of peasant agriculture and the agricultural and forestry policies of the British. But the additional pressure applied by plantation cropping of perennial crops for world markets was largely limited to two peripheries of the subcontinent. In the nineteenth century coffee and tea became India's dominant export plantation crops and were grown almost entirely in the northeastern hill region of Assam and the Nilgiri Hills and Western Ghats of Madras and Kerala in the deep south. Thus Assam and Kerala provide the two foci of this study.

ASSAM: PLANTATIONS, IMMIGRANTS, AND DEFORESTATION

On the eastern fringe of the Himalayan ranges, where the Brahmaputra River has made its great arc to the southwest toward the Bay of Bengal (see Map 6.1), Assam's dense forest belt has been under siege since the early nineteenth century.[7] By 1900 Assam's 55,156 square miles included 20,830 under government forest control, one of the highest percentages of any state in India. Until very recently, moreover, a large portion of this was inaccessible from the outside world, and particularly from commercial and demographic centers. The British raj had only rudimentary administrative operations outside the lowlands of Assam, and transport, commerce, and industry were less developed there than in other parts of India. This meant that the great forest zone of upper Assam was depleted more slowly than most parts of India; but it also meant that the government had less capacity to control the combined surge of tea plantations and immigrant peasant frontiersmen than it might have wished.

Even more so than in most parts of India, the history of Assam's forests has been intertwined with the intricate ethnic and cultural patterns of the state.[8] The remote high hills of Assam and adjacent regions are home to a wide variety of tribal groups, whose subsistence has been based primarily on shifting agriculture.[9] Until recently tribal populations were thin enough that

7 P. D. Strachey, "The Development of Forestry in Assam in the Last Fifty Years," *Indian Forester* (December 1956): 619–23; H. P. Smith and C. Purkayastha, *Assam: A Short History of the Assam Forest Service, 1850–1945* (Shillong, India, 1946). For geographical context, see H. P. Das, *Geography of Assam* (New Delhi: National Book Trust, 1970); and O. H. K. Spate and A. T. A. Learmonth, *India and Pakistan*, 3d ed. (London: Methuen, 1967), pp. 600–10.

8 For the region's general history, see E. A. Gait, *A History of Assam*, 2d ed. (Calcutta and Simla, 1926); and Amalendu Guha, *From Planter Raj to Swaraj: Freedom Struggle and Electoral Politics in Assam, 1826–1947* (New Delhi: Indian Council of Historical Research, 1977).

9 M. D. Chaturvedi and B. N. Uppal, *A Study in Shifting Cultivation of Assam* (New Delhi: Indian Council of Agricultural Research, 1953).

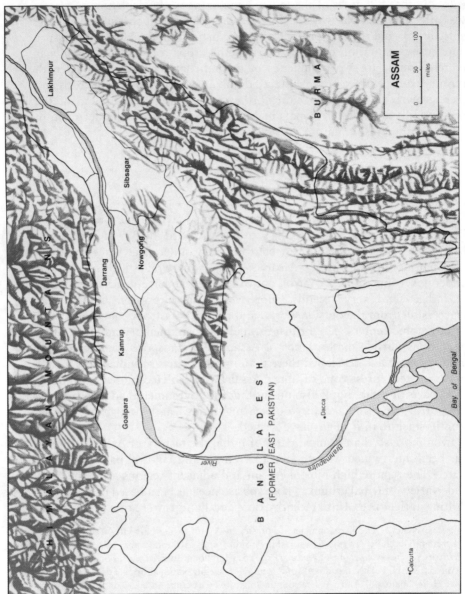

Map 6.1

they presented no fatal threat to the mixed forest, if left to themselves. But the Brahmaputra lowlands supported a much denser and rapidly growing, culturally different populace of Hindu rice farmers. In the twentieth century Assam has had the fastest growing population of any state in India: from 3.3 million in the 1901 census to 15 million in 1971, nearly all of the growth before 1947 occurring in the lower areas of settled agriculture.[10] Further, the traditional settlers of the lowlands are Assamese-speakers, while the tribals speak a totally separate set of languages. Most challenging of all, downriver in Bangladesh lies one of the densest rural populations in the world. By the late nineteenth century Bengali peasants, most of them Muslim, began surging upriver into the fertile Assamese forest fringe. Even before World War I, one cause of depletion of Assam's vegetation was the steady encroachment of these immigrant peasants on the forest lands of lower Assam.[11]

The other cause of transformation, one which quickly penetrated far into the hills, was the tea industry. The tea plantations of northeast India are a classic example of a foreign-dominated plantation economy which controlled a dependency's land-use patterns and was highly sensitive to markets in the industrialized world. After 1833, when the East India Company's new charter allowed foreigners to own rural land in India, European tea planters quickly bought large tracts of hill land in Assam and adjacent north Bengal. Most tea plantations were established by clearing natural forest on lands purchased from the government of British India; others were commandeered from village commons or bought from other private owners. By 1871 the tea planters owned 700,000 acres, of which 56,000 acres were already producing tea. By 1900 there were 764 working tea estates in Assam, producing 145 million pounds of tea annually for export.[12] Most of the plantation workers were outsiders, for local farmers and tribals were unwilling to submit to the regimentation of the plantation. By 1900, some 400,000 low-caste and tribal workers from farther west had been brought into Assam under appalling working conditions. Removed from their subsistence in ancestral soil far to the west, they became a rural proletariat whose only base of survival was the company: They were housed in company barracks, fed by company kitchens, and worked on the companies' rigorous terms.[13]

10 Myron Weiner, *Sons of the Soil* (Princeton, N.J.: Princeton University Press, 1978), chap. 2.

11 For the context in land tenure law, see J. N. Das, *An Introduction to the Land Laws of Assam* (Gauhati, 1968).

12 Sunil K. Sharma, "Origin and Growth of the Tea Industry in Assam," in T. Raychaudhuri, ed., *Contributions to Indian Economic History* (Calcutta, 1963); also Weiner, *Sons*, pp. 88–92.

13 For a recent sociological analysis, see A. C. Sinha, "Social Frame of Forest History: A Study

For many years the tea planters held dominant financial and political leverage in Assam, preventing their critics from mounting effective pressure to mitigate their labor policies,[14] and preventing the state's Forest Department, their competitor for control of forest lands, from gaining control over wide forest areas.

The impact of World War I on Assam's forest lands centered on wartime prosperity and expansion in the tea industry. Prices in Europe rose; acreage under tea in Assam extended rapidly; and dividends to the planters rose correspondingly. The first years after 1918 saw a brief oversupply in England's warehouses and a minor depression in the Assam hills, but this was succeeded by a decade of prosperity and further expansion of the acreage under tea.[15]

The global Depression of the 1930s hit the tea industry heavily. The all-India wholesale price index for tea dropped by 53 percent in four years. The planters reduced production by firing many plantation workers, men whose only livelihood was wages from work on the estates. Some returned to their homes farther west, but others moved into adjacent government forest land as squatters, growing crops in clumsy imitation of local shifting cultivation. In their desperation they damaged forest and soil cover wherever they went. Meanwhile the tea planters turned their attention to their markets. By 1933 the industry created an international system to regulate and, when necessary, limit production; this assured a rebound of profitability by 1934.[16]

Hardly had the tea industry emerged from the Depression than Assam faced another war beginning in early 1942. This war brought great military danger to Assam, but it also brought wartime profits to the tea planters again. The British government controlled all tea production and consumption from 1940 onward, and the rising competition of Indonesian tea was ended by the Japanese occupation of the islands. The tea industry in Assam and northern Bengal expanded another 20 percent by 1945. When in 1947 eastern Bengal downriver was designated part of Pakistan, the tea industry of Assam went through another period of painful disruption, but in the long run its international markets were assured.

Whenever markets for tea were strong enough to enable expansion of plantation acreage, forest cover was correspondingly reduced. Moreover, directly or indirectly, tea cultivation contributed to the commercialization

Footnote 13 (*continued*)
 in Ecologic and Ethnic Aspects of Tea Plantation in the North Eastern Himalayan Foothills" (Unpublished paper, 1985).
14 R. K. Das, *Plantation Labour in India* (Calcutta, 1936), chaps. 2–3.
15 Percival Griffiths, *The History of the Indian Tea Industry* (London, 1967), pp. 35–76.
16 For the global context of these trends, see V. D. Wickizer, *Coffee, Tea, and Cocoa: An Economic and Political Analysis* (Stanford, Calif.: Stanford University Press, 1951), pp. 155–257.

of the remaining forests, as the timber industry emerged. This process can be clearly seen through the work of the Assam Forest Department, the planters' major European competitor for control of forest lands.[17] Provincial forest departments had been established throughout British India in the 1860s; the Bengal Forest Department included in its reach the upper Brahmaputra basin until Assam's foresters became a separate cadre in the early 1870s.[18] They confronted great reserves of potentially valuable timber. In the lower reaches of the Brahmaputra, on rich alluvium, stand forests of the great hardwood *sal* (*Shorea robusta*), the easternmost extension of the great sub-Himalayan sal belt. Because of the perennially warm, moist climate of lower Assam, these are the finest quality of all sal stands. The downriver districts of Kamrup and Goalpara boast the most extensive stands; the adjacent low hills of Darrang and Goalpara also have large sal reserves. All are of great economic value, providing the wood particularly for railway sleepers or ties. Farther northeast, as the gorges become steeper and the hills higher and less accessible, lie the Lakhimpur and Sibsagar districts near the borders of Burma and China. In these still-remote forests can be found mixed subtropical broadleaf evergreen stands, including various potentially marketable species. During the late colonial era the foresters' attention focused principally on the towering *hollong* (*Dipterocarpus macrocarpus*).[19]

The combined interests of planters, imported laborers, and immigrant farmers placed such heavy and escalating pressure on the forests of Assam that the Forest Department there was one of the weaker in India's provinces. Assam's Revenue Department consistently pressed for opening more land to the plow, believing that settling immigrant peasants in the hills would stimulate economic growth while simultaneously relieving social and even political pressures. The Forest Department acquiesced on the principle that the peasants' needs for land which could be terraced for wet rice should usually take first priority in land allocation.[20] The foresters would not publicly disagree with the government's 1938 report, which stressed "that indigenous people alone would be unable, without the aid of immigrant settlers, to develop the province's enormous wasteland resources within a reasonable period."[21] However, as early as 1920 the Forest Department had

17 The standard history of the Indian Forest Service and its work is E. P. Stebbing, *The Forests of India*, 3 vols. (London, 1922–5).

18 Dietrich Brandis, *Suggestions Regarding Forest Administration in Assam* (Calcutta: Government Press, 1879).

19 M. C. Jacob, *The Forest Resources of Assam* (Shillong: Government Press, 1940); Gustav Mann, *Progress Report of Forest Administration in Assam for the Year 1874–5* (Calcutta: Government Press, 1875).

20 B. Ribbentrop, *Notes on an Inspection of the Forests of Assam during January to April 1889* (Simla, India: Government Press, 1889).

21 Guha, *Planter Raj to Swaraj*, pp. 261–2.

realized that in the long run this would threaten both timber supplies and watershed stabilization. Hence the department began to accelerate the painstaking survey of vegetation and classification of land-use potential in previously unclassified government forests, especially so as to delineate sal forests which arguably should be kept from the plow.

This was also a pragmatic response to the growing upriver movement of Bengali Muslim peasants. In lowland Goalpara district the population had risen by 2 percent between the 1891 and 1901 censuses; in the next ten years it rose by 3 percent. From there the settlers moved upriver, occupying forest lands in Nowgong and Kamrup districts; by now they were beginning to challenge tribal lands as well. They had on their side the general British assumption that settled agriculture was a far more productive and stable use of land than slash-and-burn cropping. In the 1920s the movement began to reach Upper Burma, where lowland peasants had no experience with the climate and agricultural patterns. Despite these difficulties, land hunger and political pressures continued to force Bengali peasants upriver, and when East Pakistan was created in 1947 out of eastern Bengal, a new wave of Hindu peasants moved out of Muslim Pakistan into Assam. In the twenty years ending in 1950 the immigrants turned some 1,508,000 acres of forest into settled agriculture.

How was all this reflected in timber extraction from the government forests? Before the early 1920s the Assam Forest Department was a small cadre, a few officers whose work was limited to serving short-term commercial timber demands, mostly in the sal districts. One report, surveying the seventy-five years before 1925, complained that "the provision of staff and improvements in the forests have depended upon the profit of each year, and not one single budget presented by the Department has ever emerged without large cuts by Finance."[22] By the 1920s government forests which had long been awaiting survey and reservation were so burdened with peasants' rights that purchasing those rights threatened to be prohibitively expensive for the government.

Nonetheless, the 1920s were an optimistic period for Assam's forest managers. During the highly profitable years from 1925 to 1929, the acreage in reserves increased by some 400 percent, largely in the sal belt. But in the Depression decade severe retrenchments in staff and budget left Assam's forest management able to cover little more than it had in 1918, while shifting cultivation in the unclassed State Forests of the hill regions was inexorably expanding. As so often happens in the developing world, foresters saw themselves fighting a losing battle, against their superiors on one side and villagers on the other.

World War II brought major changes in forest production. Between 1939

---

22 Smith and Purkayastha, *Assam*, p. 42.

and 1945 timber production in the reserves more than doubled, while fuelwood cutting there more than tripled. The height of this pressure came after 1942, when heavy concentrations of troops moved up the Brahmaputra valley to stem Japanese forces in Burma. Profits rose far more dramatically still: Total receipts for railway timber rose five times, and military timber use raised eight times more revenue. Much of the profits went into the hands of private contractors, from Calcutta as well as the Assamese towns. With few exceptions the contractors were small operators who cut and exported logs using only hand tools, an extremely wasteful process. And with the exception of two sawmills established in Assam in the early 1920s, no timber processing was done within the province. Thus the extreme inefficiency and wastefulness of lumbering continued well toward the present.

The war made major changes in forestry technology, not only in Assam but throughout India's Himalayan region, for the war effort required new motor roads and emergency rail lines. The roads were used by trucks and jeeps, some of which are still in operation over forty years later. The motorization of forestry which happened during the war years was a turning point in the mobility of foresters, bureaucrats, politicians, and peasants alike. The scale of timber exports could be increased to meet the economic demands of independence. And new roads could be used, as in many parts of the tropics since that time, by peasants looking for new land to till.

Assam's forests, having been put under sudden new pressures before 1945, underwent yet another major trauma in 1947, when the influx of Hindu refugees from East Pakistan moved westward into the Calcutta region and northeastward into Assam, at the same time that transport lines for Assamese timber were severed at the Pakistani border. The sudden new pressure of the immigrants accompanied severe disruptions of the state's administrative machinery and its forest management. The valuable sal forests of Sylhet district in the south became part of Pakistan, just when the Forest Department had to face severe political pressures to de-reserve existing forest tracts.

From an ecological perspective, the late 1940s was a period of temporary reprieve from commercial logging, especially in Upper Assam. The full picture of the transition in Assam's land use during the immediate aftermath of independence is still not entirely clear.[23] But it can safely be concluded that the political and ethnic turmoil of that period led to similar, but more intensive, conflicts in recent years, on a steadily shrinking base of land and

23 Farmer, *Agricultural Colonization*, pp. 13–17, 28–31, 56–9; *Progress Report of Forest Administration in the Province of Assam for the Year 1947–48* (Shillong, India: Government Press, 1948).

vegetation. Immigrant Bengali peasants, long-established Assamese Hindu rice farmers, and hill tribals now struggle to maintain a foothold on the land, often resorting to open violence.[24] Forest managers after independence struggled to maintain a remnant of the forest cover, more for commercial purposes than for preservation of the natural biota.

KERALA: THE SHRINKING FORESTS OF THE SOUTHWEST COAST

On the other subtropical fringe of India a similar process of commercialization took place, as large areas of natural forest were cleared in response to commodity markets in Europe. As in Assam, in what is now the state of Kerala, relations between peasants and planters became severely strained, and the abundant natural forests were severely depleted in the course of colonial economic expansion. In their biotic profusion Kerala's forests, like the Brahmaputra basin forests, add priceless diversity to the subcontinent's natural endowment. These mountains, called the Western Ghats, stretch along the entire west coast from north of Bombay. Rising abruptly from the Arabian Sea to elevations of three thousand feet to eight thousand feet, they then slope gradually eastward into the Bay of Bengal. Their western-facing slopes crowd the Arabian Sea, leaving only a narrow coastal belt, which varies up to forty miles in width (see Map 6.2). Their flanks produce a series of steep short rivers which have deposited rich alluvium at their feet to supplement the otherwise poor soils of the coastal region. From early June through September they confront the monsoon storms, catching up to two hundred inches of rain; thereafter there is virtually no moisture for the following eight months. The hills and valleys bask in steady high humidity and temperatures, while only the highest peaks are ever touched by winter frost.[25]

Along the coast, in the backwater estuaries of the many short rivers, mangrove forests once covered large areas.[26] But like other mangrove wetlands globally, these have been inexorably drained for such uses as rice cultivation over the past two hundred years, to feed one of the densest population concentrations in the subcontinent. Coastal backwaters lead upward into the sharply cut foothills of the ghats, where a second broad

24 S. K. Dass, "Immigration and Demographic Transformation of Assam, 1891–1981," *Economic and Political Weekly* (10 May 1980): 850–9; G. S. Ghurye, *The Burning Caldron of North-East India* (Bombay: Popular Prakashan, 1980).

25 Spate and Learmonth, *India and Pakistan*, pp. 673–81.

26 F. Blasco, *Les mangroves de l'Inde* (Pondicherry, India: Institut Français, 1975); C. Caratini, G. Thanikaimoni, and C. Tissot, "Mangroves of India: Palynological Study and Recent History of the Vegetation," *Proceedings of the Fourth International Palynology Conference, Lucknow, 1976–77*, 3 (1980): 49–59.

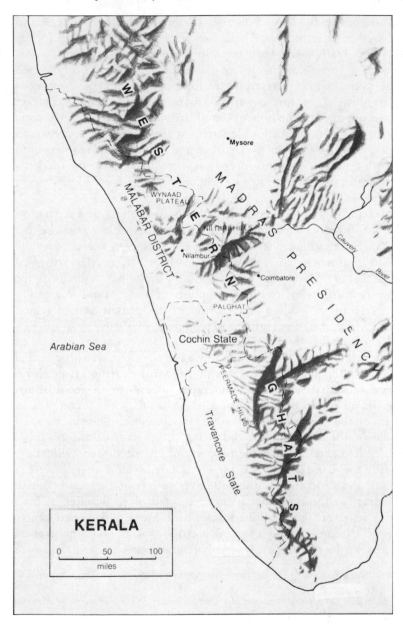

Map 6.2

Richard P. Tucker

ecological stratum on the lower hills rises to about four thousand feet and is largely based on lateritic soils. These soils leach and harden when forests are stripped, gradually losing their capacity to support vegetation.[27]

The dominant forest community of these hills is one of richly varied subtropical species, semievergreens on the lower slopes and true evergreens on the higher hills.[28] These forests provided many products for the premarket subsistence economies of the hills. As in all tropical forests, great floristic variety meant that in most locations few trees of any single species grew, and few species had any commercial use in urban and international markets until the nineteenth century. Since this forest was mere "waste," in the market's terms of reference, it was vulnerable to being removed in favor of plantation crops.

In the third and highest ecological zone of Kerala both natural vegetation and land tenure have been markedly different from that of the zones below. The lush, tangled mountainsides of subtropical evergreen vegetation were one of the subcontinent's richest floras when early British travelers struggled to penetrate them.[29] These high hills constitute the upper watersheds for Kerala's westward-flowing rivers. Disruption of the natural vegetation produces accelerating flooding and erosion in the densely settled region below, in a cycle that has recently become annual, expensive, and tragic.

The evolution of this tragedy has been inseparable from the erosion of tribal life in the hills. Until the late nineteenth century there was little settled population in the higher hills; peasants and townsmen from lower elevations toward the coast feared that the vaporous airs of the cool, moist mountain climate would be disastrous to their health. Only a complex of tribal groups on the fringes of Hindu culture inhabited the dense jungles and high grasslands, for the most part practicing shifting agriculture on lands which no one had ever declared the property of any private individual.[30]

Historically this coastal zone was largely isolated from the great centers of population and agriculture in the wide river valleys of Tamilnad (British India's Madras) to the east. The western coast evolved a series of little kingdoms at its river mouths, kingdoms whose kings and landed gentry traded pepper, cardamom, and a few other crops to Arab and other traders for export to world markets.[31] A series of small ports toward the north

27 G. Kurian, "Some Aspects of the Regional Geography of Kerala," *Indian Geographical Journal* 17 (1942): 5–8.
28 Jean-Pierre Pascal, *Les forêts denses humides sempervirentes de basse et moyenne altitudes du sud de l'Inde* (Pondicherry, India: Institut Français, 1983).
29 Francis Buchanan, *A Journey from Madras through the Countries of Mysore, Canara, and Malabar,* 3 vols. (London: Cadell and Davies, 1807).
30 P. R. G. Mathur, *Tribal Situation in Kerala* (Trivandrum, India: Kerala Historical Society, 1977).
31 For the general history of the region, see L. M. Panikkar, *A History of Kerala* (Annamalainagar, India, 1960); or A. Sreedhara Menon, *A Survey of Kerala History* (Kottayam,

comprised the Malabar coast, known to Europe from medieval times onward. Lengthy rivalries among the Portuguese, Dutch, French, and British ended with British annexation of Malabar in 1792 and its incorporation as Malabar District of Madras Presidency.[32] From then until independence in 1947, Malabar's fortunes, both political and environmental, were shaped by the British regional government headquartered in Madras.[33]

Farther south toward Cape Comorin, the most powerful of the Kerala kingdoms, Travancore, rose to prominence in the early 1700s. It remained autonomous throughout the British era, and not until 1956 was it amalgamated with Malabar and the smaller Princely State of Cochin (which lies between Malabar and Tranvancore) into the present-day Kerala State. The southern half of Kerala developed its own approach to resource exploitation, including its forests. The Princely States in general had the reputation of being far slower to modernize and establish links to the outside world than those districts which the British administered directly; in many parts of India they were backwaters that preserved the older hierarchies and rituals of aristocratic landholders against the blandishments of capitalist wealth and efficient bureaucracy. We might therefore expect the forests of the Travancore hills to have been less heavily exploited than the neighboring tree cover to the north.

The truth on the Kerala coast, however, is more complex and paradoxical. In important ways the British in Malabar avoided any economic development which might affront the entrenched landed elite there, while the rajas of Travancore endorsed capitalist transformations of their lands and forests, hiring British administrators to modernize their state and encouraging export crop plantations to supplant economically unremunerative forests.[34] By 1947 economic development, and thus the pressures on the forest cover, was further advanced in Travancore than in Malabar.

Before the British conquest of Malabar in 1792, the region had suffered the worst political turmoil and military depredations of its history. Tipu Sultan, the powerful Muslim emperor of Mysore to the northeast, had fought through the ghats to the Malabar coast. The high-caste landlords

---

India: National Book Stall, 1967). See also John Edye, "Description of the Sea-Ports on the Coast of Malabar . . . and the Produce of Adjacent Forests," *Journal of the Royal Asiatic Society* 2 (1835): 324–77.

32 N. Rajendran, *Establishment of British Power in Malabar, 1664–1799* (Allahabad: Chugh Publications, 1979).

33 For the pattern of human ecology on the eastern and western slopes of the ghats, see Joan P. Mencher, "Kerala and Madras: A Comparative Study of Ecology and Social Structure," *Ethnology* 5, no. 2 (April 1966): 135–71.

34 R. N. Yesudas, *British Policy in Travancore, 1805–59* (Trivandrum: Kerala Historical Society, 1977); Robin Jeffrey, *The Decline of Nayar Dominance: Society and Politics in Travancore, 1847–1908* (New York: Holmes & Meier, 1976).

(*jenmis*) who had consolidated their power earlier in the century had fled south beyond Tipu's armies; their low-caste tenants had been left without either their protection or their oppressive demands for produce. After the British defeated Tipu, the entire system of claims on arable and forest had to be reconstructed.

Lacking their own trained cadre of tax collectors, the European conquerors relied on the old landlord class to collect and remit tax payments. The new Malabar government declared that the jenmis were full owners of the land, not only arable but "waste" or forest land eastward into the hills as well; henceforth tenants' rights to subsistence in Malabar were among the weakest of any district in British India. For more than a century thereafter these conservative landlords controlled Malabar's land exploitation. They were slow to open new land to cultivation, and discouraged their tenants from moving upward into the forest. Further, under Malabar's joint-family property law, sale of land was extremely difficult, and until well into the twentieth century little land became a marketable commodity. Entrepreneurs wanting to grow new crops for distant markets found it almost impossible to begin in coastal Malabar.[35]

Higher into the hills, however, lies the Wynaad plateau, where events moved very differently after 1830. Wynaad is a distinctive feature of Malabar: Between the coastal lands and the high peaks, it is an undulating plateau, its broad fields cut by many low hills. In the early nineteenth century it was one of the most malarial areas of the region; its population density was considerably lower than that in the coastal lowlands.[36] Though landlord claims to the land of Wynaad were theoretically strong, Wynaad was too remote to interest them. Even Tipu Sultan had not built any all-weather roads from Wynaad to the coast.

Commander James Welsh, who succeeded in controlling the area only when he put down the last tribal rebellions there in 1812, wrote in his campaign diary of the difficulty of trapping rebels in such impenetrable terrain. His words express a sense of wonder at the lushness and potential productivity of the Wynaad forests.

This part of the country is strong, wild and beautiful, consisting of a number of small hills, covered with jungle, and separated by narrow valleys, in which there are neither rivers nor paddy fields. Yesterday we passed through a narrow defile, nearly

---

35 T. C. Varghese, *Agrarian Change and Economic Consequences: Land Tenure in Kerala, 1850–1960* (Bombay: Allied, 1970); T. Shea, Jr., "Barriers to Economic Development in Traditional Societies: Malabar, a Case Study," *Journal of Economic History* 9 (1959): 504–22. For a critique of the broader socio-economic implications of the jenmis' power and the government's role in sustaining that power, see Government of Madras, *Malabar Special (Logan) Commission, 1881–1882, Report,* 2 vols. (Madras, 1882).

36 C. Gopalan Nair, *Wynad: Its Peoples and Traditions* (Madras, 1911).

a mile in length, in which we discovered trees of such enormous height and magnitude, that I am fearful of mentioning my ideas of their measurement.[37]

The British fascination for Wynaad and its economic potential had begun to evolve. By the 1830s coffee planters began to discover that its climate and soils were well suited for their interests. But they first had to purchase land from some clearly defined owner, either private or the government, and some powerful jenmi landlords to the west began to assert their formerly shadowy claims. But the British commissioner by then was strong enough to overrule their claims in 1841. His reasons revealed what was at stake: "From its temperature and the salubrity of its climate, it is peculiarly adapted for the settlement of Europeans, and I need not dwell upon the important consequences that would follow from the planting of an European colony in such a position."[38] In the years following, some higher hill land in Wynaad came under peasant or tribal cultivation with concomitant revenue for the government; the rest was either purchased by British coffee and tea planters who cleared the forest, or it ultimately became forest reserves managed for timber production.

In the centuries of European trade with the Kerala coast since 1500, international demand for spices and coconuts had added new species to Kerala's flora and increased the concentration of others. But sudden, intensive forest clearance began only in the 1830s with the appearance of plantation monocrops, first coffee and then tea. The Madras government, determined to increase revenue by selling waste land for new cultivation, found ready buyers in the first coffee planters. A few experimental patches in the 1830s led to a rush of coffee planters after 1840, despite the total lack of good cart roads which made export of the beans to coastal ports slow, difficult, and expensive. By 1866 more than two hundred coffee plantations had been established on 14,613 acres; two-thirds of the acreage was owned by Europeans, the rest by Indian investors from the coastal towns. This was progress to European eyes. As the planters' chief ideologue of the time expressed it,

A great and important interest has thus sprung up in Wynaad, many thousands of pounds having been sunk in it, and very greatly increased wealth has resulted to the neighboring countries of Malabar and Mysore. . . . A community cultivating 15,000 acres of such products as coffee and cinchona, employing and feeding thousands of labourers, bringing wealth into the country, and paying taxes, has a right to just and effective laws for the regulation of labour, and significant staff to administer the laws, and good main lines of road through the district.[39]

Elephants and other wild animals were being brought under control. The

37 James Welsh, *Military Reminiscences* (London: Smith, Elder, 1830), p. 14.
38 Quoted in Varghese, *Agrarian Change*, p. 26.
39 Clements R. Markham, *Report on Wynaad Coffee-Planting District* (London, 1866), p. 2.

breeding grounds of the malarial mosquito were being drained, shrinking the habitat of that great enemy of progress. And mountain hideaways could be denied to potential human rebels against established government. In Manantoddy, where a tribal rebellion early in the century had centered, there were fifty-three coffee estates by 1866.[40] From the coffee planters' perspective, the provision of wages for the laborers was not the least benefit of this civilizing process on the land. In forests where the only previous subsistence laborers had been occasional Kurumbar tribals with their shifting agriculture, now dense settlements of coolie laborers were being established. Men from coastal Malabar were reluctant and unreliable coffee workers, and the hill tribals flatly refused to submit to the regimentation of the plantations. But from the districts east of the ghats Tamil-speaking untouchable laborers could be imported in adequate numbers for clearing the forest and cultivating coffee. As in plantation areas throughout the colonial world, the biotic transformation could not be accomplished without a corresponding social transformation.[41] Contract labor, its terms dictated by the planters' capital, was the key to intensive forest clearance.

Even in the railway era after 1860, the Malabar government still refused to commit major funds to construct roads and bridges, so the planters spent their own funds on a campaign of building cart roads, bridges, and embankments through Wynaad and southward. The peak of this building, and of coffee production in Malabar, came in the 1860s; then suddenly a disease far more devastating than malaria crippled the coffee boom. In 1868 the first Indian coffee planter discovered a new blight on his plants. Reported earlier on the coffee plantations of Ceylon, the blight spread rapidly through Kerala's coffee regions, and by 1876 most coffee there had been destroyed. If the planters were to survive, they had to change to other crops.

Cinchona, which had already been experimentally intercropped with coffee in some areas, was one possibility. Throughout the tropics, the nineteenth-century expansion of plantation monocropping was accompanied by a rising incidence of malaria, which threatened to debilitate the labor force and undermine the plantation economy. Cinchona, a genus of trees and shrubs whose bark produced the only known suppressant for malaria, had been introduced into Asia early in the century from its original home in the Andes.[42] Wynaad coffee planters began experimenting with it

---

40 Ibid., pp. 10–22.
41 Hugh Tinker, *A New System of Slavery: The Export of Indian Labour Overseas, 1830–1920* (New York: Oxford University Press, 1974).
42 For the British strategy throughout the Empire, see Lucille H. Brockway, *Science and Colonial Expansion: The Role of the British Royal Botanic Gardens* (New York: Academic Press, 1979). For the struggle against malaria in the Ganges valley of northern India, see Ira Klein, "Death in India, 1871–1921," *Journal of Asian Studies* 32, no. 4 (August 1973):

in the early 1870s, but it entered the international market after the superior quality cinchona from Ceylon and Dutch Java, and never succeeded in competing effectively with them. In the long run cinchona acreage in Kerala never became significant.[43]

In the hills of South India tea ultimately became the viable alternative to coffee over large areas, and was more successful than coffee at higher elevations. Coffee had rapidly invaded the middle hills between three thousand feet and five thousand feet, but tea could grow as high as seven thousand feet into the highest ranges of Kerala's ghats.[44] The East India Company's first tests with tea in the south were made around 1840. But as a major investment there, it lagged far behind Assam, and large-scale production in Kerala began only after 1870, during the worst of the coffee blight. In the long run, though coffee survived as the major plantation crop in Wynaad, tea proved far more important farther south, especially in Travancore, where it is hardier and prospers on poorer soils. The British Resident in Travancore encouraged tea planting along with coffee from 1840 onward. Under a new Indian Prime Minister, new laws enabled the raja's agents to sell forest lands efficiently, and then tea cultivation could spread rapidly.

The heart of Travancore's tea country was the Peermade hills, a region of escarpments and tangled forests so dramatic that traditionally only tribals had inhabited its mountainsides and river valleys. Then the pioneer planters appeared. They were a closely knit network of British missionaries, planters, and officials interested in both immediate profits and retirement homes. Henry Baker, the son of an Anglican missionary who had arrived in the Travancore lowlands in 1819, had worked with tribals in the lower hills since 1843. When the Travancore government began granting "waste" or uncultivated hill lands to planters in the 1860s, a large free grant went to Baker. Other planters moved in from Ceylon as the coffee disaster accelerated there, attracted by the virgin lands of the Travancore hills. Officials were equally interested in investment opportunities. John Daniel Munro, grandson of the first British diplomatic representative to the court of Travancore, established estates in the Peermade hills in the 1860s, which remained in his family for eighty years.[45]

On the London end of the trade, the 1862 Companies Act led to a change

639–59; and in western India, D. K. Vishwanathan, *Malaria and Its Control in Bombay State* (Poona, India: Chitrashala Press, 1950).

43 Nair, *Wynad*, pp. 41–7.

44 M. Viart, *Contribution a l'étude de l'action de l'homme sur la végétation dans le sud de l'Inde.* (Thèse d'Ingénieur-Docteur, Université de Toulouse, 1963, pp. 4–5, 13–19.

45 Heather Lovatt, *A Short History of the Peermade Vandiperyan Plantation District* (privately published, 1970), pp. 6–10.

from many small family firms in the import sector to the concentration of capital in limited liability corporations with hired management. Similarly in Kerala, individual tea estates in the early years were relatively modest in size, usually between two hundred and five hundred acres. But as the century wore on, the business began to be dominated by a few large firms, often with corporate connections to estates in the hills of Ceylon as well. Large-scale capitalization had not mattered decisively in the earlier years when coffee plantations were being set up, for hill wasteland had cost little or nothing, cultivation and processing could tolerate unskilled labor, and work was only seasonal; coffee plantations there as elsewhere could be competitive in international markets even on a very small scale. But with tea the process was different. Maintenance of the tea plants, harvesting the leaves, and processing them for the market are all year-round activities, and require considerably more specialized skills. With more capital at their disposal, corporate planters were better able to finance the change from coffee to tea and organize stable labor recruitment from intensely populated Tamil districts of Madras. Typical of the new twentieth-century agricultural economy was the Travancore Tea Estate Company, which began in 1897 with a capital base of £150,000. With that core, it consolidated several family estates and opened new areas as well, clearing the high forest as it went.[46]

British planters aggressively lobbied the governments whose land policies concerned them. As early as 1874 they founded the Peermade Planters Association; by the 1880s it held an annual Planters Week in Travancore, with the raja presiding over its discussions. Similar efforts were ripening farther north and in the adjacent Nilgiri Hills as well, culminating in the United Planters' Conference in 1893, when local associations merged to form UPASI, the United Planters Association of South India. In Travancore as well as the British districts the tea and coffee interest lobbied systematically for liberalized wasteland sale regulations and tighter labor control laws. The major result of the planters' lobby was its environmental impact: rapid forest clearance to make room for tea, especially in central Travancore, in the two decades before war broke out in Europe.[47] The conditions of the labor force on the plantations in these years varied somewhat, but most planters resisted reforms imposed by the government just as their colleagues in Assam did.[48]

46 Ibid., pp. 18–20.
47 Ibid., pp. 23–6. See also Usha Joseph, "History of the Central Travancore Planters Association," in *Central Travancore Planters Association Centenary Souvenir* (Kottayam, India: 1970); and *United Planters Association of South India, 1893–1953* (Madras: MacMillan, 1953).
48 See Royal Commission on Labour in India (Whitley Commission), *Report* (Calcutta,

What losses in the land's resources did this trend imply? In the early days of coffee planting, little was known about which soils and drainage patterns were most favorable for the bushes, or which climatic conditions were necessary in order to ensure financially viable operations. Plantations were attempted at elevations over the entire spectrum from four hundred feet to four thousand feet, and from the fertile alluvial soils of the bottom lands to hilltops with soils so thin and lateritic that they were adequate only for the tribals' light shifting cultivation. Many of the early plantations failed financially, their lands reverting to second-growth scrub forest with severely degraded vegetation.

More alarming still was the effect of deforestation on the higher hills, which constituted the watersheds both of the series of rivers which flow westward and of the great Cauvery river system to the east. As hilltops were stripped of their trees, rivers began flooding more severely during the rains and drying up sooner in the long dry season. Moreover, their flood waters carried increasingly high loads of silt into lowland channels. Beginning with the pioneering forester and natural historian Hugh Cleghorn around 1860, a few voices warned of disastrous erosion, landslides, and flooding stream beds as high ridges were stripped of their forests.[49] Finally in 1913 the Travancore government passed its first law limiting the extent of tea and coffee planting: There was to be no new cultivation within fifty yards of any streambed or within one-fourth mile of the crest of any hill; nor was livestock grazing to be allowed in natural second-growth forests, since that would severely inhibit regrowth of the vegetation. This first law was generally ignored in practice for many years, but at least it provided a first legal precedent and an ecological standard for later governments to follow.

The combined appearance of coffee and tea transformed wide areas of Kerala's middle hills into plantation monocrops by the first years of this century. The years after 1900 witnessed the coming of a third major plantation crop, rubber, whose role in shrinking the natural forest would be as important as coffee and tea. Like these crops, rubber is a perennial crop, but it grows well on the low-elevation terrain which coffee trees and tea plants dislike. On many hillsides, from virtually sea level to three thousand feet, uniform stands of rubber trees replaced natural forest.

With the advent of bicycles in the 1870s, the industrial economies'

1931), chaps. 19–23; D. V. Rege, *Report on an Enquiry into Conditions of Labour in Plantations of India* (Delhi: Government Press, 1950), chaps. 1–3.

49 Hugh Cleghorn, *The Forests and Gardens of South India* (London: Allen, 1861); Dietrich Brandis, *Memorandum on the Demarcation of the Public Forests in the Madras Presidency, 15 August 1878* (Calcutta, 1878); Dietrich Brandis, *Suggestion Regarding Forest Administration in the Madras Presidency* (Calcutta, 1883); and T. F. Bourdillon, *The Forest Trees of Travancore* (Madras, 1893).

demand for rubber tires led tropical botanists to study several species of trees which produced rubbery latex. Kerala, like other locations in tropical Africa and Asia, had an indigenous candidate. But none had the qualities of Brazil's *Hevea brasiliensis,* which came to dominate the world supply of natural rubber for industrial uses after 1900. The Brazilian government, aware of its potential, banned export of the tree. But the British smuggled out seedlings to Kew Gardens in 1873, and from there introduced them into Ceylon and then Malaya. In 1879 the first seedlings were brought from Ceylon to Malabar, where foresters at the Nilambur teak plantation grew them experimentally.[50]

The first *Hevea brasiliensis* rubber trees were planted in Travancore in 1904. By 1917, at the height of Europe's wartime demand for rubber, Travancore had 29,640 acres (12,000 hectares) under production, and Malabar and Cochin between them had another 17,290 acres (7,000 hectares).[51] At first this rubber production was almost entirely for European markets, since automotive transport and other industrial demand in India were still in their infancy. The rubber plantations were controlled almost entirely by British firms. But after India became independent, the picture changed greatly. In 1960 India as a whole grew 333,600 acres of rubber trees, of which the majority, 201,000 acres, were in Kerala. But by then little, if any, rubber was exported: The entire production, processed locally, met only 43 percent of India's internal demand.[52]

By the time Kerala was created in the merger of Malabar, Cochin, and Travancore in 1956, its remaining forest cover was under pressure both from one of India's densest rural populations and from the export planta-tion system. Rubber and other commercial tree crops, grown and harvested by both private landowners and the government's Forest Department, were threatening to replace the last remnants of natural subtropical jungle in southwestern India. Even timber, especially the costly teak, was a commod-ity so valuable that it was becoming the object of large-scale theft.[53] Equally alarming, the process of cutting down those forests and planting new crops was causing severe soil erosion and degradation of watersheds.[54] To small

50 Robert Cross, "The American India-rubber Trees at Nilambur," *Indian Forester* 7 (1881–2): 167–71; R. L. Proudlock, *Report on the Rubber Trees at Nilambur and at Calicut, South Malabar* (Madras, 1908).
51 "Industrial Crops of Kerala," *Journal of the Madras Geographical Association* 12, no. 1 (1937): 1–8.
52 Viart, *La végétation dans le sud de l'Inde,* pp. 160–2.
53 For a common recent occurrence, see the 1984 timber-smuggling scandal in southern Malabar, *India Today,* 31 July 1984, 52.
54 See M. A. Oommen, ed., *Kerala's Economy Since Independence* (New Delhi: Oxford University Press and India Book House, 1979); for a systematic critique of recent forestry management, see C. T. S. Nair, Mamman Chundamannil, and E. Mohammad, *Intensive*

farmers downstream from the high hills, Cleghorn's warnings a century before were starting to have daily meaning as their clean water supplies dwindled.

During the 1940s the transition of the Indian subcontinent through world war into independence, coupled with its partition into the two separate countries of India and Pakistan, was profoundly traumatic not only for the half billion humans who lived through the drama, but for the other species, notably the forest trees, which shared the subcontinent with them, notably the forest cover. Assam's forests experienced the trauma perhaps as intensely as any, situated as they were on the border of British India's defenses against Japanese armies in Burma, and upriver from the great Hindu-Muslim conflict in Bengal in 1947. Both tea growing and timber harvesting were deeply disrupted in the transitional years; both had to be reconstructed in the 1950s.

In the aftermath of independence, however, a counterevent occurred which is easily overlooked by observers of India's deforestation: the official designation of great new regions as Reserved Forests to be managed by the professional foresters. Many rajas in their Princely States had reserved large forest areas as their personal hunting reserves. They lost these reserves after 1947, and Prime Minister Nehru took a personal interest in saving many of them as permanent forest and wildlands.[55] From a 1947 total of 22.97 million acres (9.3 million hectares) covered in a recent study of India's vegetation patterns, by 1972 the system expanded by 119 percent, to 42.48 million acres (17.2 million hectares) in Pakistan, India, and Bangladesh.[56] The actual tree cover on those lands varied, of course, from remnant natural jungle in remote mountain and hill zones, to almost total denudation in many arid regions. The term "forest" was by then more a legal than a descriptive term. But at least the legal system of land use in the independent nations provided the basis for a belated surge of concern over ecological degradation, when the worldwide environmental movement of the 1970s began to accelerate.[57]

This then was the ambiguous environmental legacy of empire. Like most colonialists, the British in India expanded agricultural lands at the expense

Multiple Use Forest Management in the Tropics: A Case Study of the Evergreen Forests and Teak Plantations in Kerala, India. (Pecchi, India: Kerala Forest Research Institute, 1984).

55 For background, see Richard P. Tucker, "Resident Populations and Wildlife Reserves in India: The Prehistory of a Strategy," in Patrick West and Stephen Brechin, eds., *Resident Populations and National Parks in Developing Nations: Interdisciplinary Perspectives* (forthcoming).

56 Richards, Haynes, and Hagen, "Changes in the Land," p. 545.

57 Richard P. Tucker, "India's Emerging Environmentalists," *Sierra* (May–June 1984): 45–9; for a detailed survey, see *The State of India's Environment, 1984–85: The Second Citizens' Report* (New Delhi: Centre for Science and Environment, 1985).

of a forest mantle which had once been far greater than the needs of its human population. European legal institutions and technology accompanied the intercontinental market economy in penetrating even remote mountain and jungle lands, turning forests into commodities. Planters, traders, and landlords benefited; peasants may have benefited in some ways too, but tribals and plantation workers clearly suffered. And by 1947 nearly all of the vegetation map of India was determined by the intricate structure of power which had evolved under the British raj. The lands of the subcontinent were almost entirely domesticated, under the most complex system of resource extraction which any European empire ever established in the developing world.

7 Toward an Archaeology of Colonialism: Elements in the Ecological Transformation of the Ivory Coast

Timothy C. Weiskel

INTRODUCTION: THE PRESENT AS FUTURE RESIDUE

It is sobering to consider the present from the vantage point of a would-be archaeologist in the future. What an archaeologist would "unearth" at some such imaginary time is the residue of our daily lives and a stratigraphic record of our collective successes and failures. Adopting this vantage point alters our conception of the present and the memorable past, for by jumping into the future we are prompted to lift our gaze from the rush of daily events to ask ourselves: What, of all this that surrounds us, will endure? What will register itself in the sands and sediments of time?

While most of our familiar surroundings and habitual activities will disappear without a trace in geologic time, there are clearly several realms of human activity – to which we may not give much explicit attention in our everyday lives – that will nonetheless leave indelible and puzzling patterns for future archaeologists to contemplate. Most notably, in many areas throughout the tropics – in the regions now known loosely as the "third world" – future archaeologists will have to account for a thin, almost indistinguishable stratum in the soil profile corresponding perhaps to something as brief as one hundred to five hundred years in time depth, depending upon its location.

This archaeological stratum will be very revealing indeed. Upon laboratory analysis it will no doubt show evidence of substantial shifts in the floral and faunal populations, an efflorescence of new cultigens, a remarkable invasion of exogenous material culture, and a considerable upsurge in rates of soil erosion and sedimentation. Moreover, a future archaeologist will most probably observe evidence in this stratum for a staggering change in human population dynamics marked by an absolute growth in total numbers and a dramatic change in settlement patterns involving an exodus of rural areas and a relocation of populations at transshipment ports or in urban agglomerations along major terrestrial transportation networks which served as arteries for the distribution of imported food supplies. The evidence will probably further demonstrate that these local population dynamics were accompanied by rapid and extensive collapse of other animal and plant species in some cases leading to virtual extinction, followed by an even more rapid human population collapse, due either to massive death or accelerated out-migration.

Since these imaginary excavations will take place in the future, the full extent of what is found by our would-be archaeologist must, of course, remain speculative. Nevertheless, many of the stratum's characteristics are already determined, for the processes that leave such geologic residues for the future are by now firmly underway and seemingly irreversible.

Although this may be unsettling to contemplate, it should not be surprising. After all, the evidence about ourselves and our contemporaries that will be revealed in the soil strata of the future is already abundantly present in raw form in the historical record and in our own anthropological field notes. The problem is that as social anthropologists we have not always tried to "read" the historical record or our own field notes as an archaeologist might, in an attempt to discern the fundamental shifts in the human condition to which we have been privileged witnesses.

For their part, historians of Africa have not helped us very much in this realm. With their predilection for the narrative form, they have generally focused upon individual historical figures and political events. Despite their discussion of "the economic factor" or various aspects of "social change," few have sought to recast their narrative to depict human beings in Africa as one element in complex and evolving ecosystems.[1] They too would do well to assimilate the perspective of ecologists and archaeologists in examining the historical record.

To what, then, does the historical record attest from this perspective? What have we and our immediate forebears witnessed, albeit often unwittingly? The answer will no doubt vary widely from place to place in Africa, but it is useful to delineate the major transformations we can still document with as much precision as possible for each individual region. General patterns will no doubt emerge as comparison becomes possible between different regions.

The Ivory Coast provides a striking case study in this regard, for it is a region in which formal European control is both relatively recent and very intense. As such its history represents in encapsulated and condensed form

[1] Although this can be said to be true of historians in general, there are some notable exceptions among what might be called an emerging school of "eco-historians" working on other regions of the world. In terms of West African material there is a useful work by Kwamina Dickson, *A Historical Geography of Ghana* (Cambridge, 1971).

the kinds of transformations which were often spread over several generations in other realms of the tropics. Information in these realms is still too
disparate to provide a continuous narrative of ecological evolution in the
area, but several important interrelated elements can at least be enumerated.
These include a change in settlement patterns, the adoption of new crops, a
shift in basic foodstuff production and consumption, an increase in the size
of the overall population – accompanied by a pattern of out-migration from
rural areas, the adaptation to new types and intensities of infectious diseases,
and the adjustment of agricultural practices in the face of declining topsoil
and altered hydrologic conditions.

After an overview of the shifting forms of political control in the region,
we will consider in greater detail several specific ecological transformations
that cultures of this region have experienced since the beginning of their
relations with Europeans.

HISTORICAL OVERVIEW OF
POLITICAL CONTROL

The region between Cape Palmas and Assini on the West Africa coast was
separated on seventeenth- and eighteenth-century European maps into two
sections. The western area, from roughly Cape Palmas to Cape Lahou, at
the mouth of the Bandama river, was renowned for its export of elephant
tusks, and it became known as the "Coste d'Yvoire ou des Dents" in French
or the "Tand Kust" in Dutch. The eastern region, from roughly the mouth
of the Bandama to Assini, was known in the trading jargon of the time as the
"Coste de Quaqua," and its major exports consisted of woven cotton cloth
along with small numbers of slaves. Neither region represented a unified
political entity. Instead each appeared to contain a series of autonomous
trading policies organized on the basis of extended kin groups, each with
links to the sources of elephant ivory or cotton cloth in the interior.[2]

Despite the relative decline in the importance of the slave and ivory trade,
and the rise of the palm oil trade along both sections of the coast during the
nineteenth century, the eighteenth-century nomenclature remained in usage.
The entire region including both the western and eastern sections became
known as the Côte d'Ivoire or Ivory Coast by the mid-nineteenth century. For
a while the dominance of palm oil trading vessels from Bristol, England,
along the eastern portion of the coast earned the region the nickname of the
"Bristol Coast" in the trading jargon of the day, but the general term of the

2 For a summary of the early trading activities along this portion of the coast pieced together
  from travelers' and traders' accounts, see John Ogilby, *Africa: being an accurate description
  of the regions of Egypt, Barbary, Lybia, and Billedulgerid, the land of Negroes, Guinee,
  Ethiopia* . . . (London, 1670), pp. 416–18; and O. Dapper, *Description de l'Afrique*
  (Amsterdam, 1686), pp. 251–77.

Timothy C. Weiskel

Ivory Coast emerged firmly as the accepted designation by the end of the century.[3]

In an attempt to forestall the westward extension of British control over the active palm oil trade on the Gold Coast, the French government authorized the establishment in 1843 of small fortresses at Grand Bassam and Assini, a spot where they briefly had an onshore trading enclave in the late seventeenth and early eighteenth centuries. Official interest in developing the trading outposts into a full-fledged colony waned by the mid-1850s when the trading firm of Victor Régis decided to leave the Ivory Coast and concentrate its efforts on the Dahomey coast. From the 1860s to the late 1880s, French interests in the area were represented primarily by Arthur Verdier, a merchant from La Rochelle. Despite his appeals for more extended government commitment to colonization in the region, the French government showed little interest in extending political control over the area. On several occasions it seemed willing to abandon any claim to its presence there to the English in exchange for control over the Gambia.[4]

In any event, however, the exchange of coastal possessions with the British never took place, and by the end of the 1880s France developed a newfound interest in the Ivory Coast as a potential means of linking its inland territorial claims along the Niger river with a coastal outlet. The strategy in this age of the "scramble for Africa" was to explore simultaneously northwards from their possessions in Dahomey and the Ivory Coast and southwards from the Niger to establish treaties with chiefs in such a way as to cut off the British in the Gold Coast from the chance of extending their commercial influence and political control into the interior.[5]

In 1889 the French reasserted control over their coastal possessions, designating them "Les Etablissements Français de la Côte d'Or," as if to borrow a name from the neighboring British colony of the Gold Coast. The area was initially placed under the jurisdiction of the Lieutenant Governor of Guinea and the Southern Rivers, but in March 1893 the French formally constituted the region as an autonomous colony named "la Côte d'Ivoire," and they placed it under the governorship of Louis-Gustave Binger, the

---

3 See, particularly, John Whitford, *Trading Life in Western and Central Africa* (London, 1877 [reprint 1967]), p. 61.

4 This has been characterized as a long period of "political and commercial hesitation." See Paul Atger, *La France en Côte d'Ivoire: Cinquante ans d'hésitationes politiques et commerciales* (Dakar, 1962).

5 Debates on the strategies pursued by different European powers during the era of the "new imperialism" or the "scramble" is voluminous and expanding. For a review of some of the issues involved in West Africa, see John D. Hargreaves, *Prelude to the Partition of West Africa* (London, 1963); and his *The Loaded Pause, 1885–1889*, vol. 1 of *West Africa Partitioned* (London, 1974). For the Ivory Coast itself, Timothy C. Weiskel, *French Colonial Rule and the Baule Peoples: Resistance and Collaboration, 1889–1911* (Oxford, 1980), pp. 33–65.

explorer who had successfully traced an inland linkage between the Niger river and the coast.

These formal declarations did little at first to change the complexion of political control in the region. Declarations of colonial rule had more to do with the conventions of intra-European political disputes than they did with immediate changes in circumstances in West Africa. In what became known as the colony of the Ivory Coast, political control still resided substantially in the hands of African leaders for the first several decades of "colonial rule." The gradual erosion of that control, or its outright usurpation through military conquest, became the central focus of activity of the European colonial administration for nearly thirty years following 1893.

Thus, this period, from roughly 1890 to 1925, formed a kind of political interlude when effective French control was highly uneven and ambiguous, and African polities were in the process of reconstituting their identities in the context of a colonial economy. Despite the lack – or, indeed, maybe because of the lack – of firm political authority, it was during this interval that some of the most striking ecological transformations of the Ivory Coast began to build momentum.

It would be a fundamental mistake, therefore, to suggest that the radical ecological transformations of this period were simply or solely the result of the unilateral imposition of European colonial rule. The French were not in a position to "impose" much of anything until military conquest was complete. In some regions effective resistance continued until shortly before the outbreak of the war in 1914. During the war itself, the reduction in European administrative personnel and its preoccupation with questions of military recruitment meant that, once again, a forward policy of economic and agricultural development was not pursued, and even after the war substantial regional revolts persisted into the 1920s.[6] By that time African activities in the transformation of the region's ecology were already far ahead of the rather tentative European initiatives in agriculture. It is clear, then, that the role of purposeful European policy should not be overemphasized in discussing eco-history.

It was nonetheless true that the indirect and often unintended impact of the European presence profoundly and permanently altered the direction of the ecological evolution of the region. The transformations were accomplished in ways that were usually unanticipated and largely unnoticed in the

---

6 Unpublished achival records indicate pockets of active resistance into the 1920s, and a kind of passive resistance expressed by abandoning villages and avoiding European outposts continued for several more years. See for example the *Archives Nationales de la Côte d'Ivoire* (henceforth *A.N.R.C.I.*), XI–57–16, Le Lieut. Gouverneur de la Côte d'Ivoire à M. le Gouverneur Général de l'Afrique Occidentale Française, Cabinet Militaire, Dakar, Bingerville, April 1921; and *A.N.R.C.I.*, X–38–6, Rapport politique, Administrateur Liurette, Commandant du Baoulé, à M. le Gouverneur, no. 413, 12 May 1921.

early stages of European presence. It was not until years later that the long-term implications of government policy became fully manifest. At that point, successive forms of political control emerged largely as a means of responding to the ecological transformations engendered in an earlier era.

In short, the interaction between political form and ecological transformation has always been reciprocal and dialectical. During the colonial period policies were conceived and applied to what was perceived to be local ecological reality. While this reality had a dynamic of its own, this dynamic was in turn fashioned by policy, and in changing further, new realities subsequently evoked new forms of policy response. It is a conceptual mistake to give explanatory priority to either one or the other of these dialectical elements in retracing the evolution of colonial circumstance. Particular policies altered ecological conditions, and the ensuing transformation provoked further necessary policy choices. Thus, it is clear that basic problems of historical and social causation are embedded in this kind of investigation. As we shall see, an in-depth consideration of colonial ecology raises more general questions about the role of human agency in history.

Despite the ambiguity of political control in the first decades of colonialism, by the mid-1920s the French administration effectively established its authority over the Ivory Coast. For the next several years the administration used this authority to encourage and facilitate the arrival of European settlers to establish plantations of export crops. The intent was to build an export economy based on the expanded production of cocoa and coffee on these European-controlled estates. Ultimately this did not succeed, for African planters proved to be more efficient and effective in producing these crops for export. European plantations could only compete with African small-holder production through recourse to the colonial state as a mechanism for recruiting labor.

These forced labor exactions became more severe as market conditions of sale deteriorated during the Depression and the Vichy period in World War II. In the face of increased recruitment pressure, African planters began to resist the demands of the administration. Increased resistance among African growers of coffee and cocoa ultimately made it necessary for the administration to make a political choice between the two rival agricultural communities. When the *Comité Français de la Libération Nationale* (Free French) regained control from the Vichy forces in November 1943, the Ivory Coast administration made a strategic decision to support the African planters over the previously favored European settler community.[7] The

---

7 For details of this decision and the political circumstances determining the postwar evolution of Ivory Coast agricultural policy, see T. C. Weiskel, "Independence and the *Longue Durée:* The Ivory Coast "Miracle" Reconsidered," in William Roger Louis and Prosser Gifford, eds., *African Independence: Origins and Consequence* (New Haven, Conn.: Yale University Press, forthcoming).

choice seems to have been partially motivated by a desire to punish the European settler community for its collaboration with the Vichy regime and partially based upon the informed calculation of Governor André Latrille that African small-hold farmers held far more potential for expansion than the small and highly unpopular European settler community.

The European settlers did not accept Latrille's decision gracefully. In subsequent years they agitated successfully to have him removed from the colony, and the new administration took an avowedly prosettler stance from February 1947 until February 1951. During this period African planters, favoring a policy of small-holder production under African control, rallied mass support around the issue of eliminating forced labor – the keystone to the white settler success. As administration support for the settler community persisted, the African coffee and cocoa planters expanded their initial agricultural trade association into a full-fledged political party, the *Parti Démocratique de la Côte d'Ivoire* (P.D.C.I.), articulating the demands of an increasingly militant nationalism. Clashes between the administration and P.D.C.I. supporters became more numerous and more violent in 1949 and 1950, leading to the death of several party sympathizers and the imprisonment of numerous others.

By mid-1950 the increasing cost of repression and the growing antagonism in the colony at large gave the French government reason to rethink its policy. Impressed by the seemingly prosperous development of the neighboring Gold Coast colony after the British decided to grant a measure of autonomy to the nationalist leader, Kwame Nkrumah, the Minister of Colonies, François Mitterrand, decided in the late months of 1950 to come to terms with the leader of the P.D.C.I., Félix Houphouët-Boigny. After several meetings in Paris, the French government and Houphouët-Boigny concluded what was in effect a deal. In exchange for a French pledge to release P.D.C.I. prisoners and cease its active anti-African stance, Houphouët-Boigny, the acknowledged leader of the African planters, would break with his previous policy of militant anticolonialism and seek instead to work cooperatively with the French to transform the Ivory Coast into a prosperous member of the French Union.

The accord rested upon three essential features. First, there was a tacit assurance that African small-holder plantations would become the enduring basis for the colony's production of coffee and cocoa. Second, in the subsequent years the French made provisions to expand research on other agricultural crops and develop possible large-scale, government-controlled plantations of palm oil and rubber. Third, the government envisioned a policy of extending the trade and transportation infrastructure to facilitate the expansion of the import/export economy. All three ingredients of this political agreement were to have far-reaching and seemingly irreversible ecological implications in the following decades.

With the essential structure of the export economy preserved and strengthened, the French administration proceeded from 1951 onwards to implement progressive political reforms to transfer formal control to African leadership. For their part, the African planter class through the mechanism of P.D.C.I. – labeled by some observers as "the Planter's Party" – henceforth cooperated with the French administration to work toward a gradual devolution of authority, leading eventually to "independence" in August 1960.[8] The country has been under the formal leadership of the P.D.C.I. and President Houphouët-Boigny since then.

From 1951 to the present Houphouët-Boigny has provided the country with a political continuity and stability unparalleled in the rest of the African continent. Indeed, the Ivory Coast and its relationship to France has been a notable example of continuity among all nations of the world. In 1951 the main characters involved in forging the new political relationship between France and the Ivory Coast were François Mitterrand and Félix Houphouët-Boigny. In 1986 these same individuals remain in charge of essentially the same structures they created thirty-five years earlier. Africa may have experienced radical changes on many fronts, but politically there is far more continuity than is sometimes recognized.

Ironically, however, these thirty-five years of political stability could only be sustained by economic policies that caused a radical upheaval of the region's ecology. In the long run, the patterns of ecological transformation engendered during the late colonial period and continued by the postcolonial, successor regime threaten to undermine the country's future prospects for enduring economic prosperity and political stability in the very near future.

Elements of Ecological Transformation

From this brief overview of the political history of the Ivory Coast it is clear that the "fit" between changes in political control and phases in ecological transformation is not a tight one. As we have argued above, each realm of events is related to the other, but not always in a unidirectional, cause–effect manner. As a result, conventional political periodization is not adequate, nor is a simple chronological account of official policy concerning the environment in itself satisfactory. For the kind of study we intend, we need to develop an understanding of causation that transcends a direct mechanical model of cause→effect. In integrated systems, effects are also themselves

8 The term "planter's party" is used by Ruth Schachter Morgenthau in her *Political Parties in French-speaking West Africa* (London: Oxford University Press, 1964). In addition to this work, the most complete political history of the history of "independence" is Aristide Zolberg, *One-Party Government in the Ivory Coast* (Princeton, N.J.: Princeton University Press, 1969).

causes. Biological interactions and the evolution of ecological and cultural systems require more subtle explanatory paradigms than those derived from the laws of mechanics. Causation in these realms is best understood in terms of reciprocal and cumulative processes with escalating, sustaining, or collapsing trajectories and characteristic momenta which are often revealed only in an extended pattern of historical events. To examine this kind of causality further it is helpful to consider individually several selected elements of ecological transformation in the Ivory Coast and then discuss their interrelation and cumulative evolution.[9]

Changes in Settlement Pattern

Shifts in settlement pattern usually attest to and contribute to important ecological transformations, and future archaeologists of the Ivory Coast will uncover evidence for several abrupt shifts in population distribution. At first glance the story may seem simple – African populations lived in small dispersed villages until Europeans imposed colonial rule, and then towns and cities began to emerge. A sensitive archaeologist, however, will be able to demonstrate that the cultural evolution of settlement patterns was a far more complex process. Along the coast settlement in village systems with relatively high population densities appears to be very ancient indeed. Concentrations of shell middens along the lagoon areas near Dabou and Songon-Dagbé attest to the probable presence of sizable settlements of foragers or at least to sites of enduring resource exploitation, dating several thousand years back.[10]

Early European accounts of the trade along the Ivory Coast mention large populations with an elaborate division of labor engaged in organized production for export with other coastal groups and peoples in the distant interior. Regulated maritime trading expeditions are described as setting forth from Lahou between December and May each year with export commodities for sale to trading towns further to the east on what was then known as the Gold Coast.[11]

9   For the most part our comments will be focused upon the Baule region of the central Ivory Coast where our field and documentary research has been concentrated, but additional material from other regions in the Ivory Coast and West Africa will be mentioned where appropriate.

10 Raymond Mauny, "Contribution à la connaissance de l'archéologie préhistorique et protohistorique ivoiriennes," *Annales de l'Université d'Abidjan*, Série I, 1(1972):22–3.

11 Ogilby, *Africa: being an accurate description*, pp. 416–18; and Dapper, *Description de l'Afrique*, pp. 251–77. These early descriptions of the population represent compilations of accounts over the course of the sixteenth and early seventeenth centuries. They portray a highly segmented occupational structure and a hierarchical society that practiced the cloth trade and observed strict abstention from alcohol. There may even be evidence here that the coast itself was inhabited by Muslims linked with the large Muslim kingdoms in the Soudan

But all of this changed markedly with the ascendancy of the slave trade in the mid- to late-seventeenth century. In general the population concentrations retreated inland from the shore, and in the interior archaeological evidence indicates that populations grouped themselves in nucleated settlements forming what seem to be large, fortified villages or towns. Clay tobacco pipes of apparent Dutch origin have been unearthed in association with large earthwork enclosures in the Seguié region. The earthwork enclosures were most probably built as part of a series of defensive fortifications during the slave trade period. Such structures appear to be walls enclosing oval areas with a surface of four hundred by five hundred meters, surrounded by dry moats from three to five meters deep. Similar structures are to be found in neighboring Ghana, and it seems that the increased insecurity that accompanied the rise of the slave trade served as a strong impetus for the nucleation of African settlements for defensive purposes long before the actual arrival of Europeans on shore.[12]

This transformation occurred in a relatively short period, and aspects of it are well documented in the historical record. The immediate cause appears to have been the massive introduction of firearms as an item of the coastal commerce. This trade innovation itself reflects heightened competition among Europeans wishing to participate in what had become widely recognized as a highly profitable trade. Moreover, this competition is in part explained by episodes in European history. The Portuguese initiated sustained trading contacts with the coastal peoples, but following the conquest of Portugal by Philip II of Spain and the Dutch rebellion against Philip II, the Dutch began to encroach upon the privileged monopoly of the Portuguese in the African trade. In 1598 they established trading outposts protected by small earthwork fortresses at Mouri, Butri, Kormantin, and Komenda on the Gold Coast. From the 1630s onwards English merchants joined the trade to obtain labor for sugar plantations in the West Indies, but the Dutch remained dominant in the coastal trade. They converted their earthen fortress at Mouri to a stone fortress, and in 1637 they succeeded in capturing the principal Portuguese fortress at Elmina. In 1642 they ousted

Footnote 11 (*continued*)

region. The French historian of Africa, Yves Person, has argued that this portion of the coast enjoyed direct and continuous contact with trading groups in the north until the seventeenth-century arrival of westward migrating Akan groups cut off this trading link. See Yves Person, *Samori: Une révolution dyula* (Dakar, 1975), 3, p. 1683.

12 R. Mauny "Contribution à la connaissance," p. 23; Jean Polet, "Fouille d'enceintes à la Seguié (s.p. d'Agboville)," paper presented to the Colloque de Bondoukou, January 1974 (mimeo). For an account of the change over the period of the cloth and gold trade to intensive slave trading along this general region of the coast, see K.Y. Daaku, *Trade and Politics on the Gold Coast, 1600–1720: A Study of the African Reaction to European Trade* (Oxford: Oxford University Press, 1970).

the Portuguese from their trading fort at Axim and momentarily became the dominant European trading presence on the coast.[13]

After 1650 the intra-European competition along the coast intensified as merchants from France, Sweden, Denmark, and Brandenburg joined the Portuguese, Dutch, and English in quest of trade. During this period the volume of European manufactured goods expanded considerably, and firearms and gunpowder became dominant articles in the exchange with Africans. Between 1658 and 1661 the Dutch East India Company alone introduced more than fifty-five hundred muskets to the Gold Coast trade.[14] In a few decades the whole region became armed, and social interactions were rapidly "militarized." It is against this background that the shifts in settlement pattern toward nucleated defensive villages and towns become intelligible.

The creation of nucleated defensive settlements would most probably have been accompanied by, and in turn set in motion, a number of explicit changes in agricultural practice. Only lands within a short distance of nucleated settlements could be cultivated in safety, and these regions may well have become overexploited and depleted with repeated use. Thus, the nucleation of settlements due to the defensive imperatives of the slaving era may well have contributed in this fashion to pressure for intensified agriculture or the organized movement and migration of whole settlements from time to time. As nucleated villages converted swidden farming to more restricted bush-fallow systems, fallow times diminished and groups would have had to adopt soil restorative agricultural techniques or move period- ically to seek out new and more fertile territory. Intensified agricultural techniques do not seem to have emerged in this region as they did in other parts of Africa.[15]

Migration rather than intensification seems to have been the solution frequently adopted. Short-term sedentarization of itinerant agriculture, reflected in the growing nucleation of settlement patterns, gradually in- creased the ecological imperative for group movement on a somewhat longer time scale. Migration in the precolonial era appears to have involved

---

13 Dickson, *A Historical Geography*, pp. 45–7; and Daaku, *Trade and Politics on the Gold Coast*, pp. 1–20, 48–59.

14 Daaku, *Trade and Politics on the Gold Coast*, pp. 150–1.

15 Intensified agriculture seems to have developed where land scarcity was a problem, either because of terrain or because of the dangers of moving into open agricultural land during the era of the slave trade. Both the Tiv on the Jos Plateau in Nigeria and the Dogon in Mali, for example, appear to have developed manuring techniques in mountainous regions to restore soil fertility, largely because they did not want to expand their agriculture upon open plains where they would be vulnerable to attack and capture in the slaving period. Beyond enumerating the arrival of new cultivars, more work needs to be done by historians to examine the direct and indirect impact of the African slave trade upon the evolution of indigenous agricultural practices.

a combination of three different patterns: (1) *radiative migration,* representing the random and gradual diffusion of settlements toward new but familiar agricultural territory; (2) *directional migration,* involving the intentional movement of several groups of people in the direction of new resources or favorable trade opportunities; and (3) *disjunctive migration,* involving the massive movement of a large number of people over greater distances into new and unfamiliar territory, either as "refugees" or as "conquerers" or as both. This typology of migration behavior clearly represents a continuum, with each category merging into the next, yet over the course of the slaving period the proportion of each type of migration experience probably shifted.[16]

Further archaeological research will no doubt reveal a great deal more to us about the pattern and process of migration in the slaving period.[17] So far, however, it seems clear from the available oral histories that during the eighteenth-century peak of the slave trade, disjunctive migration became a pronounced phenomena. The movements themselves led to the elaboration of culturally important covenant and foundation myths centering upon metaphors of mass exodus and "conquest." Details of the myths differ, but many of the ethnic groups in the southeast Ivory Coast consider these movements to have been their primal, self-defining experience. The growth of nuclear settlements and the onset of soil depletion probably played only a minor causal role in these cultural transformations, especially when compared with the more direct importance of newly introduced firearms, metal blades, and exogenous cultigens, but in combination these elements led to notable ecological transformations and sociocultural upheavals. Thus, the slaving period gave birth to new social and cultural forms, and as one Ivory Coast scholar has suggested, whole towns can be considered in this sense "children" of the slave trade.[18]

With the shift from slave trading to the era of trading of palm oil in the nineteenth century, settlement patterns changed yet again. Certainly the imperative of collective security may have been reduced somewhat with the end of the export slave trade, and the logic of palm oil exploitation was compatible with dispersed settlement and decentralized production. The fortified earthworks of the seventeenth and eighteenth centuries appear to

16 For a discussion of these types of migration see T. C. Weiskel, "The Dynamics of the Akan Migrations to the Ivory Coast: Historical Process and Cultural Form" (paper presented to the conference "Open Borders: The Movement of People and Ideas in the Ivory Coast and Beyond," University of Illinois, November 1985).

17 Archaeologists have developed useful techniques for discerning the dynamics of migrations. See, for example, the evidence and logic summarized in I. Rouse, *Migrations in Prehistory: Inferring Population Movement from Cultural Remains* (New Haven, Conn.: Yale University Press, 1986).

18 Simon-Pierre Ekanza, "Aboisso, Fille du Commerce de Traite," paper presented to the Colloque de Bondoukou, January 1974 (mimeo).

have been abandoned in the regions well inland around Seguié, and their location is known today only by hunters and specialists in forest lore.

Further south, nearer the coast, however, there were good reasons for maintaining powerful nucleated settlements with relatively high concentrations of population. Slaves, formerly sold to Europeans, could be absorbed in the nineteenth century in various forms of servitude near the coast to assist in the production of palm oil or to expand fish production for trade with the interior. In either case, concepts of land tenure and territorial control became more developed as the palm oil and fish industries grew in cash value. It became increasingly important to establish effective occupation of available palm-bearing lands or exercise control over specified fishing territories in the lagoons. Both of these activities favored the growth of large towns and politically allied networks with a well-developed division of labor and defense capability. The most notable of these centers were not on the coast itself. As in the era of the slave trade, numerically significant and politically important centers of population were located on the northern side of the lagoons or even further inland.[19]

Along the Ivory Coast there were no major natural harbors like those that could be found along the Gold Coast or at Sierra Leone. Ships anchored offshore and were approached by canoes or small sailing craft from the shore. The shoreline itself consisted of a thin band of sand covered with light soil supporting palm trees, cultigens, grass, and light shrub vegetation. This coastal strip varied in width from a few hundred yards to a few miles, behind which stretched an interconnected series of freshwater lagoons, watered by a large number of small streams and a few larger rivers, including the Bandama, the Bia, the Tano, and the Comoé. The water outlets from the freshwater lagoon system to the open ocean were rare and filled with shifting sand bars, and the lagoons themselves were shallow and bordered in many cases by thick mangrove vegetation, making access to dry land difficult.

All of these features meant that penetration of deep-draft European sailing vessels into the lagoons was too hazardous to sustain on a regular basis. During the era of sailing technology and cannon shot along the Ivory Coast, Europeans contented themselves to remain offshore, while African political leaders organized their political capitals at a safe distance inland on dry land. Typically, a small coastal settlement along the coastal strip would be linked to a larger "parent" or politically dominant settlement on the mainland. These larger settlements on the mainland would themselves be linked through trading networks to other population centers further inland,

---

19 This pattern of settlement was noted as early as 1602 along the neighboring Gold Coast. See Pieter de Marees, *Description et Récit Historical du Riche Royaume d'Ore de Guinea* (Amsterdam, 1605), p. 30.

but they remained somewhat removed from the coast for reasons directly related to the nature of trade itself.

Although this pattern of linked settlement – with politically dominant "parent" communities inland and subordinate outposts on the coast – may have emerged on the Ivory Coast initially in the slaving era as it did on the neighboring Gold Coast, it clearly flourished as well in the era of the palm oil trade. Nineteenth-century Europeans seeking to establish treaties with coastal chiefs soon found that the real political power to conclude such treaties lay further inland. The narrative account of early French attempts to establish a trade agreement at Assini is instructive in this regard:

On the 4th of July, M. Fleuriot de Langle made for shore just beyond the breakers. The King sent out for them in two canoes, and M. Darricau joined them. The four village chiefs of Assinie, Aigiri called Peter, Coffee, Peter, and Guachi, and Assino Koao came out to receive them. Assino Koao, who spoke English well enough, explained to the other chiefs what the mission of M. Fleuriot de Langle was, listened to the reading of the proposed treaty, signed it with his mark, and announced that King Attacla, for whom he was only the representative, would soon come from his residence, situated several leagues up the river, in order to ratify this agreement himself. He [Assino Koao] consented, however, in his capacity as chief of the shore, to let the French officers choose the place for their future establishment.

Following the promise that had been made to M. de Langle by Aigiri, Amadifou, nephew and son-in-law of Attacla, arrived on 7 July from up river; and on the 8th M. de Langle had a first interview with him.[20]

Europeans clearly dealt in the first stages only with subordinates *(chef de la plage)* on the coast. Decisions of major importance needed to await the approval of political leaders *(le roi)* resident in the interior.

In later explorations through the lagoons the French officers reported large, fortified towns on the mainland side of the lagoons with populations of two to five thousand individuals. Krinjabo, the capital and residence of King Attacla, from which Amadifou, his nephew, had come to sign the treaty, was subsequently reported to contain twelve thousand inhabitants.[21] Other centers involved in transshipment of goods, like Tiassalé on the Bandama, or specialized production centers like the Baule gold-mining center at Kokumbo also had significant populations. In both of these centers, populations fluctuated with the seasonal nature of trading and mining activity, but as in the trading centers like Kong in the north, towns were large enough to contain permanent nonagricultural residents and professional traders.[22]

20 Amédé Tardieu, "Sénégambie et Guinée," in *L'Univers, Histoire et description des tous les peuples, vol. 3, Sénégambie, Guinée, Nubie, Abyssinie* (Paris: Firmin Didot, 1847), p. 204. [English translation by T. C. Weiskel.]
21 Ibid., pp. 199–205.
22 See Mohamed Sékou Bamba, "Bas-Bandama Précolonial: Une contribution à l'étude

With this history of fluctuating population distribution in the region, it is not surprising that the size, location, and layout of human settlements once again changed markedly in the first twenty years of formal colonial rule from 1893 to 1913. Briefly put, the transformations involved focused upon the creation of new transportation and transshipment infrastructure that became the nucleus for new centers of population concentration, as labor gravitated or was coerced into forms of wage and service employment.

Along the coast, European intentions focused upon constructing enclaves consisting of resident merchants and their supporting labor force and a small class of clerks. Their role was to act as bulkers and breakers in the import/export exchanges that the colonial regime hoped would flourish. The transportation of bulk agricultural products from West Africa to Europe became increasingly easy with the creation of regular steamship service by the mid-nineteenth century, but in the Ivory Coast the bottleneck inhibiting expanded trade centered on the problem of on/off loading. Without a natural harbor along the coast, the off-loading and on-loading was the laborious task of specialized "Kroomen" whose skills in canoe and boat handling and reputation for disciplined hard work earned them contractual employment in these coastal enclaves from the late nineteenth century onwards. The first infrastructure investments involved the construction in 1901 of a massive iron wharf jutting out into the Atlantic Ocean at Grand Bassam. These structures were equipped with mechanical cranes to facilitate the on/off-loading of barges and tender boats that shuttled goods to and from the large steamships anchored further offshore.

These wharfs were in turn connected to push-cart rail systems that enabled laborers to move large volumes of bulk items directly to the merchants' storehouses along wide streets in the onshore towns. By the turn of the century these essentially commercial enclaves, including Assine, Grand Bassam, Port Bouët, and Grand Lahou, each contained several thousand inhabitants engaged directly or indirectly in stocking and distributing trade goods. Typically they were arranged along the axis of a central "Rue du Commerce." The next major impulse for the expansion of this type of settlement came with the decision to extend the trading infrastructure inland by constructing a railroad. Abidjan, a village on the Ebrié Lagoon, was chosen as the site for the railhead, and from 1904 onwards when

historique des populations d'après les sources orales" (Thèse du Doctorat de 3e cycle, Paris, 1978), 2 vols.; Jean-Pierre Chauveau, "Production agricole et formation social baule: La Région de Toumodi-Kokumbo. Perspective historique," manuscript; and his "Note sur l'histoire du peuplement de la région de Kokumbo," O.R.S.T.O.M., *Sciences Humaines* (Abidjan), 4, 11 (1971); and his "Les cadres socio-historiques de la production dans la région de Kokumbo (Pays Baoulé, Côte d'Ivoire), 1. – La période précoloniale," Office de la Recherche Scientifique Technique d'Outre-Mer (O.R.S.T.O.M.), *Sciences Humaines* (Abidjan), 5, 7 (1972).

construction began on the Abidjan-Niger rail system, this site and surrounding areas began to grow dramatically as a permanent center of population concentration. As the railroad proceeded inland, towns located along its path grew in population in relation to the volume of commerce passing onto the rail system. In 1907 the railroad reached Agboville, and by 1912 it reached Bouaké, nearly three hundred kilometers to the interior. As a result population enclaves grew at stopping points along this new artery of transportation as it extended itself inland.[23]

A second type of population center grew steadily during the early years of colonial rule largely independent of the commercial impulse. These towns were the administrative centers of colonial government. In some cases administration centers grew as specialized *quartiers* within already established commercial centers, but in other cases they were established independently for political or strategic reasons, largely before any major commercial presence was in evidence. Grand Bassam was acknowledged as the first administrative capital of the colony, but because of repeated epidemics of yellow fever in 1899 and 1900, the French moved the administrative capital of the colony in November 1900 to Bingerville, a newly constructed colonial town on the north side of the lagoons. Its location was thought to be healthier, and for the next thirty years the administrative and commercial centers of the country were separated from one another.[24]

Ultimately the administrative and commercial centers were reunited, but only after further substantial investment on infrastructure. In 1929 the administration inaugurated a floating bridge across the lagoon, connecting the Abidjan mainland with the Isle Boulay, the major access point to traffic at sea. The bridge combined a road and rail surface to make it possible to transship bulk commodities with ease between the coast and the rail head on the mainland at Abidjan. In the same year the railway reached Ferkéssédougou in the north of the colony, making it possible to drain agricultural produce and introduce manufactures through Abidjan to vast new regions. By 1931 a 410-meter maritime wharf was completed at Port-Bouët affording a capacity of three hundred thousand tonnes of traffic per year. This was linked in turn by rail to the floating bridge and the mainland rail head at Abidjan. Finally, in August 1933 the government shifted the administrative capital from Bingerville to Abidjan, inaugurating the governor's palace there in the following year. By 1935 Abidjan's population reached an estimated twenty-five thousand inhabitants, and

---

23 For information involving the growth of infrastructure and urbanization, see Semi-Bi Zan, "La politique coloniale des travaux publics en Côte d'Ivoire (1900–1940)," *Annales de l'Université d'Abidjan, Série I Histoire*, 2 (1973–4) [special issue]; Pierre Kipré, *Villes de Côte d'Ivoire: 1893–1940* (Abidjan: Les Nouvelles Editions Africaines, 1985).

24 Christophe Wondji, "La fièvre jaune à Grand-Bassam (1899–1903)," *Revue français d'histoire d'outre-mer* 109, no. 2 (1972).

henceforth became the major pole of attraction for urban migration in the entire country.[25]

In the interior, administrative centers eventually became poles of new activity and population growth, particularly in the wake of military campaigns of conquest which dominated the government's concerns from 1908 through 1913. The resistance struggles themselves often had the effect of dispersing populations over the landscape for several years. In the Baule region in the center of the colony, for example, the population frequently abandoned their regular villages in order to avoid the exactions of the early colonial administration seeking to collect taxes or recruit forced labor. Some individuals relocated themselves in small agricultural encampments near their fields, returning to their villages only periodically. The campaigns of military conquest were in part designed to destroy these dispersed settlements and concentrate populations in regrouped villages of higher density along newly constructed roads.[26]

These newly constituted villages were in some cases organized in the same location as previously important villages, but this was not always the case. In the precolonial period the village of Ngokro among the Baule-Akoué peoples, for example, was not a particularly large or important village even in regional terms. In 1909–10, however, during a period of intense fighting in the conquest of Baule country, an individual Baule woman named Yammoussou and her nephew, Kouassi Ngo, both from the village of Ngokro, collaborated closely with the French in conquering Baule territory. Partially out of gratitude and partially for reasons of safety, the French administration decided henceforth to create an administrative center for the region in this village, renaming it Yamoussoukro, in her honor.[27]

---

25 For accounts of the planning and urban dynamics of Abidjan, see Kipré, *Villes de Côte d'Ivoire*, and his article "La Place des Centres urbains dans l'économie de la Côte d'Ivoire de 1920 à 1930," *Annales de l'Université d'Abidjan, Série I Histoire*, 3 (1975):93–120; Kathryn Kash-Weiskel, "Urban Planning in Africa," *Bulletin de Liaison*, Centre de recherches architecturales et urbaines, Université d'Abidjan, special issue, 1–2 (1974): 33–50; Michael Alan Cohen, *Urban Policy and Political Conflict in Africa: A Study of the Ivory Coast* (Chicago: University of Chicago Press, 1974); and Heather Joshi, Harold Lubell, and Jean Mouly, *Abidjan: Urban Development and Employment in the Ivory Coast* (Geneva: I.L.O., 1976).

26 Weiskel, *French Colonial Rule*, pp. 204–5, 223–5.

27 Ibid., pp. 205, 220. For the recent development of Yamoussoukro, see Françoise Grenié, "Yamoussoukro: Etude Urbaine. Contribution à l'étude des petites villes de Côte d'Ivoire" (Thèse, Institut de Géographie tropicale, Abidjan, 1973), 2 vols.; and P. Cheynier, *Yamoussoukro: Coeur de la Côte d'Ivoire* (Abidjan, n.d.).

Félix Houphouët-Boigny, the current president of the Ivory Coast, is a direct political heir of Kouassi Ngo, and he has sought to transform the modest colonial town of Yamoussoukro into a showcase example of modern urbanization in tropical Africa. Known as the "Brazilia of Africa," Yamoussoukro appears to be destined to become the administrative capital of the Ivory Coast if current plans are fulfilled.

Yamoussoukro rapidly outgrew the former dimensions of Ngokro, the village that had been in place when the French chose it as an administrative center, and its development characterized the evolution of colonial towns in general. As a rule these centers were formed on the basis of four separate *quartiers* including: (1) a military base and closely associated administrative post, which constituted a European section of the town; (2) a residential quarter for the Senegalese troops and African auxiliaries working for the administration – including in some cases freed slaves; (3) a commercial quarter, inhabited by Senegalese, Ghanaians, and increasingly, from the 1920s onward, by Lebanese and French merchants; and (4) a quartier composed of Africans from the region immediately surrounding the town.

Before 1914, the military and Senegalese quarters of town grew the mostly rapidly. In many regions Africans from surrounding areas were reluctant to go to these centers, because they had learned to associate them with the onerous demands of colonial tax collection or judicial discipline. It was difficult to attract local populations to wage-labor employment in these centers for the first several decades of colonial rule. Local populations associated salaried employment with the status of slavery at first. In effect the French administration had to import its own subordinate African personnel from Senegal or Dahomey until local school systems began to provide literate graduates in the 1920s.[28]

Changing Population Dynamics and Distribution

The evolution of urban settlements needs to be considered in light of the growth of the colony's population as a whole. The first three decades of colonial rule may well have witnessed negligible population growth or in some areas an actual decline because of the pattern of heightened mortality and out-migration provoked by wars of conquest and the famines and epidemics that spread through parts of the country in their wake.[29] After 1920, however, the growth rate of the African population appears to have gained momentum. Estimates of the colony's total population differ, and it is perhaps best to examine several estimates to discern general trends which each might reveal. The first estimate (Table 7.1) covers the years 1920–79.

A second available estimate of the population (Table 7.2) covers a somewhat different period. It gives different figures for both the initial and

28 For a discussion of the attitudes of Baule tribesmen toward the towns in their midst, see Pierre Etienne, "Les Baoulé face aux rapports de salariat," *Cahiers, O.R.S.T.M.*, *Série Sciences humaines*, 8, no. 3 (1971): 235–43; and his "Les Baoulé face au fait urbain" (Abidjan: O.R.S.T.O.M., n.d.) (mimeo).

29 Weiskel, *French Colonial Rule*, pp. 208–9.

Table 7.1. *Ivory Coast Population Growth (1920–1979)*

Date	Estimated population (no.)	Estimated average annual growth (%) (over previous interval)
1920	1,825,000	—
1930	2,075,000	1.3
1940	2,350,000	1.2
1950	2,775,000	1.7
1960	3,460,000	2.2
1965	4,000,000	2.9
1970	5,000,000	4.5
1975	6,770,000	6.0
1979	7,632,000	3.4

Source: Joel Gregory, "Burkinabé Migrations to the Ivory Coast: Old and New Hypotheses and Not-So-New Data" (paper presented at the "Open Borders" conference, University of Illinois, 9 November 1985).

Table 7.2. *Ivory Coast Population Growth (1950–1980)*

Date	Estimated population (no.)	Estimated average annual growth (%) (over previous interval)
1950	2,170,000	—
1960	3,230,000	4.1
1965	4,000,000	4.4
1970	4,660,000	3.1
1975	5,430,000	3.1
1980	6,290,000	3.0

Source: Heather Joshi, Harold Lubell, and Jean Mouly, *Abidjan: Urban Development and Employment in the Ivory Coast* (Geneva: I.L.O., 1976), p. 100.

subsequent years, and thus, the rates of growth for the respective periods. Only in 1965 do the two estimates totally agree.

Despite their differences, several common features are striking about these estimates. First, they indicate that the most dramatic upsurge of population growth occurred in the very recent post–World War II period. Secondly, the rates of growth seem to have accelerated most dramatically after formal political independence was granted in 1960. Not all of this growth is simply accounted for by an excess of birthrates over mortality rates. A good portion of the growth comes as well from the immigration of

Table 7.3. *Differential Growth Patterns over Time (average annual %)*

Period	Total (%)	Urban populations (%)			Rural populations (%)
		Total	Abidjan	Other towns	
1950–60	4.1	10.9	12.6	9.9	3.3
1960–65	4.4	16.8	12.9	19.2	1.7
1965–70	3.1	7.2	9.3	6.2	1.6
1970–75	3.1	7.6	9.2	6.5	1.0
1975–80	3.0	6.0	6.7	5.5	1.1

Source: Joshi, Lubell, and Mouly, *Abidjan,* p. 100. In these figures a "town" is considered any town with 4,000 permanent residents or more.

populations from the countries of Mali, Burkina Faso (Upper Volta), and Guinea to the north and west.[30]

Against this general background of remarkable growth, urban centers can be seen to have expanded very dramatically indeed when compared to rural areas. Abidjan grew from twenty-five thousand inhabitants in 1935 to an estimated fifty-five thousand in 1950. This represented an average annual rate of growth of nearly 5.4 percent, substantially exceeding the average annual rate of population growth for the colony as a whole. Yet even this remarkable growth was dwarfed by the staggering urbanization rates of the following three decades from 1950 to 1980. (See Table 7.3.)

Some of this urban and small-town growth seems to have resulted from the increased demand for education and the immigration of school-age children to live with relatives in towns in order to get access to school opportunities.[31] Whatever its origins or motivation, in percentage terms the overall shift in the distribution of population is remarkable indeed. As Table 7.4 indicates in summary form, all urban centers have grown as a percentage of the country's total population.

It should perhaps be remembered that these three decades correspond to a period of extraordinary continuity in population leadership. If we were to concentrate our focus upon a narrative of the population scene, we would be likely to miss the underlying, systemwide ecological convulsions going on beneath a seemingly placid political continuum. Any society that nearly triples its population and moves from a circumstance where only 7.4 percent of its population lives in urban areas to one in which fully 42.5

30 Yves Marguerat, "Des ethnies et des villes: Analyse des migrations vers les villes de Côte d'Ivoire," *Cahiers d'O.R.S.T.O.M.*, 18, no. 3 (1981–82), pp. 303–40.
31 Jean Saint-Vil, "Migrations scolaires et urbanisation en Côte d'Ivoire," *Les Cahiers d'Outre-Mer*, 34, no. 133 (January–March 1981): 23–41.

Toward an Archaeology of Colonialism

Table 7.4. *Ivory Coast Population Distribution (%)*

Date	Urban populations (%)			Rural populations (%)
	Total	Abidjan	Other towns	
1950	7.4	2.5	1.7	92.6
1960	13.9	5.6	8.3	86.1
1965	24.5	8.2	16.3	75.5
1970	29.8	11.1	18.8	70.2
1975	36.8	14.7	22.1	63.2
1980	42.5	17.6	24.9	57.5

Source: Joshi, Lubell, and Mouly, *Abidjan*, p. 101.

percent of the population lives in towns in a period of only thirty years has experienced a massive ecological transformation.

Floral and Faunal Shifts

The dramatic changes in the pattern of human settlement in the Ivory Coast have been accompanied and facilitated by equally radical shifts in local populations of flora and fauna. These include important changes in both cultivars and nondomesticates.

The shift in the range and percent of composition of domesticated plants that will be evident from studying the "colonial stratum" in the soil profile promises to be quite dramatic.[32] Once again, it is important not to be too shortsighted in our assessment of the historical depth of this process. Just as settlement patterns changed significantly throughout the four hundred years of economic exchange prior to the creation of formal colonial control, so too important shifts in domesticates long preceded colonial rule. Most new cultigens were introduced well before the twentieth century as a result of expanded exchange networks with both the New World and Asia during the slave trade period. Exogenous cultigens adapted during this period included the New World domesticates: *Manihot utilissima* (cassava); *Arachis hypogaea* (groundnut); *Lycopersicon esculentum* (tomato); *Zea mays* (maize);

---

32 A systematic history of the evolution of cultigens in the Ivory Coast has yet to be written, but information for the following summary account is drawn from Dickson, *A Historical Geography;* Marvin Miracle, *Maize in Tropical Africa* (Madison: University of Wisconsin Press, 1966); Jacques Miège, "Les cultures vivrières en Afrique Occidentale," *Les Cahiers d'Outre-Mer,* 7 (1954):25–50; and his "L'agriculture baoulé," *Conférence internationale des Africanistes de l'Ouest, 1, 1950* (Dakar: (I.F.A.N.), 1951), vol. 2, pp. 47–59; F. R. Irvine, *A Text-Book of West African Agriculture, Soils, and Crops* (London: Oxford University Press, [1934], 1957); and Bruce F. Johnston, *The Staple Food Economies of Western Tropical Africa* (Stanford, Calif., 1958).

Timothy C. Weiskel

Ipomea batatas (sweet potato); *Xanthosoma* sp. (cocoyam); *Ananas comosus* (pineapple); *Carica papaya* (papaya); *Persea americana* (avocado); *Hibiscus esculentus* (gombo); *Capsicum* sp. (various hot peppers); *Nicotinana tabacum* (tobacco); and *Gossypium hirsutum* and *G. barbadense* (New World cottons).

In addition, recently introduced Asian varieties of plants supplemented African cultigens and New World crops. Although varieties of the species *Dioscorea* were indigenous to Africa (most notably *Dioscorea cayenensis* and *Dioscorea rotundata*), new cultivars of the species were introduced by the Portuguese from Asia as well. Particularly important in this respect was *Dioscorea alata*. As one botanist has summarized it:

Recent evolution of yams as crop plants began when the paleo-colonial Lusitano-Iberian expansion into the tropics around 500 B.P. brought the Indo-Pacific area, Africa and America into regular contact. Asiatic and, later, African yams were extensively used for the victualling of ships; through this agency, *D. alata* was taken to West Africa.[33]

Further important foodstuffs introduced from Asia in the "paleo-colonial" period included: *Oriza sativa* (Asian rice); *Colocasia esculenta* (taro); *Musa sapientum* (sweet banana); *Saccharum officinarum* (sugar cane); *Citrus sinensis* (orange); *Citrus paradisi* (grapefruit); *Citrus limon* (lemon); and *Mangifera indica* (mango).

These American and Asian crops became so fully integrated into African agricultural systems that virtually all of them were referred to as "traditional" crops by Europeans at the outset of colonial rule in the Ivory Coast during the 1890s. Indeed, it is hard to conceive of describing African farming systems without reference to one or another combination of these crops, so thoroughly have they come to dominate the agricultural scene. Yet each of these crops has a particular history of introduction and diffusion which deserves more extensive research in the future. The introduction of maize, for example, enabled peoples who adopted it to develop a desiccated food supply that could be stored over a several-year period. Similarly, the characteristics of cassava allowed it to be grown on very poor soils, and this in turn enabled populations using it to exploit land that was unproductive for other crops. When we keep in mind that these two crops and the highly valued "greater yam" *(Dioscorea alata)* were adopted over the same period that machetes, firearms, and munitions were introduced into the Ivory Coast, it becomes apparent that these novel cultigens could provide expanded food supplies to assist the development of new forms of politico-military state organization, enabling populations to colonize new territory or conquer rivals with the use of mobile armies fed with dried food rations.

33 D. G. Coursey, "Yams," in N. W. Simmonds, ed., *Evolution of Crop Plants* (London, 1976), p. 72.

Toward an Archaeology of Colonialism

In short, the social impact of the introduction of new cultigens in the paleo-colonial period is something which deserves extended examination both in the Ivory Coast and elsewhere in Africa.

Not all introduced crops were foodstuffs. New World cottons, for example (*Gossypium hirsutum, Gossypium barbadense,* and *Gossypium brasilienne*), were introduced at the same time as maize, cassava, and groundnuts, and they are now widely diffused in West Africa where they have served as the basis for important local industries for hundreds of years. The case of cotton, in fact, illustrates the archetypal pattern of paleo-colonial New World crop diffusion. Initially American varieties were introduced by the Portuguese as commercial crops to be cultivated by slaves in the Cape Verde Islands. The Cape Verde Islands were discovered in 1456, and by the end of the fifteenth century a certain Marquis das Minhas had purchased slaves on the Guinea coast and installed them on the Cape Verde Island of Saint Antoine to engage in cotton production. The industry spread to the Islands of Santiago and Fogo as well, and soon merchants visiting the coast of Africa would make stops at the Islands to purchase cotton cloths, known in the trading jargon of the time as *barrful*. These cloths served as both an object and a currency of exchange along the West Africa coast. The trade soon stimulated Africans on the mainland to adopt the crop and weave cotton cloths for a booming coastal commerce in which European merchants inserted themselves as middlemen, purchasing cotton cloths at one point on the coast to sell further eastward.[34] It was on the offshore islands of San Thomé, Fernando Po, and Principe as well as the Bissagos Islands that the Portuguese first experimented with introducing one after another of the New World and Asian cultigens. From there many of the cultigens were purposefully or accidentally introduced to the African mainland.

One of the most revolutionary diffusions of an exogenous crop that followed this pattern was the introduction of cocoa. It is worth recounting as much as we know of this because no single crop has had as much influence on the contemporary development of the Ivory Coast as cocoa. Yet, oddly enough, its arrival in the Ivory Coast occurred rather recently. Moreover, its successful introduction was the result of indigenous African agricultural experimentation – not purposeful administrative policy. Only when African farmers proved it could be grown successfully did the colonial administration choose to encourage its development.

To begin with the Portuguese introduced cocoa (*Theobroma cacao* Linn.) to San Thomé in the fifteenth century. Its local history there is not well known, but unlike other paleo-colonial foodstuff crops, it does not seem to have diffused to the African mainland for several hundred years. With the

34 Charles Monteil, *Le coton chez les noirs* (Paris, 1927), pp. 24–7.

decline in the cost of bulk transport, however, after the introduction of regular steamship service to West Africa in the 1860s, it became apparent that massive weights of agricultural produce could be exported profitably to Europe. Initially, the Europeans focused upon vegetable oils from ground-nuts (*Archis hypogaea* Linn.) and the oil palm (*Elaeis guineensis* Jacq.). As more and more of these oils were produced for the European market the price they fetched began to fall. The latter part of the nineteenth century witnessed several periods of prolonged price depressions for tropical produce, and in these circumstances both European and African farmers began to experiment with new types of crops to sell for profit to European steamship merchants.

The first introduction of cocoa on the African mainland appears to have been undertaken by the Basel missionaries who brought new seed pods from Surinam in the New World and, in 1859, experimented with planting it on their missionary farm at Akropong on the Gold Coast. Their efforts were not very successful, and by 1866 there remained only a single tree on their farm, bearing fifteen healthy cocoa pods. A few of the seeds from these pods were sown on their farm at Akropong, and others were distributed to mission stations at Aburi, Mampong, and Krobo Odumase. Whatever enthusiasm may have been sparked by this first effort was not sustained. The Ashanti invasion of Akwapim and Krobo and the resulting fighting in the area between 1868 and 1873 apparently dampened the prospects of expanded production for the time being.

The next effort at cocoa growing on the mainland came from a Gold Coast farmer named Tetteh Quashie. He had spent time on the island of Fernando Po off the coast of Nigeria, and there he encountered the cocoa plant that the Portuguese had introduced centuries earlier. In 1878 he returned to Ghana with several pods and planted them on his farm in Mampong. By 1883 he enjoyed his first harvest and sold the harvested seed pods to other curious African farmers in the region. In 1885 he harvested enough to sell 121 pounds to an export firm, establishing the crop for the first time as an export commodity. In the following year, 1886, Sir William B. Griffith, the governor of the Gold Coast, imported cocoa pods from San Thomé and established a governmental agricultural experiment station with the seeds at Aburi. Over the next few years the administration actively promoted the crop by growing seedlings at the Aburi Botanical Gardens and distributing them to interested farmers.

The rapid expansion of the crop in the Gold Coast in the following years was truly phenomenal. According to one account, "by about 1895 the cocoa tree was to be seen in almost every part of Southern Ghana."[35] In addition to smallhold African production, privately owned European firms

---

35 Dickson, *A Historical Geography*, p. 166.

sought to establish plantations. By 1906 the William Cadbury firm began to purchase cocoa from farmers in Ghana on a large scale, and by 1910 that colony had become the world's second largest producer.

The arrival of the crop in the Ivory Coast followed the rapid diffusion of the crop in the Gold Coast, and the specific pattern of introduction was similar to that in the Gold Coast: After initial European failures at continuous cultivation, an innovative African farmer proved it could be grown for profit, and subsequently the colonial administration developed an enthusiastic interest in the export crop, seeking to extend it to other peasant producers. Most official accounts or secondary studies, however, have misunderstood or misrepresented this pattern of innovation and have attributed the introduction of cocoa to Governor Gabriel Angoulvant, who administered the colony from 1908 until 1916. Indeed, some accounts are as insistent as they are mistaken on this point:

The Africans [in the Ivory Coast] did not begin to plant cocoa on their own initiative, as happened in the Gold Coast and Nigeria. It is recorded that a farseeing French administrator imported cocoa seed and gave it to the Africans, but they were unwilling to plant it. After much persuasion, however, they planted the seed, but such was their resentment at having to do so, that they used to go out at night and pour hot water on it in the hope of killing it. Nevertheless, some of the seed survived and in due course cocoa became a popular crop.[36]

European experimentation with cocoa began in the Ivory Coast with the efforts of Arthur Verdier and his agent Amédée Brétignière, who established a plantation at Elima on the Aby lagoon near Aboisso in 1880. The major product of the plantation was coffee, but experimental trials of cocoa were made as well. After the turn of the century under the commercially oriented administration of governor Clozel, encouragement was given to the idea of cocoa as an export crop, and in 1905 the colony exported a total of two thousand kilos of the beans. Other European-owned cocoa ventures were established by the Société Coloniale in 1904 at Dabou and Acrédiou, by the Maison Dandy on the Potou lagoon in 1905, and by the Plantations d'Impérié on the lagoon Island of Leydet in 1906; but they were fledgling ventures and all of them collapsed by the end of World War I.[37]

Responsibility for the enduring success of cocoa, however, lies with a resident African merchant, a Fanti named Morgan Dougan. Dougan was initially from the Gold Coast, and it is perhaps there that he learned of the advantages of cocoa production for export. In any case, in the Ivory Coast his efforts were not confined to cocoa. His interests extended over the full

36 D. H. Urquart, *Report on the Cocoa Industry in the French Ivory Coast* (Bournville, 1955), p. 14.
37 Ivory Coast, Ministère de la Fonction Publique et de l'Information, *Panorama de la Côte d'Ivoire 1960* (Abidjan: la Direction de l'Information, 1960), p. 35.

range of the import-export trade. Indeed from 1905 onwards Dougan was the largest independent merchant in the important interior town of Tiassalé on the Bandama river, outcompeting both European and Senegalese merchants as an import-export agent. He employed teams of laborers and owned a steamboat on the Bandama to help carry goods to and from Grand Lahou on the coast. By 1906 he was doing over a million francs worth of business annually, principally in the export of wild rubber and the importation of English merchandise.[38] In the face of fluctuating prices paid in European markets for wild rubber, and its increased scarcity as it became overtapped in the region around Tiassalé, Dougan decided to develop a highly diverse agricultural plantation producing a variety of tropical agricultural produce to meet whatever might be demanded by the coastal merchants. Because of his connections with the Gold Coast he was aware of the potential profits that could be made by selling cocoa, and he began by establishing a small trial plantation in 1904. In 1909 his plantations consisted of over eighteen hundred seedlings over a surface of thirteen hectares. By 1912 he was the largest single producer of cocoa in the colony, and Governor Angoulvant appealed to Dougan to provide seeds for the government to initiate a new program of agricultural experimentation.[39]

This pattern of African initiative and European response was by no means rare in West Africa. Indeed, it seems to have been the general case.[40] Until the creation of scientific experiment stations from the 1920s onward European contributions to innovation in African agriculture did not match those of Africans themselves in the Ivory Coast.

The reason for recounting this pattern of innovation is not simply to set the record straight. As important as this is for the purposes of historical accuracy, it is more important to clarify these events in order to understand the fundamental dynamic of the ensuing cash crop diffusion that provoked an overall ecological transformation of the colony in the three decades from 1925 to 1955. Once the infrastructure for exporting bulk agricultural produce was firmly in place and the profits to be obtained by doing so were clearly apparent to African villagers, the logic of converting forest or fallow lands to cash-crop plantations spread rapidly with little need for government exhortation. Indeed, it can be argued that it was precisely the onerous

38 The French administrator of Tiassalé openly resented his success, for Dougan clearly favored dealing in English, rather than French, trade goods (*A.N.R.C.I.*, XIV–29–5, Rapport du Lieutenant Guese, Tiassalé, 18 April 1906).

39 *A.N.R.C.I.*, XI–43434, "Note," 3d Bureau, Agriculture, Bingerville, Le Sous Inspecteur d'Agriculture, Bervas, 14 May 1912; *A.N.R.C.I.*, XI–43–434, Télégramme Officiel, 22 Décembre, Lt. Gouvernor à Administrateur de Toumodi. See also M. Simon, *Souvenirs de Brousse* (Paris, 1965), pp. 72–3; and C. Blanc-Pamard, *Un jeu écologique différentiel: Les communautés rurales du contact forêt-savane au fond ou "V Baoulé"* (Côte d'Ivoire) (Paris, 1979), pp. 234–5.

40 See particularly Paul Richards, *Indigenous Agricultural Revolution* (London, 1985).

taxes and heavy labor exactions that the administration imposed upon the African population in the early years of colonial rule that prevented or at least slowed the development of cash cropping. Why produce goods, so the logic went, if the only result of doing so is to have them confiscated or collected by Europeans in the name of taxes?

When it became clear, however, that Africans like Morgan Dougan could retain their profits and become wealthy men by employing work teams to convert forest to cash-crop plantations, it took very little persuasion to convince villagers that they should engage in similar activity. Indeed, the resentment of Dougan as a foreigner – a Fanti from the Gold Coast – seemed to act as a further stimulus to copy his example, for local populations saw no reason why they should work their own land as wage laborers for the benefit of a foreigner. As one administrator reported in 1911, "The indigenous population, tired of seeing foreigners invade their farm lands, seem to want to apply themselves as well to cultivating cocoa."[41]

The resulting pattern of cash-crop expansion is best understood not as a gradual and progressive conversion of African "subsistence" farmers to the foreign logic of profit, but rather as a swift and assertive means of seizing control over their own resources to reestablish a measure of autonomy from further exactions of the administration. The observations of colonial administrators in the interior were clear about the mood of continued resistance:

In the course of several tours made in the district, I was able to sense the mood of the population which is considerably different than those of our other colonies.

In the beginning I attributed this state of mind to their savage nature, but I have had second thoughts and affirm simply that we have before us a population that only seeks its independence.[42]

Thus the spread of cocoa, and later coffee, among the African populations was not something that caught on gradually after a period of stubborn, atavistic resistance. Instead, it was a means of continuing a form of resistance to the administration's exactions following military defeat by working to re-create realms of economic autonomy in the wake of the brutal destruction of precolonial forms of manufacture and trade.[43] Understanding this helps to illumine the pattern and pace of cash-crop conversions in the forest areas from 1920 onwards. As African entrepreneurs were progressively displaced from their role as merchants by immigrant Syrian populations and eliminated from the export timber ventures on the coast by larger European firms with greater capital resources, they oriented their efforts

41 A.N.R.C.I., XI–43–434, Rapport économique d'ensemble, poste de Tiassalé, 15 January 1911.
42 A.N.R.C.I., X–38–6, Rapport Politique, M'Bahiakro, July–August 1971.
43 See Weiskel, *French Colonial Rule*, pp. 231–44.

increasingly toward specialization in cocoa and coffee production.[44] In the 1920s the administration favored this specialization and readily took credit for the spread of the crops, but it would be a mistake to attribute the diffusion of cash crops simply to the implementation of official policy.

During the two decades following World War I, the administration sought to encourage white farmers to emulate the success of African planters by creating cocoa and coffee plantations. The white settler community that did emerge depended upon the administration for the recruitment of forced labor, and ultimately came into conflict with successful African planters over the issue of what kind of access each would obtain to recruit laborers from the north of the Ivory Coast and Upper Volta. In the post–World War II era, however, African farmers succeeded in organizing the *Syndicat Agricole Africain* to agitate for the protection of their rights, and the administration came to the realization that African farmers held greater potential than white settlers for the future expansion of cash cropping. After a period of alternating administrations – some of which favored white settler interests and others of which openly championed the cause of African farmers – colonial authorities ultimately decided to withdraw their previous policies of support for the white settler plantations. In ecological terms, this resulted in favoring the development of numerous, dispersed, and relatively small-scale cocoa farms rather than the creation of large monocropped surfaces.[45]

The figures of overall production reflect the story of the massive ecosystemic transformations involved in cash-crop production. Whereas the colony produced 115 tonnes of cocoa in 1915, the figure rose to 14,000 tonnes by 1928 and 49,765 tonnes by 1936.[46] The post–World War II expansion was equally impressive. In 1949 the colony exported 56,000 tonnes, and in 1956 75,800 tonnes.[47] The granting of formal political independence to the Ivory Coast in 1960 appeared only to accelerate the

44 F. J. Amon d'Aby, *La Côte d'Ivoire dans la cité africaine* (Paris, 1951), p. 73.

45 A full-length history of the diffusion of cocoa and coffee in the Ivory Coast has not yet been written, but details of production in various parts of the country can be found in Hubert Fréchou, "Les plantations européennes en Côte d'Ivoire," *Cahiers d'Outre-Mer* 29 (January–March 1955): 56–83; Gabriel Rougerie, "Les Pays Agni du Sud-Est de la Côte d'Ivoire Forestière," *Etudes Eburnéennes* 6 (1957): 7–213; H. Raulin, "Mission détude des groupements immigrées en Côte d'Ivoire forestière," fasicule 3, *Problèmes fonciers dans les régions de Gagnoa et Daloa* (O.R.S.T.O.M., 1957); A. J. F. Köbben, "Le Planteur Noir: Essai d'une Ethnographie d'Aspect," *Etudes Eburnéennes* (1956); Gbazah Vrih, "La Culture du Cafe et du Cacao dans la Subdivision de Gagnoa de 1920 à 1940," *Annales de l'Université d'Abidjan, Série I,* 9 (1981): 139–52; and J. Tricart, "Le café en Côte d'Ivoire," *Cahiers d'Outre-Mer,* 10, no. 39 (1957): 209–33.

46 Abdoulaye Sawadogo, *L'Agriculture en Côte d'Ivoire* (Paris: Presses Universitaires de France, 1977), p. 205.

47 Ivory Coast, Ministère de la Fonction Publique et de l'Information, *Panorama de la Côte d'Ivoire*, p. 35.

active participation in the export economy boom. In 1961 the country produced 93,605 tonnes of cocoa beans on plantations covering a surface of 372,800 hectares. By 1977 the planted area in cocoa trees had risen to 896,500 hectares and the total production amounted to 228,328 tonnes of cocoa.[48]

The figures are equally striking for the somewhat later creation of coffee plantations and the growth in volume of coffee exports. Initially coffee was grown largely on European settler plantations. In 1934, for example, of the 30,000 hectares planted in coffee, only 6,000 belonged to African planters. In 1939 the colony exported 1,800 tonnes of coffee, but by 1946 this had risen to 36,282 tonnes. By the time of independence in 1960 this figure rose to 147,000 tonnes, more than doubling the volume of cocoa exported that year, and it was virtually all produced by African farmers.[49] Once again political independence seemed to accelerate this process. In 1961 the country exported 185,500 tonnes of coffee, and by 1976 the total volume expanded to 305,000 tonnes. By the end of the 1978 growing year there were an estimated 1,291,600 hectares of land devoted to coffee production.[50]

Coffee and cocoa, while providing dramatic cases of rapid and extensive ecosystem conversion, do not by themselves begin to tell the full story of the massive ecological conversion in the Ivory Coast. In addition to these crops, the country now has extensive agricultural surfaces dedicated to industrial plantations of oil palms, bananas, cocoa palms, sugar, pineapples, and rubber. There are, in addition, smallholder plantations of these crops and others, like cotton, for commercial sale.[51]

Yet perhaps the most staggering aspect of all the measurable biotic transformations is revealed in the story of the cataclysmic conversion of tropical rain forest of the Ivory Coast. The history of tropical hardwood exports actually precedes the creation of the colony of the Ivory Coast. In the 1880s and early 1890s, timber exporters from the Gold Coast had depleted immediately accessible reserves near water courses, and they began to develop an interest in the woods of the Ivory Coast. Working with African agents to obtain permission both to cut and for work teams to do the labor, they extended their operations into the Ivory Coast lagoons in the early 1890s. With the creation of port and dock facilities from the turn of

---

48 Ivory Coast, Ministère de l'Economie, des finances et du plan, *La Côte d'Ivoire en Chiffres: 1980–81* (Abidjan: Société Africaine d'Edition, 1981), p. 127.
49 Ivory Coast, Ministère de la Fonction Publique et de l'Information, *Panorama de la Côte d'Ivoire*, pp. 37–8.
50 Ivory Coast, Ministère de l'Economie, des finances et du plan, *La Côte d'Ivoire en Chiffres*, p. 119.
51 Government figures indicate that in 1979, for example, 107,254 hectares of land were mechanically planted with cotton to be tended by peasants as part of an arrangement with the Companie Ivoirienne pour le Dévelopement du Textile. (Ivory Coast, Ministère de l'Economie, des finances et du plan, *La Côte d'Ivoire en Chiffres*, p. 154).

the century onwards, the trade in timber expanded considerably. By 1913 the quantity exported reached 42,000 tonnes while only ten years later in 1923 the figure reached 85,000 tonnes. By 1927 there were a total of 447 timber concessions accounting for an export of 164,000 tonnes. The figures become truly astronomical after World War II. By 1958 exports reached 402,000 tonnes, and as with cash crops, the volume of exports in the domain continued to increase after 1960. Indeed, the total volume in cubic meters of hardwoods more than tripled in a little over a decade between 1960 and 1972.

These staggering figures reveal a massive and seemingly irreversible ecosystemic conversion that is occurring at a place that future archaeologists will consider to be virtually instantaneous. In 1956, for example, it is estimated that the Ivory Coast rain forest covered a total of twelve million hectares. As of 1979, however, estimates were that only four million hectares remained. This represents the conversion of two-thirds of the forested area of the country in just a little over twenty years. In percentage terms, the magnitude of this conversion probably constitutes the most dramatic transformation of tropical rain forests for any one country in the modern world. Moreover, the pace of conversion has been estimated to be catastrophic for the future survival of the forests. In 1979 the forests were being cleared at an estimated rate of five hundred thousand hectares per year – a rate which if continued would have altogether eliminated the remaining primary forest within a mere three and a half years.[52]

The consequences of this conversion will be clearly visible to future archaeologists, for the loss of forest cover on this scale in regions of heavy seasonal rainfall quickly leads to accelerated rates of soil erosion, alluvial deposition and estuary sedimentation. The muddy residues at the bottom of rivers, lakes, lagoons, and the ocean floor will constitute vital evidence for future archaeologists in understanding the dynamic of colonialism. Indeed, the increase in the soil-erosion rate, registered in large sedimentary deposits, is likely to be so striking for this period that it may well be regarded as the overwhelming diagnostic trait of the "colonial strata" in future soil profiles. Furthermore, the massive exportation from the local ecosystem of millions of tonnes of biomass in the form of timber permanently removes from these soils important restorative sources of organic and inorganic nutrients, impoverishing them to such an extent that future plant communities will increasingly require supplementary fertilizers to be able to grow on a sustained basis.

The ecological outcome is then, in systemic terms, far more damaging than the loss of several million hectares of renewable forest. In effect, this

---

52 Jean-Claude Arnaud and Gérard Sournia, "Les forêts de Côte d'Ivoire: Une richesse naturelle en voie de disparition," *Les Cahiers d'Outre-Mer* 32, no. 127 (1979): 284.

rapid and drastic transformation will look to an archaeologist like a reckless and inexplicable overexploitation of a nonrenewable resource. The resource in question here is topsoil. Strictly speaking, topsoil is a renewable resource, since under proper biological and climatological conditions it can be formed in geologic time. Thus, any soil that is destroyed or lost to a system can in principle be renewed.[53] In practical terms, however, topsoil may be called nonrenewable in that the time involved for its regeneration is so long. According to some estimates it can take ten thousand years to form an inch of topsoil, whereas it is clearly possible to destroy or export that same quantity of soil in a very few growing seasons if it is poorly managed. Because with human intervention the birth and death rates of this living community can be seen to operate on time scales that are two or three orders of magnitude apart, it is reasonable to talk of topsoil usage in the short run as if we are in the presence of a problem of primary resource depletion. From this perspective, then, the question becomes the same as with any other nonrenewable resource: What rates of depletion are evident over what time periods?

In the Ivory Coast, future archaeologists will no doubt observe, as indeed we are beginning to notice, that high rates of population growth, urban migration, export crop expansion, and primary resource depletion established in the colonial period and continued since are not compatible with the long-term stability of either ecological or political systems. Despite short-term gains, the interaction of these different elements in transforming the ecology of the Ivory Coast is likely to generate unstable circumstances prone to rapid reversals in the decades ahead. The Ivory Coast is the only state in Black Africa that has not experienced a change of its head of government since formal independence in 1960, but this seeming continuity on the political surface of things has been masking a convulsive transformation of the underlying ecological realities in this area of West Africa.

53 Moreover, it may be inappropriate to include topsoil among the nonrenewable mineral resources, for in reality it is a living community in close association with mineral elements. In this sense it would be appropriate to talk about the demography of topsoil, since it can be characterized by "birth" (or formation) rates and "death" (or erosion) rates, at least as far as local ecosystems are concerned.

The implications of changing our conceptual categories for soil in this manner would be very profound indeed for Western civilization, for we would have to adjust to the notion that in ecological terms many agricultural systems, including our own, are in reality populations of parasites or pathogens, draining the vitality of other living communities. Thus, we could no longer say we "produce food," for in ecological terms all we are doing is slowly killing off some forms of life to make other forms of life possible. For an interesting discussion suggestive of this much needed paradigm shift, see "Man as Parasite on Soil" and "Man as a Disease of Soils" in Edward Hyams's *Soil and Civilization* (New York, 1976).

CONSERVING NATURE –
PAST AND PRESENT

8 The Myth of the Southern Soil Miner: Macrohistory, Agricultural Innovation, and Environmental Change

Carville Earle

The differentiation of life is in part a matter of environmental adaptation, in part a question of cultural growth and diffusion. The origin and spread of ideas and skills is of course not to be thought of as taking place by any evolutionary sequence. There are no stages of culture; there are only inventions that make their way out into a wider world.
Carl O. Sauer, "Regional Reality in Economy," *Association of Pacific Coast Geographers' Yearbook* 46 (1984): 45

WHEN CONSERVATIONISTS OF THE 1930s wanted examples of destructive occupance on the American landscape, the American South provided them with their most dramatic horror stories. Photographs of worn-out soils, gullied fields, and streams choked with sediment offered graphic evidence of the region's environmental abuse. Regional histories, inspired by the unkind critiques of European visitors and native agrarian reformers, lent additional weight to an indictment of the South as an archetype of destructive occupance. These histories, and others since, told of over three centuries of chronic environmental exploitation; of an agrarian cycle of soil exhaustion and erosion, land abandonment, and frontier migration; and of an ecological myopia embedded within southern culture.

This critique was unsparing and relentless, if not always consistent. It represented part of a larger critique of American society initiated earlier in the century by Progressives and reinvigorated by the Great Depression. Few regions were better suited to the Progressive critique. The South was filled with ambiguities and immense ironies; so too was Progressive thought. Few regions offered more ample room for the play of their discordant ideals and goals. One wing of the critique could criticize southerners for an excess of

175

LIBRARY ST. MARY'S COLLEGE

capitalism and its wanton exploitation of land and people, while another wing accused them of infidelity to capitalist principles of efficient resource use and management. One suspects that only in the inscrutable South could such contrapuntal themes have been brought into harmony. At the empirical level, highly contradictory philosophies of economy and environment came out sounding the same. From often radically different premises, historians, geographers, conservationists, sociologists, economists, and agronomists alike came to the same conclusions about southern wastefulness. They discredited past agricultural practices and blamed the region's environmental problems on a distinctively southern agrarian trilogy – plantation economy, slavery (and its legacies), and row crop cultivation.[1] The consensus historiography roundly scorned the agent of destructive occupance, the southern planter, as lazy, slovenly, and single-mindedly pursuing short-term profit. One provocative analogy, which I borrowed for this essay's title, compared the southern planter to a "soil miner" – digging out the fertility from the soil, sifting it for short-term gains, and depositing the waste in a spoil bank of degenerate old fields. Such imagery – a legacy of the Progressive and New Deal critique of American society – has become an integral part of the lore of southern regional history.[2]

One senses, however, that the history of the southern soil miner is overdrawn, that the theme of unrelieved destructive occupance has assumed mythic proportions. Reconsideration of this bleak historical interpretation seems advisable for at least two commonsense reasons. First is the matter of economic plausibility, that is, why did southerners persistently destroy the soil that nurtured them? The familiar rejoinder of free land on the frontier is inadequate, of course, since migration to fresh lands was not costless. It

1 Hugh H. Bennett, *Soil Conservation* (New York: McGraw-Hill, 1939); and his *Soils and Southern Agriculture* (New York: Macmillan, 1921). Lewis C. Gray, *History of Agriculture in the Southern United States to 1860*, 2 vols. (Gloucester, Mass.: Peter Smith, 1958, orig. pub. 1933). Carl O. Sauer, "Theme of Plant and Animal Destruction in Economic History," *Journal of Farm Economics* 20 (1938): 765–75; also Sauer's *Land and Life: A Selection from the Writings of Carl Ortwin Sauer*, ed. John Leighly (Berkeley and Los Angeles: University of California Press, 1963). Avery O. Craven, *Soil Exhaustion as a Factor in the Agricultural History of Virginia and Maryland, 1606–1860* (Urbana: University of Illinois Press, 1925). Stanley W. Trimble, "Perspectives on the History of Soil Erosion Control in the Eastern United States," *Agricultural History* 59 (1985): 162–80. Howard W. Odum, *Southern Regions of the United States* (Chapel Hill: University of North Carolina Press, 1932). Rupert Vance, *Human Geography of the South* (Chapel Hill: University of North Carolina Press, 1932). On progressive environmental views, see Samuel P. Hays, *Conservation and the Gospel of Efficiency: The Progressive Conservation Movement 1890–1920* (Cambridge, Mass.: Harvard University Press, 1959).

2 For the "miner" metaphor, see Warren C. Scoville, "Did Colonial Farmers Waste Our Land," *The Southern Economic Journal* 20 (1953): 175–81, 178. Scoville also cites numerous postwar economic histories which incorporate the New Deal conservation critique. Other metaphors include land butchers, robbers, and killers.

entailed expenses for sale, purchase, migration travel, land clearance, and settlement creation. These cost burdens suggest that southern planters would have occasionally implemented strategies of soil maintenance as an alternative to out-migration. Second is the rather one-dimensional caricature of the southern planter that emerges from the environmental history consensus (could anyone have performed this badly all of the time?). A variety of evidence documenting southern sensitivity to agronomic practice and soil conservation contradicts the image of an historically invariant soil miner. Were his environmental sensitivities always episodic or tangential to the main business of making profit from tobacco, cotton, and other plantation staples?[3]

To these commonsensical reservations about the myth of the southern soil miner, we may add the overly simplistic equation of environmental abuse and southern slavery. The notion of the southern soil miner enters too easily into a morality play that juxtaposes southern evil and northern virtue. In this drama, southern soil abuse derives naturally from the evils of the region's plantation slave economy; the north, by contrast, enjoyed the virtues of family farms, free labor, and the ecological wisdom of mixed farming systems. These neat regional caricatures, however, are as unjust to the northern farmers as to southern planters. Northern farming, as we know, has not been immune to destructive environmental occupance, to wit the spectacles of the mud-filled Mississippi and the wind-eroded Great Plains. Nor was southern planting always and everywhere hell-bent on short-run profit to the exclusion of environmentally adaptive agronomic systems. Planters neither thought nor acted in so disjunctive a mode.[4]

A judicious reconsideration of southern environmental history, therefore, is contingent on acknowledging three possibilities for the region: its occasional sensitivity to soil abuse, its implementation of ameliorative agronomic strategies, and its measures to achieve compatibility between the institution of slavery and wise agroecological practice. If the discussion reintroduces a sense of the problematic to southern environmental history, it may be counted a modest achievement.

Fifteen years studying American agricultural history persuades me that

3 The impotence of southern conservation efforts, which came "in sporadic dribbles," is a principal theme in Trimble, "Perspectives on the History of Soil Erosion Control," p. 163; in Trimble's view, matters did not improve until the New Deal advent of the Soil Conservation Service.
4 The thesis linking slavery and destructive soil abuse is usually associated with Eugene D. Genovese, *The Political Economy of Slavery: Studies in the Economy and Society of the Slave South* (New York: Vintage Books, 1967), pp. 85–105. But the argument is older, as Genovese acknowledges. See John Taylor, *Arator: Being a Series of Agricultural Essays, Practical and Political*, 2d ed. (Georgetown, Washington D.C., 1814); Chester W. Wright, *Economic History of the United States*, 2d ed. (New York: McGraw-Hill, 1947); and Trimble, "Perspectives on the History of Soil Erosion Control, pp. 162–80.

southern planters occasionally employed agronomic practices which were ecologically as well as economically sound. On at least two occasions, southern experimentation resulted in agronomic strategies that maintained soil fertility and minimized erosion losses. These adaptive strategies emerged out of cyclic economic crises in the 1680s Chesapeake and again in the 1840s cotton belt. Agricultural experimentation took place during these depressions; in the ensuing economic upswing, these innovations diffused slowly at first and then with increasing speed throughout the Chesapeake tobacco coast (circa 1680–1740) and the cotton belt (circa 1840–80). Although similar in process and intent – to maintain soil fertility and profits – the specific innovations differed strikingly in agronomic practice. The Chesapeake tobacco system maintained soil fertility through *recyclic land rotation* in conjunction with slave labor and the by-product of diversified crops. The antebellum cotton system, in contrast, preserved soil fertility via *crop rotation* of cotton and corn intercropped with leguminous, nitrogen-fixing cowpeas. Although land rotation and crop rotation systems differed radically in agronomic organization, both maintained soil productivity, retarded soil erosion, and maximized plantation profits. And in both cases, capitalist profit and constructive environmental occupance coexisted.[5]

These wise agroecological systems, however, did not endure, and therein lies one of the principal ironies of southern history. Both land rotation and crop rotation systems were discredited and abandoned as bad times resettled over their respective regions – much as the Progressive–New Deal critique discredited previous agrarian practices. A new wave of agrarian experimentation, innovation, and diffusion swept over southern landscapes. "Bookish" and scientific agrarian reform, first in the 1780s Chesapeake and later in the eastern cotton belt during the 1870s and 1880s, introduced continuous cultivation, straight rows, clean-tilled fields, plows, and fertilizers – all of which initiated an unprecedented period of environmental destruction. When viewed in this cyclical context, the notion of a southern soil miner driven inexorably toward destructive occupance of the landscape is, at best, a semimyth. The myth is clearly inappropriate to long periods of southern history; and even when it seems to apply, the myth misinterprets environmental intentions that were well-meaning, if sadly uninformed.

---

5 Space precludes extensive documentation of these cases. The relevant citations may be found in Carville Earle, *The Evolution of a Tidewater Settlement System: All Hallow's Parish, Maryland, 1650–1783*, Research Paper No. 170 (Chicago: University of Chicago Department of Geography Research Papers, 1975). And my "Tillage Capacity and Soil Maintenance in the Nineteenth-Century Cotton South: A New Theory of Crop Choice," *Working Papers of the Social Science History Workshop*, Paper 86–7 (Minneapolis: University of Minnesota Department of History, 1986), 39 pp.; also in my forthcoming volume *Geographical Inquiry and American Historical Problems* (Stanford University Press).

The Myth of the Southern Soil Miner

AGRICULTURAL INNOVATION, MACROHISTORICAL RHYTHMS, AND ENVIRONMENTAL CHANGE

The linear conception of history which underlies the myth of the southern soil miner is indefensible from the standpoint of modern historical analysis. Three centuries is simply too long and too diverse a time for entertaining the hypothesis of unchanging human behavior toward the environment. Historical time is quite different. It ebbs and flows; it is differentiable into homogeneous periods of stasis and recurrent cycles of change. A heuristic paradigm that accommodates a dynamic environmental history and the recurrence of agricultural innovation is the by now familiar forty-five- to sixty-year long wave associated with capitalist economies. This macrohistorical rhythm, identified first by Kondratieff and popularized by Schumpeter, has been traced back to the 1790s and the early phases of the industrial revolution. Each of the waves – there have been four since 1790 – consists of several distinguishable internal phases of economic growth (see Figure 8.1). These are, in sequence, depression or bad times, takeoff, acceleration, and deceleration. Although various names have been applied to these phases, quibbling over them is less important than understanding their cyclical integrity and the context which they establish for agricultural innovation and environmental change.

Theory of the Long Wave

The long wave, of course, is controversial, but skepticism has more to do with weak theory than with insecure evidence. A brief review and critique of the theory of long waves points up certain affinities with capitalist environmental history. Long waves were discovered, if that is the word, in the 1920s by the Russian N. D. Kondratieff, but he offered little guidance on their generation. Shortly thereafter, Joseph Schumpeter's classic work on business cycles effectively introduced the long wave to an English-speaking audience. Schumpeter is best known for his emphasis on entrepreneurial innovation in the genesis of long waves; his immense erudition and, at times, prolix style, however, obscured the central problems for long-wave theory: the wave's consistent forty-five- to sixty-year duration and its clocklike recurrence.[6]

---

6 N. D. Kondratieff, "The Long Waves in Economic Life," *Review of Economic Statistics* 17 (1935): 105–15. Joseph Schumpeter, *Business Cycles: A Theoretical, Historical, and Statistical Analysis of the Capitalist Process*, 2 vols. (New York: McGraw-Hill, 1939). But see evidence of even earlier discovery of this rhythm by the Dutch scholar J. van Gelderen. Ger van Roon, "'Long Wave' Trends and Economic Policies in the Netherlands in the Nineteenth and Twentieth Century," *Journal of European Economic History* 12 (1983): 323–37.

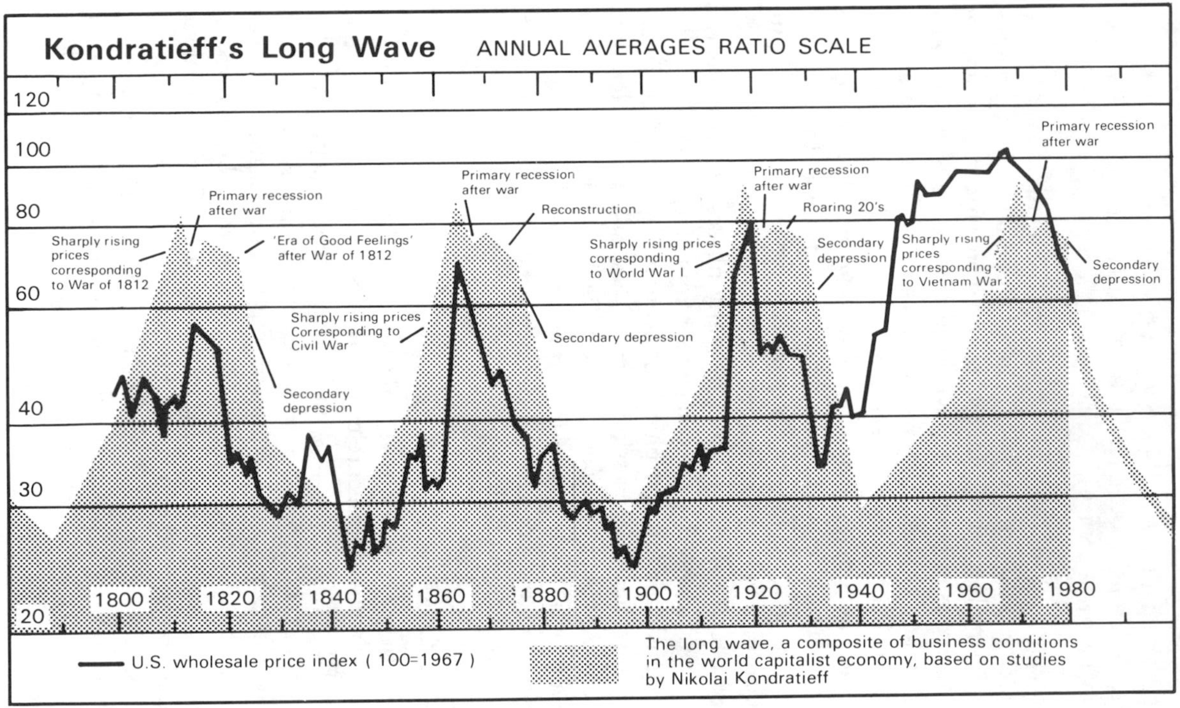
Kondratieff's Long Wave
ANNUAL AVERAGES RATIO SCALE
120
100
80
60
40
30
20
1800
1820
1840
1860
1880
1900
1920
1940
1960
1980
Sharply rising prices corresponding to War of 1812
Primary recession after war
'Era of Good Feelings' after War of 1812
Secondary depression
Sharply rising prices Corresponding to Civil War
Primary recession after war
Reconstruction
Secondary depression
Sharply rising prices corresponding to World War I
Primary recession after war
Roaring 20's
Secondary depression
Sharply rising prices corresponding to Vietnam War
Primary recession after war
Secondary depression
U.S. wholesale price index (100=1967)
The long wave, a composite of business conditions in the world capitalist economy, based on studies by Nikolai Kondratieff

Figure 8.1. The relationship of Kondratieff's four cycles to American experience. [From J. Agnew, *The United States in the World Economy: A Regional Geography* (Cambridge: Cambridge University Press, 1987), p.22]

Schumpeter's insights, however, constituted the foundation for later theoretical statements, of which Walt Rostow's offers perhaps the most sophisticated and cogent views on macrohistorical rhythms.[7] His thesis, desperately compressed, is that long economic cycles are historically specific to industrializing capitalist societies, to their dramatically increased scale of innovations and investments in basic foodstuffs and raw materials, and to the lengthening lag between an economic innovation and its productive installation. The upward shift in the scale of investment, in Rostow's view, was qualitative and not merely quantitative. It first occurred in western Europe in the second half of the eighteenth century and soon spread across the Atlantic to the United States. The new scale of innovations in railroads, new mines, and oil fields entailed massive infrastructural investments, long lags, and levels of capital mobilization unavailable before the industrial revolution.

Rostow's explanation of forty-five- to sixty-year long-wave rhythms is keyed to the lengthening lag between innovations and their full installation. The large scale of innovations and investments meant long delays between a depression innovation and its diffusion into full-capacity production. A lag of fifteen to twenty-five years became commonplace in industrializing capitalist economics. Rostow maintains that this lag, by introducing a sharp discontinuity into the economy, was responsible for long-wave generation. In the first half of the long wave, the output of the economy "undershot" demand or optimal capacity because the infrastructural investments for new innovations were incomplete. Prices rose, and economic growth slowly accelerated. The tide turned in the second half of the long wave when innovations were finally in place. Output exceeded or "overshot" optimal capacity; prices fell; economic growth decelerated toward a long-wave depression. Because of the discontinuous investment lag, the entire process unfolded over forty-five to sixty years and produced an S-shaped or logistic curve of economic growth. It commenced with depression innovation, rose slowly during the period of investment gestation, accelerated as infrastructure was put in place, and decelerated as production exceeded optimal capacity. After a half century or so, the economy fell again on difficult times. And once again, entrepreneurs sought out new innovations that would eliminate economic stagnation and lift the economy into the next long wave.

Rostow's theory of long waves, albeit a major advance, is overly restrictive in its application. It is confined to one type of society, industrializing capitalist; to one class of innovations, discontinuous larger-scale investments;

7 Walt W. Rostow, *The World Economy: History and Prospect, Part Three* (Austin: University of Texas Press, 1978); Walt W. Rostow and Michael Kennedy, with the assistance of Faisal Nasr, "A Simple Model of the Kondratieff Cycle," *Research in Economic History* 4 (1979): 1–36.

and to one type of environmental consequence, ecological neutrality. It skips over a host of capitalist innovations which were historically more extensive, smaller in scale, more continuous in their diffusion, and nonneutral in their environmental impacts. I refer, of course, to the ample record of capitalist agricultural innovations made by farmers and planters from the sixteenth century to the present.

Long-wave Theory, Agricultural Innovation Diffusion, and Environmental Change

A somewhat more liberal theory of long waves would acknowledge these innovations and their bonds with environmental change and macro-historical rhythms. Three strands of evidence encourage theoretical reconsideration. First is the remarkable symmetry in the trajectories of agrarian innovation diffusion and long waves.[8] Both are described by continuous, S-shaped, logistic curves. By way of contrast, Rostow's curves are mismatched. His long-wave curves are continuous logistic, while his curves of innovation-investment diffusion are discontinuous. His step-like diffusion model has a hard time explaining why accelerated economic growth regularly takes place prior to the installation of massive infrastructures.[9]

A second strand of evidence is the forty-five- to sixty-year simultaneity of long waves and the diffusion of agricultural innovations. To cite just a few examples (see Figure 8.2 for others), the English diffusion of clover and turnips circa 1680–1740 matches as closely with its long wave as does the diffusion of hybrid corn and cotton harvesters in the United States or combine harvesters in England circa 1930–80 with its macroeconomic rhythm. Similarly, the improvements in English wheat yields circa 1580–1640 document a close correspondence in the processes of agricultural diffusion and the long wave.[10] Such logistic symmetry and simultaneity seem more than fortuitous.

8 As noted later in the text, the correlation of agricultural diffusion and long-wave processes has gone undiscerned either by diffusionists or economists. See for example, Rostow's *World Economy* and Everett M. Rogers, *Diffusion of Innovations*, 3d ed. (New York: Free Press, 1983).

9 Rostow's theory describes discontinuous investment, yet his statistical modeling introduces continuous investment assumptions during the first 15–25 years of the long wave. Rostow and Kennedy, "A Simple Model of the Kondratieff Cycle," pp. 1–36.

10 In presenting these examples, I do not imply (a) that these are the only innovations devised and diffused in the period; nor (b) that inventions as distinct from innovations cluster in the long-wave depressions. Mark Overton, "The Diffusion of Agricultural Innovations in Early Modern England: Turnips and Clover in Norfolk and Suffolk, 1580–1740," *Institute of British Geographers, Transactions*, new ser. 10 (1985): 205–21; and the same author's "Agricultural Revolution? Development of the Agrarian Economy in Early Modern England," in Alan R. H. Baker and Derek Gregory, eds., *Explorations in Historical Geography: Interpretative Essays* (Cambridge: Cambridge University Press, 1984), pp.

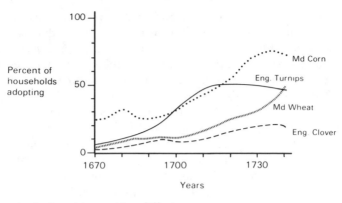

Figure 8.2. Agricultural innovation diffusion, 1670–1740.

Our final strand of evidence is a more tentative observation on long-wave–environmental interaction. The diffusion of innovation is accompanied by unanticipated, nonneutral environmental impacts. The severity of these impacts has two immediate effects. First, destructive occupance becomes evident in the deceleration phase of long waves and initiates a critique of prevailing agrarian practice. Second, the degree of environmental abuse conditions the severity of the long-wave depression that ensues. The classic American example, of course, is the Great Depression, the extensive destructive environmental occupance of its preceding logistic, and the Progressive–New Deal critique of American agricultural practice. A comparable historical case, as I will show, is the destructive occupance in the long wave that began in 1790 and culminated in the deep depression of the 1830s and 1840s.

This provisional evidence seems to implicate agricultural innovation and diffusion in an explanation of long-wave economic rhythms. The implications, of course, are far-reaching. Instead of four long waves, we may be dealing with as many as eight. Instead of regarding long waves as a product of late industrial capitalism, we may be dealing with a process inherent to the history of capitalist societies. Instead of regarding discontinuous, large-scale, corporate investments as the prime mover of long waves, we, more accurately, may be dealing with the small-scale, continuous investments of farm households. And instead of ecologically neutral innovation, we may be dealing with impacts sufficient to govern the magnitude of long-wave crises.

118–39. Zvi Griliches, "Hybrid Corn and the Economics of Innovation," *Science* 132 (29 July 1960): 275–80. David Grigg, *The Dynamics of Agricultural Change: The Historical Experience* (New York: St. Martin's, 1983).

183

Carville Earle

A theory of agricultural innovation and long-wave economic growth is not, therefore, unrelated to environmental history – indeed, that is the whole point of our interest here. Every agrarian innovation has consequences for the use or abuse of land and resources, and these consequences, in turn, reverberate upon ensuing innovation, diffusion, and long waves. Sketching these theoretical ties will bring us full circle back to our main theme, the myth of the southern soil miner. My sketch consists of three interlocking propositions which are provisional despite their declarative form: (1) long-wave depression begets agricultural experimentation and innovation; (2) the diffusion of these innovations begets long-wave curves; and (3) the attendant diffusion of unanticipated environmental impacts begets, in part, long-wave depressions and a new round of agrarian innovation.

The Source of Agricultural Innovation: Long-wave Depressions

The most critical, and certainly the most interesting, phase of capitalist agricultural history is the recurrent depressions of long waves. It is a time of great difficulty and hardship, yet of remarkable creativity, experimentation, and innovation. In a process that has rendered capitalism so remarkably successful and at the same time so deeply mysterious, the adversity of falling prices, rising unemployment, and stagnating economic growth trigger an array of agricultural experiments and speculations. Deceleration of the long wave invites critique of prevailing practice; depression demands solutions. Experimentation aims at ending economic malaise through what Schumpeter termed "creative destruction." It seeks to replace current technologies and practices, suffering from diminishing returns and low profits, with more productive alternatives.[11] Experimentation embraces the entire society, from the microscale of farm and plantation households to the mesoscale of local, state, and regional institutions to the macroscale of nation-state political economy. At the microscale, these experiments draw upon the entire reservoir of agrarian knowledge and experience. It is a time of

---

11 Innovations may be more productive in a variety of ways: by lowering costs of production; using resources more efficiently, e.g., using idle labor time to produce subsistence crop supplements to staple crop production; switching from one staple crop to another; improving quality of output; reducing through cooperative efforts the quantity of output; etc. The process of choosing from among these alternatives should be better understood if we are to develop a satisfactory theory of innovation. The risks and uncertainties of innovation in earlier times are nicely exposed in Margaret W. Rossiter, "The Organization of Agricultural Improvement in the United States, 1785–1865," in *The Pursuit of Knowledge in the Early American Republic: American Scientific and Learned Societies from Colonial Times to the Civil War,* ed. Alexandra Oleson and Sanborn Brown (Baltimore: The Johns Hopkins University Press, 1976), pp. 279–88.

reconsideration, revision, and reconfiguration – what Thomas Kuhn called, in a different context, a paradigm shift.[12]

It is, moreover, an exhilarating, heady time. The phase of depression-experimentation is filled with creative as well as crackpot ideas, with interesting speculations, with useless inventions suddenly made practical, with unlikely innovators – I think of the contributions of slaves to the emergence of wet rice culture in late seventeenth-century South Carolina – and with innovations of varying long-term utilities. It is a time, however brief, for those humanistic versions of history which celebrate "the great man (or woman)," the entrepreneurial genius, and the creative inventor. It stands in brilliant contrast to the ensuing period when the more prosaic diffusion logistic takes over and routinely plays out the plot established during the creative phase of long-wave depression, experimentation, and innovation.

Agricultural innovations have a long history of association with capitalist macrohistorical cycles. It is possible to trace the clustering of these innovations in the depression phases of eight long waves encompassing the years between 1580 and 1980.[13] The types of innovation vary from simple tools or machines to fundamental reorganizations of agrarian practice. The list is selective rather than exhaustive, and hence includes a number of familiar innovations alongside some less familiar ones which are discussed herein. A word about the list. Each macrohistorical cycle is numbered from earliest to latest; dates refer to the depression-commencement of the cycle and the end of the last deceleration phase. The listed innovations of course emerged during the period of depression-experimentation a period which lasted usually for a decade plus or minus several years.

1 (1580s–1630s):   Unspecified improvements in English wheat production nearly doubling per acre yields in the first half of the seventeenth century; Hakluyt and Stuart colonization schemes aimed at venting surplus population and tapping colonial agricultural productivity

12 To reiterate, the issue here is innovation and not invention. Indeed, inventions may be more likely in times of long-wave upswings. Innovation in long-wave depressions frequently draws upon premature inventions; revises or reconfigures them; and then applies them in new social and economic contexts. See, for example, Willis Peterson and Yoav Kislev, "The Cotton Harvester in Retrospect: Labor Displacement or Replacement?" *Journal of Economic History* 46 (1986): 199–216, 202–4. The analogy between innovation in long-wave depressions and paradigmatic revision in science is quite pertinent; the accumulation of anomalous findings in science prompts theoretical revision in the same fashion that the diminishing returns of innovations compel agrarians to seek new solutions. See Thomas S. Kuhn, *The Structure of Scientific Revolutions* (Chicago: University of Chicago Press, 1962).

13 For systematic documentation of innovation clustering in long-wave phases of deceleration and depression, see Raymond S. Hartman and David R. Wheeler, "Schumpeterian Waves of Innovation and Infrastructure Development in Great Britain and the United States: The Kondratieff Cycle Revisited," *Research in Economic History* 4 (1979): 37–85.

2 (1630s–1680s): Chesapeake tobacco yields per worker triple as a probable consequence of innovations in topping the plant and in housing (curing) the tobacco

3 (1680s–1730s): English incorporation of clover and turnips into crop rotation systems; Chesapeake adoption of land rotation in tobacco production and its integration with slave labor and crop diversification

4 (1740s–1780s): Agricultural policy innovations, most notably Chesapeake tobacco-inspection systems

5 (1790s–1830s): Cotton gin, steamboat and canals, and "high farming" reform

6 (1840s–1880s): Reaper, railroads, southern crop-rotation system (cotton, corn, cowpeas)

7 (1880s–1920s): Commercial fertilizers, tractors, threshers

8 (1930s–1970s): Hybrid corn; combine harvesters (England)[14]

This impressive list of innovations illustrates the recurrent significance of experimentation during macrohistorical depressions. The successful experiments become practical economic innovations which are subsequently diffused to and integrated within the rural economy during the forty-five- to sixty-year logistic. The temporal regularity in the diffusion of these critical innovations is remarkable. The logistic curve of the diffusion of Chesapeake slavery and diversified output (tobacco along with corn, peas, beans, and small grains), circa 1680–1740, matches almost precisely the simultaneous English diffusion of clover and turnips (see Figure 8.2). And these logistics

14 These innovations and their diffusions are documented by various sources. See especially the previously cited works for the indicated long waves: Overton (1 and 3); Earle (3, 4, 6, and 7); Griliches (8); and Hartman and Wheeler (5–8). On English overseas enterprise and colonization (1), see Theodore K. Rabb, *Enterprise and Empire: Merchant and Gentry Investment in the Expansion of England, 1575–1630* (Cambridge, Mass.: Harvard University Press, 1967). On tobacco topping and curing (2), see Russell R. Menard, "The Tobacco Industry in the Chesapeake Colonies, 1617–1730: An Interpretation," *Research in Economic History* 5 (1980): 109–77. On the Chesapeake tobacco-inspection systems (4), Earle, *The Evolution of a Tidewater Settlement System;* Mary McKinney Schweitzer, "Economic Regulation and the Colonial Economy: The Maryland Tobacco Inspection Act of 1747," *Journal of Economic History* 40 (1908): 551–69. On transport innovations (5), see Hartman and Wheeler, "Schumpeterian Waves of Innovation and Infra-structure Development," and their diffusions, John R. Borchert, "American Metropolitan Evolution," *Geographical Review* 57 (1967): 301–32. On midwestern reapers and cultivators (6), see Allan Bogue, *From Prairie to Corn Belt* (Chicago: University of Chicago Press, 1963); Paul David, *Technical Choice Innovation and Economic Growth: Essays on American and British Experience in the Nineteenth Century* (Cambridge: Cambridge University Press, 1975), pp. 195–223. On fertilizers (7), Richard A. Wines, *Fertilizer in America: From Waste Recycling to Resource Exploitation* (Philadelphia, Pa.: Temple University Press, 1985). On tractors and threshers (7), John T. Schlebecker, *Whereby We Thrive: A History of American Farming* (Ames: Iowa State University Press, 1975). Tractors display two sequential logistics in waves 7 and 8; see Allan Bogue, "Changes in Mechanical and Plant Technology: Corn Belt, 1910–1940," *Journal of Economic History* 43 (1983): 1–26. Bogue also discusses combines, corn pickers, and hybrid corn. On cotton harvesters (8), Peterson and Kislev, "The Cotton Harvester in Retrospect," pp. 199–216.

replicate the post-1930 diffusion curves for American hybrid corn and English combine harvesters. It is to these diffusion processes and their affiliation with long waves that we now turn.

The Source of Long Waves: Agricultural Innovation Diffusion

My second theoretical proposition is that capitalist long waves take their shape from the recurrent diffusion of agricultural innovations. This proposition has emerged from the tantalizing correlations between the curves of diffusion and long waves. Yet despite a massive literature on diffusion processes, these correlations have not been discerned by diffusionists – an indication, I believe, of a neglect of historical and macrohistorical context as well as an unwillingness in distinguishing critical innovations from trivial ones.[15] Thus while numerous studies have demonstrated a natural history in rural innovation diffusion in the United States and Britain, none of them have recognized that the diffusion curves of critical innovations fit approximately the forty-five- to sixty-year time frame of long-wave economic growth. Nor do the reports of S-shaped or logistic curves of diffusion acknowledge their remarkable symmetry with long-wave curves. The undiscerned parallels extend even down to the language used in categorizing phases. Diffusionists speak of four phases of adoption: innovators, early majority, late majority, and laggards – categories which in number and timing resemble the language used in describing long-wave economic growth. And when diffusion is described as a continuous logistic process – beginning slowly, accelerating, leveling off, and then decelerating – the description mimics precisely the continuous changes in the curve of long-wave economic growth.[16]

To get at the reasons for diffusion's leisurely half-century pace as well as its S-shaped curve is to move us closer to an explanation of long-wave economic growth. These reasons are hardly arcane. Agricultural diffusion is

15 The closest anyone has come is a statement of need: "Linking cycle studies with spatial diffusion remains as a challenge to human geographers and economists alike. Cycles appear to be an endemic aspect of economic processes, as does diffusion." Don Pakes and Nigel Thrift, *Time, Spaces, and Places: A Chronogeographic Perspective* (Chichester: Wiley, 1980), p. 415. Also, Rogers, *Diffusion of Innovations;* Lawrence Brown, *Innovation Diffusion: A New Perspective* (London: Methuen, 1981). The diffusion literature tends to lump innovations indiscriminately with respect to their significance to economic history. And when critical innovations have been identified, little attention has been paid to their correlations with the shape and timing of long waves. A useful critique of diffusionism, congenial with the views expressed here, is J. M. Blaut, "Diffusionism: A Uniformitarian Critique," *Annals of the Association of American Geographers* 77 (1987): 30–47.
16 Rogers, *Diffusion of Innovations*, pp. 163–209, 241–70. Rostow and Kennedy, "A Simple Model of the Kondratieff Cycle," pp. 1–36.

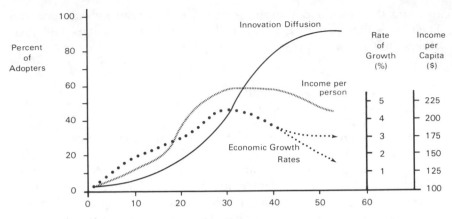

Figure 8.3. Stylized version of the long wave and diffusion. (After Rogers; Rostow and Kennedy.)

slow because its pace is constrained by several factors. Most important are the imperatives of face-to-face communication and demonstration effects and the critical role of individual rural households as the fundamental unit of adoption. The diffusion logistic, meanwhile, takes its shape from the caution and conservatism of rural households and their respect for the economic risks of introducing new technologies. Risk is especially high when innovations are incubating during long-wave depressions. When so few have adopted an innovation, rural households calculate the probabilities of economic success with great difficulty. Hence the proverbial wisdom that innovators are usually a bit odd, foolhardy, or overly venturesome. But economic risk assessment improves as the innovation diffuses. Sample size increases and the probabilities of economic success or failure are more firmly grounded.

Once under way, diffusion meshes with long-wave economic growth; the two increase simultaneously (see Figure 8.3). Economic growth is continuous because "innovators" and "early majority" earn preemptive profits or "adoption rents" from early adoption – thus improving incomes per capita. They also benefit from rising prices – a consequence of the partial diffusion of productive capacity and its undershooting of optimal capacity. About midway into the logistics, however, economic growth rates dwindle as innovation diffusion spreads to the "late majority" and then to the "laggards." Their incremental output causes productive capacity to overshoot optimal capacity; prices fall, economic growth sags, and diffusion comes to a halt ("the market is saturated" is the preferred expression in the literature). Bad times return to the region, but the cycle begins anew as agrarians search out innovations which might provide new sources of profit and economic growth in the ensuing long wave.[17] In this manner, routine diffusion of agrarian innovations generates recurrent long waves in capitalist economies.

The Ecological Consequences of Innovation Diffusion

It is a short step from macrohistorical rhythms and agricultural innovation diffusion to the problems of environmental history. The simple but inobvious point is that agrarian innovations have environmental consequences. Indeed, one of the principal aims of agricultural innovations is environmental improvement, for example, restoring, maintaining, or improving soil fertility. The innovator's dilemma, however, is that these consequences are usually unknowable. A priori or even incremental assessment of these impacts is extremely difficult because of the peculiarly long lags separating an innovation's adoption and feedback on its environmental effects. The insidious effects of soil exhaustion and soil erosion, for example, are often imperceptible for long periods. Similarly, a fertilizer may increase yields in the short run, but an unsuspected nutrient deficiency in the fertilizer may impoverish the soil in the long run – this is precisely what happened in the eastern cotton belt during the 1870s and 1880s. In sum, the environmental impacts of depression innovations are known only in retrospect. By the time environmental information is fed back – usually not until the decelerating phase of the diffusion logistic – the destructive or constructive impacts on the landscape are virtually unstoppable.

In this context of environmental uncertainty, innovating farmers and planters were at sea. They could not calculate risk as they did in assessing an innovation's short-run profit prospects. Contrary to the case of economic risk, the mathematical probabilities of ecological success or failure were unknown and incalculable. Impotent to come up with rational solutions, yet compelled to innovation by economic circumstance, rural innovators behaved in classically Weberian fashion – they relied upon nonrational sources of legitimation. Historically, these sources have arisen from one of two contending agrarian epistemologies: One derived knowledge from the practical, empirical experience of local agrarians (one is tempted to refer to them as "folk capitalists"); the other derived knowledge from the theory, inference, and speculation of scientists and agrarian reformers conveyed through books, scientific treatises, and correspondence. Although an undercurrent of

17 My interpretation of long-wave growth is more complex than this short summary allows. Of particular importance is the inextricable relationship of post-depression international war and its contribution to rising agricultural prices and innovation diffusion. A full exposition will appear in my *Geographical Inquiry and American Historical Problems* (forthcoming from Stanford University Press).

tension runs perennially between these two epistemologies, the tension surfaces dramatically when stakes are high, that is, in the critical phase of long-wave depression, experimentation, and innovation. The two sets of ideas and their agents contended vigorously for the hearts and minds of rural folk. In some depressions, innovators relied on the practical advice of respected neighbors – what contemporaries called "the testimony of practice"; in other depressions, they accepted the counsel of bookish and theoretical agrarian reformers who offered "the testimony of science." To some extent, the debate intensified in this century as "true science" aimed at discrediting both uninformed practice and ill-conceived scientific "quackery."[18]

In all frankness, we do not know for sure why one epistemology prevails over another. But it is fairly obvious that a principle of alternation is at work. The victorious epistemology in one long wave is usually discredited in the deceleration and depression that inevitably has followed. And so the field is cleared for the hegemony of the contending epistemology, its innovations, and its agents in the ensuing long wave.

The environmental consequences of the debate of science and practice, however, have been paradoxical when judged against the backdrop of southern environmental history. The more adaptive ecological innovations emanated from the practical advice of local planters; and conversely, innovations which wreaked havoc on the southern landscape emanated from agrarian reformers and their not-always-reliable "testimony of science." When "science" prevailed, the destructive occupance of soil exhaustion, erosion, and sedimentation attended the diffusion logistic and intensified the ensuing long-wave crash. Such was the case in the tobacco south between 1790 and 1840 and in parts of the cotton south between 1880 and 1930. The severity of these environmental and economic crises called for extreme remedial solutions.[19]

18 Wines, *Fertilizer in America*, pp. 41, 156–7, 167, and 170; Asa Gray, "Practice and Science Agree," *American Agriculturalist* 34 (1875): 140. See also Margaret W. Rossiter, *The Emergence of Agricultural Science: Justus Liebig and the Americans, 1840–1880* (New Haven, Conn.: Yale University Press, 1975), e.g., pp. 116–17. For the "true science" critique, see the preface to Bennett, *Soils and Southern Agriculture*.

19 The undistinguished environmental record of agricultural science and agrarian reform was the consequence, in part, of theoretical speculation uninformed by empirical method – the basis of practical farming – and, in part, of complex prescriptions that were an invitation to selective and partial adoptions by farmers and planters. By the turn of this century, however, agricultural scientists were adopting more empirical methods and insuring their full dissemination via state and local agricultural agents. Environmental catastrophes became less likely, though not improbable. Rossiter, *The Emergence of Agricultural Science;* Wines, *Fertilizer in America*, pp. 167, 170. For an example of the detrimental effects of scientific research on hybrid corn, see Bogue, "Changes in Mechanical and Plant Technology," pp. 25–6. Also, Wendell Berry, *The Unsettling of America: Culture and Agriculture* (San Francisco: Sierra Club Books, 1977).

The Myth of the Southern Soil Miner

Macrohistory and Southern Agricultural Practice

Macrohistorical analysis, thus, makes two points of significance for students of southern agricultural innovation and environmental change. First, the recurrence of bad economic times stimulated agricultural experimentation at multiple scales ranging from the folk to the nation-state. Second, ensuing innovation diffusion was accompanied by economic risk and environmental uncertainty. The former largely accounted for the S-shaped configuration of the logistic curve; the latter for unintended destructive environmental consequences. While preferring innovations that maintained soil fertility and ecological equilibrium, agrarian evaluation was handicapped by the long time lag for negative feedback. Lacking unequivocal evidence on the impact of their innovation, planters and farmers based their adoption decisions on either the local wisdom of practice or the extralocal wisdom of "science."

These points place innovation and environmental change in a dynamic, and more problematic, macrohistorical context. Therein, we may reconsider the historiographic myth of the southern soil miner. What emerges is a new southern planter – adaptive to economic change, attentive to problems of soil exhaustion and erosion, and contemplative of economic risk and environmental uncertainty – and a new history of the southern landscape which alternates cyclically between constructive and destructive occupance.

My reconsideration of southern environmental history examines two cases which, in retrospect, have a remarkable dramaturgical symmetry. Each begins with local agricultural experiments during a long-wave depression; each is followed at first by logistic diffusion of innovations which are profitable and environmentally constructive, and later, in ensuing bad times, by the abandonment of these innovations in favor of "scientific" reforms and, ironically, destructive occupance. As if to reinforce their historical symmetries, both of the ecologically adaptive innovations, arising out of the experience of local planters, have been grossly misunderstood and distorted by contemporaries and scholars alike.

The first case comes from the plantation tobacco economy of the colonial Chesapeake, 1680–1790. Constructive environmental innovations were introduced in the long depression of the 1680s and endured for two macrohistorical cycles. The innovation, a system of land rotation, succumbed to the "primitivist" critique of postrevolutionary agricultural reformers. The reformed system of plowing, clean tillage, continuous cultivation, and rude fertilizers hastened the destructive occupance of soil exhaustion and erosion – all of which was faithfully recorded in the travel narratives of the period.

The second case is the southern cotton belt, 1840–90. Its macroenvironmental history closely recapitulates the experience of the colonial Chesapeake. During the depressed 1840s, the vicious cycle of worn-out soils, land abandonment, and out-migration which had prevailed on the booming cotton frontier was replaced by an imaginative local innovation in agricultural practice. The new system of crop rotation cleverly combined cotton, corn, and leguminous cowpeas so as to maintain both profits and soil fertility. This agrarian system diffused throughout the cotton belt both before and after the war; it endured in some parts of the south until after the turn of the century. But in one subregion, the eastern cotton belt, the crop-rotation system was eliminated through the efforts of scientific and corporate reformers. In the long, downward slide to the depression of the 1880s, planters followed the advice of reformers and converted from crop rotation to cotton specialization and liberal fertilizer application. The economic consequences showed up first, as early as the 1880s, in debt peonage; the environmental consequences soon followed in the form of worn-out land and deeply gullied cotton fields – a scene graphically portrayed in the photographs within conservation textbooks in this century.

THE CHESAPEAKE TOBACCO ECONOMY, 1680–1790

The perfidious tobacco economy in the seventeenth-century Chesapeake provided two opportunities for agrarian experimentation and innovation. Long-wave bad times in the 1630s and 1680s drove tobacco prices so low that the viability of that economy was in question. In terms of price history, the 1630s were the worst of times. Prices fell thirty-six-fold from the levels which had prevailed in the boom times between tobacco's introduction (1612?) and the mid-1620s – when tobacco brought three shillings for a pound and ordinary men, producing five hundred pounds of tobacco each, earned seven times as much as their English counterparts. The sharp fall in prices, ceteris paribus, should have ended commercial tobacco production, but the economy was salvaged by experimentation and agricultural innovation. Although the evidence is fragmentary, we know that while prices plummeted between 1630 and 1650, tobacco output per worker tripled or quadrupled (from five hundred pounds to fifteen hundred to two thousand pounds). Tobacco scholars make a plausible case that productivity growth had its source in two innovations: topping the plant, thereby channeling plant nutrients from the seed to the leaves, and improvements in housing, curing, stripping, and packing the harvested leaf. These productivity innovations just barely compensated for the dramatic decline in tobacco price. Although the earnings differential between Chesapeake and English workers dropped from sevenfold to par, the innovations prevented a decline below par, at which point small planters would have considered return migration to England. In short, these innovations preserved the viability of the Chesapeake tobacco economy.[20]

Long-Wave Depression and the Reappraisal of Agrarian Practice

This story of bad times and agricultural experimentation was replayed in the 1680s. A steadily declining tobacco price hit bottom in the 1680s and early 1690s. The crisis triggered several creative experiments. Some planters called for propping up prices by a statutory stint on tobacco production; others wanted a more efficient, urban-based marketing system; and still others set about a thorough restructuring of the region's agricultural system.[21] The last of these won out. In a classic illustration of local innovation and diffusion, Chesapeake planters introduced a complex system which combined recyclic shifting cultivation (or land rotation), slave labor, and diversified crops (tobacco along with corn, beans, peas, and small grains). The new system was profitable as well as ecologically efficient.

The crisis of the 1680s, when tobacco prices dropped below a penny a pound, prompted a reevaluation of prevailing production practices. A visitor to Virginia in the 1680s provided a window on traditional practices and the problem of soil fertility. Planters, he observed, used a primitive crop-rotation system supplemented by animal manures. A few acres were devoted to tobacco (usually three acres per worker) and a few other acres were planted in corn. On these fields, which seem to have been continuously cultivated or at best subject to very short fallow, planters coped with declining soil fertility by "forcing the land" with animal manures. Vestiges of this simple rotation system survived until well into the eighteenth century.[22]

The traditional system, however simple, had certain advantages in a society which was labor-scarce and relied principally on servants for supplemental plantation labor. Servants were especially valuable because their land clearance contributed directly to plantation capital formation. Over the course of their four- to seven-year contracts, servants cleared a

20 Menard, "The Tobacco Industry in the Chesapeake Colonies," pp. 109–77. Edmund S. Morgan, *American Slavery, American Freedom: The Ordeal of Colonial Virginia* (New York: Norton, 1975).

21 John J. McClusker and Russell R. Menard, *The Economy of British America, 1607–1789* (Chapel Hill: University of North Carolina Press, 1985).

22 On cowpenning tobacco in the 1680s, see William Byrd to Father Hormonden, 5 June 1686, "Capt. Byrd's Letters," *Virginia Historical Register, and Literary Advertiser* 2 (1849): 81. Gray, *History of Agriculture in the Southern United States*, vol. 1, p. 217. Earle, *The Evolution of a Tidewater Settlement System*, pp. 28, 129. On the persistence of this old technology into the late 1750s, see Richard Corbin's letter cited in Aubrey C. Land, ed., *Bases of the Plantation Society* (New York: Harper & Row, 1969), pp. 140–3, 141.

modest amount of land for tobacco and corn. When the servant's term expired, planters used this fixed capital for continuous cultivation of tobacco and corn. Successful planters perhaps purchased another male servant to do the cultivation and to make additional land improvements.

This expansion path, however, became more difficult in the last quarter of the century when the supply of servants declined and their price rose. In the absence of servant labor increments and their clearance of fresh land, lands were continuously cultivated, soils wore out, and yields declined. Planters combated soil exhaustion by applying animal manures, but the ecological disadvantages of continuous cultivation were evident by the 1670s and 1680s. Yields declined in long-settled areas. Manures fouled tobacco's taste and lowered its price – an observation confirmed, by the way, through twentieth-century science. If the tobacco economy was to endure, the Chesapeake planter required an alternative and superior agronomic system.[23]

Chesapeake Land Rotation, 1680–1780

A new agrarian system emerged from the deep depression of the 1680s and 1690s, and it diffused widely in the region by 1740. This new system was something of an ethnic amalgam, as it were, borrowing elements from Indian, Afro-American, and European sources. The crux of the system was the Indian practice of shifting cultivation or land rotation; its indispensable source of labor was the perpetually bound Afro-American slave; and its integration of diversified crops imitated rudely and partially contemporary English innovation (that is, in the English case, clover, turnips, and small grains).

But then again, the Chesapeake's new agrarian system was *new* and it departed in several ways from its sources of inspiration. Although the new system mimicked Indian shifting-cultivation systems, it differed in its regular recycling of land back into production after a twenty-year or so fallow.[24] The Chesapeake system took full circle the vicious cycle of cultivation, exhaustion, abandonment, and out-migration. Instead of out-

---

23 Earle, *The Evolution of a Tidewater Settlement System*, pp. 24–30. On servant supply and prices, see David Galenson, *White Servitude in Colonial America: An Economic Analysis* (Cambridge: Cambridge University Press, 1981), pp. 134–68.

24 My conventional attribution of shifting cultivation to American Indians invites reconsideration. African slaves who provided the labor for the new system brought with them a long experience with shifting cultivation systems. Their contributions to Chesapeake agriculture may have been more substantial than is usually imagined. For slave contributions to wet rice agriculture further south, see Peter H. Wood, *Black Majority: Negroes in Colonial South Carolina from 1670 through the Stono Rebellion* (New York: Knopf, 1975).

migration, Chesapeake planters put their land in fallow and reclaimed it after sufficient time had elapsed for "natural" renovation.

The land-rotation system worked as follows. A typical worker beginning on fertile, virgin land haphazardly cleared three acres. Trees were girdled and left to die in the field, which was also littered with stumps and roots. In the first year, raw or "strong land" was planted in corn or beans or both. Tobacco followed during the next two to three years depending on the inherent fertility of the soil. In the fourth through seventh years, corn was intercropped with peas and beans and the whole cultivation cycle was finished off with a modest crop of small grains like wheat or rye. Thereafter, the worn-out parcel was abandoned to "old field" colonization. During the next two decades, a succession of grasses, shrubs, pines, and hardwoods restored soil fertility. At this point – indicated usually by second-growth forest – the renovated old fields were cleared and the cultivation cycle started anew. Under shifting cultivation, perpetual land clearance was assumed. "New" tobacco land was cleared every three or four years. (See Figure 8.4.) And as tobacco rotated onto renovated land, planters knocked down and reassembled their wooden tobacco houses nearby.[25]

The ecological genius of this land-rotation system was easily misunderstood. Eighteenth-century travelers in the tidewater Chesapeake universally misinterpreted what they saw. Unaware of the ecological functions of this mobile agrarian system, they hastily condemned the cosmetic appearance of the Chesapeake landscape – its unkempt fields littered with dying trees and stumps and hummocked by mini-excavation pits (the result of row crop "hilling"); its ragged old fields in various stages of succession; and its ramshackle tobacco houses in various states of decay. To be sure, the tobacco landscape after 1700 was not pretty, but it was highly functional in economy and ecology. Tobacco yields ceased their decline; soil fertility was maintained; erosion was retarded by the chaotic drainage system of typical tobacco fields, filled as they were with the numerous check dams of stumps, roots, hills, and pits. To borrow a cliché from the contemporary world of sports, the colonial system of shifting cultivation was "winning ugly."

The innovation of land rotation occurred concurrently with the massive introduction of slave labor into the Chesapeake. Indeed, the Chesapeake transformation from servant to slave labor was accomplished during this macrohistorical cycle. Slave proportions of the population rose from less than 5 percent in the 1670s to 30 percent or so in the first decades of the next century to nearly 50 percent by the 1740s. Meanwhile, indentured servants virtually disappeared except for employment in skilled tasks.

---

25 Earle, *The Evolution of a Tidewater Settlement System*. To my earlier arguments, I have given somewhat more emphasis to the late seventeenth-century emergence of the innovation of land rotation systems.

A) "Forcing" the Land, predominant before 1690

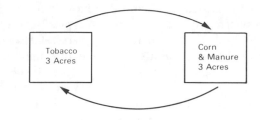

B) Land Rotation (Recycled), 1680's - 1790's

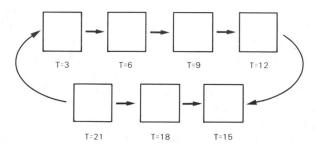

Figure 8.4. Agrarian systems in the colonial Chesapeake. (A) Continuous cultivation scheme; crops rotated on one worker's acreage. (B) One worker's acreage through time (tobacco crop); 3 acres per worker; T = time in years. Depending on the "strength" of the land, parcels were usually cultivated for 6 to 8 years before being put into fallow. Typical crop sequence on a parcel: clear-corn (1 yr.); tobacco (2–3 yr.); corn (3 yr.); wheat (1 yr.); fallow old fields (20 yr.).

Scholars have provided varying interpretations of this labor transformation. The principal arguments have focused on planter displeasure with irascible, undisciplined servants or, alternatively, relative price changes which favored slaves over servants.[26] Neither interpretation, however, is sufficient since they deal exclusively with the transformation while neglecting matters of the ongoing viability of slavery. Both issues may be addressed by examining slavery's competitive advantage in the emerging agrarian system of shifting cultivation.

The efficient functioning of Chesapeake land rotation was contingent on slavery. Perpetually bound labor was the perfect complement for an agrarian

26 Morgan, *American Slavery, American Freedom*. Russell R. Menard, "From Servants to Slaves: The Transformation of the Chesapeake Labor System," *Southern Studies* 16 (1977): 355–90. Galenson, *White Servitude in Colonial America*.

system which demanded perpetual clearance of land. In the system of land rotation, a slave cleared tobacco land as needed (usually every three to four years), and when he became "superannuated," his sons assumed the task, and then their sons. Temporary servant labor in contrast, was inadequate since land improvement continued long after the expiration of the servant's contract. This new system fundamentally redefined the meaning of land – and labor costs – in the Chesapeake. Improved land was ephemeral in status. It entered briefly into the capital stock of the plantation, and then it was "destroyed" in long fallow. The definition of land thus shifted from being a stock resource under the previous system of continuous cultivation to a flow resource under the innovation of recyclical shifting cultivation.[27]

This redefinition of land forced a revision in the planters' accounting procedures and in their labor preferences. Amortization schedules were reconfigured with adverse effects on servant labor costs. In the old system, planters amortized servant labor costs over the indefinite life of continuously cultivated, improved land; in the new system, they amortized these costs over a useful life of seven years or less – the amount of time that cleared land was in productive use before being placed in long fallow. Consequently, because of the shorter useful life of improved land, servant costs increased while slave costs remained unchanged.

Slavery's competitive advantage on the demand side received an added boost on the supply side. Relative prices for slave and servant labor moved in favor of slaves during the long-wave depression of the 1680s and 1690s. While servant prices were rising, perhaps because of the slow growth in English population as well as planter dissatisfaction with servant productivity, slave prices fell sharply. As the depression of the 1680s swept over the sugar islands in the West Indies, debt-stricken West Indian planters wholesaled their surplus slaves in an effort to make remissions on overextended credit. Many slaves were transported to the Chesapeake, where they were eagerly purchased and integrated into the emerging land-rotation system. By 1700, the Chesapeake virtually had abandoned servant labor in favor of slaves.

But supply-side explanations alone are insufficient to explain the ongoing viability of slavery, especially after 1720 when prices favored servants over slaves. What guaranteed slavery's persistence was its lower costs in the recyclical system of shifting cultivation. One might say, without risk of

---

27 The link between slavery and land rotation is strengthened by Hugh Jones' observation that tenants "forced" [manured] their lands. Lacking labor for perpetual clearing, tenants engaged in continuous cultivation practices. Hugh Jones, *Present State of Virginia, 1724* (New York: Sabin's Reprint, 1865), pp. 53–4.

exaggeration, that Chesapeake slavery was more a consequence of plantation agrarian practice than a cause of it.

The diffusion of this new agricultural system followed the logistic or
S-shaped curve. Its adoption may be observed in the diffusion of slavery, the
principal source of labor in the land-rotation system. Slaves increased from
a trivial proportion in 1680 to nearly 50 percent of the region's population
sixty years later. Diversified output followed a similar trajectory. My study
of Maryland's All Hallows Parish reports a steady increase in the frequency
of corn, peas, beans, and small grain production – crops which preceded
and succeeded tobacco on the rotating fields (see Figure 8.2). Although we
lack direct statistical evidence on the diffusion of shifting cultivation itself,
the scornful accounts of an atrophied and ugly landscape by Chesapeake
sojourners offer compelling corroboration. And finally, of course, is
evidence of worker productivity; as the land-rotation system diffused and
soil fertility was maintained, the decline in tobacco output per worker was
halted and yields edged modestly upward.[28]

The viability of recyclic shifting cultivation is attested by its survival
through two macrohistorical cycles (1680–1740, 1740–80). Despite the fall
of tobacco prices to historic lows in the long-wave depression of the 1740s,
Chesapeake planters preserved the land-rotation system. But they also
directed their experimentation toward other components of the tobacco
economy, most notably the policy innovation of a tobacco-inspection
system aimed at improving tobacco's quality and its price.

Agrarian Reform and Destructive Occupance in the Chesapeake, 1780–1840

The land-rotation system, however, did not survive into the third macrohistorical cycle that began in the 1780s. The system came under withering
attack in the postrevolutionary depression. Agrarian reformers, motivated
by hard times, population pressure, and nationalist sentiment (Americans
were acutely sensitive to European critiques of the American landscape, as
Jefferson's *Notes on Virginia* attest), discredited "primitive" agricultural
methods and advocated their abandonment in favor of modern, "high
farming" systems. The intensification arguments of John Beale Bordley,

---

28 Earle, *The Evolution of a Tidewater Settlement System.* Edward C. Papenfuse, Jr., "Planter
Behavior and Economic Opportunity in a Staple Economy," *Agricultural History* 46
(1972): 297–311. Henry M. Miller, "Transforming a 'Splendid and Delightsome Land':
Colonists and Ecological Change in the Chesapeake, 1607–1820," *Journal of the
Washington Academy of Science* 76 (1986): 173–87.

John Taylor of Caroline, and others were persuasive in full or in part. Chesapeake agriculture was transformed. Plows rapidly replaced hoe-and-ax cultivation; fields were put in good order as stumps and other rubbish were removed from them; and a more continuous system of cultivation, using fertilizers such as plaster of paris and animal manures, displaced the "primitive" land-rotation system. Improving planters thus imposed order on an unkempt, unruly landscape.[29]

The tragedy of these Enlightenment-inspired agricultural reforms is that they unleashed an epoch of devastating destructive occupance in the tobacco economy of the upper South. Clean-tilled fields accelerated erosion. Erosion stripped away vital plant nutrients and hastened soil exhuastion. Sediment flowed into Chesapeake streams, creeks, and estuaries, clogging them up and disrupting navigation. The twin evils of erosion and exhaustion forced many planters into the vicious cycle: selling off their depleted tidewater plantations and migrating west to fresh lands in the Piedmont. But there, owing to the Piedmont's steeper slopes, destructive occupance proceeded with even more intensity.[30]

For some time students of Chesapeake history have had their suspicions about the ecological abuses of agrarian reform. New physical evidence seemingly clinches the case. Recent studies of sediment cores from Chesapeake estuaries document sharp increases in the rates of sedimentation and pollen accumulation in the late eighteenth and early nineteenth centuries. Annual rates of sediment accumulation rose two- to twenty-fold over rates prevailing during the colonial period when the ecologically adaptive system of land rotation was in place. This dramatic rise in sedimentation, as well as in port and navigation siltation, was the consequence of new agricultural practices introduced in the long-wave depression of the 1780s and 1790s and diffused in the ensuing logistic.[31]

29 For a balanced view of agrarian reform, see Curtis P. Nettels, *The Emergence of a National Economy, 1775–1815* (New York: Harper & Row, 1962), pp. 243–51, and sources therein. That reformers successfully converted "rank-and-file" farmers and planters is illustrated, e.g., by the diffusion of plows almost to the bottom of the agricultural ladder in an area relatively isolated from reformist activities. Among tenants in Charles County (southern), Maryland, plows increased from 21 percent of inventories households before 1776 to 73 percent by 1820. Lorena S. Walsh, "Land, Landlord, and Leaseholder: Estate Management in Southern Maryland, 1642–1820," *Agricultural History* 59 (1985): 373–96, 385.

30 Miller, "Transforming a 'Splendid and Delightsome Land,'" pp. 173–87. In addition, a good deal of evidence on the destructive occupance from agrarian reform is unknowingly supplied by proponents of the "soil miner" thesis. Craven, *Soil Exhaustion as a Factor in the Agricultural History of Virginia and Maryland;* and Louis C. Gottschalk, "Effects of Soil Erosion on Navigation in Upper Chesapeake Bay," *Geographical Review* 35 (1945): 219–38.

31 Grace S. Brush, "Geology and Paleoecology of Chesapeake Bay: A Long-term Monitoring Tool for Management," *Journal of the Washington Academy of Science* 76 (1986): 146–60.

Coda

By the end of this macrohistorical cycle, circa 1840, the Chesapeake tobacco economy had sunk into an impoverished state. Although the depression stimulated a new round of agricultural reformers, including Edmund Ruffin, their attempt to reverse the vicious cycle was unsuccessful. The region was beyond agricultural and environmental salvation. Consequently, the most popular depression-experimentations dealt not with agronomic practice but rather with radical political economy. These radical ideologies confronted an almost overwhelming set of regional problems – worn-out and worn-down land; poverty; a dual economy of poor whites and threadbare planter elites; and a bewildering mix of plantation slaves, hired slaves, and free Negroes created by slave owners trying to cut costs by manumitting or hiring out slaves. Ideological experimentation led at one extreme to George Fitzhugh's prescription of a paternal, feudal order. He advocated enslaving all men, black and white, under the authority of a natural planter elite. At the opposite, though equally radical, extreme, Hinton Rowan Helper blamed the poor whites' problems on slavery. His racist tract urged the immediate removal of all blacks from the region and the nation. Such were the twisted and deformed ideologies which emerged from the tobacco South following one long cycle of extremely destructive environmental occupance.[32]

In retrospect, Enlightenment agrarian reform in the upper South eliminated an ugly landscape in exchange for the ugliest set of regional ideologies that this nation has yet created. The region and the nation might have been better served by the persistence of the "primitive" colonial system of land rotation. That adaptive ecological system, though dependent on slave labor, had at least the redeeming values of maintaining soil fertility and retarding soil erosion. Ironically, the system's success proved to be its undoing. This "primitive" agronomic system was the point of departure for an enlightened, republican ideology – an ideology embarrassed by landscape appearances, dedicated to agrarian reform, and, in retrospect, implicated in the ascent of the southern soil miner.[33]

---

32 On Fitzhugh, see his writings and their interpretation (to which I demur) by Eugene D. Genovese, *The World the Slaveholders Made: Two Essays in Interpretation* (New York: Random House, 1969), pp. 118–224. See also Hinton Rowan Helper, *Compendium of the Impending Crisis of the South* (New York, 1860).

33 Morgan has pointed out the irony of republican ideology arising out of slavery; the irony is deeper still since slavery is contingent on agrarian systems, and agrarian systems on ideology. To oversimplify the causal chain, land rotation led to slavery which led to republican ideology which led to reform in agrarian practice which led to the twisted racist and quasi-feudal ideologies of Helper and Fitzhugh, respectively. At some point herein,

The Myth of the Southern Soil Miner

THE SOUTHERN COTTON BELT, 1840–1890

The erosional cycle (1780–1840) that plagued the upper South also swept across the emerging cotton belt. Following the invention of the cotton gin, a sharp rise in cotton prices ignited a half century of destructive occupance. The vicious cycle of clearing, planting, abandoning, and migrating to virgin frontier lands was extended from coastal Georgia and South Carolina to the Mississippi. The legendary profits from cotton made planters oblivious to the landscape they left in their wake. In this macrohistorical cycle, the myth and the reality of the southern soil miner were one.[34]

Crop Rotation in the Antebellum Cotton Belt

The collapse of cotton prices during the 1830s and 1840s put a stop to headlong expansion and destructive occupance. A new round of agrarian reflection and experimentation commenced. Potential solutions for cotton's problems proliferated. Ideas ranged from regional cooperative controls on supply to railroad building, and from economic diversification to applications of Peruvian guano.[35] Although these solutions cluttered the pages of the popular press, the innovations having the most far-reaching impact began without fanfare in local experiments with crop-rotation systems. As is the case with most local innovation, publicity is meager and documentation is scarce. Geographic origins are particularly difficult to pin down, but the fragmentary evidence points toward planters in northern and central Mississippi and Alabama. Perhaps aware of the discovery in 1838 that leguminous plants fixed nitrogen from the air, cotton planters devised a crop rotation system which combined the cotton staple with corn and soil-renovating leguminous cowpeas.[36]

This diversified agrarian system, which replaced staple monoculture and its vicious cycle, was organized as follows. Each planter or slave was allocated, on average, eighteen acres for row-crop production. This relatively fixed amount of land was determined by the slow rates of row-crop

---

when unsuspected opposites became the expected, irony ended and dialectics began. Morgan, *American Slavery, American Freedom*.

34 The most eloquent statement remains W. J. Cash, *The Mind of the South* (New York: Knopf, 1941).

35 Genovese, *The Political Economy of Slavery*; Harold Woodman, *King Cotton and His Retainers* (Lexington: University of Kentucky Press, 1968).

36 Here and below, see sources cited in Earle, "Tillage Capacity and Soil Maintenance in the Nineteenth-Century Cotton South."

tillage and the short two-month cultivation period each spring. Under the old monocultural system, virtually all of the eighteen acres went into cotton; but under the new system, best practice called for twelve acres in cotton, six in corn intercropped in July with leguminous cowpeas. As cotton depleted the soil of plant nutrients, especially nitrogen – usually after two years – cotton land was rotated into fields renovated by nitrogen-fixing cowpeas intercropped with corn. The latter crops gave an added twist to the new system – its integration of swine raising and pork production. Following the corn harvest, planters put their hogs upon the corn fields where they mowed down the cowpeas, vines, and corn stalks.[37]

The rotational sequence was slightly more complicated than might initially appear (see Figure 8.5). The planter divided the eighteen acres into three equal parcels. One parcel of newly renovated land was planted in cotton; a second was planted in cotton for a second straight year; and the third, following two years in cotton, was renovated with corn and cowpeas. In the succeeding year, parcel one continued in cotton for one more year; parcel two rotated into corn-cowpeas for one year; and parcel three was planted with cotton for two years. And so on.

This tight crop-rotation scheme accomplished four plantation objectives: Soil fertility was maintained; profits equaled or exceeded cotton monoculture; corn met most of the plantation's grain subsistence needs; and swine, fed on corn stalks and cowpea vines, satisfied most of the pork needs. Given these virtues, this local innovation of a cotton-corn-cowpeas rotation diffused rapidly.

The new agrarian system seems to have spread widely throughout the antebellum South during the 1840s and 1850s. Literary evidence and plantation account books document a cotton-belt consensus on the best-practice ratio of two units of cotton land to one of corn – and cowpeas. Although the ratio varies in accordance with local soils (fertile soils had higher ratios), rainfall, and tillage implements (mules and plows versus hoes), these variances all fall within a narrow range, for example, 9:5; 10:5; 11:6. Census figures provide further confirmation of diffusion during the 1850s. These report an increasing output of corn and hogs from the cotton belt relative to areas which had traditionally supplied these subsistence commodities. The new crop-rotation system thus had the simultaneous effect of providing the bulk of regional subsistence needs while reducing cotton-belt dependence on provisions from the upper South (Kentucky and Tennessee) and the Midwest.[38]

37 The best guides to this agrarian system are John Hebron Moore, *Agriculture in Antebellum Mississippi* (New York, 1971), pp. 59–60, 123–7; Sam B. Hilliard, *Hog Meat and Hoe Cake: Food Supply in the Old South* (Carbondale: Southern Illinois University Press, 1972).

38 Genovese writes that the only rotation practiced on a large scale was that of cotton and

The Myth of the Southern Soil Miner

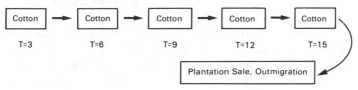

A) The "Vicious Cycle" of Shifting Cultivation, 1790's - 1840's

| Cotton | → | Cotton | → | Cotton | → | Cotton | → | Cotton |

T=3   T=6   T=9   T=12   T=15

Plantation Sale, Outmigration

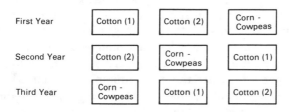

B) Cotton-Corn-Cowpeas Crop Rotation, 1840's - ca. 1900

First Year	Cotton (1)	Cotton (2)	Corn - Cowpeas
Second Year	Cotton (2)	Corn - Cowpeas	Cotton (1)
Third Year	Corn - Cowpeas	Cotton (1)	Cotton (2)

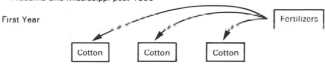

C) Cotton Monoculture and Fertilizers, Eastern Cotton Belt post-1870; Alabama and Mississippi post-1890

First Year

Fertilizers

Cotton   Cotton   Cotton

Second Year ... Tn

Figure 8.5. Agrarian systems in the cotton belt. (A) One worker's acreage capacity = 12 to 18 acres; T = time in years. (B) Total acreage for one worker = 18 acres divided into 3 parcels of 6 acres; numbers in parentheses refer to the number of years cotton had been planted on a particular parcel. (C) Total acreage for one worker = 18 acres; continuous cultivation in cotton.

Perhaps the most dramatic example of the interregional impact of the new plantation economy comes from Cincinnati. As late as the 1840s and early 1850s, that city shipped most of its provisions trade downriver; by 1857, virtually everything was dispatched upriver to Pittsburgh or Wheeling. While eastern railroads contributed to the reorientation of Cincinnati's

corn, and even an enlightened planter such as M. W. Philips generally ignored legumes (*The Political Economy of Slavery*, p. 97). But here is the said Philips speaking in 1846: "I plant thin land two years in corn and cowpeas and one in cotton and feel well-assured that with peas I improve my land" (*Southern Cultivator* 4 (1846): 78–9). On good land, Philips switched the ratio to the more usual two in cotton to one in corn – doubtless intercropped with cowpeas.

trade, their role was necessary but not sufficient. Two decades of cotton-belt crop rotation and attendant crop diversification had nearly eliminated Cincinnati's traditional southern market for provisions. Corn and hog farmers in Kentucky and Tennessee also felt the squeeze. This new agrarian system thus hastened the disengagement of southern and midwestern trade – a disengagement with portentous sectional overtones on the eve of the American Civil War.[39]

The subtlety and intelligence of antebellum crop rotation has been regrettably overlooked by students of southern history. The leading geographer of the southern environment assumes that agricultural practices were unchanging. In his view, soil destruction accelerated in conjunction with slavery, cotton production, and the "land-killing technology" of use, exhaustion, and abandonment.[40] More appreciative of the fundamental change in southern agriculture are the new economic historians, but even they have been baffled by unanticipated plantation diversification during a period of rapidly rising prices. Their best-known examination of crop choice seriously misinterprets the reasons for planting corn along with cotton.[41] According to this thesis, planters fearful of the cotton market and staple specialization behaved in peasantlike fashion. They averted market risk, provided for subsistence first, and treated cotton as a production residual after corn and pork needs had been met. Although the argument is new, its portrayal of southern planters is stereotypic. Planters take the role of passive reactants to a world market beyond their control; ignored are their contributions to one of the South's most brilliant agrarian innovations.

Both geographers and economic historians have missed the main point of diversified production, namely that corn, swine, and cowpeas were integral elements in a radically new agrarian system – one which was at once ecologically and economically superior to its predecessor. As I have suggested above and document elsewhere, diversification sprang not from fear of the market, but rather from a conjuncture of capitalist motive, environmental sensitivity, and local innovation during the macrohistorical depression of the 1830s and 1840s.

39 Carville Earle, "Regional Development West of the Appalachians, 1815–1860," in *North America: The Historical Geography of a Changing Continent,* ed. Robert D. Mitchell and Paul A. Groves (Totowa, N.J.: Rowman and Littlefield, 1987), pp. 172–97. Sam Bowers Hilliard, *Atlas of Antebellum Southern Agriculture* (Baton Rouge: Louisiana State University Press, 1984), pp. 47, 49, 50, 64–7, 73.

40 Trimble, "Perspectives on the History of Soil Erosion Control," pp. 162–80; and his *Man-Induced Soil Erosion on the Southern Piedmont, 1700–1970* (Ankeny, Iowa: Soil Conservation Service of America, 1974).

41 Gavin Wright, *The Political Economy of the Cotton South* (New York: Norton, 1978).

The Myth of the Southern Soil Miner

A New Agrarian System: Fertilizer and Cotton Specialization in the Postbellum Eastern Cotton Belt

The innovation of a cotton-corn-cowpeas crop rotation survived the Civil War and persisted, with one subregional exception, partway into the next macrohistorical cycle (that is, 1880–1930). The exception was the eastern cotton-belt states of Georgia and South Carolina wherein planters adopted a new cropping system with fateful environmental consequences. During the long depression of the late nineteenth century, eastern cotton planters abandoned the cotton-corn-cowpeas rotation in favor of higher profits from cotton specialization and intensive fertilizer application. In this system, soil fertility was maintained by commercial fertilizers instead of the botanic solution of a cowpeas rotation. Agrarian reformers and "the testimony of science" were mobilized in behalf of the new system. State scientists and the agents of fertilizer companies recommended highly the adoption of mono-culture and fertilizers. The new system revolutionized the region's agrarian economy and environment in five ways: first, cotton specialization expanded rapidly; second, market dependency for provisions of corn and pork increased as diversified output was abandoned; third, following an early spike, cotton yields and profits experienced a long decline; fourth, as profits declined, credit dependency, crop liens, and debt peonage ensued; and fifth, soil exhaustion and soil erosion were accelerated by deficient fertilizers and perennially exposed soils, respectively. A regional tragedy of destructive social and environmental occupance was about to unfold.[42]

The victory of cotton and fertilizers depended on a particular conjuncture in time and space, in macrohistorical cycles and mesoregional conditions – all boosted along by well-intentioned scientific reformers. With respect to time, the so-called Guano Craze that swept Georgia and South Carolina in the 1870s and 1880s coincided with the long-wave decline in cotton prices. By now it should be evident that the onset of bad times increased the propensity for agrarian experimentation and the predisposition to innovation adoption. With respect to space, the specific innovation – cotton specialization and fertilizer – was contingent upon mesoregional economic and environmental factors. Two were significant in localizing innovation diffusion to the eastern cotton belt. First was the spatial economic factor of relatively low-cost fertilizers. Fertilizer in Georgia, for example, was twelve to fifteen dollars cheaper per ton than it was further west. Proximity to phosphate rock mines opened in 1868 in coastal South Carolina and the

---

42 My attention was first alerted to the peculiar agrarian changes in the eastern cotton belt by Peter Temin, "Patterns of Cotton Agriculture in Post-Bellum Georgia," *Journal of Economic History* 43 (1983): 661–74.

manure manufacturers clustered around this basic raw material meant lower fertilizer prices for the eastern cotton belt.[43] Second was the ecological factor of fertilizer efficiency: The region's heavier spring rains which hastened chemical activation of fertilizers combined with a natural soil deficiency in phosphorous assured maximum improvements in yields when phosphorous-rich fertilizers were applied. When scientists reported that fertilizers improved cotton yields by anywhere from 25 to 60 percent, the brief for adoption of the new system was complete and ineluctable.[44]

The misnomered Guano Craze ensued. But what initially seemed a foolproof, riskless agrarian system devolved swiftly into economic and ecological crisis. The mysteries of soil chemistry and fertilizer-plant exchange had eluded planter and scientist alike. Although phosphorous-rich fertilizers produced an initial spike in cotton yields, these declined after a few years of continuous cultivation. Fertilizer deficiencies in nitrogen – the most important plant nutrient for cotton – took their toll.[45] Planters, tenants, and croppers responded by applying even more of the deficient fertilizer; debts spiraled out of control. To service their mounting debts, planters attached liens to their cotton crops, which locked them into cotton monoculture. Or put another way, the cotton liens prevented them from abandoning monoculture and reverting to the old crop rotation of cotton-corn-cowpeas.

L. W. Jarman, a local witness to the devastation wrought by fertilizer and monoculture, summarized the situation so perceptively and so plaintively that his words deserve full quotation.

Who said fertilizer? Well, that's just it. Every farmer says it, every tenant says it, every merchant says it, and even the bankers must speak of it at times. . . . The trouble is that in times past the easy purchase and use of fertilizer has seemed to many of our Southern farmers a short cut to prosperity, a royal road to good crops of cotton year after year. The result has been that their lands have been cultivated clean year after year, their fertility has been exhausted, . . . their soils have largely

43 Wines, *Fertilizer in America,* pp. 112–61, and sources therein.
44 Earle, "Tillage Capacity and Soil Maintenance in the Nineteenth-Century Cotton South." For scientific claims on fertilizer's effects on yields, see David F. Weiman, "The Economic Emancipation of the Non-Slaveholding Class: Up-Country Farmers in the Georgia Cotton Economy," *Journal of Economic History* 45 (1985): 71–93.
45 Cotton is not an especially exhaustive crop, but soils do require nitrogen replacement either through legumes or nitrogen-enriched fertilizers. B. A. Waddle, "Crop Growing Practices," in R. J. Kohel and C. F. Lewis, eds., *Cotton,* No. 24 Agronomy Series (Madison, Wisconsin: American Society of Agronomy, Crop Science Society of America, and Soil Science Society of America, 1984), pp. 233–63, 244. Contemporary critics of excessive fertilizer usage, nonetheless, described approvingly fertilizer mixes overloaded with phosphorous relative to nitrogen. Charles W. Burkett and Clarence H. Poe, *Cotton: Its Cultivation, Marketing, Manufacture, and the Problems of the Cotton World* (New York: Doubleday, Page & Co., 1906), pp. 109–46.

washed away, and much land that formerly would make good crops without fertilizer now makes but poor returns with fertilization. . . . [Fertilizers] have caused them to fall into a system of all cotton farming that looked alone to present gain, and not to the improvement of the soil. To say the least of it, the use of commercial fertilizer has not been an unmixed blessing to the Southern farmer. Like all other good things, it can be abused. It has enriched thousands of good farmers . . . on the other hand, it has caused thousands of poor farmers to fall into a system of farming that impoverished them and their lands as well.[46]

By the 1890s, debt peonage was diffusing in the wake of the new agricultural system. Moreover, the signs of destructive occupance spread beyond the region into Alabama and Mississippi.[47] In Georgia and South Carolina, meanwhile, years of deficient fertilizer application and cotton monoculture had worn out the land. Erosion made matters worse. Unlike the old crop-rotation system, with its periodic respite to erosion when fields were intercropped with corn and cowpeas, the clean-tilled fields of Georgia and South Carolina were subject to constant soil wash, stripping, rilling, and gullying. Descriptions of erosion and sedimentation in the Georgia piedmont suddenly became commonplace in the 1880s and the worst effects were associated with planters rather than croppers and tenants.[48] Compounding the regional erosion problem were spring rains 10 to 20 percent higher than those of the western cotton belt in the 1870s. The eastern cotton belt thus provided textbook horror stories for the conservationists who wrote during the downswing of the 1880–1930 macrohistorical cycle – and

46 L. W. Jarman, "About Fertilizers," in *Southern Crops: As Grown and Described by Successful Farmers and Published from Time to Time in the Southern Cultivator*, comp. G. F. Hunnicutt (Atlanta: The Cultivator Publishing Co., 1911), pp. 370–3. Agricultural chemists strenuously debated the scientific methods and results of fertilizer analyses. State chemists tended to the farmer; industry chemists, the firm. On this interesting controversy that reveals a Kuhnian view of science, see Alan I. Marcus, "Setting the Standard: Fertilizers, State Chemists, and Early National Commercial Regulation, 1880–87," *Agricultural History* 61 (1987): 47–73.
47 On the westward diffusion of fertilizer by 1900 – probably accompanying the opening of phosphate mines in Tennessee – see Roger L. Ransom and Richard Sutch, *One Kind of Freedom: The Economic Consequences of Emancipation* (Cambridge: Cambridge University Press, 1977), pp. 188–9. I of course disagree with their view that fertilizers were a mild palliative to crushing merchant exploitation; nor do I share Gavin Wright's position that war debts were the cause of debt peonage; planter abandonment of crop rotation and the overzealous acquisition of fertilizers for monoculture are sufficient. Gavin Wright, *Old South, New South: Revolution in the Southern Economy since the Civil War* (New York: Basic Books, 1986), pp. 30–1, 107–15.
48 Stanley W. Trimble's master's thesis carefully demonstrates the lack of destructive occupance in the Georgia Piedmont before the 1880s; and after large-scale soil erosion commenced, it was dissociated from areas of tenancy – evidence he seems to have overlooked in his later writings. "Culturally Accelerated Sedimentation on the Middle Georgia Piedmont" (Master's Thesis, Geography, University of Georgia, 1969).

who, while discrediting past agrarian practice, gave rise to the myth of the southern soil miner.

SOUTHERN ENVIRONMENTAL HISTORY IN MACROHISTORICAL CONTEXT

Neither history nor environmental history is linear. Conversely, that is not to say that history is everywhere and always recurrent, for it may just as easily consist of short random bursts up and down or steplike ascents and descents. Whatever the historical tempo appropriate to specific times and places, environmental history benefits from a keen sensitivity to changing economic and social conditions. In the case of the southern soil miner, the linear myth of three centuries of destructive occupance ceases to be problematic. The myth's unilinearity eliminates most of what is interesting about past human behavior. The presumption that ten generations of southerners committed one environmental blunder after another obscures their environmental acuity and sensitivity as well as their ignorance and naïveté.

The story of southern environmental history, therefore, is much richer than is usually allowed by regional historiography. It is full of irony, uncertainty, experimentation, and paradox (for example, the contrasting environmental achievements of practical and "scientific" innovations). One means of re-creating the wit and folly of southern environmental history, though not the only means to be sure, is to structure that experience within the paradigm of macrohistorical rhythms in the American past. Although these forty-five- to sixty-year rhythms are controversial (much less so today than a decade ago) and their dating is approximate, their macrostructure has the heuristic virtue of helping synthesize an array of otherwise disparate evidence and argument. These long rhythms simplify the complexity of the American past and differentiate good economic times from bad ones, and , periods of creative experimentation and innovation from those of routine diffusion. The macrohistorical paradigm offers a refreshing perspective on southern environmental history, but the merits of its reinterpretation remain to be judged. A succinct summary of that reinterpretation seems a fitting way of closing this essay.

Viewed from the perspective of macrohistory, our survey of three centuries of southern environmental history identifies two symmetrical cycles of local innovation and constructive occupance followed by cycles of scientific reform and destructive occupance. The constructive phases were initiated in cyclical bad times (the 1680s and 1840s). In the ensuing cycle, agrarian innovations that emerged from depression experimenting diffused in accordance with the S-shaped logistic curve. As proof of the economic and ecological viability of local innovations based on practice, they endured through two entire cycles until succumbing finally to the depression innovations of scientific reform.

More specifically, these cycles of constructive landscape occupance occurred in the colonial Chesapeake (1680–1790) and in the nineteenth-century cotton belt (1840–1930). Both of these long epochs of benign environmental impact were initiated by folk agricultural innovation and diffusion. Although the macrohistorical structure of these two cases is identical, the particular sets of innovations were distinctive to the regions. The colonial tobacco planters devised a system of land rotation; the cotton planters, in contrast, established a system of crop rotation. In the Chesapeake, tobacco planters maintained soil fertility through an intricate system that integrated shifting cultivation, slavery, and crop diversification. Renovating their worn-out fields through natural ecological succession, planters later recycled these old fields back into tobacco production. Equally subtle and creative were the folk innovations of antebellum cotton planters. Their crop-rotation system restored soil fertility by rotating cotton with corn intercropped with nitrogen-fixing cowpeas. Corn and pork were profitable by-products of this complex agricultural system. In both of our cases, soil fertility was maintained and the vicious cycle of land abandonment was broken. Erosion too seems to have been retarded, though perhaps more effectively in the chaotic fields of the colonial Chesapeake. And in both times and places, the notion of a southern soil miner is an unfounded myth.

The myth has foundation however in the macrohistorical cycles which succeeded the constructive occupance just described. From the standpoint of the southern environment, the most destructive agricultural innovations emerged from scientific agrarian reform innovations in macrohistorical depressions circa the 1790s in the Chesapeake and circa the 1870s and 1880s in the eastern cotton belt. In the former, advocates of "high farming" damned as primitive the prevailing system of land rotation. In its place, they helped install an environmentally destructive system of clean tillage, plowing, and limestone-based fertilizers. The erosional consequences were severe. A similar story unfolded in the eastern cotton belt a century later. Scientists and fertilizer companies argued persuasively in behalf of the diffusion of cotton specialization linked with fertilizers. Neither they nor the adopting planters perceived the nitrogen deficiencies in these fertilizers, nor the devastating economic (debt peonage) and ecological (worn-out soils, eroded lands, and falling yields) consequences of using them. In these sad times, the myth and the reality of the southern soil miner were one and the same.

The great paradox of southern environmental history is, of course, that practical wisdom was invariably superior to science as a guide to the future environmental consequences of agricultural innovation. The southern soil miner, then, was the progeny not of plantation economy and slavery (nor their legacies), but of premature epistemologies of scientific agrarian reform. Fortunately, these destructive cycles of occupance did not last. In succeeding cycles, when the practical wisdom of local experience prevailed, the environmental impacts of southern agrarian innovation were benign. And given these cyclical changes in the region's exploitation of the landscape, what then remains of the myth of the southern soil miner? It is in truth a semimyth, the reality of which is always contingent on proper specification in time and space.

9 Toward an Interactive Theory of Nature and Culture: Ecology, Production, and Cognition in the California Fishing Industry

Arthur F. McEvoy

ONE OF THE GREAT MYTHIC CASES in the history of Anglo-American property law is that of *Pierson v. Post,* which reached the New York Supreme Court of Judicature in 1805.[1] This was a contest between competing fox hunters. Post, the plaintiff at trial, had flushed his prey and was about to shoot it when Pierson came along, killed the animal, and carried it off. The question presented to the justices on appeal, then, was when a wild animal became somebody's property: Did Post own the fox once he invested his labor in the chase, or did it remain in a "state of nature" until someone (Pierson, in this case) took actual possession of it?

The court found for the usurper Pierson. The majority reasoned that finding a "capture rule" – where property rights in a previously unowned resource came into being at the moment of possession, not before – would cut down on future litigation by providing a clear standard for hunters to follow. A capture rule would, moreover, encourage competition and economic growth by rewarding hunters who took their game more cleanly and efficiently than their rivals. The dissent, on the other hand, argued that Post had invested his labor in the chase and ought not to be robbed of the

An earlier version of this paper was presented at the Conference in World Environmental History held at Duke University, 30 April–2 May 1987, as a synopsis of research published in Arthur F. McEvoy, *The Fisherman's Problem: Ecology and Law in the California Fisheries, 1850–1980,* Studies in Environment and History (Cambridge: Cambridge University Press, 1986). I am grateful to Elizabeth Bird, William Cronon, Barbara Leibhardt, Carolyn Merchant, Richard White, and Donald Worster for their comments and suggestions.
1 *Pierson v. Post,* 3 Cai. R. 175, 2 Am. Dec. 264 (N.Y. Sup. Ct. 1805).

fruits thereof. Rewarding claim jumpers like Pierson, indeed, might even discourage people from hunting in the first place.

Pierson v. Post is a famous decision because of its mythic quality: It offers a nicely distilled picture of how property rights come into being. A valuable resource was up for grabs; a dispute between would-be takers forced a court to lay down a rule that would allow business to proceed efficiently and equitably.[2] Inasmuch as property rights constitute the basic structure of natural resource use in common-law countries like the United States, moreover, the case offers a look at a broader issue – how judges at the time understood the relationships between law, economic enterprise, and the natural environment.[3]

That understanding, of course, was a product of the justices' time, culture, experience, and ambitions: A modern reader, for example, might find the opinions strange because none of the justices seems to have given much thought to the fox. "Poor Renard," as the dissent called it, was of no particular concern in and of itself. Foxes were, rather, part of the environment in which the dispute arose: They were at best a source of income for Pierson and Post and at worst a menace to local henhouses and the sooner the state was rid of them all, the better. Nobody at the time thought that "poor Renard" might perform some ecological purpose such as controlling rats or gophers, or indeed that there might someday be money in sustaining a supply of the animals for the benefit of furriers or well-to-do hunting clubs.

Most people in the nineteenth-century United States approached natural

2 For an interpretation of the origin of property rights along these lines, see Harold Demsetz, "Toward a Theory of Property Rights," *American Economic Review* 57 (Papers and Proceedings, 1967): 347–57. Carol Rose offers another interpretation, which emphasizes possession as an act of communication between people, in "Possession as the Origin of Property," *University of Chicago Law Review* 52 (1985): 73–88.

3 Treating legal materials as "texts" in this way and subjecting them to literary interpretation is common to a branch of legal scholarship known as critical legal studies. For introductions to this method of study, see Roberto Mangabiera Unger, "The Critical Legal Studies Movement," *Harvard Law Review* 96 (1983): 563–675; David Kairys, ed., *The Politics of Law: A Progressive Critique* (New York: Pantheon, 1982); and Robert W. Gordon, "Critical Legal Histories," *Stanford Law Review* 36 (1984): 57–126. Such scholars frequently draw inspiration from the work of the anthropologist Clifford Geertz. See Geertz, "Ideology as a Cultural System," in *The Interpretation of Cultures: Selected Essays,* ed. Geertz (New York: Basic, 1973), pp. 193–233.

The basic text for U.S. legal history is Lawrence M. Friedman, *A History of American Law,* 2d ed. (New York: Simon & Schuster, 1985). For the history of economic regulation in particular, see J. Willard Hurst, *Law and Markets in United States History: Different Modes of Bargaining among Interests* (Madison: University of Wisconsin Press, 1982). For an introduction to the literature, see Robert W. Gordon, "J. Willard Hurst and the Common Law Tradition in American Legal Historiography," *Law and Society Review* 10 (1975): 9–56; and Harry N. Scheiber, "Public Economic Policy and the American Legal System: Historical Perspectives," *Wisconsin Law Review* 1 (1980): 159–90.

resource problems in much the same way as did the court in *Pierson v. Post;* the opinions of the judges in that case are of particular interest because such people had power to structure social relations according to their particular views of the world and thus to guide behavior in many areas of public and private life.[4] At the core of their understanding, then, was a radical division between the human world and the natural world. In the early nineteenth-century United States the main task at hand, for private citizens and public officials alike, was to get the new nation's economy rolling. There was so much unexploited natural wealth to be had, relative to short supplies of capital and labor, that abundant resources were taken as a fact of life, one of the given conditions that made up the environment in which entrepreneurs and lawmakers went about their businesses.[5] To call something "natural" meant to divide the world into that which was human and that which was not and to place the naturalized thing, cognitively, into the realm of things to be contemplated, loathed, or turned into a dollar, but in no case thought of as active participants in human affairs.[6] Understanding the problem in that way, of course, had profound ecological consequences: Foxes soon became quite rare, as did passenger pigeons, buffalo, whales, and a great many other wildlife resources over the course of the nineteenth century.[7]

A more recent addition to the mythology of resource use is "The Tragedy of the Commons," a kind of heuristic fable that takes its name from an

---

4 Morton Horwitz described how early nineteenth-century legal elites imposed their social thought on the rest of the nation in *The Transformation of American Law, 1790–1860* (Cambridge, Mass.: Harvard University Press, 1977).

5 See J. Willard Hurst, "The Release of Energy," in *Law and the Conditions of Freedom in the Nineteenth-Century United States* (Madison: University of Wisconsin Press, 1956), pp. 3–31.

6 On the division between systems under study and their environment, see Arnold M. Schultz, "The Ecosystem as a Conceptual Tool in the Management of Natural Resources," in *Natural Resources: Quality and Quantity,* ed. S. V. Ciriacy-Wantrup and James J. Parsons (Berkeley and Los Angeles: University of California Press, 1967), pp. 139–61, pp. 139, 147.
   Poverty, for example, was until the late nineteenth century something that belonged in this outer realm. It was not until the economy was fully industrialized that people began to find social causes and programmatic cures for it. For an excellent discussion of this change in view, see Calvin Woodard, "Reality and Social Reform: The Transition from Laissez-Faire to the Welfare State," *Yale Law Journal* 72 (1962): 286–328.
   On the alienation of humankind from nature, see Roderick Nash, *Wilderness and the American Mind,* 3d ed. (New Haven, Conn.: Yale University Press, 1982), which analyzes the dichotomy in United States intellectual history without calling it into question. See also Lynn White, Jr., "The Historical Roots of our Ecologic Crisis," *Science* 155 (10 March 1967): 1,203–7, which finds the dichotomy fundamental to Judeo-Christian culture.

7 On the development of U.S. wildlife law, see Michael S. Bean, *The Evolution of National Wildlife Law,* rev ed. (New York: Praeger, 1983); and James A. Tober, *Who Owns the Wildlife? The Political Economy of Conservation in Nineteenth-Century America,* Contributions in Economics and Economic History, no. 37 (Westport, Conn.: Greenwood, 1981).

article published by the biologist Garrett Hardin in 1968.[8] Hardin's tale concerned a group of competing farmers grazing cattle on a common pasture. What was tragic was that each farmer found it more profitable to graze more cows than the pasture could support in the long run because each took all the profit from her extra cows but bore only her pro rata share of the cost of destroying the pasture. Economic rationality thus drove the farmers to the irrational result of ruining their pasture and ultimately their own livelihoods.

As Hardin saw it, annihilation was thus the inevitable fate of resources that were shared in common by competing users. The model applied, he thought, not only to common pastures but also to national parks, to clean air and water, and ultimately to the planet's capacity to sustain the ever-increasing numbers of new people that individual families bring into the world. So powerful a heuristic was the commons tragedy that through the 1960s and 1970s it supplied the framework in which most economists, lawyers, scientists, and environmentalists understood natural resource issues. Just as *Pierson v. Post* is a myth that explains the emergence of property rights, then, the commons tragedy is a model in narrative form for the genesis and essence of environmental problems.

A key source of a model's authority – its power to organize our view of the world – is its (usually implicit) claim to universality and ahistoricity.[9] Neither eighteenth-century Social Contract theory, for example, nor social Darwinism (nor Euclidean geometry, for that matter) purported to describe the world only as it exists under particular conditions. Rather, each of these theories ostensibly explained the way things *are* in the world, independent of time, place, and circumstance. Such theories do, in a way, create the world in their own image as they structure people's perceptions and guide people's actions as they transform the world through their work. But just as people develop their views of the world through interaction with their social and material environments, so, too, do those views change as people continually make the world over in response to changing ways of understanding it.[10] The devastation of North American wildlife by the end of the nineteenth century, for example, was proof enough that the worldview implicit in *Pierson v. Post* was myopic and in need of correction.

8 Garrett Hardin, "The Tragedy of the Commons," *Science* 162 (13 December 1968): 1,243–8.

9 See Geertz, *Interpretation of Cultures*, p. 90.

10 See, generally, Thomas S. Kuhn, *The Structure of Scientific Revolutions*, 2d. International Encyclopedia of Unified Science, vol. 2, no. 2 (Chicago: University of Chicago Press, 1972). Some of the most exciting recent work in ecological history deals with the role of consciousness in mediating relations between humankind and nature. See Elizabeth Ann R. Bird, "The Social Construction of Nature: Theoretical Approaches to the History of Environmental Problems," *Environmental Review* 11 (1987): 255–64; also Carolyn Merchant, "The Theoretical Structure of Ecological Revolutions," ibid., pp. 265–74.

Hardin's article drew from a body of research in law and economics that began to appear shortly after World War II, when emerging conflicts over high-seas fisheries and mineral resources drew attention to the problem of exploiting unowned resources.[11] Fisheries, indeed, are the classic instance of the commons tragedy and provided the illustrative example used in the early literature on the problem.[12] Few fisheries conform to boundaries of property or legal jurisdiction. They are typically the object of fierce, highly atomized economic competition. They are ecologically volatile and vulnerable to any number of external influences, whether generated by humans or as impersonally as a change in the weather. Fisheries are, finally, renewable resources that will degrade if harvesters do not leave enough behind to regenerate future supplies.[13]

The fisheries of California provide an exceptionally good case with which to test the ability of Hardin's model to explain the origin and essential nature of resource problems. The waters off the California coast make up the best-studied oceanic ecosystem in the world. Records of the region's climate go back to the beginning of U.S. occupation in the 1840s. California scientists, in addition, have been able to count the number of fish scales in layered sediments taken from the ocean floor and from them have derived population estimates for several key species that go back several centuries. The aggregate levels of these populations and the relative abundance of different species provide direct evidence of changing conditions in offshore waters.[14] It is thus possible to reconstruct the ecological history of the

---

11 McEvoy, *The Fisherman's Problem,* pp. 190–96, 210–11. On the development of the law of the sea after World War II, see Ann L. Hollick, *U.S. Foreign Policy and the Law of the Sea* (Princeton, N.J.: Princeton University Press, 1981).

12 The first systematic treatment of the problem was in H. Scott Gordon, "The Economic Theory of a Common-Property Resource: The Fishery," *Journal of Political Economy* 62 (1954): 124–42. See also Carol M. Rose, "The Comedy of the Commons: Culture, Commerce, and Inherently Public Property," *University of Chicago Law Review* 53 (1986): 711–81, p. 748; S. V. Ciriacy-Wantrup, "The Economics of Environmental Policy," *Land Economics* 47 (1971): 37–45, pp. 42–5; Ciriacy-Wantrup and Richard C. Bishop, "'Common Property' as a Concept in Natural Resources Policy," *Natural Resources Journal* 15 (1975): 713–28, p. 722.

    R. H. Coase generalized the problem in his now-famous article, "The Problem of Social Cost," *Journal of Law and Economics* 3 (1960): 1–44; see also Steven N.S. Cheung, "The Structure of a Contract and the Theory of a Non-Exclusive Resource," ibid., 13 (1970): 49–70.

13 The best introduction to fisheries management issues is Francis T. Christy, Jr., and Anthony Scott, *The Common Wealth in Ocean Fisheries: Some Problems of Growth and Economic Allocation,* Resources for the Future (Baltimore: Johns Hopkins University Press, 1965). A basic text for fisheries biology is William F. Royce, *Introduction to the Fishery Sciences* (New York: Academic Press, 1972).

14 See Andrew Soutar and John D. Isaacs, "Abundance of Pelagic Fish during the Nineteenth and Twentieth Centuries as Recorded in Anaerobic Sediments off the Californias," *Fishery Bulletin U.S.* 72 (1974): 257–73; Paul E. Smith, "Biological Effects of Ocean Variability:

Arthur F. McEvoy

region's fisheries, both so as to understand why fisheries problems came into public view when and how they did, and to analyze the impact on the resources of whatever action people took in response to those problems. Records left by people permit comparison of that history with what people *thought* was happening and how their perceptions influenced what they did.

In one representative resource industry – the California fisheries – and its management by public agencies, there has been since the industry began a progressive diminution of what people have understood as "environment," that is, the set of given, autonomous conditions surrounding policy problems (like the abundance of foxes in *Pierson v. Post*), and a correspondingly greater inclusiveness to public comprehension of resource issues. "The Tragedy of the Commons," rather than expressing some metaphysical or metahistorical truth about society-environment relationships, may express only one, historically contingent, and perhaps too-narrow view of those relationships. The history of California's fishing industry suggests a different, more inclusive approach to the relationship between people, their work, and the world they live in.

THE LAISSEZ-FAIRE VIEW

In the late nineteenth century, environmental problems typically came into public view in the form of conflicts between resource users like Pierson and Post, who typically accused each other of threatening to destroy everybody's livelihood. There are a number of reasons why people in the United States would perceive resource problems in that way. Most simply, no one would have paid much attention to an ecological change unless someone with enough power to secure public attention thought she was losing money on account of it. The two-party suit at common law, in which one aggrieved party sought judicial relief from the harmful activities of another, was the classic forum for resolving public disputes in the days before collective bargaining and government bureaucracy. The country's unquestioning faith in individual market initiative as an engine of social progress, finally, had its logical converse in an instinct for seeking individuals or identifiable groups to blame when social problems arose.[15] Corollary to that instinct was an inability to see the nonhuman environment as an active participant in social change.

Nineteenth-century lawmakers "naturalized" – set beyond the realm of

Footnote 14 (*continued*)

Time and Space Scales of Biological Response," *Rapports et Procès-Verbaux des Réunions, Conseil International pour l'Exploration de la Mer (Denmark)* 173 (1978): 111–27.

15 See Hurst, *Law and Social Order in the United States* (Ithaca, N.Y.: Cornell University Press, 1977), p. 214; Jan G. Laitos, "Continuities from the Past Affecting Resource Use and Conservation Patterns," *Oklahoma Law Review* 28 (1975): 60–96.

the knowable and the controllable – not only the ecology of natural resources but the market forces that disrupted that ecology. Consider, for example, the British response to conflicts over declining fisheries in the North Sea. Oceanic fisheries, reported one Royal Commission in the 1880s, were *by their nature* inexhaustible. If particular fishing grounds declined from time to time, market forces would lead creative fishers to new grounds and give old ones time to replenish themselves, in slash-and-burn fashion. Burdening the industry with regulations, on the other hand, would unjustly infringe upon the fishers' liberty and might, in the Commission's words, "disturb in an unknown manner the balance existing between the conservative and destructive forces at work" on the stocks.[16]

Implicit in the Commission's laissez-faire approach to fishery depletion was a tripartite, hermetic system of boundaries between social thought, market behavior, and ecology. Fishing in the long run could have no meaningful impact on the ocean environment, which in any case was beyond the grasp of human understanding and thus not a socially cognizable thing. Unfettered competition, meanwhile, was the mode of social interaction most consonant with essential human nature and thus not to be interfered with without some compelling, articulable reason. The law, in sum, had no business interfering with the "natural," that is to say ineluctable, course of events.

Fisheries were among the first natural resources to receive organized public attention in the United States because competition and industrial development had such an early and pronounced effect on them. California quickly emerged as a leader in the field. Policing local economic activity was a state responsibility in the nineteenth century, so in 1870 the legislature at Sacramento established a Board of Fish Commissioners "to provide for the restoration and preservation of fish in the waters of this State."[17] Congress created a federal fishery agency to undertake research and development on the industry's behalf a year later.[18] U.S. authorities recognized, as to be fair did the British, that inland fisheries at least could be degraded by pollution and overharvesting. The problem was, however, that those forces were so diffused over society, every individual contributing her own, individually negligible share, as to be legally uncontrollable. The working assumption on which U.S. fishery agencies proceeded, then, was resource depletion was a necessary complement to economic progress, and no less inevitable than the

16 Quoted in Larry A. Nielsen, "The Evolution of Fisheries Management Philosophy," *Marine Fisheries Review* 38 (December 1976): 15–23, pp. 15–16; Gordon, "Economic Theory of a Common-Property Resource," p. 126.
17 1869–1870 *California Statutes* 663.
18 On the early history of the U.S. Fish Commission, see Dean Conrad Allard, Jr., *Spencer Fullerton Baird and the U.S. Fish Commission* (Ph.D. diss., George Washington University, 1967 [Reprint, New York: Arno Press, 1978]).

passing of the buffalo or the Indians. To modern readers, the fatalism with which even sympathetic observers discussed the issue is striking.[19]

With this view of the problem in mind, late nineteenth-century U.S. authorities responded to it in two characteristic ways. What regulations over fishing there were boiled down to the law's choosing sides in conflicts between different kinds of harvesters: in the New England fisheries between operators of set gear and floating gear, and in California between the roughly one-third of the state's fishery workers who were Chinese and just about everybody else. The California agency earned nationwide prestige by retaining distinguished scientists to study local fisheries problems. Typically, their conclusion was that the only practicable solution to those problems was to drive the Chinese out of business.[20]

There was, as it turns out, a coincidence between Chinese success in the fishing business and hard times for everybody else in the 1880s. Brutal overexploitation by non-Chinese crippled important fisheries for salmon and marine mammals. Pollution from the gold mining industry seriously damaged non-Chinese fisheries in San Francisco Bay, while generally low populations of nearshore market species gave ocean-going fishers cause to complain. The Chinese, who primarily fished abalone, squid, and shrimp, seem not to have been affected by these changes to the same degree as non-Chinese. But when the 1890s brought higher levels of productivity in offshore waters and as inshore waters gradually cleaned themselves of what debris remained from a now-defunct mining industry, non-Chinese fishers attributed their renewed prosperity to state harassment of the Asians.[21]

Legislators and government bureaucrats were happy to take credit for the revival. The causal relation between the removal of a distinctive, powerless minority from the business and the return of good times for others seemed too obvious to question, however bizarre the reasoning might appear to us today. As the California Fish Commissioners put it in 1886, "The oft-repeated and serious complaint that fish food is becoming scarce in California furnishes a powerful reason why the Chinese exhaustion should cease, and the cause of the complaint be removed."[22] The effects of pollution, habitat degradation, and changes in the balance of species in the system were not even investigated to the level which current advances in biology suggested they might be; they were not amenable to public intervention in

---

19 See, for example, U.S. Fish Commission, *Report* (1878): xlv; Hugh M. Smith, "The United States Bureau of Fisheries," U.S. Bureau of Fisheries, *Bulletin* 27 (1908): 1371.

20 See, for example, N. B. Scofield, "Shrimp Fisheries of California," *California Fish and Game Quarterly* 5 (1919): 1–12, pp. 2–3.

21 McEvoy, *The Fisherman's Problem*, pp. 79–88. See also McEvoy, "In Places Men Reject: The Chinese Fishermen at San Diego, 1870–1893," *Journal of San Diego History* 23 (Fall 1977): 12–24.

22 California Commissioners of Fisheries, *Report* (1885–6): 12–13.

any case. The shared responsibility of many water-using industries, fisheries included, likewise remained legally and politically invisible.

The second response was to re-stock depleted waterways with exotic species of fish and to propagate especially valuable ones like salmon and trout artificially in government hatcheries. As it turned out, a few successful transplants to California waters were at least counterbalanced by the baleful effects of others, while observed increases in the salmon catch at the turn of the century were almost certainly due, not to the hatchery work, but rather to changes in climate, changes in the distribution of the salmon's prey species, the opening of an offshore fishery for immature salmon, and the steady decline of pollution from the mining industry.[23]

To harvesters and the public officials whose job it was to oversee their industry, commercial fish were like gold nuggets: valuable commodities to be recovered from a state of nature and transformed into cash. So long as government sustained a supply and drove unwanted competitors out of business, further inquiry into their lives had little point. Nature was thoroughly plastic and could be manipulated in the service of enterprise to the limit of human ingenuity and political will. That observed changes in the fishing business might have been due to the collective behavior of harvesters, to changes in other industries, or even to the weather was simply not a legally meaningful question. Inasmuch as most fishery research was paid for with public funds, it was not a scientifically meaningful one either.

PROGRESSIVE CONSERVATION

What we recognize as modern conservation came into being during the Progressive Era at the beginning of the twentieth century, when interdependence became a major theme in debates over social problems. "In modern societies," wrote Justice Holmes in 1903, "every part is so organically related to every other that what affects any portion must be felt more or less by all the rest."[24] Conservation as Theodore Roosevelt and Gifford Pinchot preached it, with its emphasis on impartial scientific expertise, economic efficiency, and centralized planning in the public interest, epitomized everything that was new, modern, and progressive about Progressivism.[25]

The Progressive goal was to manage the economy's human and material resources scientifically, so as to produce the greatest good for the greatest number over the longest time. For the management of forests, fisheries, and

23 McEvoy, *The Fisherman's Problem*, pp. 104–8.
24 *Diamond Glue Co. v. United States Glue Co.*, 187 U.S. 611, 616 (1903).
25 Samuel P. Hays, *Conservation and the Gospel of Efficiency: The Progressive Conservation Movement, 1890–1920* (1959; reprint, New York: Atheneum, 1980), esp. chap. 12. See also Gifford Pinchot, "How Conservation Began in the United States," *Agricultural History* 11 (1937): 255–65.

other renewable resources, the key to this goal was what came to be known as the "sustained yield" model. Unlike the laissez-faire approach to resource problems, the sustained yield theory recognized a systematic relationship between harvesting and resource productivity. A stock's capacity to produce fish in any year was a linear function of the number of breeding adults left after the previous year's harvest. The number of fish left in the population after harvest, meanwhile, was inversely proportional to fishing effort. There was thus an inverse quadratic relation between sustainable yield and fishing effort: Productivity increases with added effort up to a point of "maximum sustainable yield" (MSY) and then declines as additional harvesting removes more fish than the population can replace from year to year.[26] The Progressives' idea was that government scientists would pinpoint each stock's MSY and present their findings to lawmakers, who would then limit the harvest to that level.

Biologists developed the sustained yield theory out of their experience with the kinds of fisheries that presented problems in the late nineteenth century: seals on the one hand and oceanic groundfishes such as plaice and halibut on the other.[27] All of these organisms were relatively easy to study for the same reason that they were easy to harvest and thus to deplete. They are large animals, have relatively orderly life histories, and are relatively tolerant of short-term changes in their environment. The kinds of fish that became commercially important in the early twentieth century, when fossil fuel engines and mechanized processing made more highly intensive fishing possible, behaved very differently.[28] The sustained-yield model, however, remained the standard approach to fisheries management until it came under criticism in the 1960s.[29]

26 One of the earliest articles on the theory was C. G. J. Petersen, "What Is Over-Fishing?" *Journal of the Marine Biological Association* (U.K.) 6 (1903–6): 587–95. On the history of fisheries science, see Nielsen, "The Evolution of Fisheries Management Philosophy"; also J. L. McHugh, "Trends in Fishery Research," in *A Century of Fisheries in North America,* ed. Norman G. Benson, American Fisheries Society Special Publication No. 7 (Washington, D.C.: American Fisheries Society, 1970), pp. 25–56. An excellent introduction to the politics and economics of sustained-yield conservation is S. V. Ciriacy-Wantrup, *Resource Conservation: Economics and Policies,* 3d ed. (Berkeley: University of California Division of Agricultural Sciences, Agricultural Experiment Station, 1968).

27 See, e.g., Peterson, "What Is Over-Fishing?"; William F. Thompson and Norman C. Freeman, "History of the Pacific Halibut Fishery," International Fisheries Commission, *Report No. 5* (Vancouver: Wrigley Publishing Co., 1930). For the history of sealing, see Briton Cooper Busch, *The War against the Seals: A History of the North American Seal Fishery* (Kingston and Montreal: McGill-Queens University Press, 1985).

28 McEvoy, *The Fisherman's Problem,* p. 160. On the effects of mechanization on the fishing industry and its public oversight, see McEvoy, "Law, Public Policy, and Industrialization in the California Fisheries, 1900–1925," *Business History Review* 57 (1983): 494–521.

29 The model reached its peak sophistication in the 1950s. See, e.g., Milner B. Schaefer, "Some Aspects of the Dynamics of Populations Important to the Management of

One reason for the theory's success was that it fit well with the ways in which Progressive reformers understood relationships between nature, market behavior, and lawmaking. It described the resource in terms of only one variable — fishing effort — and that a strictly economic one. Climate, interactions between species, and other variables that might affect productivity were so little understood that the model treated them essentially as random noise having no significant effect on the system.[30] Also external to the theory were the forces that drove the harvest: demand, technology, and so on were givens with which fishery managers had to cope, not variables to be controlled. Perhaps most crucially, the Progressives assumed that lawmaking was hermetically sealed off from competition in the marketplace. In their view, the objective findings of expert scientists would lead automatically to an impartial law which would then command instant, absolute obedience from market actors. The model was very tidy and worked well, for example, to rehabilitate the stock of fur seals in the northern Pacific, but failed utterly to meet the challenge of the Pacific Coast sardine fishery.

The sardine fishery was in its day probably the most intensive fishery in history; its destruction ranks with that of the passenger pigeon as one of the great disasters in U.S. wildlife management. Despite its economic importance and the great deal of public attention paid to it, the sardine fishery appeared, exfoliated, and collapsed in the pattern typical of unregulated fisheries. Harvesters and processors began experimenting with sardines at the turn of the century. After 1915 the fishery grew exponentially as it tapped foreign markets for inexpensive canned fish. Even more voracious was the domestic market for fishmeal, a flourlike substance made first from cannery waste but increasingly from whole fish, which was a valuable supplement to commercial feeds for poultry and livestock. Coastwide yields reached six hundred thousand tons per year in the mid-1930s and remained at that level for about a decade.[31]

This was a safe yield so long as climate and currents favored the sardine's reproduction, but a very dangerous one when they did not. Because it is

Commercial Marine Fisheries," Inter-American Tropical Tuna Commission, *Bulletin* 1 (1954): 26–56. For a detailed critique of the model from a scientific standpoint, see P. A. Larkin, "An Epitaph for the Concept of Maximum Sustained Yield," *Transactions of the American Fisheries Society* 106 (1977): 1–11.

30 See, e.g., William F. Thompson, "The Scientific Investigation of Marine Fisheries as Related to the Work of the Fish and Game Commission in Southern California," California Fish and Game Commission, *Fish Bulletin No. 2* (1919); Thompson, "The Fisheries of California and Their Care," *California Fish and Game* 8 (1922): 170–5.

31 On the rise and fall of the sardine fishery see McEvoy, *The Fisherman's Problem*, chap. 6; John Radovich, "The Collapse of the California Sardine Fishery: What Have We Learned?" in *Resource Management and Environmental Uncertainty: Lessons from Coastal Upwelling Fisheries*, eds. Michael H. Glantz and J. Dana Thompson (New York: Wiley, 1981), pp. 107–36.

lower on the food chain than a seal or a halibut, the sardine is much more sensitive to random changes in the ocean environment, especially in its first few days of life.[32] Depending on conditions, a spawning may produce huge numbers of viable young or very few. The sardine had adapted to the ecological volatility that is a fact of life in California waters by living long enough to allow each generation to breed in at least one good year. By 1940, however, no sardine lived longer than a year or two before being fished up out of the water. The fishery thus stripped the stock of its natural buffer against ecological shock. In the late 1940s, as fishing pressure steadily increased through a number of bad spawning years, the stock suddenly collapsed.[33]

What destroyed the sardine fishery, then, was the interaction between harvesting pressure and random ecological change. At the time, however, and well into the postwar period, political debate over conserving the fishery turned on the binary question of whether observed fluctuations in the harvest were due to overfishing *or* to "natural," that is to say unpredictable, unavoidable, and thus legally irrelevant, causes.[34] Human activity was one thing, ecology another entirely. The concept of synergy, familiar to post–World War II generations thanks to their experience with such modern ecological phenomena as radioactive fallout and pesticides, was simply not available for use in a political contest at the time.[35] Scientists in the California Department of Fish and Game, who called for restrictions

32 Paul E. Smith, "Year-Class Strength and Survival of O-Group Clupieods," *Canadian Journal of Fisheries and Aquatic Sciences* 42 (1985): 69–82.

33 Precisely the same series of events, with many of the same businesses, boats, and scientists playing supporting roles, took place in the Peruvian anchoveta fishery between the early 1950s and the early 1970s. See G. J. Paulik, "Anchovies, Birds, Fishermen and the Peru Current," in *Environment: Resources, Pollution, and Society,* ed. W. W. Murdock (Stamford, Conn.: Sinaur, 1971), pp. 156–85; also Georg Borgstrom, "Ecological Aspects of Protein Feeding – The Case of Peru," in *The Careless Technology: Ecology and International Development,* ed. M. Taghi Farvar and John P. Milton (Garden City, N.Y.: Natural History Press, 1972), pp. 753–4.

34 See (Seattle) *Pacific Fisherman* (August 1935), p. 60; also the testimony taken in U.S. Congress, House, Committee on Merchant Marine and Fisheries and Committee on Commerce, Subcommittee on Fisheries, *Sardine Fisheries,* 74th Cong., 2d sess. (March 10–11, 1936). The same division of opinion appeared in a postwar report on the collapse, Frances N. Clark and John C. Marr, "Population Dynamics of the Pacific Sardine," California Cooperative Oceanic Fisheries Investigations, *Reports* 4 (1956): 11–48. The controversy was finally settled by Garth I. Murphy, "Population Biology of the Pacific Sardine *(Sardinops caerulea),*" *Proceedings of the California Academy of Sciences,* 4th ser., 34(1).

35 On the development of postwar environmentalism, see Samuel P. Hays, *Beauty, Health, and Permanence: Environmental Politics in the United States, 1955–1985,* Studies in Environment and History (Cambridge: Cambridge University Press, 1987); Donald Fleming, "Roots of the New Conservation Movement," *Perspectives in American History* (1971): 7–91.

on the harvest as early as 1929, made little headway in the state legislature against a highly capitalized and politically muscular fishing industry and its even more powerful allies in California agribusiness, who could muster tangible evidence of money being made in the here and now, which would be lost to no apparent purpose were the state to limit the harvest to guard against some uncertain future disaster.[36]

As fatal to Progressive-style management of the sardine fishery as the implicit dichotomy between ecology and human action was the implicit but pervasive distinction it made between market forces and lawmaking. Progressive conservation envisioned a powerful central state made up of impartial experts who would command automatic obedience to efficient laws from a passive citizenry. Rather than correcting the market failures that, left unimpeded, would lead to Hardin's tragedy of the commons, however, the structure and processes of lawmaking for the fishery merely duplicated them in a different forum.[37] Not only did the California legislature have to balance the articulate claims of the industry against the inchoate fears of state biologists, but it had also to consider the sure knowledge that any fish left in the ocean by California boats would surely be snapped up by boats from Oregon, Washington, British Columbia, and, later, Mexico.[38] Federal controls might have alleviated much of this problem, but policing fishery use was traditionally a state function. The federal fishery agency, while agreeing with the state biologists that the sardine's future was highly uncertain, had no incentive to dissipate the political capital it had built up with the industry over years of promotional support over what it saw as an uncertain and probably futile effort to rein in the harvest.[39]

There was thus a tragedy of the commons not only in the fishery itself, but also in the very legal processes that were supposed to correct such failures in the market. Too many government bodies competed with each other for political resources for any of them to take account of such diffused,

36 The first published warning was in California Division of Fish and Game, *Biennial Report* (1928–30): 108. See also W. L. Scofield, "Sardine Oil in Our Troubled Waters," *California Fish and Game Quarterly* 24 (1938): 210–33; and Frances N. Clark, "Can the Supply of Sardines Be Maintained in California Waters?" ibid. 25 (1939): 172–6.

37 Hurst, *Law and Markets in United States History*, esp. chap. 3; Richard A. Walker and Michael Storper, "Erosion of the Clean Air Act of 1970: A Study in the Failure of Government Regulation and Planning," *Boston College Environmental Affairs Law Review* 7 (1978): 189–257, pp. 198, 252–4.

38 Mexico did not enter the fishery until the early 1950s, after it had already collapsed. The other jurisdictions had restrained their sardine fishers until about 1935, but turned them loose rather than close them out of the bonanza that California boats were enjoying in the depths of the Depression. M. T. Hoyt, "Report of the Pilchard Fishery of Oregon" (Salem: Oregon Fish Commission, 1938), p. 5 (copy on file, California State Fisheries Laboratory Library, Long Beach); 1935 *Washington Laws* 403; 1935 *Oregon Laws* 678.

39 McEvoy, *The Fisherman's Problem*, pp. 162–6, 182–3.

intangible, and long-term values as were at stake in the sardine controversy. The mutually constitutive relationship between the legal system and the private economy was as invisible to Progressive conservation as the fox's life was to the judges in *Pierson v. Post*.

THE TRAGEDY REVISITED

Hardin's article was a synthesis and popularization of a body of scholarship that began in the early 1950s as a critique of the Progressive distinction between economic behavior and legal organization. The reformers' idea was that fishery depletion and other tragedies had their origins in the common-property legal regimes in which such industries operated. Placing the resources under the management of a single owner, whether private or public, would allow that owner to internalize the social cost of overharvesting, that is, make it worthwhile to limit harvesting effort to that level which produced the greatest difference between yields or income and operating costs. Because yields increase with added effort only up to the point of MSY and then decline while costs rise steadily with increased effort, the theory went, the point of maximum economic yield (MEY) theoretically would lie at a lower (hence safer) level of effort than the stock's MSY.[40]

In a privatized fishery, then, market incentives would lead harvesters to behave in an ecologically prudent fashion automatically, in a way that competitors for shared resources, each scrambling over the other to take as much as she could before all the wealth disappeared, could not. This is the lesson implicit in the tragic myth of the commons; it underlies much of the modern literature on environmental problems.[41] Developments in environmental law since 1970, however, suggest that a new understanding is taking shape; as an explanation of the origins and essence of environmental problems, the tragic myth of the commons may be only slightly less myopic than the story in *Pierson v. Post*.

To begin with, the only measure of value against which the commons myth compares common-property and privatized harvesting regimes is the profit of the harvesters. As in the Progressive Era, sustained-yield model, the only meaningful variable is economic effort. The only meaningful output is cash or its equivalent. Yet at the core of most environmental problems is the

40 See generally Gordon, "Economic Theory of a Common-Property Resource," passim.
41 See especially the studies of fisheries, water, and other resources underwritten by Resources for the Future in the 1960s, including Christy and Scott, *The Common Wealth in Ocean Fisheries;* James A. Crutchfield and Giulio Pontecorvo, *The Pacific Salmon Fisheries: A Study of Irrational Conservation*, Resources for the Future (Baltimore: Johns Hopkins University Press, 1969); and Joe S. Bain, Richard E. Caves, and Julius Margolis, *Northern California's Water Industry: The Comparative Efficiency of Public Enterprise in Developing a Scarce Economic Resource*, Resources for the Future (Baltimore: Johns Hopkins University Press, 1966).

fact that the price measure does not account for many values which are important but are too long-term, too diffuse, or too uncertain to register in the calculations of market bargainers. Some values, indeed, are sacral in nature and thus not open to market bidding at any price.[42]

A number of post-1970 environmental statutes take the inherent weakness of the price measure into account, either by removing some values from cost-benefit considerations as do the Endangered Species Act, the Marine Mammals Protection Act, and parts of the Clean Air Act of 1970 and the Occupational Health and Safety Act, or by explicitly requiring regulators to balance economic and noneconomic values in their decision making.[43] The Fishery Conservation and Management Act of 1976, for example, sets up as a management standard what it calls "optimum yield" (OY), which it defines as "maximum sustainable yield as modified by any relevant economic, social, or ecological factor."[44]

The OY standard lacks the tidy objectivity of its predecessors. It does, however, reflect a new awareness that natural resources are more than passive inputs to economic production – ultimately the economic interests of human beings and the survival interests of their resources are one. That awareness, still imperfectly formed and even less coherently put into practice, stems from the radically different ways in which people have interacted with the rest of Creation since 1945. As one team of fishery managers put it, "the conclusion that arises from [such] ecological considerations is that benefit to the nation occurs by leaving fish in the ocean."[45] To the federal scientists of the 1930s, who maintained that "resources must not be permitted to lie in a state of unproductive idleness," such a notion would have seemed absurd.[46]

A second shortcoming of the commons tragedy is its implicit view of the way in which government makes decisions. Hardin's solution to the commons problem, his use of metered parking and private landownership

42 On the limits of economism, see Steven Kelman, "Cost-Benefit Analysis: An Ethical Critique," *Regulation* 5, no. 1 (January/February 1981): 33–40; also Laurence H. Tribe, "Ways Not to Think about Plastic Trees: New Foundations for Environmental Law," *Yale Law Journal* 83 (1974): 1,315–48.
43 Endangered Species Act of 1973, as amended, 16 U.S.C. § 1,531–43; Marine Mammal Protection Act of 1972, 16 U.S.C. § 1,361–1,407; on the Clean Air Amendments of 1970, see Walker and Storper, "Erosion of the Clean Air Act"; on the Occupational Health and Safety Act, see Paolo F. Ricci and Lawrence F. Moulton, "Risk and Benefit in Environmental Law," *Science* 214 (4 December 1981): 1,096–100.
44 Fishery Conservation and Management Act of 1976, 16 U.S.C.A. §1,801–81. "Optimum yield" is defined at 16 U.S.C. §1,802(18).
45 National Oceanic and Atmospheric Administration, "Implementation of Northern Anchovy Fishery Management Plan: Solicitation of Public Comments," 43 *Federal Register* 31,651–879, p. 31,699 (21 July 1978).
46 Elmer Higgins, "Memorandum to Mr. Kerlin," (22 June 1936), U.S. Bureau of Commercial Fisheries, General Files, Record Group 22, Series 121, Box 486, file 825.9, National Archives, Washington, D.C.

as examples of the "mutual coercion mutually agreed upon" he thought necessary to discipline the use of shared resources, implied an independent observer of nature and a neutral rulemaker somehow external to and immune from the interests being disciplined. The common myth thus shares with Progressive conservation an assumed dichotomy between market struggle and lawmaking.

The California sardine catastrophe exposed the ways in which lawmaking only reproduced in different guise the competition for resources that depleted the fishery. Scientific, supposedly "objective" – note once again the implicit distancing between human observers and observed Nature – information did not lead automatically to effective law, but only amounted to evidence offered by one faction in a political struggle for resources with other factions, better organized and with more articulable interests at stake. After 1970, by contrast, government began to use biological data in a different way. The federal plan for managing the anchovy fishery and the state plans for the sardine and mackerel fisheries keyed harvesting quotas directly, in the text of the law, to specific shares of the measured population above some safe minimum level.[47] No longer must the accuracy of the measurements be tested in a political forum; the objectivity of the data is no longer at issue. Observation and regulatory consequence thus form a continuum, and there is one less opportunity for necessarily uncertain scientific data to be overwhelmed by the quite tangible evidence of fish left uncaught in the ocean. If the first shortcoming of Hardin's myth is that there is no such thing as a "human" interest apart from that of the resources on which people rely, the second is that there is no such thing as an "objective" knowledge of nature apart from the political and economic perspectives from which people view it.

A third shortcoming of the tragic myth of the commons is its strangely unidimensional picture of *human* nature. The farmers on Hardin's pasture, for example, do not seem to talk to one another. As individuals, they are alienated, rational, utility-maximizing automatons and little else. The sum total of their social life is the grim, Hobbesian struggle of each against all and all together against the pasture in which they are trapped. Culture and community are no more relevant to what happens on the pasture than the biology of foxes was to the outcome of *Pierson v. Post*.

The commons myth thus misrepresents the way in which common lands were used in the archetypical case, that is, in England before the privatiza-

---

47 NOAA, "Implementation of Northern Anchovy Fishery Management Plan," p. 31,664 (anchovy); *Cal. Fish and Game Code* § 8150.7 (West 1984) (rehabilitation of sardine resource); *Cal. Fish and Game Code* §8411–8412 (allowable catch of mackerel 20 percent of total population over 20,000 tons total; "total population" defined in terms of agency determination).

tion of property in land.[48] English farmers met twice a year at manor court to plan production for the coming months and on those occasions would certainly have exchanged information about the state of their lands and picked out for sanctioning those who took more than their fair share from the common pool. Likewise, Italian, Chinese, and other immigrant fishing groups in late nineteenth-century California kept very tight control over the harvest and allocation of their resources so as to produce what we would now call an optimum yield for their group. As the *San Francisco Chronicle* put it in 1907, "if any Italian thinks it is possible to catch crabs for the market without joining the association, let him try it."[49] In the same way, the adamant refusal of some Pacific Northwest Indian groups to abdicate control over their traditional fisheries has stymied effective management for most of the Pacific Coast salmon industry. Indian fishers insist on their right to manage their traditional resources in their own way because not only the harvest but the social edifice in which it is embedded are crucial to the survival of their communities, their cultures, and thus to their sense of themselves as Indian *people,* which is a moral obligation and thus has no price.[50] This is, perhaps, "mutual coercion mutually agreed upon," but of a radically different sort from the grim, totalitarian variety that Hardin envisioned.[51]

Philippe Nonet described the law of administrative agencies, to which

48 See William S. Cooter, "Ecological Dimensions of Medieval Agrarian Systems," *Agricultural History* 52 (1978): 458–77; S. V. Ciriacy-Wantrup, "Soil Conservation in European Farm Management," *Journal of Farm Economics* 20 (1938): 86–101; see especially Carol Rose's discussion of "custom and the managed commons," in Rose, "The Comedy of the Commons," pp. 739–42.

49 *San Francisco Chronicle* (8 September 1907), p. 40.

50 For an excellent treatment of the significance of native culture in a modern resource conservation dispute, see Barbara Leibhardt, "Among the Bowheads: Legal and Cultural Change on Alaska's North Slope Coast to 1985," *Environmental Review* 10 (1986): 277–301.

On the importance of traditional culture to salmon-fishing Indians in northwestern California, see John H. Bushnell, "From American Indian to Indian American: The Changing Identity of the Hupa," *American Anthropologist* 70 (1968): 1,108–16; U.S. Department of Agriculture, Forest Service, "Draft Environmental Statement: Gasquet-Orleans Road, Chimney Rock Section, Six Rivers National Forest, California Region," USDA-FS-R5-DES (Adm.) (San Francisco: U.S. Forest Service, 1977), Appendices K-T, pp. 217–485. On conflicts over the salmon fishery of the Klamath River, California, see U.S. Department of the Interior, Fish and Wildlife Service, "Environmental Impact Statement on the Management of River Flows to Mitigate the Loss of the Anadromous Fishery of the Trinity River, California" INT/FES 80–52 (Sacramento: U.S. Fish and Wildlife Service, 1980), p. C7-8, p. C8-12, n. 51.

51 Barry Commoner early grasped the implications of Hardin's model in *The Closing Circle: Nature, Man & Technology* (New York: Knopf, 1971), pp. 295–6. The darker implications of Hardin's original article emerge somewhat more clearly in his "Living on a Lifeboat," *BioScience* 24 (1974): 561–8.

modern society entrusts the management of its natural resources, as "a structure of opportunities for participation and criticism."[52] A crucial reason why fishing people of all ethnicities notoriously resist government efforts to manage their resources is that conservation in the Progressive mold envisions no such opportunity, but only the promulgation of rules by a distant, centralized authority on the basis of ostensibly neutral fact-finding and lawmaking.[53] The dissenting judge in *Pierson v. Post* may have sensed this: He would have referred the dispute to a tribunal of fox hunters for disposition according to community practice.[54] Many of the changes that the effort to cope with modern environmental problems have brought to U.S. administrative law look directly to this problem: Environmental impact statements, citizen-suit provisions, broadened opportunities for private groups to take part in the rulemaking process and to be heard in court on environmental issues, all have enhanced public participation in environmental decision making and thereby given added weight to interests and values normally overlooked in the competition for resources that takes place in government no less than it does in the marketplace.[55]

CONCLUSION

In 1982 one federal official suggested that the chief task of public fishery agencies was less to develop economically efficient or biologically sound plans for managing the industry than it was to "keep the various groups off each other's necks, keep people feeling that there is some fairness in the system so that they don't become obstructionists."[56] The statement evinces an understanding of environmental issues that differs markedly from those implicit in the story of the fox hunters in *Pierson v. Post,* in the Progressive theory of conservation, and in the tragedy of the commons. Resource depletion may be more a social problem, that is, evidence of a community's inability to integrate its social order in a self-sustaining way, than it is a necessary product of the alienated, self-regarding profit motive that Hardin posits as simple human nature.[57]

52 Philippe Nonet, *Administrative Justice: Advocacy and Change in Government Agencies* (New York: Russell Sage Foundation, 1969), p. 6.
53 Hays nicely exposed the antidemocratic character of Progressive conservation and the contradiction between it and the self-determination that nourished the vitality of U.S. culture. See *Conservation and the Gospel of Efficiency,* esp. chap. 12.
54 *Pierson v. Post,* 3 Cai. R. at 180 (Livingston, J., dissenting).
55 See Robert L. Rabin, "Federal Regulation in Historical Perspective," *Stanford Law Review* 38 (1986): 1,189–326, pp. 1,278–315.
56 Personal interview with Dan Huppert, Fishery Economist, National Marine Fisheries Service, Southwest Fisheries Center, La Jolla, California, 17 December 1982.
57 Mildred Dickeman put this point nicely in "Demographic Consequences of Infanticide in Man," *Annual Review of Ecology and Systematics* 6 (1975): 107–37, p. 133.

Consecutively, the four visions incorporate a gradually more inclusive view of the essence and genesis of environmental problems. It makes no difference to the story in *Pierson v. Post* whether the fox is alive or dead. The Progressive, sustained-yield model of fishery management described a dynamic interaction between a living resource and a harvesting industry, but presupposed a government hermetically insulated from pressures arising out of that interaction. The tragic tale of the commons, finally, recognized that legal structure influences the way people use their resources but portrays people themselves as profit-maximizing automatons, without culture, without feeling for their work, and without community.

Any explanation of environmental change should account for the interembeddedness and reciprocal constitution of ecology, production, and cognition, the last either at the level of individuals, which we call ideology, or at the societal level, which in the modern world we call law. First, people adapt to the world around them, which consists not only of a nonhuman environment, evolving partly on its own and partly in response to what people do to it, but also of other people as well. Second, what distinguishes humanity as a species is its capacity to produce, to alter its environment, more or less deliberately, so as to ensure its survival and propagation. Finally, people organize their behavior according to particular worldviews, whether expressed or implicit. As people act on the basis of one or another understanding of how the world works and their place in it, finally, what they do inevitably changes their social and natural environments, to which they then must adapt anew.

All three elements, ecology, production, and cognition, evolve in tandem; each partly according to its own particular logic and partly in response to changes in the other two. To externalize any of the three elements, to place it in the set of given, "environmental" conditions within which one explains an ecological change, is to miss the crucial fact that human life and thought are embedded in each other and together in the nonhuman world. Insofar as the tragic myth of the commons does this, it may serve less well as a heuristic device for understanding environmental problems than as a recipe for exacerbating them.

IO Efficiency, Equity, Esthetics: Shifting Themes in American Conservation

Clayton R. Koppes

A NEW CHAPTER IN THE HISTORY of the American environment opened about 1900. For several decades discontent with the way Americans dealt with the natural world had been mounting. Three centuries of unbridled capitalism had produced a monumental transformation in the American environment. The relatively pristine environment encountered by the European settlers in the 1600s had been turned into a world of agriculture, industry, and urbanism. These developments enjoyed almost universal acclaim among Americans. Precisely planted rows of corn and wheat, neat white farm houses, and a one-room country school represented civilization, democracy, and progress. On the seal of the Northwest Territory a fruit-bearing tree towers over an ax-felled tree, while in the background the rising sun and commercial boats plying the Ohio River represent the dawn of a new era. The seal bears the motto *Meliorem lapsa locavit* – "From the fallen tree a better one has grown." Belching smokestacks, noisy locomotives, and smelly oil wells conveyed prosperity and national greatness.

But by the late 1800s growing numbers of Americans grew increasingly worried about the costs of this edition of progress. They began to fear that something valuable and irreplaceable was being lost in the headlong rush to expand and grow richer. They feared, too, that unrestrained capitalist expansion was undermining the very resource base of national prosperity. Hence by the 1890s there was widespread recognition that old patterns of economic development needed drastic change. From a mixture of concern about irreversible changes in the natural world and anxiety about the future course of American capitalism, Americans began to redefine their relationship to their environment. In this crucible the conservation movement was

This essay is a revision of the author's presidential address for the American Society for Environmental History in 1986, which was printed in "Efficiency/Equity/Esthetics: Towards a Reinterpretation of American Conservation," *Environmental Review* 11 (Summer 1987): 127–46.

forged. The ideas, politics, and policies that emerged at the turn of the century set the tone of intellectual and political debate for the next half century and laid the basis for the environmental movement of the late twentieth century. The compromised, even contradictory, impulses of the early conservation movement were to be reflected in a mottled record of gains and losses in the face of a still-dominant developmental ethic.

The American environment in 1900 reflected three reigning assumptions about the use of natural resources since the early 1600s. First, Americans believed that an abundance of natural resources existed in an unclaimed state. Indians used the land, of course, but not in ways whites felt bound to respect. The native Americans were often migratory and observed communal ownership patterns rather than a system of individual title. From the arrival of the Puritans to 1890, when the last Indians were herded onto reservations, Anglos expected to appropriate what they regarded as unused lands. As John Winthrop, governor of the Massachusetts Bay Colony, explained: "They inclose no land neither have they any settled habitation nor any tame cattle to improve the land by & so have no other but a natural right to those countries. So if we leave them sufficient for their use we may lawfully take the rest."[1] Indeed, for a combination of economic incentives and religious constraints, Americans felt a virtual compulsion to convert unclaimed natural resources into productive goods.

Second, Americans believed that natural resources were inexhaustible. So it seemed! Forests were vast, streams surged with fish, flights of birds blotted out the sun, and an expanding nation believed it had a manifest destiny to annex enormous tracts stretching to the Pacific and perhaps beyond. Such attitudes sanctioned inordinate waste of natural resources. Farmers who cleared their land of trees celebrated with joyous bonfires that illuminated the night for miles around; loggers often denuded huge areas but used only the finest specimens; early oil drillers struck gushers that spewed plumes of petroleum into the air for days at a time and then turned to polluting torrents. Depletion of natural resources became evident early; Boston experienced shortages of firewood as early as 1638, as did most Eastern cities by the 1700s. It seemed there was always more wood in the next mountain range or that one could shift to a new resource, such as coal for home heating. Only in the late 1800s as a shortage of natural resources, particularly timber, became a serious threat was an economic imperative created for conservation.[2]

Third, Americans believed that it was best to use natural resources immediately. They believed that the people who had done the hard work of

---

1 Winthrop quoted in Cecelia Tichi, *New World, New Earth: Environmental Reform in American Literature from the Puritans through Whitman* (New Haven, Conn., 1979), p. 8.
2 William Cronon, *Changes in the Land: Indians, Colonists, and the Ecology of New England* (New York, 1983), pp. 121–2.

converting the wilderness into usable resources should reap the benefit of their labor as soon as possible. There was little philosophical rationale to conserve for future generations, and capitalism's emphasis on turning a quick profit worked against long-term calculations.

These assumptions were written into the public policies and laws of the new nation, and thereby received decisive encouragement from the power of the state. The legal historian James Willard Hurst has identified three key principles of American law in the period from 1789 to roughly the 1890s. Each has important implications for Americans' approach to the environment. First, human nature is creative, and society should provide "broad opportunity for the release of creative human energy." Second, humans should have as wide a range of freedom as possible. Third, blessed by a combination of "unclaimed natural abundance" and unparalleled technological means to alter nature, Americans may realize their creative potential primarily through economic activity. The internal market was largely unfettered; one could sell the fruits of one's labor for whatever it would bring. Governments at all levels fostered the "release of energy" by financing infrastructure development, such as canals and railroads. Such activity was designed to assist private economic activity, not supplant it.[3]

Translated from legal abstractions to real world policies, these concepts had a great effect in shaping national development. Consider just two examples. One was the disposal of the public lands. The federal government elected to convey much of its unused land to private owners quickly and cheaply so that individuals' creative energies would transform it for immediate economic use. The crowning statement of this principle was the Homestead Act of 1862 by which one could acquire title to 160 acres simply by making it productive. The other is the law of capture, which after its enunciation by the Pennsylvania Supreme Court in 1889, became the basis of petroleum law. The court viewed oil and gas as analogous to migratory wild animals, which had to be pursued and captured. Whoever applied his energy and capital in this way earned the ownership of this otherwise unclaimed resource and was entitled to its immediate, unrestrained exploitation.[4] In both instances the weight of law and public policy rewarded the person who through his initiative transformed unused, unclaimed nature into something economically valuable.

Bolstered by these principles, Americans devoted prodigious energy to the transformation of the continent. A world that had been touched only lightly by humans became, in a remarkably short time, a realm of advanced agriculture and burgeoning industry. Americans congratulated themselves on having fashioned a nation of rising material living standards and of growing

---

3 James Willard Hurst, *Law and the Conditions of Freedom in Nineteenth-Century America* (Madison, Wis., 1956), pp. 5–6.
4 *Westmoreland Natural Gas Company v. DeWitt*, 130 Pa. 235.

international power. No account of environmental history should ignore the very real achievements wrought by millions of capitalists applying their creativity to the natural world they encountered.

By the 1890s, however, the costs of this tranformation grew evident, and the fin de siècle celebrations were laced with anxiety, tension, and doubt. Many Americans feared that a continuation of traditional modes of operation threatened irreparable harm to the environment which had undergirded national growth and irreversible damage to the country's scenic splendor. The Census Bureau concluded in its famous report of 1890 that the frontier was closed. That bland factual statement carried immense symbolic meaning, for it suggested to a generation of Americans that the process of exploiting inexhaustible resources was coming to an end. Natural resources were no longer substantially unclaimed; they had been mostly appropriated. And in keeping with the ineluctable unfolding of an unrestrained capitalism, control of resources often became concentrated in the hands of speculators and large corporations, in contrast to the democratic ideal of widely distributed ownership. Growing numbers of citizens realized that this pattern of development needed to be restrained in order to reduce waste and to insure future production. Forestry, for example, had been essentially extractive. Now it had to be transformed into an industry that practiced sustained yield production through controlled cutting schedules and systematic replanting. Water resources needed to be developed and their distribution made more democratic. Great scenic wonders should be preserved free from development. Although there was widespread agreement on these basic ideas, translating such ideas into practice posed a monumental challenge for the nascent conservation movement.

This shift away from a focus on immediate economic use diluted the primacy of the market, but it did not necessarily entail an anticapitalist stance. Resource regulation might be undertaken by the government to smooth out fluctuations in the business cycle or to introduce long-range calculations, which individual entrepreneurs found hard to do when their competitors were intent on immediate use. Thus environmental policies, like other government regulations, might intrude on the market with the idea of making capitalism work better in the long run. The conservation movement numbered many fervent critics of laissez-faire capitalism among its ranks, but most conservationists wanted to reform capitalism, not abolish it.

The conservation movement took its distinctive political form in the Progressive Era and under the particular aegis of the Theodore Roosevelt presidency. Three ideas were dominant in Progressive-Era conservation thinking – efficiency, equity, and esthetics. The efficiency school wanted to manage natural resources by applying modern engineering and managerial techniques, in contrast to the haphazard, short-run practices of the past. Advocates of equity wanted to insure that the benefits of natural resources development, such as federal irrigation projects, were widely distributed rather than concentrated in a few hands. Supporters of esthetics campaigned to preserve great scenic wonders free from ruinous development. Most Progressive-Era conservationists, though subscribing to all three ideas, differed on their emphases. These approaches often proved incompatible. The potential for conflict between the efficiency and esthetic wings was particularly strong. The potential fissures in the conservation movement became dramatically apparent when the efficiency faction succeeded in 1914 in having a federal dam built in the beautiful Hetch Hetchy Valley (a part of Yosemite National Park) over the anguished opposition of the esthetic school. The Progressive conservation movement was a volatile compound in which the relative strengths of the three components fluctuated over time and according to the issue.

The efficiency exponents enjoyed the most strength in the early twentieth century. In a germinal work historian Samuel P. Hays argued that the crux of their approach lay in "a rational and scientific method of making basic technological decisions through a single, central authority."[5] The efficiency conservationists wanted to bring the techniques of applied science to environmental management, chiefly through the executive branch of the federal government. What Hays termed "the gospel of efficiency" had several implications. First, cadres of scientifically trained experts – mostly male – would in theory apply their expertise to take an objective, disinterested, comprehensive view of environmental issues. Decisions about resources would be based on a concept of the long-term public interest instead of short-term political maneuvering. Second, as an elite corps within the federal bureaucracy, these experts would be insulated from the corrupting pressures of politics and hence carry out objective planning. Third, these experts had a strong developmental bias. Not wilderness preservationists, they saw the environment as something to be made productive with minimum waste. Sometimes, as in the national forests, efficiency dictated that resource use be postponed, but this was to insure their availability for future generations, not for preservation of natural beauty per se. The embodiment of the efficiency conservationist was Gifford Pinchot, the patrician, European-trained forester who built the Forest Service and was Roosevelt's unappointed secretary of conservation.

The gospel of efficiency entailed some interference in the market, but its practitioners believed they were not supplanting capitalism, only making it work better. They often enjoyed support from corporations, who realized that only government measures could ameliorate the short-run orientation and cutthroat competiton of the unregulated marketplace. The efficiency

5 Samuel P. Hays, *Conservation and the Gospel of Efficiency: The Progressive Conservation Movement, 1890–1920* (Cambridge, Mass., 1959), p. 69.

Efficiency, Equity, Esthetics

conservationists were not socialists; they did not want the government to take over the means of production or go into business for itself. Resources might be set aside in the national forests or mining on the public land might be subject to government control, but the federal government allowed private industry to carry out the actual exploitation of the resources; it did not set up its own lumber mills or go into the mining business. Businessmen feuded with conservationist bureaucrats over the best way to manage federal resources, but both had a common interest in the perpetuation of the resource.

To many conservationists efficiency was not enough; they were also concerned for greater equity. Indeed, it would not be too much to say that, for many conservationists, efficiency was but a means to the greater goal of equity. The equity advocates stressed that natural resources, which belonged to all the people, should be retained in public control in order to insure that the benefits of resource development were distributed fairly. Conservationists such as Pinchot believed that concentration of resources in the hands of a few was both inefficient and unfair. He repeatedly stressed that the end of efficient development was equity; equal opportunity recurs frequently in his writing. "For whose benefit shall they [natural resources] be conserved – for the benefit of the many, or for the use and profit of the few?" he asked. Public ownership and control was essential to prevent further monopolization of resources.[6]

The equity school saw wise use of the environment as a tool to foster grass-roots democracy. Previously free or cheap land had been sufficient to promote economic democracy; the application of individual energy had done the rest. But now governmental intervention was needed, for individual initiative was not adequate in itself. Federal irrigation works in the West became a key conservation measure in the Progressive Era for both efficiency and equity advocates. To the efficiency faction irrigation promised more rational use of a scarce resource: Water that would otherwise be wasted would transform arid regions into fruited plains and slake the thirst of alabaster cities. To equity proponents irrigation opened vistas and arid-lands democracies: The government would limit each recipient of the federally financed water to a mythic 160 acres, thus preventing further concentration of resource holding. Congressman Francis G. Newlands of Nevada saw his reclamation act of 1902 as a way to "break up existing land monopoly in the West."[7]

6 Gifford Pinchot, *The Fight for Conservation* (New York, 1910), p. 109 and passim (esp. pp. 24, 26, 27, 79–82, 88, 103, 133).
7 Arthur B. Darling, ed., *The Public Papers of Francis G. Newlands*, 2 vols. (Boston, 1932), 1: 62; Donald J. Pisani, *From the Family Farm to Agribusiness: The Irrigation Crusade in California and the West* (Berkeley, Calif., 1984), pp. 316–17, 321, 325. On the 160-acre law, see Clayton R. Koppes, "Public Water, Private Land: Origins of the Acreage Limitation

Clayton R. Koppes

However luminous in principle, the dream of the Bureau of Reclamation as a catalyst for democracy proved flawed in practice. Historian Donald J. Pisani has shown that early reclamation projects, including the acreage limitation, encountered severe problems.[8] The Reclamation Bureau's big dams generated not only hydroelectricity but serious environmental problems of their own making, such as siltation and misplaced urban development, that led latter-day analysts to question whether they actually fit any sensible definition of efficiency. And in a bitter irony, the reclamation program eventually helped reinforce land monopoly when its cheap water was poured on the lands of agribusiness corporations without regard to the acreage limitation. A similar problem afflicted the forestry program. Pinchot often found large lumber companies more receptive to his long-range managerial strategy than small operators, who needed immediate access to a particular parcel of timber in order to stay in business.

Programs such as reclamation and the management of national forests were thus halfway measures. They attempted to introduce efficiency and equity considerations within the existing capitalist structure. Progressive-Era conservation shrank from more radical steps, such as greater state control of resources or the state's actually engaging in production, which was tried at times on the local level and in some capitalist societies abroad. Many local governments experimented with ownership of their own utilities, such as water and electricity. But any attempt to expand beyond the local level or to move outside water and electricity met determined opposition. The oil industry – a leading case of the concentrated control of natural resources – was a frequent but unavailing target. Trying to break the regional stranglehold of Standard Oil's subsidiary Prairie Oil Company, the state of Kansas tried to build its own refinery, but this measure was declared unconstitutional. Woodrow Wilson's secretary of the navy, Joseph Daniels, failed in his efforts to have the government, rather than private industry, pump oil from the naval reserves. In periods of energy crises government operation of the oil industry was suggested but never implemented. Not until the New Deal did federal participation in energy production become significant, and that was limited chiefly to hydroelectricity. In Australia and other outposts of the

Footnote 7 (continued)

Controversy, 1933–1953," Pacific Historical Review 47 (1978): 607–36. Donald Worster has pointed out that, however appealing the rhetoric of agrarian democracy in the passage of the reclamation act, the underlying appeal of power and empire was perhaps compelling. This may help explain why the efficiency aspects of reclamation have overwhelmed the equity principles for most of the Reclamation Bureau's history. See Donald Worster, Rivers of Empire: Water, Aridity, and the Growth of the American West (New York, 1985), pp. 160–9.

8 Elwood Mead, "What Australia Can Teach America," Independent 71 (17 August 1911): 369. I am indebted to Donald Pisani for information on British Commonwealth water practices. John G. Clark, Energy and the Federal Government: Fossil Fuel Policies, 1900–1946 (Urbana, Ill., 1987), p. 131.

British Commonwealth water rights belonged to the crown or the state and were licensed for specified periods, thus avoiding the problems of monopoly control in perpetuity that bedeviled the American West.[9]

The developmental ethos of both the efficiency and equity schools coexisted uneasily with the third conservation principle – esthetics – the desire to preserve areas of natural beauty or scientific importance. The conservationists' appreciation of the beauty of the natural world found enthusiastic acceptance in many quarters. For many people it was a rekindling of the romantic interpretation of sublime nature – sweeping vistas, picturesque scenes, dramatic landscape features. They shared either directly or vicariously the rush you get standing at the edge of the Grand Canyon and seeing aeons spread before you, the spiritual communion you experience as you walk among the towering, fog-shrouded redwoods, and the sense of liberation you feel as you discern a panorama of mountain peaks. For others it was an apprehension of natural beauty as order – a sense of organization outside of human framing.

The esthetic ideal also embraced wilderness preservation. By 1900 Americans partook of a veritable wilderness cult, historian Roderick Nash has written.[10] To some wilderness was necessary for the psychological rejuvenation of an overwrought urban population. To others wilderness should be preserved in order to keep alive the possibility of a reenactment of the national epic of heroic struggle with nature. (Enter the wilderness a citified weakling and come out a man – so went the cry of those who, like Theodore Roosevelt, feared American men were becoming effete.) Others found in wilderness an argument for diversity. They feared that the numbing uniformity of modern industrial civilization would destroy all natural coherence, order, and beauty. John Muir, the arch druid of the early twentieth century, asserted the rights of nature on a par with humans', but few devotees of esthetic conservation went so far. Nonetheless, whatever their differing rationales, defenders of natural beauty and wilderness fought the tendency of their onrushing industrial civilization to turn all of nature into a commodity with a price tag.

The chief political victory of the esthetic wing – the creation of the National Park Service in 1916 and the accompanying rationalization of the park system – reflected contradictions implicit in the preservationists'

9 Although historians have often focused on changing attitudes toward the wilderness, it may be that many Americans came to believe in preservation because they saw the disappearance of pastoral landscapes they had known under the onrush of industrialization. For a suggestive reading of the appreciation of nature, and such a transition, see Henry Seidel Canby, *The Age of Confidence* (New York, 1935), chap. 12.
10 Roderick Nash, *Wilderness and the American Mind*, rev. ed. (New Haven, 1967), chap. 9. On the history of the national parks, see Alfred Runte, *The National Parks: The American Experience* (Lincoln, Nebr., 1976).

positions. Congress told the park service to both preserve areas in their natural state and provide for the public's enjoyment. The trouble was that access threatened to destroy preservation. Progressive-Era conservationists tried to balance the competing goods. Even Muir and the Sierra Club initially favored steps to make wilderness more accessible. The first directors of the park service, Stephen Mather (1916–29) and Horace M. Albright (1929–33), worked eagerly to promote tourism in the parks in the belief, probably correct, that visitors would become supporters of the park system. They endorsed sumptuous hotels, such as Yosemite's Ahwahnee, the epitome of genteel rusticity, so that well-heeled vacationers could take nature with all the comforts of home. In 1918 they made the fateful decision to allow automobiles in the parks. The trickle of tourists would become a torrent after World War II and bring to the fore a very nearly insoluble conflict between access and preservation.

By World War I the conservation movement counted notable achievements for efficiency, equity, and esthetics. The efficiency branch could point to major changes in the way the country approached its natural resources. To cite but two: The system of national forests gave Pinchot and his successors the tools to exercise their vision of rational, expert management; the Bureau of Reclamation promised to develop Western water resources for greater productivity. Equity advocates endorsed such measures, particularly the 160-acre limitation, as decisive steps toward fairer distribution of nature's riches. The esthetic school, though dismayed at the loss of Hetch Hetchy, took comfort in the establishment of a system dedicated to preservation. None of these victories was complete, however, and the internal contradictions of the conservation movement itself were not resolved. The pace of capitalist development sharpened conservation dilemmas, and posed new ones, over the next decades.

The conservation movement's momentum faltered in the 1920s. Suspicious of anything that interfered with capitalist expansion, the Harding, Coolidge, and Hoover administrations tried to fuse government and business operations in what some historians have termed the "associative state."[11] The chief casualty of such an approach in conservation matters were equity-oriented policies. Presidents who placed Andrew W. Mellon, one of the world's richest men, in charge of the Treasury Department and endorsed his efforts to reduce income taxes for the rich were not likely to promote policies designed to counteract concentrations of wealth. Measures that impinged on the market, such as early efforts to deal with water pollution by the oil industry, were greatly diluted. Hoover tried to cede the

---

11 For a perhaps too positive assessment of conservation from 1921 to 1933, see Donald C. Swain, *Federal Conservation Policy, 1921–1933* (Berkeley, Calif., 1963). On the "associative state" see Ellis W. Hawley, *The Great War and the Search for a Modern Order: A History of the American People and Their Institutions, 1917–1933* (New York, 1979), pp. 90–105.

public domain to the states for their administration, or more likely, the devolution of its most valuable parcels into private hands. With the Great Depression, however, these vast areas seemed unprofitable, and the public domain remained in federal hands – a crucial foundation for later efforts to deal with the Western environment. The conservation programs that fared best politically were efficiency measures, for they often dovetailed with business interests. The Forest Service tailored its policies to suit the lumber trade associations. Reclamation projects expanded slowly. What seemed to be a major departure – the authorization of the giant Boulder (later Hoover) Dam on the lower Colorado River – was carefully hedged so that its hydroelectric production did not interfere with private utilities.

The esthetic wing saw few victories, since expanding preservation areas took areas out of production. The huge Death Valley National Monument was authorized late in Hoover's term, but was compromised by the anomalous provision that borax mining could continue inside the monument. Acadia and Shenandoah were added to the roster of national parks largely for their scenic and recreational appeal. Conservationists of all persuasions campaigned actively during the 1920s, but their goals needed the catastrophe of the Great Depression, and the resulting shift in intellectual and political climate, to prosper.

Franklin D. Roosevelt and his administration reinvigorated conservation politics.[12] As avid a conservationist as his cousin Theodore, the squire of Hyde Park, who once listed his occupation as "tree farmer," put his personal imprint on environmental measures. The depression gave FDR and his administration an unusually broad field in which to expand on the Progressive-Era conservation legacy. The economic crisis discredited the business-oriented policies of the 1920s and dealt advocates of bold governmental action a strong hand. Although some people thought federal action should primarily assist business, many others favored measures that would curb the market and enhance government's role as a counterweight to business power. Elements of social democracy enjoyed more legitimacy than probably at any time in American history.

For conservationists a key concept was planning – comprehensive, expert designs for vast sections of the country. Environmental planning drew on the intellectual legacy of John Wesley Powell, who had proposed organizing the development of the West by river basins, and on the heretofore rather feeble efforts of the Reclamation Bureau. But planning in the 1930s far outstripped

---

12 The author has considered some of these questions in relation to American liberalism; this essay represents a rethinking of the environmental issues of the period. See Clayton R. Koppes, "Environmental Policy and American Liberalism: The Department of the Interior, 1933–1953," *Environmental Review* 7 (Spring 1983): 17–41. The earlier article contains fuller citations.

even Powell's vision. "We now undertake to achieve a grand vision for the whole country," averred Harold L. Ickes upon taking office as secretary of the interior. In this breathtaking vision planners would assess the optimum environmental uses of millions of parcels of land, and decide "this land shall be cropped, this shall be range, this shall be forest, this shall be worked for minerals." Ickes believed such planning was essential both for efficiency and for "a more equable distribution" of the bounties of natural resources. What lay behind this expansive vision was the ideal of achieving ecological harmony and social justice through state action. He borrowed a concept of community from the natural world: "A forest is a community of trees, as a city is a community of human beings," he said. A struggle for existence took place in nature, to be sure, "but, on the other hand, a forest is a cooperative community in which each tree helps its neighbor and contributes its part to the common protection of the young."[13] For probably the first time in history a cabinet officer suggested Americans might emulate nature. The most fully realized planning program was the Tennessee Valley Authority, a product of the first hundred days of the Roosevelt presidency. Myriad planning groups toiled throughout the federal bureaucracy, spinning plans that proved politically impossible. Where conservationists saw planning as etching dreams of a cooperative commonwealth, conservatives and business interests feared the substitution of state directives for market incentives.

In environmental policy, as in other areas of national life, the power of the federal government grew markedly under the New Deal. Conservationists tried to incorporate local decision making within the overall scheme of national planning and policy. Soil-conservation district boards exercised considerable power at the local level, as did the district advisory boards of the Grazing Service (predecessor of the Bureau of Land Management). The TVA had a decentralist vision. Yet conservationists often found decentralization frustrating, for it tended to reflect the immediate economic interests of powerful regional elites rather than environmental priorities. Arguing that natural resources belonged to the whole country, conservationists thus usually tried to have environmental policy made at the national level. They did not anticipate that federal conservation policies might prove to be environmentally destructive or that local autonomy would emerge as a rallying cry of the post-1960s environmental movement.

Though each branch of the conservation movement received new impetus in the 1930s, the equity wing found its position most enhanced. In the face of the depression's agonies, who but ideologues could believe the market

---

13 Marquis James interview with Harold L. Ickes, "The National Domain and the New Deal," *Saturday Evening Post* 206 (23 December 1933): 55, 10. On the emergence of ecology to prominence in the 1930s, see Donald Worster, *Nature's Economy: The Roots of Ecology* (San Francisco, 1977), chap. 12.

provided fairly for citizens' welfare? Arthur Morgan, first chairman of the Tennessee Valley Authority, pointed out: "Economic surplus does not necessarily result in a prosperous and happy people. We need a greater sharing." This sense of a need for equity was closely linked to the management of natural resources. The National Resources Committee called for reducing "glaring inequalities of wealth and income." Some New Dealers believed that a better distribution of income would help stave off future depressions. For many conservationists equity was an ethical imperative, especially as applied to the environment. As Morgan said: "We are not complete owners of the soil, but only trustees for a generation." Ickes believed "we must get a sense of personal responsibility toward the national resources as a whole."[14]

If the Progressive-Era efficiency wing had achieved its greatest impact through federal forest management, the hallmark of New Deal efficiency was federal dam building. Today environmentalists view big dams as ecological disasters, but to New Deal conservationists dams were hydroelectric liberators. Boulder, Grand Coulee, and the TVA were powerful cultural symbols. The British dramatist J. B. Priestley devoted a dozen pages to a celebration of the great icon, Boulder Dam. In Stuart Chase's *Rich Land, Poor Land* a dam is the centerpiece in a planned river valley in which eroded submarginal land gives way to a reservoir, state park, and reclaimed farmland; pollution is cleaned up; navigation is enhanced; a gas works is supplanted by a park and waterfront drive; and a suburb built on the grid pattern undergoes a metamorphosis into a greenbelt-protected haven of curvilinear streets.[15] Dams symbolized both humans' control of nature and the nation's triumphant combat with the depression. Armies of foreign visitors, trooping through the turbine rooms and gazing down spillways, absorbed the vision of concrete harnessing natural resources for social progress. Big dams became a staple of American foreign aid after World War II as its technical advisers carried the gospel of hydroelectric efficiency to the third world. Just as the TVA had rescued the Tennessee Valley – or thus the legend went – so too valley authorities on the Jordan or the Mekong would bring progress and peace to the developing world.

Dams linked efficiency with equity. They stood for public power – hydroelectric development carried out by the government, and hence presumably more attuned to the public interest, rather than by private

14 Harold L. Ickes, "Saving the Good Earth: The Mississippi Valley Committee and Its Plan," *Survey Graphic* 23 (February 1934): 93; Arthur E. Morgan, "Bench-Marks in the Tennessee Valley," *Survey Graphic* 23 (January 1934): 8, 9; National Resource Committee, "Our Cities: Their Role in the National Economy," February 1937, National Resources Committee Files, Franklin D. Roosevelt Library, Hyde Park, N.Y.

15 Stuart Chase, *Rich Land, Poor Land: A Study of Waste in the Natural Resources of America* (New York, 1936); J. B. Priestley, *Midnight on the Desert* (New York, 1938).

Clayton R. Koppes

utilities which were wracked by scandals in the 1930s. Some conservationists argued that government hydroelectric projects would provide a yardstick against which to measure the fairness of private companies' rates and service. Others favored production by the state for its own sake. Private industry bitterly fought government production.

Many conservationists saw dams as the cornerstone of social policy extending well beyond cheap hydroelectricity. They envisioned regional development programs that would bring a variety of benefits, both economic and social, to the disadvantaged population. These goals were frequently large-scale applications of the grass-roots democracy implicit in Reclamation's acreage limitation: an attempt to target the lower class, usually rural, as the particular beneficiaries of government programs. Franklin Roosevelt emphasized that these programs should not benefit existing landlords but provide small tracts to give "the *Grapes of Wrath* families of the nation" a new start. He envisioned a string of dams in the Columbia basin of the Pacific Northwest that would be the basis for a planned society supporting eighty thousand families in agriculture and twenty thousand more in small industries. Arthur Morgan saw the mission of TVA as not simply building dams or generating hydroelectricity but as an experiment in building a viable rural community with a strong indigenous base.

Conservationists tried to implement these goals with administrative structures that challenged market-oriented policies – the independent valley authority, such as the TVA, and regional development agencies within the Department of the Interior. Business interests and economic conservatives, fearing the expanding role the state played in production, fought them bitterly. The TVA won a crucial battle when it established a monopoly over electricity production in its service region by forcing private utilities there to sell out to it. The Interior Department established the right to build steam-generating plants, which would provide power if their dams' production fell short, and to string transmission lines directly to their customers. Federal hydroelectric installations grew impressively. The capacity of Reclamation Bureau generating plants increased from a minuscule 30,000 kilowatts in 1933 to 2,178,197 kilowatts in 1946, making the agency the largest generator of electrical power in the world. Ambitious plans to extend these programs were blocked, however, by the enduring controversy over the role of the state in production. A plan to establish seven "little TVA's" failed in Congress, and the Interior Department met recurrent opposition to its attempts to expand in the West.

It proved easier to fulfill the goals of efficiency than equity. Morgan's vision of the TVA as a model for the development of cooperative communities was scrapped after a few years. Instead the TVA focused on power production and accommodated itself to the regional political structure. "By 1936 TVA should have been called the Tennessee Valley Power Produc-

242

tion and Flood Control Corporation," wrote Rexford Tugwell and E. C. Banfield.[16]

Indeed, the TVA foreshadowed the way in which efficiency conservation devoid of equity concerns could dovetail with capitalist expansion and bolster the national security state. Progressive-Era advocates of efficiency conservation, such as Theodore Roosevelt and Pinchot, were often visceral nationalists and saw the wise use of natural resources as a crucial underpinning of a vigorous foreign policy. But it was with America's vast new global role during World War II and the cold war that efficiency conservation became most closely identified with foreign policy. Instead of assisting cooperative communities and *Grapes of Wrath* families, New Deal hydroelectric projects during World War II were harnessed to that most alien of technologies: nuclear power. The dams of the TVA and of the Bonneville Power Administration in the Pacific Northwest provided the cheap, abundant electricity necessary for the manufacture of the atomic bomb. The TVA went on to become a leading producer of nuclear energy in the 1960s and 70s, and, with its coal-fired generating plants, to establish an air pollution record as bad as many private utilities. By the 1980s the TVA icon was badly smudged, and analysts such as the eminent urbanologist Jane Jacobs were explaining "Why TVA Failed."[17]

The goal of efficiency would eventually overwhelm aspirations toward equity in the Department of the Interior as well, but that would not become clear until after World War II. In the more liberal climate of the 1930s and early war years, and under the leadership of Secretary Ickes, the department made some brave attempts to use efficiency to promote equity. Previously much of the electricity produced at federal installations had been sold to private utilities which, in turn, sent the electricity over their lines and turned a profit. Instead Ickes gave primacy to public bodies and announced the department would assist in organizing cooperatives. His aim was to retain federal control and eliminate private profit in the areas where government production was dominant. He achieved his goals only in part, for after World War II private utilities whittled away at his empire and redistributive purposes.

He also made a significant attempt to reinvigorate the 160-acre law. One of the principal equity measures of Progressive-Era conservation, the acreage limitation had been all but forgotten in the 1920s. Efficiency-minded reccamation bureaucrats advised Ickes that the law had been "a dead letter for years" and urged him to "let sleeping dogs lie." The lack of enforcement

16 Rexford G. Tugwell and E. C. Banfield, "Grass Roots Democracy – Myth or Reality?" *Public Administration Review* 10 (1950): 50.
17 Jane Jacobs, "Why TVA Failed," *New York Review of Books* (10 May 1984): 41–7. For a more nuanced assessment, see Erwin C. Hargrove and Paul K. Conkin, eds., *TVA: Fifty Years of Grass-Roots Democracy* (Urbana, Ill., 1984).

limitation had not been especially detrimental, since early reclamation projects had been relatively small and land ownership was fairly equally distributed. But on the department's biggest project, the multibillion-dollar Central Valley Project in California, landholding was sharply skewed toward large owners. Ickes saw acreage limitation as a way to insure the wide distribution of the project's benefits, but even more, as a lever to correct the valley's land concentration. Here was the strongest echo yet in policy of Newlands' dream of using the tool of efficiency – federal irrigation – to promote equity by breaking up land monopoly. Ickes managed to keep the acreage limitation in the Central Valley Project's authorizing legislation only with difficulty. Politically powerful groups were eager to benefit from efficiency conservation but wanted to thwart the equity measures. The secretary's blueprint faced an uncertain future after World War II.

Ickes's concern for equity surfaced in his effort to curb the rich salmon fishery monopoly under the jurisdiction of the Fish and Wildlife Service (F&WS) in the territory of Alaska. The fishery was dominated by technologically superior firms headquartered in Seattle. In a textbook study of firms capturing their regulators, the big canning companies maneuvered F&WS , which issued fishing permits, to protect their access to the resource better than they could have done in a competitive market. The F&WS saw its mission simply in terms of efficiency; it was interested only in maintenance of the resource and opposed redistribution of permits "to accomplish social objectives." Ickes persisted in his plans to "smash the salmon monopoly" and divide the permits among small fishermen (many of them Alaska natives) and cooperatives. Unable to move during the war, he took his first steps toward this policy in late 1945. But when he left office in early 1946, his successors retreated to the simpler goal of efficiency.[18]

Complementing these efforts in the Interior Department was a revived interest in equity issues in forest and range management. Ferdinand A. Silcox, chief forester of the Forest Service, delivered wide-ranging critiques of forestry as currently practiced. Reflecting the community ethos of other New Deal conservationists, he believed wise environmental practices fostered healthy communities. "The issue, in a nutshell, is selfish private interest against social stability," he said. He envisioned public foresters as acting for the common good as against predatory interests. "Forestry not backed up with social ideals is merely a job," he said.[19]

Silcox blended efficiency and equity in a comprehensive program that gave

18 Charles E. Jackson to Ickes, 16 March 1944, File 3–4, Records of the Office of the Secretary of the Interior, Record Group 48, National Archives, Washington, D.C.
19 F. A. Silcox, "Foresters Must Choose," *Journal of Forestry* (March 1935): 203. For a stimulating interpretation of the relationship between public and private forestry, see William G. Robbins, *Lumberjacks and Legislators: Political Economy of the U.S. Lumber Industry, 1890–1941* (College Station, Tex., 1982).

primacy to public control over private profit. He advocated a vastly increased federal role in forestry. As a minimum he wanted to extend federal supervision over private holdings and to substantially increase the size of national and state forests. He even proposed that the federal and state governments go into production by logging their own timber and perhaps milling it. These steps might be taken to provide stable communities with permanent employment and cheap local supplies. Silcox's proposals raised a howl of protest from private foresters since they crossed the crucial divide between regulation for efficiency, which business found congenial, and state production for equity, which raised a fundamental threat to capitalist interests.[20]

On the range, too, concerns about equity and efficiency were intertwined. With the passage of the Taylor Grazing Act in 1934, one of the oldest land-use traditions in America came to an end; the public domain, open to all, was effectively closed and placed under federal regulation. This great grazing commons – equal in size to California and Oregon combined – had suffered the serious deterioration that often afflicts unregulated commons in which each individual's incentive is to maximize his use even though it may destroy the common resource. Stock raisers and conservationists agreed that the range needed federal regulation to promote efficient use over wasteful exploitation. The Taylor Grazing Act offered the possibility of combining efficiency and equity, but its implementation was flawed. Bowing to the power of western ranchers, the Department of the Interior's Grazing Service allowed the larger stock growers to claim a disproportionate number of the new grazing permits. (Seven percent of the permit holders controlled 44 percent of the allotted cattle, and 4 percent of the permittees ran 22 percent of the designated sheep.)[21] Ironically, the biggest losers were the itinerant sheepherders, who had trailed small, but highly destructive, flocks across the western meadows. In the name of efficiency they were all but frozen out in favor of large, settled ranchers. The situation was analogous to that of Southern agriculture, where New Deal policies enabled large landowners to invest in new technology, consolidate their holdings, and dislodge their tenants and sharecroppers.

A related problem on the western range was Ickes's promise to limit grazing fees to the cost of administration of the Grazing Service. This ploy, which resulted in lower fees than those charged for comparable resources by the Forest Service, was designed to win support for his drive to make his department a comprehensive conservation agency. But his pledge was ill

---

20 Silcox, "Foresters Must Choose," p. 202.
21 William D. Rowley, *U.S. Forest Service Grazing and Rangelands: A History* (College Station, Tex., 1985), p. 155. Donald Worster has noted the inability of New Deal planners, even in the midst of the environmental disaster of the Dust Bowl, to get away from the idea of increasing capacity. See *Dust Bowl: The Southern Plains in the 1930s* (New York, 1979), pp. 196–7.

advised, for since the cost of administration was well below the actual market value of the grazing resource, permit holders in effect received a substantial subsidy. Ickes tried to correct both the fee structure and skewed distribution of permits late in his term, but this effort was doomed in the changed postwar political climate.

By the end of World War II, New Deal conservationists had greatly expanded the scope of the efficiency doctrine, especially through their dam-building activities. They had also given new prominence to a number of equity issues. Most of the latter were raised rather late in the day, however. The timing was probably unavoidable, for the question of how to distribute the benefits of federal projects became acute only when the projects neared completion, which often entailed several years of lead time. The timing was nonetheless unfortunate for equity advocates. By the late 1930s the resurgent conservative coalition in Congress made it difficult to realize such goals. During World War II the economic boom and national security consciousness made it even harder to advance equity issues; the salmon and grazing permit problems were placed on hold during the war as maximum production, not social justice, was paramount. The best, perhaps only, chance to attain the sweeping equity goals lay early in the New Deal. The dominance of the efficiency school threatened to create a postwar developmental juggernaut that would harm not only redistributive goals but esthetic and ecological concerns as well.

The esthetic phase of the conservation movement gained power during the New Deal. The economic failure encouraged Americans to recapture spiritual and community values. The criticism of America as a "business civilization" – narrow, materialistic, hostile to things of the spirit – expanded from artistic and intellectual circles to politics. Secretary of Agriculture Henry A. Wallace hoped the New Deal would contribute "toward giving life meaning, joy and beauty for generations to come." Robert Marshall, founder of the Wilderness Society and sometime federal bureaucrat, placed spiritual needs in the natural world. "It is more vital for many humans to view the sunset across some wilderness lakelet or scale the summit of a deeply wooded mountain, than it is to enjoy any material comfort which twentieth-century mechanization has bestowed."[22]

Esthetic conservation underwent a critical transition as it felt the influence of the emerging science of ecology. In the hands of Aldo Leopold and others, ecology offered both a technique for the management of the environment and an elegant, artistic appreciation of the wholeness of nature. For a pragmatic society, ecology provided a crucial scientific underpinning which had over-tones of objectivity and utility. Ecology shifted the focus from the scenic and

22 Henry A. Wallace, *New Frontiers* (New York, 1934), p. 273; Robert Marshall, *The Social Management of American Forests* (New York 1930), p. 9.

246

monumental. Though spectacular scenery might still be protected, an eco-logical perspective gave primacy to the preservation of large areas repre-sentative of what Leopold called "biotic communities." In turn, emphasis shifted toward visitors' having a more authentic encounter with nature. Making wilderness areas accessible met increasing opposition; efforts were made to limit the impact of visitor accommodations; and false theatrics, such as the "fire fall" at Yosemite, were eliminated. "I am death on roads," Ickes told a parks convention in 1934. Skyline drives and similar motorways may sound "poetical" but may in fact be "atrocities." The esthetic and ecological rationales became fused, laying the foundation for the emergence of the new preservationist philosophy in the 1960s and 1970s.[23]

The esthetic/ecological attitude found expression in policy through the growth of preserved areas and a change in their orientation. The acreage included in the national park and monument system grew from 14,739,405 in 1933 to 20,346,249 in 1946, and the number of national monuments increased from thirty-three to eighty-six. The Forest Service and the Bureau of Indian Affairs designated large areas as wilderness zones. A host of wildlife refuges were added. But more revealing than these quantitative measure-ments was the changing orientation of the National Park Service. Five new parks – Olympic, Kings Canyon, Big Bend, Isle Royale, and Everglades – were chiefly wilderness units, and their boundaries were drawn with new-found attention to ecological principals. Visitor accommodations were kept to a minimum. Everglades represented the sharpest break with the monu-mentalist tradition. It lacked visually spectacular landforms – the change in elevation was all but imperceptible – and owed its importance to the abun-dance of wildlife and its unique role in the ecology of South Florida.

The depression created economic conditions conducive to implementation of the ecological approach. Much of the land incorporated into the parks and monuments seemed of little economic value or was in the national forest system and could be transferred relatively easily. If timber had been more valuable the size of Olympic National Park would have been much smaller. The malaise in the forest products industry also made possible what could have been one of the greatest additions to the national park system – a sizable, ecologically sound Redwoods National Park composed of old-growth tim-ber. Lumber companies were willing to sell, cheap. The Interior Department was interested. The opportunity passed, however, largely because of oppo-sition from the Save-the-Redwoods League, which was dominated by con-servatives who both feared federal government action and failed to absorb the new ecological philosophy. After bitter controversy, an ecologically compromised Redwoods National Park was finally established in the 1960s

23 Quoted in Stephen Fox, *John Muir and His Legacy: The American Environmental Movement* (Boston, 1981).

Clayton R. Koppes

and 1970s, and at great cost. The missed opportunity in the redwoods in the 1930s was as tragic for the preservation movement as Hetch Hetchy.[24]

Although World War II posed serious threats to the esthetic/ecological wing of conservation, Ickes maintained the inviolability of the parks and monuments. He turned back an attempt to raid Olympic National Park for Sitka spruce, which was needed for aircraft production; an alternative supply was found in British Columbia. Sheep and cattle did not trample the parks' meadows, as in World War I. Roosevelt and Ickes succeeded in creating Jackson Hole National Monument by means of a controversial, high-handed executive order.

Preservation had been less costly politically and economically during the depression when pressure to use resources was minimal. And despite mounting ecological understanding, opposition on preservationist grounds to dams outside national parks and monuments was minimal. Paradoxically the New Deal's invigoration of the great dam-building agencies, the Bureau of Reclamation and the Corps of Engineers, created severe postwar pressures against preservation.

The postwar economic revival made natural resources valuable again and restored business legitimacy. As government agencies sought to expand their efficiency programs in line with a resurgent capitalism, they raised profound dangers for equity and esthetics/ecology. The shift in tone was most evident in the Department of the Interior, where Ickes's successors, Julius A. Krug (1946–9), a former TVA power engineer, and Oscar L. Chapman (1949–53), a longtime departmental assistant secretary, devoted most of their efforts to efficiency programs. Economic growth constituted "the very essence of our development as a nation," said Chapman, who had once championed equity and esthetic goals as well. "Conservation does not mean . . . the locking up of some resource in order to keep people from touching or using it. It means to develop the resource in a wise way." David Lilienthal, who had spearheaded the TVA's buy outof private utilities, penned an appreciation of large corporations in his early 1950s tract *Big Business: A New Era.* Efficiency conservation could provide the infrastructure development that would spur regional economic growth and provide the material basis for national security.[25]

Controversy still surrounded some efficiency programs, particularly the extension of costly Reclamation Bureau facilities. Generally speaking, however, equity issues raised the most troublesome political problems. The Bureau of Reclamation and the Forest Service learned that their efficiency programs would prosper if they abandoned the politically troublesome

24 Susan Schrepfer, *The Fight to Save the Redwoods: A History of Environmental Reform, 1917–1978* (Madison, Wis., 1983), pp. 72–9.
25 U.S. Senate, 81st Cong., 2nd Sess., Committee on Interior and Insular Affairs, *Hearings, Nomination of Oscar L. Chapman to Be Secretary of the Interior* (1950), p. 6.

248

equity issues. In effect conservation bureaus of the Truman-Eisenhower era chose to increase capacity (in Reclamation's case) and maintain stability (in the case of the Forest Service) and not try to redirect the distribution of benefits.

The growing dominance by the efficiency forces was particularly striking in the Reclamation Bureau's transition under its expansion-minded commissioner Michael Straus from 1945 to 1953. By the early 1950s the once anemic bureau dominated the Interior Department, commanding 61 percent of its budget. Under Straus the bureau was "principally interested in obtaining work and jurisdiction and is not greatly interested in the social and economic problems," said Undersecretary Abe Fortas in 1945. Three major developments confirmed Fortas's warning. First, dam projects in the Columbia Valley, once an empire of dreams for equity-minded New Dealers, became strictly efficiency oriented. The Bureau of Reclamation and the Army Corps of Engineers signed the so-called Newell-Weaver agreement in 1949 in which they divided the choice sites between them. In so doing they effectively killed a regional planning agency and the equity goals such a body might have attempted. Second, through administrative subterfuges and ingenious legal opinions, Straus reduced the 160-acre law to a dead letter. The heavily subsidized water of the Central Valley Project in California, which had once seemed a way to combat the pyramidal land ownership structure, became a bulwark of the status quo. Third, the bureau retreated from Ickes's position of giving preference to cooperatives and municipalities in the distribution of electricity from its dams. Instead Reclamation entered into a series of wheeling agreements in which federally generated power was turned over to private utilities for transmission to consumers. The companies turned a handsome, all but guaranteed profit in the deal. Shorn of the equity provisions that had originally leavened the reclamation vision, these projects fit the mid-century emphasis on capitalist expansion.

Other programs fell into the same pattern. Upon Ickes's departure the Interior Department abandoned efforts to break the Alaska salmon monopoly. The department squelched a program to mitigate grazing abuse on the western range and instead augmented the power of the district advisory boards, which were dominated by the big ranchers. The Forest Service retreated from Silcox's vision. Efforts to foster community stability — admittedly a difficult proposition — were largely abandoned. Certainly the federal foresters dared not propose government involvement in lumber production. Secretary of Agriculture Charles F. Brannan halted the redistribution of grazing permits in the national forests.[26]

26 David A. Clary, "What Price Sustained Yield? The Forest Service, Community Stability, and Timber Monopoly under the 1944 Sustained-Yield Act," *Journal of Forest History* 31 (January 1987): 4–18.

The gospel of efficiency mid-century style provoked a reenactment of the Progressive-Era conflict with the esthetic/ecological school. The principle of national park sanctity was first challenged in 1947 when timber interests won Interior Department support for a time to delete fifty-six thousand acres from Olympic National Park; eventually the move failed, however. Of the utmost seriousness was the threat of a reprise of Hetch Hetchy. The Bureau of Reclamation, seconded by Secretary Chapman, proposed to build a dam at Echo Park, in the heart of Dinosaur National Monument. A key structure in the bureau's fondest dream, the massive Upper Colorado River Basin Program, Echo Park Dam provoked a *High Noon* showdown between the efficiency and esthetic traditions. Chapman agreed that Dinosaur was "potentially a good park unit." But he decided that "the growth and development of the West" required the dam and "this is the most important consideration to be faced in this matter."[27]

Preservationists countered that the dam would obliterate impressive scenery. The ecological argument was not directly applicable to Dinosaur National Monument. But in a larger sense the ecological argument for a world of diversity was at stake in the Echo Park imbroglio, for the Reclamation Bureau had dams on the drawing board for Glacier, Big Bend, Kings Canyon, and Grand Canyon national parks. Preservationists believed, rightly, that the future of esthetic/ecological conservation was at stake in Echo Park. Ultimately political pressure made Chapman back down on his support for the dam, and the issue remained deadlocked until 1955, when an alternative site outside the park and monument system was chosen.

Although the inviolability of the park and monument system was sustained, other rich scenic areas were lost to the dam builders. Glen Canyon Dam inundated a 186-mile stretch of the spectacular canyon country of the Colorado River in southeastern Utah, which Ickes had wanted to protect in a spectacular national monument. Like the failure to establish a Redwoods National Park in the 1930s, this was one of the great missed opportunities of esthetic conservation. The Bureau of Reclamation, again supported by Chapman, also wanted to build a giant dam in Hells Canyon of the Snake River, the deepest canyon in North America. Opposition from a private utility, which wanted to build its own dam on the site, blocked the dam for a time. For preservationists, including Ickes, the crucial thing was to stop any dam, public or private. Indicative of their growing strength, the esthetic/ecological forces were able to block construction until the 1960s, when the Supreme Court and Congress gave Hells Canyon protection. At mid-century preservationists found themselves most sharply in conflict not with private

27 Chapman to Arthur Carhart, 6 November 1951, box 122, Oscar L. Chapman Papers, Harry S. Truman Library, Independence, Mo.

developers but with another wing of the conservation movement that also traced its roots to the Progressive Era.

Six decades of American conservation had brought significant change to the American environment and had produced a rapidly maturing conservation movement on the brink of transition to the environmental movement. Conservation's fate had been closely related to economic changes as reflected in political transitions, as well as scientific evolution. The efficiency school of conservation was dominant in the 1950s, and its programs had brought substantial environmental change to the country, particularly the West. Yet the efficiency wing stood at the peak of its power and legitimacy. The esthetic/ecological school, having survived the crucial challenge at Echo Park, had established the inviolability of the national park and monument system; this was an indispensable basis for the growth of broader preservationist and environmental movements from the 1960s onward. The equity branch of the movement proved to be the least successful. Using the benefits of efficiency programs for redistributive purposes always aroused political opposition, and efficiency-oriented bureaucracies usually had little sympathy for such troublesome issues. Moreover, in the absence of grass-roots organizations, change from the top posed grave difficulties. Some of the changes in the way Americans approached their environment had averted disaster, others contributed to the deepening of environmental problems. The necessary emergence of a dramatically transformed environmental perspective in the 1960s testified to the ambiguous legacy of the conservation movement.

I I The Changing Face of Soviet Conservation

Douglas R. Weiner

To readers familiar with the history of American conservationism, the fate of the Russian and Soviet movement offers both striking parallels as well as some notable divergences. Who could fail to appreciate, for example, the similar upwellings of national indignation among Soviets and Americans during the 1960s when such national treasures as Lake Baikal and the Grand Canyon became the objects of development schemes? Indeed, the decades-long struggle between Soviet preservationists and logging, agricultural, and other economic interests echoes our own continuing war between the children of John Muir and those of Gifford Pinchot. Recent Soviet interest in outdoor recreation and national parks has also been a feature of modern American life, especially among our urban-educated population.

Yet, the differences in our two national experiences stand out just as dramatically. Where the American conservation movement's attention early became firmly focused on the protection of recreational amenities, preeminently national parks and game resources, the efforts of its Soviet counterpart were long directed at advancing a program for the ecological study of nature in order to guide economic development scientifically. Correspondingly, the Soviet conservation movement for most of its existence has been dominated to a far greater extent than the American by professional scientists, and its fate has been more closely linked to that of ecology as a science. The reasons for these significant differences lie in the realms of politics, culture, and social structure, and will be explored in this essay.

BRIEF HISTORICAL BACKGROUND

The existence of conservation as a programmatic movement in Russia, as in the United States, really only begins about the turn of the century, although individual voices were raised decades earlier in both lands.[1] Like its

1 An extended description and analysis of the Russian and Soviet conservation movement prior to World War II may be found in Douglas R. Weiner, *Models of Nature: Conservation,*

Progressive-Era American counterpart, the Russian conservation movement embraced a multiplicity of approaches and positions. It is helpful to divide these into three main groupings: utilitarian, cultural-esthetic-ethical, and scientific.

Crowning the utilitarian's view of creation were those animals and plants that could be directly put to economic use. Other life forms providing indirect benefit to the economy, such as insectivorous birds, were also deemed worthy of protection. Occupying the lowest rung of this chain of being were animals which were seen to pose threats to human life and livelihood while presenting no discernible economic benefit themselves; this group, which by consensus included almost all of the rare, large predators of the Russian Empire (snow leopard, Siberian tiger, cheetah, wolf), was fit only for extermination. Utilitarians were well represented among governmental game-management officials, who saw through the legislative establishment, by the Imperial Duma, of the Barguzin sable preserve along the shores of Lake Baikal – the empire's first – just three months before the February 1917 revolution. Additionally, utilitarian conservation thinking was strong among progressive biologists, particularly in Moscow, who hoped to one day create an earthly paradise through the scientific "conquest" of nature. Many political radicals, with their uncritical faith in science and their distaste for the spontaneous and the unplanned, nourished these same hopes.

In sharp contrast were arguments for nature protection based on cultural, esthetic, or moral grounds. Looking to Swiss and German models, Russian exemplars of this trend, such as botanist Ivan Parfen'evich Borodin, emphasized landscape protection and the preservation of unique "monuments of nature," a term, incidentally, which he adopted from the German *Naturdenkmal*. Nature, it was thought, was the source of all noble values, especially love of one's native land, respect for life, and love of beauty. These neo-romantic beliefs were hostile to the emerging bustling, dirty, atomized, modern, industrial era Russia was now entering.

Lastly, an ecological approach was developed – during the 1890s – which aimed at the protection and long-term study of what were believed to be pristine, integral ecological communities incorporated in reserves called *zapovedniki*. Such study would, it was hoped, reveal the secrets of the structures of such communities. Using a tract of land under study as a baseline (*etalon*, in Russian), scientists would then be able to recommend appropriate economic uses for surrounding lands in conformity with their ecological carrying capacity as established in the *etalon*. Severely degraded lands could be rehabilitated using the protected *etalon* as a model of healthy

Ecology, and Cultural Revolution in Soviet Russia (Bloomington: Indiana University Press, 1988). This discussion has been synopsized from that account.

Douglas R. Weiner

nature. More than any other individual, Professor Grigorii Aleksandrovich Kozhevnikov, director of the Moscow University Zoological Museum, emerged as an exponent of this approach.

Despite the rich variety of perspectives, from a numerical standpoint the infant Russian conservation movement was not terribly extensive. It did claim the support of the prestigious elite hunting societies, such as the Moscow Society of Hunters and the Imperial Society for Responsible Hunting (Imperatorskoe obshchestvo pravil'noi okhoty), composed largely of estate holders and urban professionals. But the movement's generals were a still smaller band of academic biologists. With backing from the Academy of Sciences (where he had served as vice-president) and from the Imperial Russian Geographical Society, Borodin founded (1911) and led the Society's Permanent Conservation Commission, a governmental advisory body of thirty-one prominent science and government leaders. Also in 1911, fellow botanist Professor Valerii Ivanovich Taliev of Khar'kov founded a society of naturalists there devoted above all to nature protection. This came close on the heels of the creation the previous year of Russia's first citizen conservation group, the Khortitsa Society of the Defenders of Nature, whose primary mission was to save some picturesque cliffs overlooking the Dnieper River. Although conservation groups coalesced in some provincial towns as well, by World War I the number of activists in the empire could not have exceeded much more than a thousand. Still, the movement exercised an influence out of proportion to its numbers, and the creation of a number of nature reserves, notably in the Caucasus and the Baltic, date from this period. It also may be added that, with the participation of Borodin and Kozhevnikov in the 1913 First International Conference for the Protection of Nature in Bern, the Russian conservation movement made its debut on the world scene.

While the war exerted a purely debilitating influence, the February revolution, and later, the Bolshevik accession to power, presented new opportunities for conservationists, which they quickly seized. With the personal encouragement of Lenin, the People's Commissariat of Education, led by the cosmopolitan Anatolii Vasil'evich Lunacharskii, was entrusted with supervision and leadership in conservation matters for the whole of Soviet Russia. By the mid-1920s, a governmental apparatus was in place, featuring a Conservation Department within the commissariat's Main Administration for Scientific Institutions, the Arts, Museums and Conservation, plus an Interagency State Committee for Conservation uniting a number of ministerial bureaucracies. Also, in the last weeks of 1924, an All-Russian Society for Conservation (VOOP) was started up, at the initiative of Kozhevnikov and others, with a membership of about one thousand. By 1928, the Society was publishing an attractive bimonthly *Okhrana prirody* (Conservation) and had built up an impressive network of foreign contacts. Enhancing the movement's clout was the solid support it received from the one hundred thousand-member Society for the Study of Local Lore (the kraevedy).

This postrevolutionary period of the New Economic Policy (NEP) (1921–1928/9) is also noteworthy as a time when the scientific, ecological rationale for conservation rose to preeminence among the different currents. This may be explained both as a negative reaction among Bolshevik leaders to the explicitly anti-industrialist, philosophically idealist teachings of the cultural-esthetic-ethical approach, and as a function of their belief that ecology had an important part to play in placing the economy on a rational, scientifically run basis. That it contributed to furthering a scientific, materialist view of the world enhanced its attractiveness to Bolshevik enlighteners in the realms of science and culture. Support for the ecological program was reflected in Soviet Russia's pioneering establishment of reserves of what was thought to be pristine nature for the purpose of ecological research (*zapovedniki*) under the aegis of the Education Commissariat. By 1933, these numbered thirty-three with an aggregate area of 2,698,527 hectares (6,666,000 acres), and were the loci for significant research, including the development of ecological energetics by Professor Vladimir Vladimirovich Stanchinskii, a zoologist.[2] Two large conservation congresses held in Moscow, in 1929 and 1933, and the widespread observance of "Bird Day" as a school holiday, testified to the vigor of the movement.

The passage of time, however, unfolded increasingly adverse conditions for conservation, including its scientific variety. Some of these had been present from the start, while others arose later, but all of these became vastly intensified with the advent of the First Five-Year Plan (1928–33) and the largely overlapping period of Cultural Revolution. Although utilitarian currents were well represented in Lenin's government, especially in the Commissariats of Agriculture and Foreign Trade, Lenin's personal support for the Education Commissariat offset their influence. With the triumph of the Stalin faction in the late 1920s, however, these currents were given full leeway to press their agenda: hyperindustrialization, vocationalism, working-class upward mobility, and a radical transformation of nature, both human and nonhuman. The consequences of this for the conservation movement were ultimately fatal; the Education Commissariat's missions of enlightenment and the scientific organization of economic life were derided as elitist

---

2 In addition, there were reserves, confusingly called *zapovedniki* as well, that pursued the utilitarian objective of the maximal propagation of selected economically desirable species of animals, usually game. In 1933, these included 13 reserves with a total area of 3,056,477 hectares that had been administered by the Russian Socialist Federated Soviet Republic (RSFSR) People's Commissariat of Agriculture but that had recently passed to the auspices of the USSR People's Commissariat of Foreign Trade. See Appendix 1, "Soviet *zapovedniki*: Affiliation, Area, and Administrative Status, 1925–1933," in Weiner, *Models of Nature*.

and reformist. Conservationists were attacked for their "bourgeois" social origins, for setting themselves up as a technocratic opposition to economic policies decided upon by the party, for pursuing "science for science's sake," and, most crucially, for arguing limits to successful human transformation of nature given existing levels of scientific knowledge. This last point was especially emphasized by Isai Izrailovich Prezent and Trofim Denisovich Lysenko in their successful campaign – first against ecological conservation, and later against genetics – to become arbiters of biological science. It might be added that the radical critiques of ecological conservation contained a fair measure of truth. After all, activists' insistence on the power to veto economic projects and activities that they considered antithetical to the interests of environmental quality (especially to those of "pristine" nature) did represent an elitist challenge to the party's monopoly of economic decision making. This was underscored by the conservationists' proven efforts to curtail the heroic projects of the First Five-Year Plan, including collectivization, introduction of exotic fauna and flora, and the construction of hydroelectric dams and canals, on the basis of ecological considerations. Finally, did not the ecological conservationists have the temerity to fight for their right to determine the research agendas of the *zapovedniki* in the face of conflicting demands on the part of the party and the state?

By the late 1930s, the conservation movement was vitiated. Membership in VOOP, which had peaked at 15,000 in 1932, sank to 2,553 by 1940,[3] and its publications ceased to appear. Its ally, the Society for the Study of Local Lore, was abolished. More indicative, perhaps, was the forced change of mission of the *zapovedniki*. No longer inviolate centers for the study of ecological dynamics, they were now converted into bases for the introduction of exotic life forms and other transformation-of-nature schemes.

WORLD WAR II AND AFTER

War's carnage took its toll not only on the vegetation and wildlife of the Soviet Union, but foremost on its people.[4] Among the millions who perished were many conservation activists; some died at the front, while others, such as Professors Andrei Petrovich Semenov-tian-shanskii, his brother Veniamin, and Daniil Nikolaevich Kashkarov were claimed by the Leningrad siege and famine. Despite the hardships, nature reserve staff scientists and other conservation workers tried to save what they could, all the while straining to make a parallel contribution to the war effort; work on natural

3 Otchet VOOP o rabote obshchestva za 1939 god. TsGAOR (Central State Archive of the October Revolution), fond 494, op. 1, list 1.
4 A special article devoted to the environmental consequences of World War II is Yu. G. Noskov, "Environmental Devastation in the USSR during the Second World War," in *Environmental Management in the USSR* (1985), fasc. 4, pp. 87–95.

substitutes for rubber, and on vegetation cover suitable for airfields, was vigorously pursued in the *zapovedniki*. Officials of VOOP, led by its leader and deputy president Vasilii Nikitich Makarov, successfully lobbied for a continued ban on the trapping of the desman, a rare aquatic shrew, and on moose hunting.[5]

The war's end was greeted as a time to rebuild by an exhausted population. Yet, hopes for material improvement in living conditions and, among intellectuals, for a freer, richer, cultural life – including conservation – were once again dashed as the cold war cast its grey shadow. Despite the convocation of a VOOP Congress in April 1947 and the government's disbursement of one hundred thousand rubles to the society for organizational activities, resulting in a membership spurt to 136,195 by late 1951,[6] VOOP found its freedom of action constricted. Its protests were bootless to prevent the liquidation of more than 85 percent of the territory of Soviet *zapovedniki* in 1951. The terrorized atmosphere of the last years of Stalin's rule further trivialized the society's agenda; with the exception of the society's Crimean Commission, which bravely continued to oppose uplands deforestation, efforts were channeled into the harmless pastimes of gardening and urban beautification.[7] As in the early 1930s, the society's very existence was in jeopardy. A conference meeting in the summer of 1951 concluded that there was no further need for VOOP and resolved to liquidate it. To the good fortune of the society, the economic ministers failed to get enough support in the end.[8]

At this juncture, energetic defense of conservation passed to the Academy of Sciences, which was perhaps the one remaining Soviet institution with enough autonomy to resist the utilitarian tide. On 28 March 1952, its new, liberal president A. N. Nesmeianov, approved the creation of a new Commission for Zapovedniki to be led by Academician Vladimir Nikolae-

5 I. F. Barishpol and V. G. Larina, *U prirody druzei milliony* (Moscow: Lesnaia promyshlenost', 1984), p. 49.

6 Ibid., p. 59. The enormous growth of membership in the postwar period is in part attributable to the incorporation of entire factories and institutions, together with their staff, as "juridical" or "collective" members. By 1981, there were 80,543 organizations that had joined VOOP in that manner. A single such organization, such as Uraltiazhmash in Sverdlovsk, could add more than 10,000 new members to the society. See Barishpol and Larina, *U prirody druzei milliony*, p. 91. Needless to say, the level of commitment of the individuals thus inscribed as members would be expected to be much lower than those who joined on the basis of individual choice.

7 In September 1953, the All-Russian Society for the Promotion and Protection of Urban Greening was incorporated into VOOP. The merged organization then became known as the All-Russian Society for the Promotion of Conservation and Urban Greening. See Barishpol and Larina, *U prirody druzei milliony*, p. 65. Readers are also referred to local VOOP publications such as: *Ob opyte raboty Leningradskogo gorodskogo otdeleniia obshchestva* (Moscow: VOSOPIONP, 1956), pp. 3–8.

8 Barishpol and Larina, *U prirody druzei milliony*, p. 60.

vich Sukachev, an ecologist and director of the Academy's Institute on Forests.[9] With its aim the reversal of the recent setbacks, the committee seized the moment of "thaw" following Stalin's death in March 1953 to promote a carefully researched plan, drafted by Academician Evgenii Mikhailovich Lavrenko, the botanical ecologist, for the reestablishment of the *zapovedniki* as ecological *etalony*.[10] Increasing freedom of action for individual agencies in the early years of Khrushchev's rule allowed the Russian Republic's newly established Main Administration for Zapovedniki and Hunting (Glavokhota), supported by VOOP, successfully to restore many of the liquidated reserves in the face of "raids" and opposition on the part of the conservative USSR Ministry of Agriculture. This struggle, it may be observed, almost exactly recapitulated that between the Commissariats of Education and Agriculture during the 1920s and 1930s, testifying to the continued institutionalized polarization of the "enlightening" and utilitarian camps.

VOOP ASCENDANT

The breakup of the political ice jam from the mid-1950s also augured an unheralded era of membership growth for VOOP. Kozhevnikov and his colleagues would have been astonished to learn, for instance, that membership had reached 916,000 by 1959[11] and 32 million by 1981[12]; it is more than 37 million currently.[13] Annual gross income totaled 9.5 million rubles in 1976,[14] deriving in part from sales of game, forest crafts, pesticides, fertilizers, and other items in the society's network of retail stores "Priroda" (Nature). The price the society has paid, however, for the honor of becoming the largest conservation organization in the world has been high: lush bureaucratization and co-optation.

Organizationally, the society's highest body is its congress, which meets every five years. In recent years, these meetings have tended to be ponder-

9 Ibid., p. 61.

10 See "Khronika," *Okhrana prirody i zapovednoe delo v SSSR* (1958), builleten' no. 3, pp. 112–13, and *Botanicheskii zhurnal* (1955), no. 5, pp. 773–4.

11 *Vserossiiskoe obshchestvo sodeistviia okhrane prirody i ozeleneniiu naselennykh punktov, Materialy vtorogo s"ezda, prokhodivshego 15–18 dekabria 1959 goda v gorode Moskve* (Moscow, 1960), p. 12. Of these, 561,000, or more than 60 percent, were schoolchildren and others in the youth section. A further 300,000 members were reported for the Ukrainian republic's society (p. 74).

12 Barishpol and Larina, *U prirody druzei milliony*, p. 89.

13 This last figure, from 1985, was reported by V. N. Vinogradov, president of VOOP, in "The All-Russia Nature Conservation Society Marks Its 60th Anniversary," *Environmental Management in the USSR* (1985), fasc. 4, p. 84.

14 *Vserossiiskoe obshchestvo okhrany prirody, VI s"ezd, Materialy* (Moscow: Lesnaia promyshlennost', 1976), p. 22.

ous, ceremonial affairs; the Fourth Congress in 1962 had 550 delegates,[15] the Sixth, in 1976, had 615 delegates plus over 500 guests,[16] while the number of delegates alone at the Seventh, which met in Moscow in June 1981, numbered 726.[17] Conspicuous in their attendance have been such Soviet celebrities as A. G. Nikolaev, the cosmonaut, as well as oblast (province) party secretaries and members of the arts, letters, and the highest circles of Soviet science.

To manage the affairs of the society on an ongoing basis, the congress elects a Central Council, which has recently numbered more than one hundred members, and which in turn selects a Praesidium of about twenty-five. In the past two decades the Praesidium's chair has been a senior member of the Academy of Sciences. As late as VOOP's Second Congress in 1959, the society's president, G. P. Motovilov, could inform the delegates that nonactive members had been removed from the Praesidium, and he went on to declare that the "Central Council and its Praesidium's members must be elected on the basis of their ability to work, their love of nature, and their desire to help . . . and not on the basis of their famous names or the fact that they occupy high positions."[18] By the 1960s, however, it became a standard practice to name the deputy leader of the oblast, city, or *raion* (district) soviet to a top leadership position in the local VOOP organization of the corresponding territorial division. From the start, a few warned of the danger that these politicians might treat their conservation responsibilities as a formality.[19] Nevertheless, in VOOP's drive to move in from the margins of official life to prosperous respectability, purity has given way to realpolitik.

Like other Soviet organizations, VOOP has an auditing commission to look after financial matters. In addition, there is a Scientific-Technical Board, an Editorial Board, a Propaganda Department, a Department for Administration and Training, a Central Wholesale Store, and numerous sections attached to the central apparatus: soil conservation; water conservation; forest protection; protection of the atmosphere; wildlife preservation; and sections for the protection of fish, wild birds, useful insects, and relics of nonliving nature. Rounding out the picture are a youth section, one devoted to beautification, one to general horticulture, and one to the protection of subsoil mineral deposits. These sections are replicated in the local branches of the society. It should be noted that VOOP has managed to involve large numbers of people in conservation activities, however tame.

15 Barishpol and Larina, *U prirody druzei milliony*, p. 74.

16 Ibid., p. 84.

17 Ibid., p. 89.

18 *Vserossiiskoe, Materialy vtorogo*, pp. 32–3.

19 *Vserossiiskoe obshchestvo sodeistviia okhrane prirody i ozeleneniiu naselennykh punktov. Tsentral'nyi sovet, Materialy seminara rukovodiashchikh rabotnikov otdelenii obshchestva (15–20 oktiabria 1958 goda)* (Moscow, 1959), p. 134.

Under its sponsorship, for example, more than one hundred thousand people participated in a series of mass "raids" or inspections over the period 1981–4 to identify environmental malpractices. The appropriate ministries and agencies were then informed of these so that they could be corrected. VOOP has also been active in promoting the cleanup of small rivers through its project "Blue Meridian" and other efforts.[20]

In contrast with its forcefully oppositional infancy in the 1920s and early 1930s, the society has now settled into a comfortable, if not complacent, middle age. True, there have been powerful prophetic voices within VOOP even in recent years; did not the writer O. N. Pisarzhevskii warn at the 1959 Congress that "industrial growth even under socialism doesn't come with automatically acting 'safety' levers" and that "social forces must play an important role"?[21] Another participant at the same meeting, the delegate from Leningrad, G. I. Rodionenko, pointedly asked: "Have [the members of the Central Council] raised even one problem of national scope, such as the fate of lakes Sevan or Baikal, or of a large *zapovednik?* Nothing has been said about these problems."[22]

Indeed, as such dramatic problems as the fate of the Soviet Union's major lacustrine bodies (lakes Sevan, Balkhash, and Baikal; and the Aral and Caspian seas) burst suddenly into prominence by the early 1960s, other, more vibrant social forces took the lead in championing natural integrity. Of these, the student movement has proven to be the most durable as well as militant.

THE STUDENT CONSERVATION BRIGADES

One measure of the flood of social energies unleashed by the Khrushchev thaw was the emergence of independent student activism in the area of conservation. Not surprisingly, the first *druzhina* (brigade) made its appearance in progressive Estonia, at the Tartu State University. At about that same time, a student subsection was formed within the Conservation Section of the Moscow Society of Naturalists (MOIP). In this, the students were fortunate to enlist some very prestigious patrons, such as Nikolai Sergeevich Dorovatovskii, president of the section, K. M. Efron, leader of MOIP's Biological Sciences Division, and Fedor Nikolaevich Petrov, a founding member of VOOP in 1924 and an influential Old Bolshevik. MOIP, which at the time was led by Sukachev, had served from the forties

20 G. G. Gahn, "The Role of the Public of the Russian Federation in Implementing Principles of 'The World Strategy' of Nature Conservation," in *Environmental Management in the USSR* (1985), fasc. 4, pp. 58–9.
21 *Vserossiiskoe, Materialy vtorogo*, p. 63.
22 Ibid., p. 71.

as a refuge of anti-Lysenko scientists and of liberal opinion generally. Protecting conservationists against state encroachment on intellectual autonomy was one of MOIP's historic missions, and it now opened its doors wide to the militant students.[23] Unhappily, the logistical side of things turned out to be less than satisfactory; MOIP was located downtown in the Zoological Museum, far from the main Lenin Hills campus of Moscow State University (MGU), which most of the students attended. When some energetic freshmen members managed to locate some sympathetic faculty members, notably Konstantin Nikolaevich Blagosklonov, biology docent and VOOP veteran of the 1930s, it was decided to move the operation to campus and seek official certification as a *druzhina*.[24]

Recalling as it did the fighting cohorts of Kievan days, "*druzhina*" evoked unmistakable overtones of determination and comradeship. As its longtime faculty sponsor, Professor Vadim Nikolaevich Tikhomirov, a botanist, described it:

The very word *druzhina*, so happily chosen, precisely framed the group's future activity. In it was reflected the striving for deeds, for struggle, and not for mere round-table discussions on conservation themes. It presupposed a certain level of cohesion, of solidarity, and, above all, of strict social responsibility while respecting the spirit of free choice that motivated members to join.[25]

Like Khrushchev's bumpy course of liberalization itself, the *druzhina*'s progress was not unremittingly forward. Highly placed academic bureaucrats at MGU were fearful of the group's militance and did not understand its mission. "You want to what? Protect nature? From whom? From our own Soviet citizen?" – these questions reflected some of the challenges to the *druzhina*.[26] The Siberian biologist Fedor Eduardovich Reimers reported that during summer field trips the students' outspoken, critical remarks "frightened some of the faculty." Students who urged caution in selecting tracts of virgin land for cultivation were accused of opposing the Virgin Lands program as a whole.[27] Their forays into protected territories and hunting grounds to apprehend poachers and their "Operation Fir Tree" campaign to stem the illegal felling of coniferous trees at New Year's fed fears of vigilantism and of potential scandal. Only the determined support of N. P. Naumov, dean of the Biological Faculties, saved the day.[28]

By 1972 there were already thirty-four brigades, all sponsored by their

---

23 This account is taken from interviews with A. A. Nasimovich, 10 and 18 April 1980, and from Vadim Nikolaevich Tikhomirov, *Studenchestvo i okhrana prirody* (Moscow: MGU, 1982), pp. 12–22.
24 Ibid.
25 Tikhomirov, *Studenchestvo i okhrana prirody*, p. 14.
26 Ibid., p. 15.
27 *Vserossiiskoe, Materialy vtorogo*, p. 64.
28 Ibid., and Tikhomirov, *Studenchestvo i okhrana prirody*, p. 15.

Douglas R. Weiner

universities' Young Communist League (Komsomol) branches, and that year marked the first of what has become annual convocations of all the brigades in the USSR (which currently comprise over 140 with more than 5,000 members).²⁹ However, the druzhina movement has no aspirations to grow so great as to dilute its impressive esprit de corps; as Tikhomirov declared at a recent All-Union convocation of *druzhiny, VOOP*, with its thirty-odd million members, should not serve as a model either organizationally or substantively.³⁰ After all, the *druzhiny* emerged in opposition to VOOP, rejecting what they considered to be the trivialized preoccupations of urban greening and vegetable gardening. Another implicit contrast with VOOP made by Tikhomirov concerned the relative autonomy of the two organizations; "the most important fact about the brigades," he emphasized, "is that they are guided by the principle of independence. They are not subordinated to anyone," he continued, "and pursue activities suggested by no one other than themselves."³¹ In this the *druzhiny* continue an important mission of the Soviet conservation movement – exemplified by the prewar VOOP – serving as a haven for minority viewpoints and for the defense of the autonomy of the intelligentsia from state infringement generally.

With the passage of time, the student movement has accrued much knowledge and experience. The antipoaching campaigns (Operation 'Shot') have led to a serious study of poaching as a social phenomenon, for example, as well as to a physical and moral testing for the students themselves. Their philosophy was to educate and publicize. If a violator was caught, the *druzhina* would send letters to his workplace. "This was like tossing a pebble into the water; the pebble itself is not terribly big, but the waves it generates can travel a great ways," explained Tikhomirov. Other programs focused on identifying nesting sites of rare and endangered species and other territories in need of protection (Operation Fauna), involving the organization of expeditions staffed by graduate students representing a variety of relevant disciplines. For many students, these activities resulted in their accreditation as "Voluntary Citizens Inspectors" for conservation. Frequently this experience has led to careers as official state inspectors with the forestry, fishing, hunting and nature reserve, or other conservation agencies, which are regarded as high-prestige vocations by *druzhina* members.³² Quantitatively,

29 Speech by Vadim Nikolaevich Tikhomirov to the All-Union Convocation of Student *druzhiny* for Conservation, 3 February 1986, at MGU. See as well I. I. Rusin, "Youth Environmental Protection Movement in the USSR," *Environmental Management in the USSR* (1985), fasc. 4, pp. 96–111.
30 Tikhomirov speech, 3 February 1986.
31 Ibid.
32 On training of voluntary inspectors, see Rusin, "Youth Environmental Protection Movement," pp. 106–7. The MGU *druzhina* operates under a broader student umbrella organization called the MGU Youth Council for Conservation, which has over 600 members and a 10,000-ruble annual budget (ibid., p. 105).

the MGU *druzhina* alone was responsible, over a twenty-year period, for the detention of over five thousand violators of conservation statutes, for the establishment of twelve local-level nature preserves, and for the organization of over one thousand lectures and excursions.[33]

While the student movement through the 1960s was preoccupied with the old agenda of protecting animate nature, by the 1970s it assumed a more assertive posture and began to tackle "socio-political problems," in the words of a prominent student leader. Within their sights now is the synergistic interaction of "cultural-historical, national, . . . ecological . . . and socio-economic issues."[34] One example of this new social-planning role is the *druzhina* program "Ecopolis," developed by Dr. Aron Brudnyi, a philosopher with the Kirghiz Academy of Sciences, and by Dr. Dmitrii Mikhailovich Kavtaradze, head of MGU's Laboratory of Ecology and Conservation (Biological Faculties). Using the town of Pushchino, the Academy of Sciences' Biological Research Center on the Oka River about seventy miles south of Moscow, as an experimental "subject," Brudnyi and Kavtaradze have sought to design the new town's services, amenities, and physical features to achieve maximum environmental and esthetic quality for its residents. Groves have been left standing, ecologically sensitive paths wind through forests connecting the town with the accessible, undeveloped riverfront, and conservation educational materials are abundant. Surveys of residents have been extensively used; the designers have been mindful of getting as much feedback from residents as possible so that "Ecopolis" does not become simply two men's vision of an ecological utopia.[35]

Another program sponsored by the *druzhiny* of particular note is "Operation Cruelty," which began in 1969. Focusing on the roots of cruel or sadistic behavior toward animals (again, utilizing polling) has led to both a broader discussion about "the phenomenon of cruelty" in general and to a widening of the debate beyond the walls of the brigade itself. Perhaps the most significant breakthrough in confronting this issue was the convening of a round-table discussion sponsored by the Conservation Section of MOIP on 19 April 1974, which was subsequently published in the Academy of Science's widely read monthly, *Priroda* (Nature). Professor Ksenia Semenova, a child psychiatrist specializing in the rehabilitation of children with cerebral palsy, linked cruelty to animals and to fellow humans as due to a common failure on the part of many people to develop empathic responses to the pain of others. This, in turn, Semenova attributed to the cruel individual's inability to find any constructive avenues in society for self-

33 Tikhomirov, *Studenchestvo i okhrana prirody*, p. 23.
34 Rusin, "Youth Environmental Protection Movement," p. 99.
35 On "Ecopolis," see E. E. Bozhukova and D. N. Kavtaradze, *Main Works on the Programme "Ecopolis" [Synopses of the Publications, 1979–1982]* (Pushchino: Scientific Center for Biological Research of the Academy of Sciences of the USSR, 1983).

affirmation. As a rule, she noted, low academic achievers were overrepresented in this group, which pointed to an implicit socioeconomic pattern; in the Soviet Union, as elsewhere, low academic achievement is highly correlated with poor, low-prestige backgrounds.[36] Again, this may be interpreted as an expression of intelligentsia revulsion at what is considered to be "lower-class" violent behavior.

It must be noted, however, that urban professionals are not exempt from this behavior. Semenova relates the case of three young female medical students who were photographed laughing as a just-dissected dog, entrails extruding, regained consciousness from anesthesia. Written just as Peter Singer published his controversial *Animal Liberation* (New York: Random House, 1975), Semenova's piece was perhaps the first in the USSR to call attention to the ethical problems of vivisection and scientific experimentation upon animals. Perhaps the most radical social critique was that uttered by Academician E. M. Kreps, director of the Academy's I. M. Sechenov Institute of Evolutionary Physiology, who placed much of the responsibility for cruelty on "our, that is, adult, cruelty and indifference."[37] As Pogo once memorably uttered, "we have met the enemy, and he is *us!*"

LAKE BAIKAL

Until the late 1950s, the growing but still barely tolerated postwar Soviet conservation movement continued to direct its attention to such traditional concerns as *zapovedniki*, other protected territories, wildlife conservation, and, in the case of VOOP, beautification and gardening. However, by the close of the decade, several new developments – the striking demographic expansion of an urban professional stratum, its increasing attention to health and recreational issues, the rise of a new Great Russian nationalism to fill the void of a decaying allegiance to a Marxist-Leninist worldview, and, finally, Khrushchev's headlong campaign to develop a chemical industry in the USSR – combined to produce an unprecedented environmentalist outcry heralding the birth of a new Soviet environmental movement.

Others, notably Philip R. Pryde, Marshall I. Goldman, Thane Gustafson, and Ze'ev Vol'fson (Boris Komarov, pseudonym) have ably recounted the story of the Baikal controversy,[38] so I will only provide the briefest of

36 "Fenomenologiia zhestokosti," *Priroda* 1 (1975): 89–90.
37 Ibid., p. 101.
38 Philip R. Pryde, *Conservation in the Soviet Union* (Cambridge: Cambridge University Press, 1972), chap. 8; Marshall I. Goldman, *The Spoils of Progress* (Cambridge, Mass.: MIT Press, 1972) chap. 6; Thane Gustafson, *Reform in Soviet Politics: Lessons of Recent Policy on Land and Water* (New York: Cambridge University Press, 1981); and Ze'ev Vol'fson [Boris Komarov, pseud.], *The Destruction of Nature in the Soviet Union* (White Plains, N.Y.: M. E. Sharpe, 1978), chap. 1.

outlines. Generally accepted as the oldest lake in the world (approximately thirty million years old) as well as the deepest (5,346 feet), Baikal also contains more water than any other body of fresh water on the planet. The unique habitat of the world's only fresh-water seal as well as for more than seven hundred endemic organisms, the lake is truly a place of superlatives. With its fierce beauty and historic associations with Russian explorers, pioneers, and, not least, czarist-period political exiles, Baikal resonantly symbolized the *Russian* claim to Siberia for ethnic Russians. For the liberal intelligentsia, moreover, it symbolized one of the last major natural features of the Soviet Union unmarred by heroic construction projects. It was a place where civil society could take a stand and say to the state: "Enough! Your aggrandizing, transforming hand stops here!"

Until the late 1950s, the lake's basin was not subject to intensive development. All that changed in 1957, when the decision was made to construct two large viscose rayon plants on the southern rim of the lakeshore to produce cord for the Soviet air force. For three years, these plans remained largely unknown to the public, including the scientific elite, whose experts were not consulted on the ecological consequences of such construction. When the plans were revealed in a letter by Grigorii I. Galazii, director of the Limnology Institute of the Siberian Division of the Academy of Sciences, to the mass daily *Komsomolskaia pravda* on 26 December 1961, they therefore came as a great shock. As the possible implications of the construction became increasingly publicized, the *druzhiny* were among the first (1962) to mobilize; with the national Komsomol press on its side, opposition to the pulp-and-paper-processing plants took on the coloration of a protest movement of both "official" and "unofficial" youth.

While the main burden of opposition to the project, as in the past, continued to be shouldered by subdivisions of the Academy of Sciences and the scientific societies (particularly those of biologists, geographers, and theoretical physicists), wholly new groups were drawn into the struggle. First, an entire group of Russian writers, many of whom later were described as members of the "Village Prose" school, began to raise their voices both in their prose and in public statements. Of the prose works, best known is Valentin Rasputin's *Farewell to Matyora* (New York: Macmillan, 1979; originally published in the USSR in 1961), which chronicles the anguished destruction of a rural island community, along with the natural environment that sustained it, by the construction of the Bratsk Hydroelectric Dam on the Angara River, near Baikal. This theme – that rural life, functioning within the sustainable carrying capacity of the environment, was a valuable source of nourishing values (indeed *Russian* values) – ran through the works of kindred writers such as Sergei Zalygin, Viktor Astaf'ev, Oleg Volkov, and, of course, Vladimir Chivilikhin. Ethnic Russians, with little outlet, paradoxically, for expression of their own *national*

Douglas R. Weiner

identity (not *Soviet* identity) as compared with many of the other Soviet nationalities, were ripe for such cryptonationalist appeals. Another aspect of "Village Prose" was its romanticization of the rustic; such a perspective could only originate in a disillusioned urbanized milieu, and, as such, could not have arisen before the late 1950s, when the USSR's urban population reached majority status for the first time.[39]

Other sociological changes were reflected in the public reaction to Baikal. From 1950 to 1960, the number of professionals with higher education increased from 1,443,000 (of a population of 181,600,000) to 3,545,000 (of 216,300,000). This group further increased by 1972 to 7,700,000 (of 248,600,000).[40] The numerical growth of engineers, from 400,200 to 2,820,000 over this period, was the most dramatic, but that of other scientists (from 162,508 to 1,056,017) was impressive nonetheless.[41] These new white-collar, white-coated legions supported an equally striking expansion of scientific literature. In particular, scientific periodicals of both a general and a specialized nature experienced an unprecedented boom. And these began to publish features about Baikal and conservation generally in a growing tide; regular conservation columns were initiated in *Priroda* (Nature), *Nauka i zhizn'* (Science and Life), and *Khimiia i zhizn'* (Chemistry and Life).[42] Added to these was the not inconsequential *Literturnaia gazeta* (The Literary Gazette), the voice of the urban intelligentsia as a whole. Additionally, there was an enormous spurt of growth in the membership of the twenty-three branch scientific and technical societies, embracing ten million managers, engineers, and technicians. These societies naturally gravitated toward concern about pollution, low-waste technology, and rational and complex use of resources.[43] Perhaps the most extraordinary indication of the breadth and daring of this new environmental coalition was a letter published on 11 May 1966 in *Komsomolskaia pravda,* signed by a vice-president of the Academy of Sciences and more than thirty leaders of science, culture, and the arts calling for the removal of the already

---

39 On the "Village Prose" school and its connection with nationalist sentiments, the best introduction is John B. Dunlop, *The Faces of Contemporary Russian Nationalism* (Princeton, N.J.: Princeton University Press, 1983).

40 D. M. Gvishiani, S. R. Mikulinsky, and S. A. Kugel, eds., *The Scientific Intelligentsia in the USSR (Structure and Dynamics of Personnel)* (Moscow: Progress, 1976), p. 123 (table 8).

41 Ibid., and table 9 (p. 124).

42 Tat'iana Vladimirovna Vasil'eva, *Ekologicheskaia propaganda v sovetskom nauchno-populiarnom zhurnale: Stanovlenie, sovremennoe sostoianie, i tendentsii razvitiia* (Dissertation for candidate of science in Journalism, Moscow State University, 1984), and Tat'iana Vladimirovna Vasil'eva, chap. 2 "Ekologicheskaia propaganda v nauchno-populiarnom zhurnale (1917–1983 gg.)," in D. M. Gvishiani, ed., *Ekologicheskaia propaganda v SSSR* (Moscow: Nauka, 1984), pp. 27–53.

43 L. N. Efremov, "Environmental Protection and Natural Resources Management in the USSR: A Nation-wide Task," *Environmental Management in the USSR* (1982), pt. 1, p. 15.

operating Baikal mills.[44] While the mills were not dismantled (although the Gorbachev regime, it is rumored, has been considering that step), the unprecedented social pressure – together with the conservationists' skillful exploitation of foreign public opinion – greatly influenced the Brezhnev regime's decision to invest tens of millions of rubles in pollution abatement facilities for the plants. True, the circumstances were unique[45] – just as they were when the Grand Canyon was threatened by the proposed Hualapai Dam in 1966 – and the resolution of the problem was far from satisfactory in the eyes of many scientists, not to mention purists; nonetheless, it constituted a signal victory for social forces in their defense of a different idea of development from that of the party-state.

Indicative of the continuing vibrancy of this conservation coalition of students, scientists, and the urban-educated stratum generally has been the vigorous opposition to the rerouting of northward-flowing rivers to the drier southern regions of the USSR. As with Baikal, it is important to note that these protests have been allowed to continue as outspokenly as they have because they coincide with the priorities and approaches of at least a segment of the party's leadership. Beginning with Brezhnev and Kosygin and greatly intensifying under Gorbachev, the Soviet leadership itself has been adopting a new model of development. Indisputably, there is now far less emphasis on heroic projects as a means of establishing regime legitimacy and prestige. The watchword instead is intensive (not extensive) development; a new sense of realism is in the air. Thus, Gorbachev's recent cancellation of the Siberian river diversion project is as much or more the result of an economic cost-benefit analysis than of a desire to maintain the natural environment in an unmodified state. The true test of strength of the conservation movement will come on an issue where the interests of economic rationality and nature protection do not coincide.

More evidence of urban professional interest in conservation is the proliferation from the 1970s of popular-scientific periodicals specifically devoted to conservation. The oldest of these, actually founded in 1955 and published under the aegis of the USSR Ministry of Agriculture (now State Agroindustrial Committee of the USSR) together with the Russian Socialist Federated Soviet Republic (RSFSR) Union of Hunters and Fishermen (since the mid-1980s) is *Okhota i okhotnich'e khoziaistvo* (Sport and Commercial Hunting). This is a principal forum for discussion of wildlife issues and those concerning protected territories, especially in its lively "round-tables." Of special note is the popular series *Chelovek i priroda* (Humans and

44 See Philip R. Pryde's discussion of this in *Conservation in the Soviet Union*, p. 148.
45 One of the most crucial factors was the recent technological obsolescence of the viscose fiber in the making of jet plane tires and its replacement by nylon. Therefore, the plant did not have the strategic importance it had in the late 1950s, allowing for a greater degree of published criticism than otherwise would have been the case.

Nature) published from 1975 by the "Knowledge" Society Publishing House and enjoying a circulation of over 100,000. Conceived as an instrument of continuing education of the society's so-called People's University for Conservation, the journal devotes each of its twelve issues a year to a different conservation theme, for example, architecture and nature (1987, no. 3), the "ecologization" of technical processes (1987, no. 4), and recreation and water resources (1987, no. 5). Almost every aspect of resource use or nature/human interaction has been treated in these accessibly written pamphlets. The third journal, which made its appearance in 1981, is the monthly *Priroda i chelovek* (Nature and Humans) (circulation: 93,000) of the USSR State Committee for Hydrometeorology and Monitoring of the Natural Environment, which combines literary essays with a wide range of informational articles and announcements.

RECREATION

One feature of social change in postwar Soviet Russia has been the summer migration of urbanites "back to nature," so familiar in the American experience. This does not denigrate the laudable success of Soviet urban planners in retaining large areas of open space in the USSR's greatly expanded cities,[46] but rather it is testimony to the great attraction of untended landscape for modern Soviet urbanites. In the early 1980s, more than half of the Soviet population took vacations outside of their places of residence – a modern revolution in lifestyle. Of these, 25.4 million tourists were officially accommodated in nearly 1,000 "tourist bases." Clearly, such dimensions of recreational demand and mobility, aside from creating a mighty constituency for recreational amenities, has likewise created its share of logistical problems for recreational managers. An entire science of recreational planning has emerged, pursued in such institutions as the Academy of Sciences' Institute of Geography and in the Central Scientific-Research Laboratory of the Central Tourism and Excursions Council, successor to the old Society for Proletarian Tourism and Excursions of the 1930s.[47]

One of the problems-cum-opportunities for the conservation movement was the increasing use of *zapovedniki*, which in theory were to remain inviolate except for ecological research by accredited scientists, to accommodate backpackers and other tourists. On the one hand, such use was a show of public support for the nature reserves, helped to propagandize their natural beauty, and contributed to a hands-on ecological education. On the other, heavy public use of the reserves, which in actuality began in the late

46 For example, the city of Moscow includes about 10,000 hectares [24,000 acres] of forests. N. S. Kazanskaia, "Forests near Moscow as Territories of Mass Recreation and Tourism," *Urban Ecology* 2 (1977), pp. 371–95, p. 371.
47 See B. N. Likhanov, *Geografiia otdykha* (Moscow: "Znanie" RSFSR, 1985), pp. 4–10.

1930s, disrupted the habitat, ruined conditions for scientific investigation, and was a transgression by untrained outsiders on the turf of what the biological sciences' elite always considered "its own territory."[48]

The solution hit upon by the scientific leaders of conservation in the late 1960s was to add a new category of protected territory – the "national park" – to serve the needs of tourists and take the pressure off the *zapovedniki*. Currently, there are at least twelve such national parks.[49] A note should be added about the Baltic republics, which have been in the forefront of the creation of national parks as well as in regional zoning with conservation objectives. In addition to the obvious fact that Estonia, Latvia, and Lithuania are among the most modern, best educated, and most urbanized of all the Soviet republics, there is perhaps another factor which may help to explain their leadership in conservation: a desire to prevent further industrialization. This becomes understandable when we realize that industrial development in those republics over the past four decades has served as a rationale for bringing in large numbers of ethnic Russians and Ukrainians. Owing to their extremely low population growth during this period, the Baltic nationalities are fearful of being "swamped" by eastern Slavs. Conservation plausibly has become another weapon in their arsenal of national self-defense.[50] It goes without saying that champions of Russian culture have been equally energetic in their promotion of national parks of typical "Russian" landscapes in the RSFSR, but for somewhat different reasons.[51]

INTERNATIONAL LINKS

One notable by-product of Khrushchev's liberalization and the subsequent period of détente has been the restoration of the formerly flourishing ties with foreign conservation organizations and vigorous participation in international programs. Although rebuffed twice in the mid-1950s, VOOP finally gained membership in the International Union for the Conservation

48 On this interesting debate, see L. S. Belousova, "Ob organizatsii prirodnykh parkov v Sovetskom Soiuze," in *Primechatel'nye prirodnye landshafty SSSR i ikh okhrana* (Moscow, 1967); I. I. Puzanov, "Nam nuzhny natsional'nye parki," *Okhota i okhtnich'e khoziaistvo* (1968), no. 2; A. G. Bannikov and V. V. Krinitskii, "Uskorit' organizatsii natsional'nykh parkov," ibid., (1975), no. 4.; and the valuable work of N. F. Reimers and F. R. Shtil'mark, *Osobo okhraniaemye prirodnye territorii* (Moscow: Mysl', 1978), passim.

49 As of 1985, according to V. A. Borisov, L. S. Belousova, and A. A. Vinokurov in their *Okhraniaemye prirodnye territorii mira* (Moscow: Agropromizdat, 1985), p. 7. These incorporated an aggregate area of 950,000 hectares.

50 I am indebted to Kristian Gerner and Lars Lundgren for this idea, presented at the First Conference on Environmental History, Irvine, California, 1–3 January 1982.

51 The example of Academician Dmitrii Likhachev is instructive, as he has championed protection of both nature and historical monuments as the chairperson of the All-Russian Society for the Protection of Monuments of History and Culture.

of Nature (IUCN) in 1960; more recently, Soviets have participated energetically in UNESCO's Man and the Biosphere Program, the International Biological Program, and in cooperative work with both individual governments as well as private groups such as the Crane Foundation. In particular, the Man and the Biosphere Soviet National Committee, coordinated by Valerii Mikhailovich Neronov, and occupying part of a modest Moscow-style townhouse, has achieved notable success in raising conservation's visibility in the USSR while building international cooperation in such areas as the Biosphere Reserves Program. The committee's ecological working groups have sponsored countless scientific studies, many of which have been synopsized in *Priroda,* while its Working Group on Education and Training, led by Drs. German Gapochka and Dmitrii Kavtaradze of Moscow State University, has displayed great energy and creativity. In addition to sponsoring an array of teaching texts and aids of the more conventional sort, Kavtaradze and his colleagues have developed strategic games involving the simulation of environmental problems and choices. In general during the past two decades there has been a broad increase in environmental education in the USSR at all levels.[52]

THE BROADENING SCOPE OF SOVIET CONSERVATION

Up to now, we have reviewed how conservation's constituency has expanded since the days when it was the concern of a small band of stalwarts. The spectrum of conservation concerns has expanded no less. VOOP remains, but with bureaucratization and co-optation its importance in the movement has been marginalized even as its membership has ballooned. And its old baton of militancy was passed to the scientific societies and to the student movement. But while some militants of the old-style intelligentsia are still preoccupied with preserving the inviolability of what they believe to be pristine, discrete, self-regulating ecological communities as represented by *zapovedniki,* those concerns have now been pushed from center stage by new ones linked to newer constituencies.

Understandably, the masses of engineers, the great rank and file of the new, postwar Soviet-educated elite, by their very position in the economy would be hard put to sympathize with a severe, antidevelopmental perspective. Rather, they are interested in harmonizing production values with

52 Readers are referred to the excellent article by Elizabeth Koutaissoff, "Environmental Education in the USSR," chap. 4 in Janusz J. Tomiak, ed., *Soviet Education in the 1980s* (Beckenham, England: Croon Helm Ltd., 1983), pp. 85–105. See also I. D. Zverev, "Ecology in the School: A New Aspect of Education," *The Soviet Review* 23, no. 3 (Fall 1982): 3–26; *Prirodookhrannoe obrazovanie v universitetakh* (Moscow: MGU, 1985); and *Prirodookhrannoe vospitanie i obrazovanie* (Moscow: MGU, 1983).

ecological possibilities and with environmental quality. Their very pattern of thought is concrete and pragmatic, not schematic or theoretical. For them, air and water quality and recreational opportunities are central. They are not as sensitive as the academic elite (or the students) to the confining authority of the state in the area of intellectual expression, and do not chafe under the conviction that politicians have unfruitfully usurped decision-making powers that should rightfully belong to them on the basis of their professional expertise or social position. Consequently, most technical "new men" are not especially looking to do battle with the state, but are simply seeking a better material life. One of the quintessential spokespersons for this new scientific stratum was the ecologist Stanislav Semenovich Shvarts, head of the Institute for the Ecology of Plants and Animals of the Academy's Ural Scientific Center in Sverdlovsk. Shvarts held that the earth could not remain pristine, if it ever had been in recent times, and called for an ecology that would guide the scientific "creation of a transformed world." His description of the preservationist position as "reactionary" and as "antiscientific" emotionalism appealed to the new engineers' sense of progress and aversion to sentimentality.

Most recently, a new synthesis has emerged in the form of a new conceptualization of the nature/society relationship by highly placed philosophers, including Ivan Timofeevich Frolov, the recently named chief editor of the party's theoretical journal, *Kommunist*. They have advanced a wholly new discipline, social ecology, which rejects both the extremes of dogmatic antidevelopmentalism and Shvarts's blind technological optimism. Instead, social ecology directs our efforts toward the identification of a "socio-economic-ecological equilibrium," which represents the maximal level of sustainable economic activity, socially agreed upon, consistent with the existing ecological constraints presented by the environment. At the same time, it underscores the need to incorporate such intangibles as esthetic, psychological, and health considerations into our calculus.[53] It would not be surprising if the Gorbachev regime moves to incorporate core elements of this perspective at least formally into a new social contract appealing to all of urban-educated society.

CONCLUSION

Differences in social structure between the Soviet Union and the United States go far toward explaining the differences in the characters of the

53 For a dramatic presentation of the new social ecology, see I. T. Frolov and V. A. Los', "Filosofskie osnovaniia sovremennoi ekologii," in *Ekologicheskaia propaganda v SSSR* (Moscow: Nauka, 1984), pp. 5–26. I have discussed these views at greater length in "Prometheus Rechained: Ecology and Conservation in the Soviet Union," in Loren R. Graham, ed., *Humanistic Dimensions of Science and Technology in the Soviet Union* (Cambridge, Mass.: Harvard University Press, forthcoming).

Douglas R. Weiner

conservation movements in the two countries. In the United States, with the brief exception of the Progressive Era, scientists had few pretensions about their natural right to lead the nation, and their use of conservation as a weapon in their technocratic campaign was brief.[54] By contrast, the Russian scientific and intellectual elite historically nourished a view of their social role as one of natural leadership. When these pretensions were threatened, and then denied, by the Bolshevik regime, scientists tried to exploit the regime's self-professed commitment to the ideal of the scientific management of society to press their claims for greater input into decision making. Conservation, in its ecological permutation, became enlisted in this struggle – a struggle which collaterally involved educated society's attempts to defend its sphere of intellectual autonomy from an increasingly intrusive and controlling regime. *Zapovedniki* became symbols of this inviolable, fiercely defended social turf, were derided as such by radical critics during the Cultural Revolution, and were ultimately liquidated during the apogee of Stalin's autocracy after World War II. Because these broader issues of power, values, and freedom remained unresolved even after Stalin's death and through the Khrushchev and Brezhnev eras, ecological conservation continued to figure in the armamentarium of the scientific elite in its struggle with the state. Whether it will continue to play that role in the Gorbachev era, it seems, will depend first on how far the regime goes toward meeting the agenda of this elite, and secondly, whether more suitable vehicles to advance the elite's agenda emerge.

Although scientists have not figured so prominently among environmental purists in the United States as in the USSR,[55] there are similarities between the two groups: elitism, strong feelings of being disempowered, and an alienation from production values.[56] Students and the intellectual elite have been heavily represented in both societies; both have placed the preservation of "untouched nature" at the top of their agendas. Nevertheless, I wish to point out two crucial divergences. First, because of the Soviet Union's overwhelming emphasis on heavy industry during its first five decades, a correspondingly overwhelming majority of its educated urban

54 See Samuel P. Hays's classic study *Conservation and the Gospel of Efficiency: The Progressive Conservation Movement, 1890–1920* (Cambridge, Mass.: Harvard University Press, 1959). The "Technocracy, Incorporated" movement in the United States, which flourished in the early 1930s under the leadership of Howard Scott, is described in Howard P. Segal, *Technological Utopianism in American Culture* (Chicago: University of Chicago Press, 1985), pp. 123–9.
55 An interesting treatment of this tradition is Stephen Fox, *The American Conservation Movement: John Muir and His Legacy* (Madison: University of Wisconsin Press, 1985).
56 A very strong but somewhat schematic and ahistorical statement of this is contained in Mary Douglas and Aaron Wildavsky, *Risk and Culture: An Essay on the Selection of Technological and Environmental Dangers* (Berkeley and Los Angeles: University of California Press, 1982).

272

professional stratum was drafted into industry, usually as engineers. That has meant the dilution, not the strengthening, of the relative weight of the creative intelligentsia with its own values cut off from the "vulgar" world of production. By contrast, in the United States, along with a decline in our industrial base, we have seen a huge increase in those occupied in the service sector (plus the phenomenon of a sizable number of baby-boomer humanities majors who have become economically marginalized). Correspondingly, the relative weight of ecological "radicals" has increased from both those sources.[57] Finally, there is a nuanced difference in the form of struggle of Soviet and American elite conservationists. American preservationists, from Muir on, have raised their banner against what they saw as the tyrannizing, philistine majority. Preservationism was a cultural crusade against Babbittry. While this element is present in the Soviet case, the struggle has largely been one waged with the state as principal adversary. Moreover, the stakes have been immeasurably higher in the Soviet Union; the struggle over intellectual freedom and the ability of scientists to control the conditions of their work possesses an immediacy there that is absent to a great degree here.

Now, however, the Soviet Union is undergoing an unprecedented process of reform. Should this process deepen, the old relationships between regime and intelligentsia are likely to be profoundly altered in the coming months and years. Complicating the picture, Soviet society and its leaders will have to choose some mix of two antithetical ingredients of an improved standard of living: environmental quality and increased economic growth. This poses an especially difficult choice for the new technologists, who support both values. We shall eagerly follow how the various strands of the Soviet conservation movement affect, and are affected by, that crucial choice.

57 This is the argument made by Samuel P. Hays in his new analysis *Beauty, Health, and Permanence: Environmental Politics in the United States, 1955–1985* (New York: Cambridge University Press, 1987). While Mary Douglas stresses the role of the marginalized, Hays emphasizes the development of new sets of culturally constructed desires on the part of the newly affluent service-sector professionals.

CONCLUSION

I 2 Toward a Biosphere Consciousness

Raymond F. Dasmann

SOME YEARS AGO I found myself guilty of categorizing people into two groups. The occasion was a meeting of anthropologists and ecologists held at Cambridge University, where I was asked to consider the ecological relationships of "primitive people," meaning hunter-gatherers, hunter-gardeners, nomadic pastoralists, and others who had retained a self-sufficient existence, largely cut off from the influence of the dominant cultures of the earth. What categorized these people, from one viewpoint, was their ability to survive, year after year and often for centuries or longer, on the resources of a single ecosystem or contiguous and related ecosystems. Through one means or another, they had achieved a sustainable way of life that did not bring about changes in the natural biota deleterious to their continued existence. I called these "ecosystem people."[1]

By contrast, apparently since the rise of civilization, the societies and cultures that are featured in the history books have demonstrated a capacity to overexploit and convert productive ecosystems into near barren wastelands. Although this capacity has in the past contributed to the collapse of kingdoms and empires, the practice of overexploitation (or the consumption of natural resource capital) continues today.[2] Now those who are tied in with the global economy can continue to survive despite destructive exploitation

---

1 The concept of ecosystem people and biosphere people was first presented in a paper titled "Difficult Marginal Environments and the Traditional Societies Which Exploit Them: Ecosystems" at the Symposium on the Future of Traditional "Primitive" Societies at Cambridge University, England, 16–20 December 1974. It was published in *News from Survival International* 11 (July 1975):11–15. The idea was further elaborated in "National Parks, Nature Conservation, and Future Primitive," a paper presented at the South Pacific Conference on National Parks, Wellington, New Zealand (February 1975), published in *The Ecologist* 6 (1977): 164–7, and later in "Toward a Dynamic Balance of Man and Nature" 13th Technical Meeting, International Union for the Conservation of Nature and Natural Resources, Kinshasa, Zaire (September, 1975), *The Ecologist* 6 (1977): 2–5.
2 See W. C. Lowdermilk, *Conquest of the Land through 7000 Years* (U.S. Department of Agriculture, Washington, D.C., 1953). Tom Dale and V. C. Carter, *Topsoil and Civilization* (Norman: University of Oklahoma Press, 1955).

Raymond F. Dasmann

of local environments. Through the exchange of the products of industry they can draw on the total resources of the biosphere to override the controls previously exercised through the productive limits of local animal and plant populations. One needs only to look at the source of origin of most of the foods consumed by city populations in the industrialized world to visualize the trade routes that pour resources from throughout the biosphere into their hands. I have used the term "biosphere people" to categorize those who are linked to and dependent on the continued functioning of global trade in resources. I now regard the term as unfortunate since it suggests that we of the global economy have achieved the same sort of symbiosis with the total biosphere that characterizes ecosystem people and their home environments.

Obviously, this categorization is oversimplified. Certainly most people in the world are neither one nor the other, but caught somewhere in between these two positions. Since the contact between the biosphere cultures and ecosystem people is usually destructive to the ways of life of the latter, many of these have lost their ability to survive as they had in past times, but usually have gained little of the security that for the more fortunate derives from being part of the global economy.

It is also true enough that there have been tribal people who did overexploit local resources. Paul Martin has pointed out the apparent role that early North Americans played in exterminating the megafauna of this continent.[3] More certain is the role of ecosystem people in bringing about extinction for many species that once occupied islands such as New Zealand, Hawaii, and Madagascar. I have suggested, however, that a distinction must be made between invaders and natives. When humans occupy new and unfamiliar ecosystems, their effect on the biota is likely to be devastating initially. As they settle down, learn the ecological realities of their new home, and come to terms with its limits, this destructive impact is mitigated until they achieve the level of symbiosis with their environment that characterizes long-settled natives.

The invader effect, however, can be renewed when ecosystem people take up new technologies — particularly where these are brought from outside. An obvious example involved the introduction of the horse into Plains Indian culture, which brought a new and potentially destructive relationship with the bison herds. Whether or not a new balance was being reached can no longer be answered since both Plains Indians and bison were decimated by the new wave of exotic invaders, the Europeans. Similarly, the introduction of a new trapping technology to the Indians of northeastern America combined with a shattering of their religious contract with wild animals to bring a devastating impact upon the wildlife of that region.[4]

3 Paul Martin, "The Discovery of America," *Science* 179 (1973): 969–74.
4 Calvin Martin, *Keepers of the Game. Indian-Animal Relationships and the Fur Trade* (Berkeley and Los Angeles: University of California Press, 1978).

Most who have studied ecosystem people believe that the balance between human populations and the resources of their environment is not maintained through conscious decision or overall awareness on the part of individuals. Rather an intricate pattern of behavior, strongly reinforced by religious belief and social pressure, governs the relationship with nature for the individual, without he or she having conscious knowledge of why a particular action at a particular time is required or forbidden. In the terms used by L. P. Vidyarthi, a nature-spirit-culture triangle develops in which each side reinforces the other and together determine the actions of individuals and groups.[5]

There is no way that we who have been caught in the meshes of the global economic web can go back to "primitive" ways. We no longer have the possibility of developing unconscious behavior patterns that will lead to a restored and sustainable relationship with nature. The religious props have been removed, the sociocultural reinforcement of appropriate behavior no longer exists. From here on we are doomed to consciousness. We must know, understand, be aware of, comprehend our relationships with the total biosphere on which our future depends.

I have used the term "biosphere" in the sense that it is used in the UNESCO Man and the Biosphere Programme (MAB). Some ecologists prefer the term "ecosphere" and restrict the use of "biosphere" to only the living components of the ecosphere. However, since it is impossible to separate life from its inorganic environment, the most inclusive definition seems preferable. The biosphere then consists of all life and the environment that supports it — atmosphere, hydrosphere, and the upper layers of the lithosphere. The biosphere is thus the actively functioning part of the planet, and as James Lovelock and Lynn Margulis have pointed out in their Gaian hypothesis, it is to a high degree self-regulating, and self-sustaining, and to some extent behaves almost as a total living organism.[6] In the long run the activities of the human species probably cannot impair the functioning of the biosphere, although there is a strong likelihood that we can make the planet uninhabitable for ourselves. Writing in *The Ecologist* with reference to the effects of nuclear war, Margulis has stated:

Following detonation of nuclear weapons extermination of "western culture" is a certainty, extinction of *Homo sapiens* by the destruction of our environment is a high likelihood, but the continuity of Gaia will probably not be affected at all. Weedy, fast-growing, habitat-threatening species have "bloomed" ever since the

5 L. P. Vidyarthi, Paper presented at the Symposium on the Future of Traditional "Primitive" Societies at Cambridge University, England, 1974.

6 J. E. Lovelock and Lynn Margulis, "Atmospheric Homeostasis by and for the Biosphere," *Tellus* 26 (1973):2. See also J. E. Lovelock, *Gaia: A New Look at Life on Earth* (New York: Oxford University Press, 1982), or "Daisy World: A Cybernetic Proof of the Gaia Hypothesis," *Coevolution Quarterly* 38 (1983): 66–72.

earliest biospheres of Earth. Such weeds, by destroying their habitat for themselves, prepare the environment for others. . . .

We delude ourselves if we believe that as 3 million year old punks we can threaten the 3,500 million year old planetary patina in which we are embedded. However, that we can foul our nest, convert the garden of Babylon to the sands of the Sahara and even change the planetary albedo by felling forest trees and paving over with cement – in short that we can make our habitat hideous for our children – is certain.[7]

Some may find a certain grim comfort in the knowledge that we are incapable of wiping out all life on earth, and that some forms of life will survive our worst efforts. However, most of us find that the prospect of wiping out the human species and those friendly animals and plants on which we have thus far depended is sufficient incentive to search for other ways to solve political problems.

Among those aspects of human behavior that I find depressing when considering the need for achieving a biosphere consciousness are two features that in themselves have made it possible for humanity to spread itself over the face of the earth. One is the sheer adaptability of humans, their tolerance for adversity; the other is the shortness of individual and group memory. One needs only visit Los Angeles on a smoggy day and gaze from the mountain down on the layer of brown gaseous substance that covers the city to wonder how and why people can tolerate living in such conditions. But one adjusts to slow, deleterious changes in the environment and begins to accept them as normal. Young people, growing up in the smog, have no basis for believing that things were better in the past, and could be better in the future if certain actions were taken. The abnormal is accepted as normal and becomes the standard by which future change is measured. Even those who have lived under better conditions seem to forget what it was like to have clear air, or accept the words of industry and civic leaders that any serious effort to improve conditions would bring economic disaster.

Environmental events that approach the level of catastrophes, at least on a local scale, tend to be quickly discarded from active memory unless they occur with a high frequency. How many people, during the severe African drought of the early 1980s, remembered that a similar drought took place in the early 1970s? Ten years is long enough for memories to fade. Droughts, floods, hurricanes, tornados, earthquakes, volcanic eruptions seem inevitably to find people unprepared if their frequency is one in ten, or longer.

Perhaps most disturbing is our ability to accept, as though it were some form of inevitable doom, the global effects of our industrial activity. Carbon dioxide accumulates in the atmosphere and the likelihood of adverse, destructive climatic change increases. We are faced with the probability that

7 Lynn Margulis, letter in *The Ecologist* 16, no. 1 (1986):52–3.

rising sea levels will flood our coastal cities unless we can unhook ourselves from a dependence on the burning of fossil fuel. But we make no serious effort to shift to nonpolluting energy sources, and instead heave a sigh of relief when the price of petroleum falls, and we can return to our old ways of over-consumption.[8] Acid rain is killing our northern forests and we quibble about the costs of removing sulfur dioxide and related contaminants from our industrial effluent. We are unable to do something relatively simple, like reducing the output of chlorofluorocarbons into the atmosphere, even though depletion of the ozone layer is becoming obvious, and the danger of increased levels of ultraviolet radiation has been made abundantly clear. Most prefer to remain unconscious and not read, look at, or listen to the warnings. Those that are aware are caught in a feeling of helplessness, feeling unable to bring about the necessary changes in our ways of doing things.

Does there appear to be any hope that the human race can become aware of what is happening to their planet and act to prevent further deterioration? The logical answer would have to be no, unless we experience something like Ken Keyes's hundredth monkey syndrome, where suddenly a critical mass of people learn enough and begin to behave in ways appropriate to their own survival, and at that point everyone begins to behave in the same ways.[9] But to have the hundredth monkey, we must have the first monkey picking up the new ways – and perhaps that is what we must look for today.

Perhaps one of the more hopeful changes that has taken place in recent years has been the interest taken in the state of human well-being by those who were previously concerned mostly with the fate of wild species of animals and plants, and with environments relatively untouched by human activity. The change in attitude on the part of conservationists and environmentalists is frequently dated back to the United Nations Confer-ence on the Human Environment, held in Stockholm in 1972.[10] Of course, its beginnings are much earlier, although the Stockholm conference gave it a focus and an emphasis not previously available. The idea that conserva-tionists could never attain their long-term goals without paying attention to the needs of human populations, and that economic developers could not bring sustainable gains without facing up to the ecological conditions and the conservation requirements of the environments being affected by

8 For an exploration of some of the political and economic complexities of the carbon dioxide/climatic change problem, see Garrett Hardin, *Filters against Folly* (New York: Viking, 1985), pp. 145–63.

9 Ken Keyes, Jr., *The Hundredth Monkey* (St. Mary, Ky.: Vision Books, 1981). The original account of the monkeys on the island of Koshima, Japan, is attributed to Lyall Watson, *Lifetide* (New York: Bantam, 1980), pp. 147–8. I am unable to evaluate the scientific credibility of the tale, but it makes a good story.

10 United Nations Environment Programme, *In Defence of the Earth* (Nairobi, Kenya: UNEP, 1981).

development, has been widely accepted by the conservation community. This is evidenced, among other ways, by the publication of the *World Conservation Strategy* by the International Union for the Conservation of Nature and Natural Resources (IUCN) in 1980.[11] This publication, also sponsored by the World Wildlife Fund, UNESCO, the United Nations Environment Programme (UNEP), and the Food and Agricultural Organization of the United Nations (FAO) has since been accepted by many governments and has guided many of the world's conservation organizations. One would like to say that it has also been adopted as a guide for action by the multinational banks and corporations, but such success can hardly be claimed. In truth, although many ecologists and conservationists have moved toward recognition of economic and social needs, relatively few economists and engineers have moved to recognize ecological limits or conservation needs.

Nevertheless the concept of sustainable development, based on ecological awareness, is becoming accepted, in principle at least. Few want to admit that their brand of economic development is not sustainable. Arguments develop over the meaning of "sustainability." Agribusiness based on monoculture has its defenders who will maintain that they can keep up high yields and even increase productivity just as long as energy supplies are available at reasonable costs, relative to the prices they receive for their produce. Their faith in the ability of agricultural science and technology to find new varieties of disease-resistant, high-yielding crops and to find more effective pesticides is almost unbounded. They remain certain that fossil fuels and nuclear power can provide for their energy needs indefinitely. In fact, even among its greatest advocates, the meaning and full implications of the term "sustainable," when applied to development, are only now being faced.

In a recent paper prepared primarily by Thomas Stoel for the Global Tomorrow Coalition to submit to the World Commission on Environment and Development, sustainable development is defined as:

Process of change to meet the needs of people, as defined by them, without lessening the potential for meeting their future needs, the needs of other societies, or those of future generations. The purpose of development is not simply material advancement; societies or individuals may conclude that they prefer fewer material goods and more leisure or other amenities. Development is not for this generation alone; those living now must not leave a denuded polluted planet for generations to come.

The paper goes on to examine the elements essential to sustainable development: satisfaction of human needs, freedom from unwanted dependence, control of population growth, and maintenance of natural and life-support systems. Under the heading of "what must be done" the following

11 IUCN, *World Conservation Strategy* (Gland, Switzerland: IUCN, 1980).

actions are proposed: "promote decentralized, small-scale, community-based development; ensure that people are able to participate in decisions; encourage appropriate changes in lifestyles and values; protect natural resources and the environment; improve efficiency of resource use; change aid, trade, and investment practices; and reduce arms expenditures and the risk of nuclear war."[12]

If nothing else, this paper is evidence of a major shift in outlook among many of the principal conservation organizations, and reflects a new way of looking at conservation problems. It is, however, an expansion of the concept of "ecodevelopment" which was first advanced by Maurice Strong, then director-general of the United Nations Environment Programme, in 1973 – shortly after Stockholm. This concept was further expanded and explored in the Cocoyoc Declaration – the statement of a joint symposium sponsored by the United Nations Environment Programme and the United Nations Commission on Trade and Development, at Cocoyoc, Mexico, in October 1974.[13] Cocoyoc was hardly a gathering of conservationists, and the declaration is significant for expressing a new approach to development originating to a great extent among third world countries rather than being predetermined by representatives of the richer nations of the world.

The declaration is critical of approaches to development undertaken in past decades, and of the operations of global market mechanisms: "The traditional market makes resources available to those who can buy them rather than those who need them, it stimulates artificial demands and builds waste into the production process, and even under-utilizes resources." Stressing how the rich countries have continued to benefit at the expense of the poor, the report goes on to state:

Nor are the evils which flow from excessive reliance on the market system confined to international relationships. The experience of the last 30 years is that the exclusive pursuit of economic growth, guided by the market and undertaken by and for the powerful elites, has the same destructive effects inside developing countries. The richest 5 per cent engross all the gain while the poorest 20 per cent can actually grow poorer still. And at the local as at the international level the evils of material poverty are compounded by the people's lack of participation and human dignity, by their lack of any power to determine their own fate.

The declaration then redefines the purpose of development:

This should not be to develop things but to develop man. Human beings have basic needs: food, shelter, clothing, health, education. Any process of growth that does

---

12 Thomas B. Stoel, Jr., and Donald R. Lesh, *Sustainable Development and How to Achieve It* (Washington, D.C.: Global Tomorrow Coalition, 1986).
13 UNEP, The Cocoyoc Declaration, *In Defence of the Earth* (Nairobi, Kenya: UNEP, 1981). This is reproduced as an appendix to R. F. Dasmann, *Environmental Conservation,* 5th ed. (New York: Wiley, 1984), pp. 453–62.

not lead to their fulfillment – or, even worse, disrupts them – is a travesty of the idea of development. We are still in a stage where the most important concern of development is the level of satisfaction of basic needs for the poorest sections in each society which can be as high as 40 per cent of the population. . . .

Development should not be limited to the satisfaction of basic needs. There are other needs, other goals, and other values. Development includes freedom of expression and impression, the right to give and to receive ideas and stimulus. There is a deep social need to participate in shaping the basis of one's own existence, and to make some contribution to the fashioning of the world's future. Above all, development includes the right to work, by which we mean not simply having a job but finding self-realization in work, the right not to be alienated through production processes that use human beings simply as tools.

The need to shape development strategies to fit the variety of different cultures, bearing in mind the limits imposed by the finite carrying capacity of the biosphere, is emphasized, as is the necessity to develop increased national self-reliance. At the same time the declaration warns:

There is an international power structure that will resist moves in this direction. Its methods are well known: the purposive maintenance of the built-in bias of the existing international market mechanisms, other forms of economic manipulation, withdrawing or withholding credits, embargoes, economic sanctions, subversive use of intelligence agencies, repression including torture, counter-insurgency operations, even full-scale intervention. To those contemplating the use of such methods we say: "Hands-off. Leave countries to find their own road to a fuller life for their citizens."

Cocoyoc has called for revolutionary changes in our way of dealing with each other, but not revolution intended to bring the centrally planned economy instead of the operation of the market system. Rather, as Johan Galtung has stated it, midway in the spectrum between the deep red of central planning and the deep blue of the free market economy, we find the color green.[14] This is the more hopeful color to follow, and seems to lead in the direction that the ecodevelopment movement is trying to go.

The Cocoyoc Declaration, the proposals for ecodevelopment, and the demand for a new international economic order have all encountered the expected opposition from the "international power structure." Those that try to move too strongly in a program for meeting basic needs find the International Monetary Fund threatening to withdraw or withhold credits. Countries that seek to follow their own road to a fuller life for their citizens, such as Nicaragua, encounter "subversive use of intelligence agencies, repression including torture, counter-insurgency operations," and are threatened with even full-scale intervention. The rich do not willingly part

14 Johan Galtung, Regent's lectures at the University of California, Santa Cruz, 1986. The idea is developed in part in "Development Theory – Notes for an Alternative Approach" in *Entwicklungstheorie-Entwicklungspraxis* (Berlin: Duncker & Humblot, 1986), pp. 73–89.

with their wealth. The old guard does sometimes retreat but seems in no mood to surrender.

Yet I find it both strange and hopeful that the conservation movement, which has tried very hard in the past to maintain an apolitical stance, is becoming politicized. It is not necessarily involved in party politics in the Republican versus Democratic sense, nor in the more extreme politics of capitalism versus socialism. The conservation movement is questioning more deeply the political, social, and economic roots that support a social order in which pollution is acceptable and the destruction of natural resources is considered necessary, and in which the rich become extremely rich at the expense of those who have trouble finding enough for bare survival. In demanding participatory democracy, even in the economic marketplace; in calling for the development of local self-reliance; in strengthening the village vis-à-vis the city, and the periphery against the center, the conservation movement runs contrary to the rules of the entrenched socialist bureaucracies as much as to the ways of multinational corporations.

Meetings and conferences, essays and declarations may give some hope that humanity is developing a new consciousness concerning its role in the life of the biosphere, but one needs more evidence that people are taking these ideas seriously. It seems appropriate that third world countries should be taking a lead in finding new ways, since they have benefited least from the old directions. The island nation of Sri Lanka today provides an interesting contrast between old and new. On the one hand the government is backing the accelerated Mahaweli Development Programme, a scheme which could find its model in the California Water Project or the Tennessee Valley Authority's activities. The major river, the Mahaweli, which drains through the dry half of the island, is being captured in a system of dams, hydropower installations, and irrigation canals which are totally changing the landscape of what was once dry tropical forest country on the east side of the island. Wild species and patterns of shifting cultivation are giving way to irrigated rice paddies. Tens of thousands of people are being moved about, and encouraged to take up new ways of farming. The development is intended to provide food for the people of Sri Lanka and for export as well, along with power for developing industries around the capital and elsewhere. It has all of the modern trappings, including an Environmental Impact Statement leading to a Mahaweli Environment Programme, intended to mitigate or compensate for environmental damage. It has the support of Swedish, Canadian, German, and American development agencies.[15]

15 Ministry of Lands and Land Development/Ministry of Mahaweli Development, *Mahaweli Projects and Programme, 1985* (Colombo, Sri Lanka, 1984). This is the official version of the project. For a more critical review see Carel Drijver, et al., *Mahaweli Ganga Project in Sri Lanka*, Evaluation of environmental problems and the role of settler-households in

On the other hand, in the same country, with little or no government support, the *Sarvodaya* movement, a grass-roots development effort, seems to be spreading from village to village. According to recent reports it has reached seven thousand villages and affected millions of people. It has its roots in Buddhist principles, but follows the pathway of Mahatma Gandhi. It involves the Hindu Tamils as well as the Buddhist Sinhalese. Its origins were with a high school teacher, A. P. Ariyaratna, in the capital city of Colombo, who decided to take his class, for a vacation project, to live in and work with an agricultural village, helping the people accomplish a local project which would make their life a little easier. The idea spread to other schools and villages. Next it spread from village to village with mutual assistance programs. The Sarvodaya network developed with regional centers working to help villagers to help themselves, with problems of health, water supply, roads, education, child care – all of the local needs. It avoided the trap of being channeled for the benefit of the village elite. It drew on the help of the village monks to get women and whole families involved in each project and to more truly accomplish what the people wanted to have done. It has no massive international support, but has had assistance from private foundations and religious groups. In many ways it appears to follow the directions of ecodevelopment – meeting basic needs, developing local self-reliance, working in harmony with the environment. But it is too early to tell.[16]

Both development efforts are handicapped by the presence of an ongoing and vicious civil war between Tamils and Sinhalese as the former seek to establish their own independent nation in the east and north of the island. It may be that in the long run the Mahaweli project will improve the conditions of life for millions of Sri Lankans. It may be that the new system of nature reserves being created in the Mahaweli area will compensate in part for the destruction of nature that has already taken place. The whole system may stabilize at a more productive level. It will take another twenty years or longer before the results are in. It is easier to evaluate Sarvodaya, since it is on a smaller scale and more direct, with its benefits easier to recognize and its shortcomings easier to correct. It is one way to go, regardless of what happens with the Mahaweli scheme.

North of Sri Lanka, on the Indian subcontinent, another grass-roots movement has been achieving some remarkable results. This is the Chipko, or "Hug-a-Tree" movement. It had its origins among the women of one village who were protesting the logging of trees in the woodland on which they were

Footnote 15 (*continued*)
    conservation, Centre for Environmental Studies (Netherlands, State University of Leiden, 1985).
16 Joanna Macy, *Dharma and Development*, rev. ed. (West Hartford, Conn.: Kumarian Press, 1985).

dependent for many products. By hugging a tree they interposed their bodies between the loggers with their chain saws and the trees of the village forest. The trees were saved, and the idea spread from village to village to become what is now a national movement for forest conservation.[17]

An attempt to bring representatives of many of these grass-roots movements together in one place was carried out by the Environmental Liaison Centre in Nairobi, Kenya, in February of 1985. Peace, Environment, Consumer Action, Women's Liberation, Public Health, and other areas were represented by the delegates who found a common interest in a sustainable development program. One offshoot of this meeting was the formation of an African Environmental Network, to bring together nongovernmental, voluntary organizations throughout that continent.[18]

Among those surviving members of groups that are, or have recently been, among the ranks of ecosystem people there are now activities taking place that would not have been predicted twenty years ago. In efforts to retain or regain their cultural identity and their lands, many of these people are forming international coalitions and joining together in international conferences. The Inuit of Canada have not only formed action groups within Canada but are reaching out to Arctic peoples in Europe and Asia by way of circumpolar conferences. South of Inuit lands, the Indians of Canada are also forming coalitions for reaching common goals and carrying out political action. World congresses of indigenous people have occurred under United Nation's auspices, bringing together those fourth world people who have lacked effective political representation in third world countries, as well as in the industrialized world. A concern for the environment and conservation has led, for example, to the formation of the Yukon National Park in Canada, where the subsistence hunting and fishing rights of native Americans are guaranteed, and far south in Panama to the establishment of a tribal nature reserve, equivalent to a national park, by the Kuna Indians, who see it as a means for protecting their forests and lands from the encroachment of outside groups.[19]

Within the industrialized world there is a plethora of organizations, movements, groups, and activities, all of which are more or less directly concerned with maintaining the green and blue colors of the lands and seas of the planet. While it cannot be doubted that these collective groups have an influence on national policies, they represent no "clear and present danger" to the "international power structure." Even when a million people hit the streets in New York and Washington to demand a nuclear freeze, they fail to cause a minor blip in the upward climb of the budget of the

17 Vandana Shiva, "Ecology Movements in India," *Alternatives* II (1986): 255–73.
18 Environmental Liaison Centre, *Sustainable Development*, (Nairobi, Kenya: ELC, 1985).
19 Reports and discussion at the World Conservation Strategy Conference held in Ottawa, Canada, June 1986. (Gland, Switzerland: IUCN, forthcoming).

Department of Defense, and are ignored by the administration and the majority in Congress.

There is really little doubt that there is a growing awareness of the necessity for modifying human ways to ensure the survival of the natural world on which the future of the human race depends. There is a rapidly growing biosphere consciousness, which is reaching the higher levels of many governments and has often found its expression at the level of the United Nations. One regrets that it is less evident in the United States government than it has been in the past, but it is certainly expressed among many members of the Congress, and one can expect future changes in the national leadership which will reflect the growing public awareness. The real question is whether or not the human race can modify its ways of behavior rapidly enough, because the majority continues to pursue pathways that lead toward the ecological impoverishment of the planet. The increase in awareness does not keep pace with the rate of destruction of tropical forests, the spread of deserts, the erosion of agricultural soils, the depletion of wildlife, or the growing pollution of the atmosphere and hydrosphere. Those who exercise the greatest political and military power still threaten a war that can bring the whole edifice built by civilization crashing down into the wreckage of the biosphere, while in the meanwhile dozens of little wars forestall efforts to achieve sustainable ways of life.

There is also a reasonable fear that if the power and influence of those who work for conservation of nature, sustainable development based on social justice and equity, and a more reasonable approach to human use of the biosphere, begins to reach a critical mass there will be attempts at massive repression by those who feel threatened by such changes. In other terms, if we begin to approach the hundredth monkey level, the "international power structure" will declare an open season on monkeys. If that happens then the real question will be whether anyone will be left to write the environmental history of our times.

Appendix: Doing Environmental History

Donald Worster

IN THE OLD DAYS, the discipline of history had an altogether easier task. Everyone knew that the only important subject was politics and the only important terrain was the nation-state. One was supposed to investigate the connivings of presidents and prime ministers, the passing of laws, the struggles between courts and legislatures, and the negotiations of diplomats. That old, self-assured history was actually not so old after all – a mere century or two at most. It emerged with the power and influence of the nation-state, reaching a peak of acceptance in the nineteenth and early twentieth centuries. Often its practitioners were men of intensely nationalistic feelings, who were patriotically moved to trace the rise of their individual countries, the formation of political leadership in them, and their rivalries with other states for wealth and power. They knew what mattered, or thought they did.

But some time back that history as "past politics" began to lose ground, as the world evolved toward a more global point of view and, some would say, toward a more democratic one. Historians lost some of their confidence that the past had been so thoroughly controlled or summed up by a few great men acting in positions of national power. Scholars began uncovering long submerged layers, the lives and thoughts of ordinary people, and tried to reconceive history "from the bottom up."|Down, down we must go, they maintained, down to the hidden layers of class, gender, race, and caste.| There we will find what truly has shaped the surface layers of politics. Now enter still another group of reformers, the environmental historians, who insist that we have got to go still deeper yet, down to the earth itself as an agent and presence in history. Here we will discover even more fundamental forces at work over time. And to appreciate those forces we must now and then get out of parliamentary chambers, out of birthing rooms and factories, get out of doors altogether, and ramble into fields, woods, and the open air. It is time we bought a good set of walking shoes, and we cannot avoid getting some mud on them.

So far this extending of the scope of history to include a deeper and

289

Donald Worster

broader range of subjects has not challenged the primacy of the nation-state as the proper territory of the historian. Social, economic, and cultural history are all still commonly pursued within national boundaries. Thus, to an extent that is quite extraordinary among the disciplines of learning, history (at least for the modern period) has tended to remain the insular study of the United States, Brazil, France, and the rest. Such a way of organizing the past has the undeniable virtue of preserving some semblance of order in the face of a threatening chaos – some way of synthesizing all the layers and forces. But at the same time it may set up obstacles to new inquiries that do not neatly fit within national borders, environmental history among them. Many of the issues in this new field defy a narrow nationality: the wanderings of Tuareg nomads in the African Sahel, for instance, or the pursuit of the great whales through all the world's oceans. Other environmental themes, to be sure, have developed strictly within the framework of single-nation politics, as a few of the essays in this book illustrate. But not all have done so, and in the history that will be written tomorrow, fewer and fewer will be.

Environmental history is, in sum, part of a revisionist effort to make the discipline far more inclusive in its narratives than it has traditionally been. Above all, it rejects the conventional assumption that human experience has been exempt from natural constraints, that people are a separate and "supernatural" species, that the ecological consequences of their past deeds can be ignored. The old history could hardly deny that we have been living for a long while on this planet, but it assumed by its general disregard of that fact that we have not been and are not truly part of the planet. Environmental historians, on the other hand, realize that we can no longer afford to be so naive.

The idea of environmental history first appeared in the 1970s, as conferences on the global predicament were taking place and popular environmentalist movements were gathering momentum in several countries. It was launched, in other words, in a time of worldwide cultural reassessment and reform. History was hardly alone in being touched by that rising mood of public concern; scholarship in law, philosophy, economics, sociology, and other areas was similarly responsive. Long after popular interest in environmental issues crested and ebbed, as the issues themselves came to appear more and more complicated, without easy resolution, the scholarly interest continued to expand and take on greater and greater sophistication. Environmental history was, therefore, born out of a moral purpose, with strong political commitments behind it, but also became, as it matured, a scholarly enterprise that had neither any simple, nor any single, moral or political agenda to promote. Its principal goal became one of deepening our understanding of how humans have been affected by their natural environment

290

through time and, conversely, how they have affected that environment and with what results.

One of the liveliest centers of the new history has been the United States, a fact that undoubtedly stems from the strength of American leadership in environmental matters. The earliest attempt to define the field was Roderick Nash's essay, "The State of Environmental History."[1] Nash recommended looking at our entire surroundings as a kind of historical document on which Americans had been writing about themselves and their ideals. More recently, a comprehensive effort by Richard White to trace the development of the field credits the pioneering work of Nash and that of the conservation historian Samuel Hays, but also suggests that there were anticipations before them in the frontier and western school of American historiography (among such land-minded figures as Frederick Jackson Turner, Walter Prescott Webb, and James Malin). Those older roots became increasingly recalled as the field moved beyond Hays's politics of conservation and Nash's intellectual history to focus on changes in the environment itself and consider, once more, the environment's role in the making of American society.

Another center of innovation has been France, particularly the historians associated with the journal *Annales*, who have been drawing attention to the environment for several decades now. That journal was founded in 1929 by two professors at the University of Strasbourg, Marc Bloch and Lucien Febvre. Both of them were interested in the environmental basis of society, Bloch through his studies of French peasant life and Febvre as a social geographer. The latter's protégé, Fernand Braudel, would also make the environment a prominent part of his historical studies, notably in his great work on the Mediterranean. For Braudel, the environment was the shape of the land – mountains, plains, seas – as an almost timeless element shaping human life over the long duration *(la longue durée)*. There was, he insisted, more to history than the succession of events in individual lives; on the grandest scale, there was history seen from the vantage of nature, a history "in which all change is slow, a history of constant repetition, ever-recurring cycles."

Like the frontier historians in the United States, the *Annalistes* in France found their environmental interests reanimated by the popular movements of the sixties and early seventies. In 1974, the journal devoted a special issue to "Histoire et Environnement." In a short preface Emmanuel Le Roy Ladurie, himself one of the leading lights in the field, gave this description (my translation) of the field's program:

Environmental history unites the oldest themes with the newest in contemporary historiography: the evolution of epidemics and climate, those two factors being

1 All authors referred to in this essay are fully cited in the Bibliography.

integral parts of the human ecosystem; the series of natural calamities aggravated by a lack of foresight, or even by an absurd "willingness" on the part of the simpletons of colonization; the destruction of Nature, caused by soaring population and/or by the predators of industrial overconsumption; nuisances of urban and manufacturing origin, which lead to air or water pollution; human congestion or noise levels in urban areas, in a period of galloping urbanization.

Denying that this new history was merely a passing fashion, Le Roy Ladurie insisted that the inquiry had in truth been going on for a long time as part of a movement toward "histoire écologique."

Much of the material for environmental history has indeed been around for generations, if not for centuries, and is only being reorganized in the light of recent experience. It includes data on tides and winds, on ocean currents, on the position of continents in relation to each other, on the geological and hydrological forces creating our land and water base. It includes the history of climate and weather, as these have made for good or bad harvests, sent prices up or down, ended or promoted epidemics, led to population increase or decline. All these have been powerful influences over the course of history, and continue to be so, as when massive earthquakes destroy cities or starvation follows in the wake of drought or rivers determine the flow of settlement. The fact that such influences continue in the late twentieth century is evidence of how far we are yet from controlling the environment to our complete satisfaction. In a somewhat different category are those living resources of the earth, which the ecologist George Woodwell calls the most important of all: the plants and animals (and one might add the soil as a collective organism) that, in Woodwell's phrase, "maintain the biosphere as a habitat suitable for life." These resources have been far more susceptible to human manipulation than the abiotic ones, and at no point more so than today. But pathogens are also a part of that living realm, and they continue, despite the effectiveness of medicine, to be a decisive agency in our fate.

Put in the vernacular then, environmental history is about the role and place of nature in human life. By common understanding we mean by "nature" the nonhuman world, the world we have not in any primary sense created. The "social environment," the scene of humans interacting only with each other in the absence of nature, is therefore excluded. Likewise is the built or artifactual environment, the cluster of things that people have made and which can be so pervasive as to constitute a kind of "second nature" around them. That latter exclusion may seem especially arbitrary, and to an extent it is. Increasingly, as human will makes its imprint on the forest, on gene pools, on the polar ice cap, it may seem that there is no practical difference between "nature" and "artifact." The distinction, nonetheless, is worth keeping, for it reminds us that there are different forces at work in the world and not all of them emanate from humans; some remain spontaneous and self-generating. The built environment is wholly expressive of culture; its study is already well advanced in the history of architecture, technology, and the city. But with such phenomena as the forest and the water cycle, we encounter autonomous energies that do not derive from us. Those forces impinge on human life, stimulating some reaction, some defense, some ambition. Thus, when we step beyond the self-reflecting world of humankind to encounter the nonhuman sphere, environmental history finds its main theme of study.

There are three levels on which the new history proceeds, three clusters of issues it addresses, though not necessarily all in the same project, three sets of questions it seeks to answer, each drawing on a range of outside disciplines and employing special methods of analysis. The first deals with understanding nature itself, as organized and functioning in past times; we include both organic and inorganic aspects of nature, and not least the human organism as it has been a link in nature's food chains, now functioning as womb, now belly, now eater, now eaten, now a host for microorganisms, now a kind of parasite. The second level in this history brings in the socioeconomic realm as it interacts with the environment. Here we are concerned with tools and work, with the social relations that grow out of that work, with the various modes people have devised of producing goods from natural resources. A community organized to catch fish at sea may have very different institutions, gender roles, or seasonal rhythms than one raising sheep in high mountain pastures. Power to make decisions, environmental or other, is seldom distributed through a society with perfect equality, so locating the configurations of power is part of this level of analysis. Then, forming a third level for the historian is that more intangible and uniquely human type of encounter – the purely mental or intellectual, in which perceptions, ethics, laws, myths, and other structures of meaning become part of an individual's or group's dialogue with nature. People are constantly engaged in constructing maps of the world around them, in defining what a resource is, in determining which sorts of behavior may be environmentally degrading and ought to be prohibited, and generally in choosing the ends of their lives. Though for the purposes of clarification, we may try to distinguish between these three levels of environmental study, in fact they constitute a single dynamic inquiry in which nature, social and economic organization, thought and desire are treated as one whole. And this whole changes as nature changes, as people change, forming a dialectic that runs through all of the past down to the present.

This in general is the program of the new environmental history. It brings together a wide array of subjects, familiar and unfamiliar, rather than setting up some new, esoteric specialty. From that synthesis, we hope, new questions and answers will come.

Donald Worster

The environmental historian must learn to speak some new languages as well as ask some new questions. Undoubtedly, the most outlandish language that must be learned is the natural scientist's. So full of numbers, laws, terms, and experiments, it is as foreign to the historian as Chinese was to Marco Polo. Yet, with even a smattering of vocabulary, what treasures are here to be understood and taken back home! Concepts from geology, pushing our notions of history back into the Pleistocene, the Silurian, the Precambrian. Graphs from climatology, on which temperatures and precipitation oscillate up and down through the centuries, with no regard for the security of kings or empires. The chemistry of the soil with its cycles of carbon and nitrogen, its pH balances wavering with the presences of salts and acids, setting the terms of agriculture. Any one of these might add a powerful tool to the study of the rise of civilizations. Together, the natural sciences are indispensable aids for the environmental historian, who must begin by reconstructing past landscapes, learning what they were and how they functioned before human societies entered and rearranged them.

But above all it is ecology, which examines the interactions among organisms and between them and their physical environments, that offers the environmental historian the greatest help. This is so in part because, ever since Charles Darwin, ecology has been concerned with past as well as present interactions; it has been integral to the study of evolution. Equally significant, ecology is at heart concerned with the origins, dispersal, and organization of all plant life. Plants form by far the major portion of the earth's biomass. All through history people have depended critically on them for food, medicine, building materials, hunting habitat, and a buffer against the rest of nature. Far more often than not, plants have been humans' allies in the struggle to survive and thrive. Therefore, where people and vegetation come together more issues in environmental history cluster than anywhere else. Take away plant ecology and environmental history loses its foundation, its coherence, its first step.

So impressed are they with this fact that some scholars speak of doing, not environmental, but "ecological history" or "historical ecology." They mean to insist on a tighter alliance with the science. Some years back the scientist and conservationist Aldo Leopold projected such an alliance when he spoke of "an ecological interpretation of history." His own illustration of how that might work had to do with the competition among native Indians, French and English traders, and American settlers for the land of Kentucky, pivotal in the westward movement. The canebrakes growing along Kentucky bottomlands were a formidable barrier to any agricultural settlement, but as luck would have it for the Americans, when the cane was burned and grazed and chopped out, bluegrass sprouted in its place. And bluegrass was all that any farmer, looking for a homestead and a pasture for his livestock, could want. American farmers entered Kentucky by the thousands, and the struggle was soon over. "What if," Leopold wondered, "the plant succession inherent in this dark and bloody ground had, under the impact of these forces, given us some worthless sedge, shrub, or weed?" Would Kentucky have become American property as and when it did?

Shortly after Leopold called for that merging of history and ecology, the Kansas historian James Malin brought out a series of essays leading to what he termed "an ecological reexamination of the history of the United States." He specially had in mind examining his native grasslands and the problem in adaptation they had set for Americans, as they had for the Indians before them. From the late nineteenth century on, white settlers, coming out of a more humid, wooded country, had tried to create a stable agriculture on the dry, treeless plains, but with only mixed results. Malin was impressed that they had succeeded in turning the land into prosperous wheat farms, but not before they had had to unlearn many of their old agricultural techniques. Dissatisfied with traditional history, which did not give such matters any prominence, Malin found himself reading ecologists to find the right questions to ask. He read them with a certain freedom, as a source of inspiration rather than a set of rigid models. "The ecological point of view," he believed, "is valuable to the study of history; not under any illusion that history may thus be converted into a science, but merely as a way of looking at the subject matter and processes of history."

Those were alliances sought some thirty or forty years back. Since then, as ecology has developed into a more rigorously mathematical science, with more elaborate models of natural processes, neither Malin's nor Leopold's casual sort of alliance has seemed adequate. Environmental historians have had to learn to read at a more advanced level, though they are still faced with Malin's problem of deciding just how scientific their history needs to be and which ideas in science can or ought to be adopted.

Today's ecology offers a number of angles for understanding organisms in their environment, and they all have their limits as well as uses in history. One might, for example, examine the single organism and its response to external conditions; in other words, study adaptation in individual physiological terms. Or one might track the fluctuations in size of some plant or animal population in an area, its rates of reproduction, its evolutionary success or failure, its economic ramifications. Although both sorts of inquiry may have considerable practical significance for human society, there is a third strategy that holds the most promise for historians needing to understand humans and nature in the composite.

When organisms of many species come together, they form communities, usually highly diverse in makeup, or as they are more commonly called now, ecosystems. An ecosystem is the largest generalization made in the science, encompassing both the organic and inorganic elements of nature bound together in a single place, all in active, reciprocating relationship.[2] Some ecosystems are fairly small and readily demarcated, like a pond in New England, while others are sprawling and ill-defined, as large as the Amazonian rain forest or the Serengeti plain or even the whole earth. All are commonly described, in language derived heavily from physical mechanics and cybernetics, as self-equilibrating, like a machine that runs on and on automatically, checking itself when it gets too hot, speeding up when it slows and begins to sputter. Outside disturbances may affect that equilibrium, throwing the machine temporarily off its regular rhythm, but always (or almost always) it returns to some steady state condition. The numbers of species constituting an ecosystem fluctuate around some determinable point; the flow of energy through the machine stays constant. The ecologist is interested in how such systems go on functioning in the midst of continual perturbations, and how and why they break down.

But right there occurs a difficult issue on which the science of ecology has reached no clear consensus. How stable are those natural systems and how susceptible to upset? Is it accurate to describe them as balanced and stable until humans arrive? And if so, then at what point does a change in their equilibrium become excessive, damaging or destroying them? Damage to the individual organism is easy enough to define: It is an impairment of health or, ultimately, it is death. Likewise, damage to a population is not very hard to determine, simply, when its numbers decline. But damage to whole ecosystems is a more controversial matter. No one would dispute that the death of all its trees, birds, and insects would mean the death of a rain-forest ecosystem, or that the draining of a pond would spell the end of that system. But most changes are less catastrophic, and the degree of damage has no easy method of measurement.

The difficulty of determining ecosystem damage applies to changes worked by people as well as nonhuman forces. A South American tribe, for instance, may clear a small patch in the forest with their machetes, raise a few crops, and then let the field revert to forest. Such so-called swidden, or slash-and-burn, farming has usually been regarded as harmless to the whole ecosystem; eventually, its natural equilibrium is restored. But at some point, as this farming intensifies, the capacity of the forest to regenerate itself must be permanently impaired and the ecosystem damaged. What is that point? Ecologists are not sure and cannot give precise answers. For that reason the

2 "Systems" talk can be rather mystifying and jargonized. The *American Heritage Dictionary* defines a system as "a group of interacting, interrelated, or interdependent elements forming or regarded as forming a collective entity." One may then speak of systems in nature, in technology and economics, or in thought and culture. And all these, in turn, may be described as interacting systemically, until the mind reels before the complexity.

ecological historian more often than not ends up talking about people inducing "change" in the environment – "change" being a neutral and indisputable term – rather than doing "damage," a far more problematical concept.

Until recently the ruling authority in ecosystem science has been Eugene Odum, through the various editions of his popular textbook, *Fundamentals of Ecology*. Odum is a system man nonpareil, one who sees the entire realm of nature as hierarchically organized into systems and subsystems, all made up of parts that function harmoniously and homeostatically, the rhythm of each system rather resembling the eighteenth-century's watchlike nature that never missed a tick. That earlier version was supposed to reveal the contriving hand of its divine maker; Odum's, in contrast, is the spontaneous work of nature. But increasingly, ecologists are retreating from his picture of order. Led by paleoecologists, especially paleobotanists, who collect core samples from peat bogs and, through pollen analysis, try to reconstruct ancient environments, they are finding Odum's blueprint a bit static. Looking backward in time to the Ice Age and before, they are discovering plenty of disorder and upheaval in nature. Abstracted from time, the critics say, ecosystems may have a reassuring look of permanence; but out there in the real, the historical, world, they are more perturbed than imperturbable, more changing than not.

This scientific difference of opinion is partly over evidence, partly over perspective, like disputing whether a glass is half empty or half full. Stand back far enough, stand off in outer space as the British scientist James Lovelock has tried imaginatively to do, and the earth still looks like a remarkably stable place, with organisms maintaining conditions highly suitable for life for over a billion years: all the gases in the atmosphere properly adjusted, fresh water and rich soil preserved in abundance, though evolution rages on and on, ice sheets come and go, and continents go drifting off in all directions. That may be how things look to the cosmic eyeball. Seen up close, however, the organic world may have a very different aspect. Stand on any given acre in North America and contemplate its past thousand years or so, even a single decade, and the conclusion ecologists are coming to these days is change, change, change.

There is a further unresolved problem in translating ecology into history. Few scientists have perceived people or human societies as being integral parts of their ecosystems. They leave them out as distractions, imponderables. But people are what the historian mainly studies; consequently, his or her job is to join together what scientists have put asunder.

Human beings participate in ecosystems either as biological organisms akin to other organisms or as culture bearers, though the distinction between the two roles is seldom clear-cut. Suffice it here to say that, as organisms, people have never been able to live in splendid, invulnerable isolation. They

Donald Worster

breed, of course, like other species, and their offspring must survive or perish by the quality of food, air, and water and by the number of microorganisms that are constantly invading their bodies. In these ways and more, humans have inextricably been part of the earth's ecological order. Therefore, any reconstruction of past environments must include not only forests and deserts, boas and rattlesnakes, but also the human animal and its success or failure in reproducing itself.

HUMAN MODES OF PRODUCTION

Nothing distinguishes people from other creatures more sharply than the fact that it is people who create culture. Precisely what culture really is, however, is anybody's guess. There are literally scores of definitions. For preliminary purposes it can be said that the definitions tend to divide between those including both mental and material activities and those emphasizing mental activities exclusively, and that these distinctions between the mental and material correspond to the second and third levels of analysis in our environmental history. In this section we are concerned with the material culture of a society, its implications for social organization, and its interplay with the natural environment.

In any particular place nature offers the humans dwelling there a flexible but limited set of possibilities for getting a living. The Eskimos of the northern polar regions, to take an extreme case of limits, cannot expect to become farmers. Instead, they have ingeniously derived a sustenance, not by marshaling seed, plows, and draft animals of other, warmer latitudes, but through hunting. Their food choices have focused on stalking caribou over the tundra and pursuing bowhead whales among floating cakes of ice, on gathering blueberries in season and gaffing fish. Narrow though those possibilities are, they are the gift of technology as much as nature. Technology is the application of skills and knowledge to exploiting the environment. Among the Eskimos technology has traditionally amounted to fish hooks, harpoons, sled runners, and the like. Though constrained by nature, that technology has nonetheless opened up for them a nutritional field otherwise out of reach, as when a sealskin boat allowed them to venture farther out to sea in pursuit of prey. Today's Eskimos, invaded as they are by the instruments of more materially advanced cultures, have still more choices laid before them; they can, if they desire, import a supply of wheat and oranges by cargo plane from California. And they can forget how their old choices were made, surrender their uniqueness, their independence of spirit, their intimacy with the icy world. Much of environmental history involves examining just such changes, voluntary or imposed, in subsistence modes and their ramifications for people and the earth.

As historians address these elemental issues of tools and sustenance, they

298

soon become aware that there have been other disciplines at work here too, and for a long time. Among them is the discipline of anthropologists, and environmental historians have been reading their work with great interest. They have begun to search for clues from anthropologists to critical pieces of the ecological puzzle: What is the best way to understand the relation of human material cultures to nature? Is technology to be viewed as an integral part of the natural world, akin to the fur coat of the polar bear, the sharp teeth of the tiger, the fleet agility of the gazelle, all adaptive mechanisms functioning within ecosystems? Or should cultures be viewed as setting people apart from and outside of nature? Everything in the ecosystem, we are told by natural scientists, has a role and therefore an influence on the workings of the whole; conversely, everything is shaped by its presence in the ecosystem. Are cultures and the societies that create them also to be seen in that double position, both acting on and being acted on? Or are they better described as forming their own kind of "cultural systems" that mesh with ecosystems only in rare, isolated cases? Or, to make the puzzle more complicated still, do humans create with their technology a series of new, artificial ecosystems – a rice paddy in Indonesia or a carefully managed German forest – that require constant human supervision? There is, of course, no single or consistent set of answers to be given to such questions; but anthropologists, who are among the most wide-ranging and theory-conscious observers of human behavior, can offer some provocative insights.

Anthropological thinking on such questions goes back well into the nineteenth century, but it has been particularly the last three or four decades that have seen the emergence of an ecological school (one with no settled curriculum, bearing such contending labels as cultural ecology, human ecology, ecological anthropology, and cultural materialism). The best guide to this literature is probably John Bennett's *The Ecological Transition,* though there are other useful surveys by Emilio Moran, Roy Ellen, Robert Netting, and others. Bennett defines the ecology school as the study of "how and why humans use Nature, how they incorporate Nature into Society, and what they do to themselves, Nature, and Society in the process." Some of these anthropologists have maintained that culture is an entirely autonomous and superorganic phenomenon, emerging apart from nature and understandable only in its own terms – or at least, as Bennett himself would have it, modern culture is trying to become so. Others, in contrast, have argued that all culture is, to some important degree, expressive of nature and ought not be rigidly set off in its own, self-contained sphere. Both positions are illuminating to the environmental historian, though for the historical era that is the main focus of this book, Bennett's is surely the more plausible one.

No one did more to found the ecological study of culture than Julian Steward, who published in 1955 his influential work, *Theory of Culture*

Change, from which comes the idea of "cultural ecology." Steward began by examining the relationship between a people's system of economic production and their physical environment. He asked what resources they chose to exploit and what technology they devised for that work. This set of subsistence activities he called the "cultural core." Then he asked how such a system affected the behavior of people toward one another, that is, how they organized themselves to produce their living. Social relations in turn shaped other aspects of culture. Some of the most interesting case studies for him were the great irrigation empires of the ancient world, in which large-scale control of water in arid environments led again and again to parallels in sociopolitical organization. Such regularities, he hoped, would suggest a general law of human evolution: not the old Victorian scheme that had all cultures moving along a single, fixed line of progress from hunting and gathering to industrial civilization, but rather one that explained the multilinear evolution of cultures, now diverging, now converging, now colliding with one another, with no end point in sight.

Steward's leadership in the new ecological approach inspired, directly or indirectly, a younger generation of field researchers who fanned out to all parts of the globe. John Bennett went to the Canadian prairies, Harold Conklin to the Philippines, Richard Lee to the !Kung Bushmen of Africa, Marshall Sahlins to Polynesia, Robert Netting to Nigeria to observe the hillside farmers there, Betty Meggers was off to the Amazon basin, Clifford Geertz to Indonesia, and there were still others. But above all, it has been Marvin Harris who has taken Steward's ideas and transformed them into a comprehensive and, some would complain, a highly reductive theory of the relationship between nature and culture. Like Steward, he has identified the "techno-environment" (i.e., the application of technology to environment) as providing the core of any culture, the main influence over how a people live with one another and think about the world. He has been even more rigidly deterministic than Steward was about that core. He has also been more interested in its dynamics. The techno-environmental system is not at all stable, he insists, certainly not forever. There is always the tendency to intensify production. It may come from population increase, climate change, or competition between states. Whatever the cause, the effect is always the same: depletion of the environment, declining efficiency, worsening living standards, pressures to move on – or if there is no new place to go, then pressure to find new tools, techniques, and resources locally, creating thereby another techno-environment. In other words, the degradation of the environment can be tragic, unhappy, or if people rise successfully to the challenge, it can mean the triumphant birth of a new culture. Harris calls this theory "cultural materialism." Clearly, it draws not only on Steward but on recent energy shortages, the present decline of a techno-environment based on the fossil fuels, and the revival of Malthusian anxieties about world resource scarcity, though Harris would argue that a time of scarcity can also be a time of opportunity and revolution.

Marvin Harris has explicitly compared his theory of cultural materialism to that of Karl Marx, who gave the world "dialectical materialism," a view of history impelled forever forward by the struggle of one economic class to dominate another. The contrast between the two theories is emphatic: One sees change coming from the struggle of whole societies to exploit nature, with diminishing returns; the other points to internal conflicts within societies as the prime historical agency, with nature serving as a passive background. Perhaps, however, the distance between the two men is not hopelessly unbridgeable. One might put a little more Marxism into Harris by arguing that, among the factors leading to depletion and ecological disequilibrium, is competition between classes as well as states. Capitalists devise a social and technological order that makes them rich and elevates them to power. They set up factories for mass production. They drive the earth to the point of breakdown with their technology, their management of the laboring class, and their appetites. Subsistence gets redefined as endless want, endless consumption, endless competing for status. The system eventually self-destructs, and a new one takes its place. Similarly, we might improve Marxism by adding Harris's ecological factors to help explain the rise of classes and class conflict. Neither theory, taken alone, adequately accounts for the past. Together, they might work more effectively, each supplying the other's shortcomings. In so far as the course of history has been shaped by material forces, and hardly anyone would deny that they have indeed been important, we will undoubtedly need something like that merger of the two theories.

The modes of production are an endless parade of strategies, as complex in their taxonomies as the myriad species of insects thriving in the canopy of a rain forest or the brightly colored fish in a coral reef. In broad terms, we may speak of such modes as hunting and gathering, agriculture, and modern industrial capitalism. But that is only the bare outline of any full taxonomy. We must also include, as modes, submodes, or variations on them, the history of cowboys herding cattle across a Montana grassland, of dark-skinned fishermen casting their nets on the Malabar coast, of Laplanders trailing after their reindeer, of Tokyo factory workers buying bags of rice and seaweed in a supermarket. In all these instances and more, the environmental historian wants to know what role nature had in shaping the productive methods and, conversely, what impact those methods had on nature.

This is the age-old dialogue between ecology and economy. Though deriving from the same etymological roots, the two words have come to denote two separate spheres, and for good reason: Not all economic modes are ecologically sustainable. Some last for centuries, even millennia, while others appear only briefly and then fade away, failures in adaptation. And ultimately, over the long stretch of time, no modes have ever been perfectly adapted to their environment, or there would be little history.

PERCEPTION, IDEOLOGY, AND VALUE

Humans are animals with ideas as well as tools, and one of the largest, most consequential of those ideas bears the name "nature." More accurately, "nature" is not one idea but many ideas, meanings, thoughts, feelings, all piled on top of one another, often in the most unsystematic fashion. Every individual and every culture has created such agglomerations. We may think we know what we are saying when we use the word, but frequently we mean several things at once and listeners may have to work at getting our meaning. We may suppose too that nature refers to something radically separate from ourselves, that it is "out there" someplace, sitting solidly, concretely, unambiguously. In a sense, that is so. Nature is an order and a process that we did not create, and in our absence it will continue to exist; only the most strident solipsist would argue to the contrary. All the same, nature is a creation of our minds too, and no matter how hard we may try to see what it is objectively, in and by and for itself, we are to a considerable extent trapped in the prison of our own consciousness and web of meanings.

Environmental historians have done some of their best work on this level of cultural analysis, studying the perceptions and values people have held about the nonhuman world. They have, that is, put people thinking about nature under scrutiny. So impressed have they been by the enduring, pervasive power of ideas that sometimes they have blamed present environmental abuse on attitudes that go far back into the recesses of time: as far back as the book of Genesis and the ancient Hebraic ethos of asserting dominion over the earth; or the Greco-Roman determination to master the environment through reason; or the still more archaic drive among patriarchal males to lord it over nature (the "feminine" principle) as well as women. The actual effects of such ideas, in the past or in the present, are extremely difficult to trace empirically, but that has not deterred scholars from making some very large claims here. Nor should it altogether. Perhaps we have too wildly exaggerated a notion of our mental prowess and its impact on the rest of nature. Perhaps we spend too much time talking about our ideas, neglecting to examine our behavior. But however overblown some of these claims may be, it is certainly true that our ideas have been interesting to contemplate, and nothing among them has been more interesting than our reflections on other animals, plants, soils, and the entire biosphere that gave birth to us. So, for good reason, environmental history must include in its program the study of aspects of esthetics and ethics, myth and folklore, literature and landscape gardening, science and religion – must go wherever the human mind has grappled with the meaning of nature.

For the historian, the main object must be to discover how a whole culture, rather than exceptional individuals in it, perceived and valued nature. Even the most materially primitive society may have had quite sophisticated, complex views. Complexity, of course, may come from unresolved ambiguities and contradictions as well as from profundity. People in industrial countries especially seem to abound in these contradictions: They may chew up the land wholesale and at a frightful speed through real estate development, mining, and deforestation but then turn around and pass laws to protect a handful of fish swimming in a desert spring. Some of this is simply confusion, some of it may be quite reasonable. Given the protean qualities of nature, the fact that the environment presents real dangers as well as benefits to people, this contradictoriness is inescapable. It has everywhere been true of the human reaction. Yet not a few scholars have fallen into the trap of speaking of "the Buddhist view of nature" or "the Christian view" or "the American Indian view," as though people in those cultures were all simple-minded, uncomplicated, unanimous, and totally lacking in ambivalence. Every culture, we should assume, has within it a range of perceptions and values, and no culture has ever really wanted to live in total harmony with its surroundings.

But ideas should not be left floating in some empyrean realm, free from the dust and sweat of the material world. They should be studied in their relations with those modes of subsistence discussed in the preceding section. Without reducing all thought and value to some material base, as though the human imagination was a mere rationalization of the belly's needs, the historian must understand that mental culture does not spring up all on its own. One way to put this relationship is to say that ideas are socially constructed and, therefore, reflect the organization of those societies, their techno-environments and hierarchies of power. Ideas differ from person to person within societies according to gender, class, race, and region. Men and women, set apart almost everywhere into more or less distinctive spheres, have arrived at different ways of regarding nature, sometimes radically so. So too have slaves and their masters, factory owners and workers, agrarian and industrial peoples. They may live together or in close proximity but still see and value the natural world differently. The historian must be alert to these differences and resist easy generalizations about the "mind" of a people or of an age.

Sometimes it is maintained that modern science has enabled us to rise above these material conditions to achieve for the first time in history an impersonal, transcultural, unbiased understanding of how nature works. The scientific method of collecting and verifying facts is supposed to deliver truth pure and impartial. Such confidence is naive. Few scholars writing the history of science today would accept it uncritically. Science, they would caution, has never been free of its material circumstances. Though it may indeed be a superior way of arriving at the truth, certainly superior in its capacity to deliver power over nature, it has nonetheless been shaped by the techno-environment and social relations of its time. According to historian Thomas Kuhn, science is not simply the accumulating of facts but involves fitting those facts into some kind of "paradigm," or model of how nature works. Old paradigms lose their appeal, and new ones rise to take their place. Although Kuhn does not himself derive those paradigm shifts from material conditions, other historians have insisted that there is a connection. Scientists, they say, do not work in complete isolation from their societies but reflect, in their models of nature, their societies, their modes of production, their human relations, their culture's needs and values. Precisely because of this fact, as well as the fact that modern science has had a critical impact on the natural world, the history of science has a part in the new environmental history.

Finally, the historian must confront the formidable challenge of examining ideas as ecological agents. We return to the matter of choices that people make in specific environments. What logic, what passion, what unconscious longings, what empirical understanding go into those choices? And how are choices expressed in rituals, techniques, and legislation? Sometimes choices are made in the halls of national governments. Sometimes they are made in that mysterious realm of the zeitgeist that sweeps across whole eras and continents. But some are also made, even in this day of powerful centralized institutions, by scattered households and farmsteads, by lumberjacks and fishing crews. We have not studied often or well enough the implementation of ideas in those microcosms.

Once again, it is anthropologists who have a lot to offer the historian seeking insight and method. One of the most intriguing pieces of fieldwork that comes from them bears directly on this question of ideas at work in the small setting. It comes out of a mountain valley in New Guinea, where the Tsembaga people subsist on taro, yams, and pigs. Published by Roy Rappaport under the title *Pigs for the Ancestors,* it exemplifies brilliantly how one might conceive of humans and their mental cultures functioning within a single ecosystem.

The Tsembaga appear in Rappaport's study as a population engaged in material relations with other components of their environment. Unlike their plant and animal congeners, however, they create symbols, values, purposes, and meanings, above all, religious meanings, out of the world around them. And that culture performs, though at points obscurely and indirectly, an important function: It encourages the Tsembaga to restrain their use of the land and avoid its degradation. For long periods of time, up to twenty years, these people busy themselves raising pigs, which they accumulate as payment to their ancestral spirits for help in battles with their neighboring enemies. Then at last, when they feel they have enough pigs to satisfy the spirits, a ritualistic slaughter ensues. Hundreds of the animals die and are consumed on behalf of the ancestors. Now, the debt paid, the Tsembaga are ready to go back to war, confident that they will have divine power on their side again. So their lives go round, year after year, decade after decade, in a ritualistic cycle of pig-raising, pig-slaughtering, dancing, feasting, and warring. The local explanation for this cycle is wholly religious, but the outside observer sees something else going on: an elaborate ecological mechanism at work, keeping the number of pigs under control and the people living in equilibrium with their surroundings.

In this forested valley Rappaport has found an example, assuming the validity of the study, of how a culture can take shape through addressing the problems of living within a peculiar ecosystem. The harmony between the two realms of nature and culture seems in this case to be nearly perfect. But the historian wants to know whether human populations are always as successfully adaptive as the Tsembaga. Moreover, are the people that the historian is most likely to study – people organized in advanced, complex societies, relating to nature through modern rituals, religions, and other structures of meaning and value – quite so successful? Rappaport ventures to suggest that the "ecological wisdom" embodied unconsciously in the New Guinea ritual cycle is by no means common. It is most likely to be found where the household is the primary unit of production, where people produce for immediate use rather than for sale and profit, and where "signs of environmental degradation are likely to be apparent quickly to those who can do something about them." Modern industrial societies, on the other hand, he finds culturally maladaptive. In them an economic and technological rationality has replaced the Tsembaga's ecological rationality. Rappaport's case is therefore of limited application elsewhere. Nor does it explain why a change in rationality has occurred, why cultures have drifted away from ecosystem harmony, why modern religion fails to restrain our environmental impact. Generally, anthropology bows out as those issues arise, retiring to its remote green valleys and leaving the historian to face the grinding, shrieking disharmonies of modernity alone.

As it tries to redefine the search into the human past, environmental history has, as indicated above, been drawing on a number of other disciplines, ranging from the natural sciences to anthropology to theology. It has resisted any attempt to put strict disciplinary fences around its work, which would force it to devise all its own methods of analysis, or to require all these overlapping disciplines to stay within their own discrete spheres. Each may have its tradition, to be sure, its unique way of approaching questions. But if this is an age of global interdependence, it is surely also the

Donald Worster

moment for some cross-disciplinary cooperation. Scholars need it, environmental history needs it, and so does the earth.

One discipline not so far explicitly discussed is geography. Environmental historians have leaned on many geographers for insight, on names like Michael Williams and Donald Meinig among presently active scholars, and from the recent past, names like Carl Sauer, H. C. Darby, and Lucien Febvre. Over the last century scholars from the two disciplines have crossed into one another's territory often and found that they share much in temperament. Geographers, like historians, have tended to be more descriptive than analytical. Taking place rather than time as their focus, they have mapped the distribution of things, just as historians have narrated the sequence of events. Geographers have liked a good landscape just as historians have liked a good story. Both have shown a love of the particular and a resistance to easy generalizing – a quality that may be their common virtue and strength. But they also bear a neighborly resemblance in their weaknesses, above all in their recurring tendency to lose sight of the elemental human-nature connection: historians when they have measured time only by elections and dynasties, geographers when they have tried to reduce the earth and its complexities to the abstract idea of "space." Nature, the land, climate, ecosystems, these are the entities that have relevance. When and where geographers have talked about such forces, they have offered much in the way of information to the new history. More, it has preeminently been geographers who have helped us all see that our situation is no longer one of being shaped by environment; rather, it is increasingly we are doing the shaping, and often disastrously so. Now the common responsibility of both disciplines is to discover why modern people have been so determined to escape the restraints of nature and what the ecological effects of that desire have been.

Put so comprehensively, with so many lines of investigation possible, it may seem that environmental history has no coherence, that it includes virtually all that has been and is to be. It may appear so wide, so complex, so demanding as to be impossible to pursue except in the most restricted of places and times: say, on a small, scarcely populated island well isolated from the rest of the world and then only for a period of six weeks. Historians of every sort will recognize that feeling of being engulfed by one's subject. No matter how inclusive or specialized one's perspective, the past seems these days like a vast buzzing confusion of voices, forces, events, structures, and relationships defying any coherent understanding. The French speak bravely of doing "total history." History is everything, they say, and everything has a history. True and noble that realization may be, but it does not give much ease of mind. Even delimiting some part of the totality as "environment" may seem to leave us with the still unmanageable

306

burden of trying to write the history of "almost everything." Unfortunately, there is no feasible alternative open to us any longer. We did not make nature or the past; otherwise, we might have made them simpler. Now we are challenged to make some sense of them – and in this case, to make sense of their working intricately together.

Bibliography

A complete listing of titles in a field as wide-ranging and ambitious as environmental history would require a volume or two in itself. This bibliography is only a selection for those seeking further reading. It emphasizes the major book-length works that have appeared in English in recent years, along with a few older titles and journal articles, and largely confines itself to the modern period. The heavy preponderance of American titles may indicate the compiler's bias in background and approach, or it may suggest the extent of American dominance in the field. In any case, there is a considerable literature in other languages that must be omitted here. Many of the items listed contain extensive bibliographies, which should be consulted for a fuller view of the subject.

INTRODUCTION TO THE FIELD

Bailes, Kendall E., ed. *Environmental History: Critical Issues in Comparative Perspective.* Lanham, Md.: University Press of America, 1985.

Bilsky, Lester J., ed. *Historical Ecology: Essays on Environment and Social Change.* Port Washington, N.Y.: Kennikat Press, 1980.

"Environmental History." *Pacific Historical Review* 41 (1972): 271–372. (A special theme issue.)

Environmental Review 1 (1976–).

"Environnement et histoire." *Annales: Economies, Sociétés, Civilisations* 29 (1974): 537–647.

Journal of Forest History 1 (1956–).

Journal of Historical Geography 1 (1975–).

Nash, Roderick. "Environmental History." In *The State of American History,* edited by Herbert J. Bass, pp. 249–60. Chicago: Quadrangle Press, 1970.

Tate, Thad W. "Problems of Definition in Environmental History." *American Historical Association Newsletter* (1981): 8–10.

White, Richard. "American Environmental History: The Development of a New Historical Field." *Pacific Historical Review* 54 (1985): 297–335.

Worster, Donald. "History as Natural History: An Essay on Theory and Method." *Pacific Historical Review* 53 (1984): 1–19.

STUDIES IN NATURAL AND HUMAN ECOLOGY

Natural Ecology

Andrewartha, H. G., and L. C. Birch. *The Ecological Web: More on the Distribution and Abundance of Animals.* Chicago: University of Chicago Press, 1984.

I wish to thank my research assistant, Ruth Friedman, for her help in compiling this bibliography.

Bibliography

Billings, W. D. *Plants and the Ecosystem*. Belmont, Calif.: Wadsworth, 1964.
Dasmann, Raymond. *Environmental Conservation*. 3d ed. New York: Macmillan, 1972.
Davis, Margaret B. "Palynology and Environmental History during the Quaternary Period." *American Scientist* 57 (1969): 317–32.
Dodd, J. Robert, and Robert J. Stanton, Jr. *Paleoecology, Concepts and Applications*. New York: John Wiley, 1981.
Ehrlich, Paul, Anne Ehrlich, and John Holdren. *Ecoscience: Population, Resources, Environment*. San Francisco: Freeman, 1977.
Elton, Charles. *The Ecology of Invasions by Animals and Plants*. London: Methuen, 1958.
Gall, Jean-Claude. *Ancient Sedimentary Environments and the Habitats of Living Organisms: Introduction to Paleoecology*. Translated by P. Wallace. Berlin: Springer, 1983.
Goudie, Andrew. *Environmental Change*. Oxford: Oxford University Press (Clarendon Press), 1977.
   The Human Impact on the Natural Environment. 2d ed. Cambridge, Mass.: MIT Press, 1986.
Hutchinson, G. Evelyn. *An Introduction to Population Ecology*. New Haven, Conn.: Yale University Press, 1978.
Kormondy, Eugene. *Concepts of Ecology*. Englewood Cliffs, N.J.: Prentice-Hall, 1969.
MacArthur, Robert H. *Geographical Ecology: Patterns in the Distribution of Species*. New York: Harper & Row, 1972.
Odum, Eugene P. *Fundamentals of Ecology*. 3d ed. Philadelphia: Saunders, 1971.
Ricklefs, Robert E. *Ecology*. 2d ed. New York: Chiron Press, 1979.
Ruddiman, W. F., and A. McIntyre. "Northeast Atlantic Paleoclimatic Changes over the Past 600,000 Years." In *Investigation of Late Quaternary Paleoceanography and Paleoclimatology, The Geological Society of America, Inc., Memoir 145*, edited by R. M. Cline and J. D. Hayes, pp. 111–46. Boulder, Colo.: Geological Society of America, 1976.
Shelford, Victor E. *The Ecology of North America*. Urbana: University of Illinois Press, 1963.
Whittaker, R. H. *Communities and Ecosystems*. 2d ed. New York: Macmillan, 1975.
Woodwell, George. "On the Limits of Nature." In *The Global Possible*, edited by Robert Repetto, pp. 47–65. New Haven, Conn.: Yale University Press, 1985.
Wright, H. E., Jr., ed. *Late-Quaternary Environments of the United States*. Vol. 1, "The Late Pleistocene," edited by Stephen C. Porter; vol. 2, "The Holocene," edited by H. E. Wright, Jr. Minneapolis: University of Minnesota Press, 1983.

Human Ecology
Asch, Michael. "The Ecological-Evolutionary Model and the Concept of Mode of Production." In *Challenging Anthropology*, ed. David Turner and Gavin Smith, pp. 81–101. Toronto: McGraw-Hill Ryerson, 1979.
Bennett, John W. *The Ecological Transition: Cultural Anthropology and Human Adaptation*. Elmsford, N.Y.: Pergamon, 1976.
Burton, Ian, Robert W. Kates, and Gilbert F. White. *The Environment as Hazard*. New York: Oxford University Press, 1978.

Bibliography

Buttel, Frederick H. "Social Science and the Environment: Competing Theories." *Social Science Quarterly* 57 (1976): 307–23.

Coates, Ken, ed. *Socialism and the Environment.* Nottingham: Spokesman Books, 1972.

Darling, F. Fraser. "The Ecological Approach to Social Science." *American Scientist* 39 (1951): 244–54.

Dunlap, Riley E., ed. "Ecology and the Social Sciences." *American Behavioral Scientist* 24 (1980): 3–151.

Durham, William H. "The Adaptive Significance of Cultural Behavior." *Human Ecology* 4 (1976): 89–121.

Ellen, Roy F. *Environment, Subsistence and System: The Ecology of Small-Scale Social Formations.* Cambridge: Cambridge University Press, 1982.

Hardesty, Donald. *Ecological Anthropology.* New York: Wiley, 1977.

Hardin, Garrett. "The Tragedy of the Commons." *Science* (13 December 1968): 1243–8.

Harris, Marvin. *Cultural Materialism: The Struggle for a Science of Culture.* New York: Random House, 1979.

Ingold, Tim. *The Appropriation of Nature: Essays on Human Ecology and Social Relations.* Iowa City: University of Iowa Press, 1987.

Leeds, Anthony, and Andrew P. Vayda, eds. *Man, Culture, and Animals: The Role of Animals in Human Ecological Adjustments.* Washington, D.C.: American Association for the Advancement of Science, 1965.

Leopold, Aldo. "The Land Ethic." In *A Sand County Almanac.* New York: Oxford University Press, 1966.

MacCormack, Carol P., and Marilyn Strathern, eds. *Nature, Culture and Gender.* Cambridge: Cambridge University Press, 1981.

Moran, Emilio F. *Human Adaptability: An Introduction to Ecological Anthropology.* North Scituate, Mass.: Duxbury Press, 1979.

Netting, Robert McC. *Cultural Ecology.* Menlo Park, Calif.: Benjamin-Cummings, 1977.

Norton, William. *Historical Analysis in Geography.* London: Longman Group, 1984.

Odum, Howard T. *Environment, Power, and Society.* New York: Wiley-Interscience, 1971.

Ophuls, William. *Ecology and the Politics of Scarcity: Prologue to a Political Theory of the Steady State.* San Francisco: Freeman, 1977.

Ortner, Sherry. "Is Female to Male as Nature Is to Culture?" In *Woman, Culture, and Society,* edited by M. Z. Rosaldo and L. Lamphere, pp. 67–88. Stanford: Stanford University Press, 1974.

Parsons, Howard L., ed. *Marx and Engels on Ecology.* Westport, Conn.: Greenwood Press, 1977.

Rappaport, Roy A. "Nature, Culture, and Ecological Anthropology." In *Man, Culture, and Society,* ed. Harry L. Shapiro, pp. 237–67. London: Oxford University Press, 1956.

Pigs for the Ancestors: Ritual in the Ecology of a New Guinea People. Rev. ed. New Haven, Conn.: Yale University Press, 1984.

Sauer, Carl. *Land and Life: A Selection from the Writings of Carl Ortwin Sauer.* Edited by John Leighly. Berkeley and Los Angeles: University of California Press, 1963.

Schmidt, Alfred. *The Concept of Nature in Marx.* Translated by Ben Fowkes. London: New Left Books, 1971.

Bibliography

Schnaiberg, Allan. *The Environment: From Surplus to Scarcity.* New York: Oxford University Press, 1980.

Sprout, Harold, and Margaret Sprout. *The Ecological Perspective in Human Affairs: With Special Reference to International Politics.* Princeton, N.J.: Princeton University Press, 1965.

Steward, Julian. *The Theory of Culture Change: The Methodology of Multilinear Evolution.* Urbana: University of Illinois, 1955.

Evolution and Ecology: Essays on Social Transformation. Edited by Jane C. Steward and Robert F. Murphy. Urbana: University of Illinois Press, 1977.

Stretton, Hugh. *Capitalism, Socialism, and the Environment.* Cambridge: Cambridge University Press, 1976.

Vayda, Andrew P., ed. *Environment and Cultural Behavior: Ecological Studies in Cultural Anthropology.* Garden City, N.Y.: Natural History Press, 1969.

Vayda, Andrew P., and Roy A. Rappaport. "Ecology, Cultural and Noncultural." In *Introduction to Cultural Anthropology: Essays in the Scope and Methods of the Science of Man,* edited by James A. Clifton, pp. 477–97. Boston: Houghton Mifflin, 1968.

Vayda, Andrew P., and Bonnie J. McCay. "New Directions in Ecology and Ecological Anthropology." *Annual Review of Anthropology* (1975): 293–306.

Wagner, Philip H., and Marvin W. Mikesell, eds. *Readings in Cultural Geography.* Chicago: University of Chicago Press, 1962.

World History in Environmental Perspective

Boserup, Ester. *The Conditions of Agricultural Growth: The Economics of Agrarian Change under Population Pressure.* Chicago: Aldine, 1965.

Bryson, Reid A., and Thomas J. Murray. *Climates of Hunger: Mankind and the World's Changing Weather.* Madison: University of Wisconsin Press, 1977.

Colinvaux, Paul. *The Fates of Nations: A Biological Theory of History.* New York: Simon & Schuster, 1980.

Cowgill, George. "On Causes and Consequences of Ancient and Modern Population Change." *American Anthropologist* 77 (1975): 505–25.

Crosby, Alfred W. *The Columbian Exchange: Biological and Cultural Consequences of 1492.* Westport, Conn.: Greenwood Press, 1972.

Ecological Imperialism: The Biological Expansion of Europe, 900–1900. New York: Cambridge University Press, 1986.

East, W. Gordon. *The Geography behind History.* Rev. ed. London: Nelson, 1965.

Febvre, Lucien. *A Geographical Introduction to History.* Translated by E. G. Mountford and J. H. Paxton. London: Kegan Paul, Trench, Trubner, 1932.

Glacken, Clarence. *Traces on the Rhodian Shore: Nature and Culture in Western Thought from Ancient Times to the End of the Eighteenth Century.* Berkeley and Los Angeles: University of California Press, 1967.

Hughes, J. Donald. *Ecology in Ancient Civilizations.* Albuquerque: University of New Mexico Press, 1975.

Huntington, Ellsworth. *Civilization and Climate.* 3d ed. New Haven, Conn.: Yale University Press, 1924.

Hyams, Edward. *Soil and Civilization.* New York: Harper & Row, 1976.

Lamb, H. H. *Climate: Present, Past, Future.* 2 vols. London: Methuen & Co., 1972–7.

Bibliography

Le Roy Ladurie, Emmanuel. *Times of Feast, Times of Famine: A History of Climate since the Year 1000*. Translated by Barbara Bray. Garden City, N.Y.: Doubleday, 1971.

McEvedy, Colin, and Richard Jones. *Atlas of World Population History*. Harmondsworth: Penguin Books, 1978.

McNeill, William H. *The Human Condition: An Ecological Perspective*. Princeton, N.J.: Princeton University Press, 1980).

Plagues and Peoples. New York: Doubleday, 1979.

Parry, J. H. *The Discovery of the Sea*. Berkeley and Los Angeles: University of California Press, 1981.

Passmore, John. *Man's Responsibility for Nature: Ecological Problems and Western Traditions*. New York: Charles Scribners' Sons, 1974.

Pepper, David. *The Roots of Modern Environmentalism*. London: Croom Helm, 1984.

Richards, John F. "World Environmental History and Economic Development." In *Sustainable Development of the Biosphere*, edited by William C. Clark and R. E. Munn, pp. 53–74. Cambridge: Cambridge University Press, 1986.

Richards, John F., and Richard P. Tucker, eds. *World Forests and the Global Economy in the Twentieth Century*. Durham, N.C.: Duke University Press, 1987.

Rotberg, Robert I., and Theodore K. Rabb, eds. *Climate and History: Studies in Interdisciplinary History*. Princeton, N.J.: Princeton University Press, 1981. *Hunger and History: The Impact of Changing Food Production and Consumption Patterns on Society*. Cambridge: Cambridge University Press, 1985.

Russell, W. M. S. *Man, Nature and History: Controlling the Environment*. Garden City, N.Y.: Natural History Press, 1967.

Seymour, John, and Herbert Girardet. *Far from Paradise: The Story of Man's Impact on the Environment*. London: British Broadcasting Corporation, 1986.

Thomas, William L., Jr., ed. *Man's Role in Changing the Face of the Earth*. Vol. 1, *Through the Corridors of Time*, pp. 115–398. Chicago: University of Chicago Press, 1956.

Toynbee, Arnold. *Mankind and Mother Earth: A Narrative History of the World*. New York: Oxford University Press, 1976.

Tuan Yi-Fu. *Topophilia: A Study of Environmental Perception, Attitudes, and Values*. Englewood Cliffs, N.J.: Prentice-Hall, 1974.

Tucker, Richard P., and J. F. Richards, eds. *Global Deforestation and the Nineteenth-Century World Economy*. Durham, N.C.: Duke University Press, 1983.

Walters, A. Harry. *Ecology, Food and Civilisation: An Ecological History of Human Society*. London: Charles Knight, 1973.

Webb, Walter Prescott. *The Great Frontier*. Boston: Houghton Mifflin, 1952.

White, Lynn, Jr. "The Historic Roots of Our Ecologic Crisis." *Science* 155 (10 March 1967): 1202–7.

Wigley, T. M. L., M. J. Ingram, and G. Farmer, eds. *Climate and History: Studies in Past Climates and Their Impact on Man*. Cambridge: Cambridge University Press, 1981.

Wilkinson, Richard G. *Poverty and Progress: An Ecological Perspective on Economic Development*. New York: Praeger, 1973.

Wittfogel, Karl A. *Oriental Despotism: A Comparative Study of Total Power.* New Haven, Conn.: Yale University Press, 1957. Reprint 1981.

Zinsser, Hans. *Rats, Lice, and History.* Boston: Little, Brown, 1935.

MAJOR REGIONS OF THE EARTH

Europe

Bertrand, Georges. "Pour une histoire écologique de la France rurale." In *Histoire de la France rurale,* edited by Georges Duby, vol. 1, pp. 32–113. Paris: Seuil, 1975.

Bloch, Marc. *French Rural History: An Essay on Its Basic Characteristics.* Translated by Janet Sondheimer. London: Routledge & Kegan Paul, 1966.

Braudel, Fernand. "The Role of the Environment." Chap. 1 in *The Mediterranean and the Mediterranean World in the Age of Philip II.* Vol. 1. Translated by Sîan Reynolds. New York: Harper & Row, 1972.

Darby, H. C. *The New Historical Geography of England.* Cambridge: Cambridge University Press, 1973.

Darling, F. Fraser. *West Highland Survey: An Essay in Human Ecology.* Oxford: Oxford University Press, 1955.

Fleure, H. J., and Margaret Davies. *A Natural History of Man in Britain: Conceived as a Study of Changing Relations between Men and Environments.* London: Collins, 1970.

Flinn, Michael. *The European Demographic System, 1500–1850.* Baltimore: Johns Hopkins University Press, 1981.

Hackett, L. W. *Malaria in Europe: An Ecological Study.* Oxford: Oxford University Press, 1937.

Herlihy, David. "Ecological Conditions and Demographic Change." In *One Thousand Years: Western Europe in the Middle Ages,* edited by Richard DeMollen, pp. 3–43. Boston: Houghton Mifflin, 1974.

Hoskins, W. G. *The Making of the English Landscape.* London: Hodder and Stoughton, 1977.

Howe, George Melvyn. *Man, Environment and Disease in Britain: A Medical Geography of Britain through the Ages.* Newton Abbot: David & Charles, 1972.

Jones, Eric L. "The Environment and the Economy." In *The New Cambridge Modern History,* edited by Peter Burke, 13, Companion Volume, pp. 15–42. Cambridge: Cambridge University Press, 1979.

The European Miracle: Environments, Economics, and Geopolitics in Europe and Asia. Cambridge: Cambridge University Press, 1981.

Langer, William L. "Europe's Initial Population Explosion." *American Historical Review* 69 (October 1963): 1–17.

Le Roy Ladurie, Emmanuel. *The Peasants of Languedoc.* Translated by John Day. Urbana: University of Illinois Press, 1974.

Merchant, Carolyn. *The Death of Nature: Women, Ecology, and the Scientific Revolution.* San Francisco: Harper & Row, 1980.

Nef, John U. "An Early Energy Crisis and Its Consequences." *Scientific American* 237 (November 1977): 140–51.

Netting, Robert. *Balancing on an Alp: Ecological Change and Continuity in a Swiss Mountain Community.* New York: Cambridge University Press, 1981.

Pipes, Richard. "The Environment and Its Consequences." Chap. 1 in *Russia under the Old Regime.* New York: Charles Scribner's Sons, 1974.

Bibliography

Post, John D. *The Last Great Subsistence Crisis in the Western World.* Baltimore: Johns Hopkins University Press, 1977.

Pounds, Norman J. G. *An Historical Geography of Europe.* Cambridge: Cambridge University Press, 1985.

Pryde, Philip R. *Conservation in the Soviet Union.* Cambridge: Cambridge University Press, 1972.

Skipp, Victor. *Crisis and Development: An Ecological Case Study of the Forest of Arden, 1570–1674.* Cambridge: Cambridge University Press, 1978.

TeBrake, William R. "Air Pollution and Fuel Crises in Preindustrial London, 1250–1650." *Technology and Culture* 16 (1975): 337–59.
Medieval Frontier: Culture and Ecology in Rijnland. College Station: Texas A & M University Press, 1985.

Thomas, Keith. *Man and the Natural World: A History of the Modern Sensibility.* New York: Pantheon, 1983.

Tubbs, Colin. *The New Forest: An Ecological History.* Newton Abbot: David & Charles, 1968.

Weiner, Douglas R. *Models of Nature: Conservation, Ecology, and Cultural Revolution.* Bloomington: Indiana University Press, 1988.

Woodham-Smith, Cecil. *The Great Hunger: Ireland, 1845–1849.* New York: Harper & Row, 1962.

Wrigley, E. A., and R. S. Schofield. *The Population History of England, 1541–1871: A Reconstruction.* Cambridge, Mass.: Harvard University Press, 1981.

Africa and Latin America

Brush, Stephen B. *Mountain, Field, and Family: The Economy and Human Ecology of an Andean Valley.* Philadelphia: University of Pennsylvania Press, 1977.

Bunker, Steven. *Underdeveloping the Amazon: Extraction, Unequal Exchange, and the Failure of the Modern State.* Urbana: University of Illinois Press, 1985.

Dean, Warren. *Brazil and the Struggle for Rubber: A Study in Environmental History.* New York: Cambridge University Press, 1987.
Confronting the Environmental Crisis in Latin America. New York: New York University, Ibero-American Language and Area Center, 1973.

Dickson, Kwamina B. *A Historical Geography of Ghana.* Cambridge: Cambridge University Press, 1969.

Elphick, Richard. *Kraal and Castle: Khoikoi and the Founding of White South Africa.* New Haven, Conn.: Yale University Press, 1977.

Franke, Richard W., and Barbara H. Chasin. *Seeds of Famine: Ecological Destruction and the Development Dilemma in the West African Sahel.* Montclair, N.J.: Allanheld, Osmun, 1980.

Harms, Robert. *Games Against Nature: An Eco-cultural History of the Nunu of Equatorial Africa.* New York: Cambridge University Press, 1987.

Hartwig, Gerald W., and K. David Patterson. *Disease in African History: An Introductory Survey and Case Studies.* Durham, N.C.: Duke University Press, 1978.

Kiple, Kenneth. *The Caribbean Slave: A Biological History.* New York: Cambridge University Press, 1984.

Kjekhus, Helge. *Ecology Control and Economic Development in East African History: The Case of Tanganyika, 1850–1950.* Berkeley and Los Angeles: University of California Press, 1977.

Bibliography

Meggers, Betty J. *Amazonia: Man and Culture in a Counterfeit Paradise*. Chicago: Aldine-Atherton, 1971.

Meggers, Betty J., Edward S. Ayensu, and W. Donald Duckworth, eds. *Tropical Forest Ecosystems in Africa and South America*. Washington, D.C.: Smithsonian Press, 1973.

Reichel-Dolmatoff, Gerardo. *Amazonian Cosmos: The Sexual and Religious Symbolism of the Tukano Indians*. Chicago: University of Chicago Press, 1971.

Sanchez-Albornoz, Nicolas. *The Population of Latin America*. Translated by W. A. R. Richardson. Berkeley and Los Angeles: University of California Press, 1974.

Sponsel, Leslie. "Amazon Ecology and Adaptation." *Annual Reviews in Anthropology* 15 (1986): 67–97.

Weiskel, Timothy. "Nature, Culture and Ecology in Traditional African Thought Systems." *Cultures* 1 (1973): 123–44.

Asia and the Pacific

Bolton, Geoffrey. *Spoils and Spoilers: Australians and Their Environment, 1788–1980*. Sydney: Allen & Unwin, 1981.

Clark, Andrew H. *The Invasion of New Zealand by People, Plants, and Animals: The South Island*. New Brunswick, N.J.: Rutgers University Press, 1949.

Fosberg, Francis Raymond, ed. *Man's Place in the Island Ecosystem*. Honolulu: Bishop Museum Press, 1963.

Geertz, Clifford. *Agricultural Involution: The Process of Ecological Change in Indonesia*. Berkeley and Los Angeles: University of California Press, 1971.

Hancock, William Keith. *Discovering Monaro: A Study of Man's Impact on His Environment*. Cambridge: Cambridge University Press, 1972.

Jacobs, Wilbur R. "The Fatal Confrontation: Early Native-White Relations on the Frontiers of Australia, New Guinea, and America – A Comparative Study." *Pacific Historical Review* 40 (1971): 283–309.

McKean, Margaret. *Environmental Protest and Citizen Politics in Japan*. Berkeley and Los Angeles: University of California Press, 1981.

McLennan, Marshall S. "Changing Human Ecology on the Central Luzon Plain: Nueva Ecija, 1705–1939." In *Philippine Social History: Global Trade and Local Transformation*, edited by Alfred W. McCoy and Edward C. de Jesus, pp. 57–90. Quezon City: Ateneo de Manila University Press, 1982.

Mulvaney, D. J., and J. Golson, eds. *Aboriginal Man and the Environment*. Canberra: Australian National University Press, 1971.

Pearson, Richard. "Paleoenvironment and Human Settlement in Japan and Korea." *Science* 197 (23 September 1977): 1239–46.

Pelzer, Karl. *Pioneer Settlement in the Asiatic Tropics: Studies in Land Utilization and Agricultural Colonization in Southeastern Asia*. New York: American Geographical Society, 1945.

Pluvier, Jan. *South-East Asia from Colonialism to Independence*. New York: Oxford University Press, 1974.

Powell, Joseph M. *Environmental Management in Australia, 1788–1914*. Melbourne: Oxford University Press, 1976.

Powell, Joseph M., and Michael Williams, eds. *Australian Space, Australian Time: Geographical Perspectives*. Melbourne: Oxford University Press, 1975.

Pyne, Stephen. *The Ice: A Journey to Antarctica*. Iowa City: University of Iowa Press, 1986.

Bibliography

Richards, John F., James R. Hagen, and Edward S. Haynes. "Changing Land Use in Bihar, Punjab and Haryana, 1850–1970." *Modern Asian Studies* 19 (1985): 699–732.

Roll, Eric C. *They All Ran Wild: The Story of Pests on the Land in Australia.* Sydney: Angus & Robertson, 1969.

Stover, Leon E. *The Cultural Ecology of Chinese Civilization: Peasants and Elites in the Last of the Agrarian States.* New York: Pica Press, 1974.

Totman, Conrad. *The Origin of Japan's Modern Forests: The Case of Akita.* Honolulu: University of Hawaii Press, 1985.

Watters, R. F., ed. *Land and Society in New Zealand: Essays in Historical Geography.* Wellington: A. H. & A. W. Reed, 1965.

North America

Albion, Robert, William A. Baker, and Benjamin W. Labaree. *New England and the Sea.* Middletown, Conn.: Wesleyan University Press, 1972.

Allard, Dean C. *Spencer Fullerton Baird and the U.S. Fish Commission.* New York: Arno Press, 1978.

Ashworth, William. *The Late, Great Lakes: An Environmental History.* New York: Knopf, 1986.

Bartlett, Richard A. *Nature's Yellowstone.* Albuquerque: University of New Mexico Press, 1974.

Yellowstone: A Wilderness Beseiged. Tucson: University of Arizona Press, 1985.

Blake, Nelson M. *Land into Water – Water into Land: A History of Water Management in Florida.* Tallahassee: University Presses of Florida, 1980.

Blouet, Brian, and Frederick C. Luebke, eds. *The Great Plains: Environment and Culture.* Lincoln: University of Nebraska Press, 1979.

Bogue, Joseph J. *The Population of the United States.* Glencoe, Ill.: Free Press, 1959.

Brown, Ralph H. *A Historical Geography of the United States.* New York: Harcourt Brace & World, 1948.

Carroll, Charles F. *The Timber Economy of Puritan New England.* Providence, R.I.: Brown University Press, 1973.

Caudill, Harry M. *Night Comes to the Cumberlands: A Biography of a Depressed Area.* Boston: Little, Brown, 1963.

Clark, Andrew H. *Acadia: The Geography of Early Nova Scotia to 1760.* Madison: University of Wisconsin Press, 1968.

Three Centuries and the Island: A Historical Geography of Settlement and Agriculture in Prince Edward Island, Canada. Toronto: Toronto University Press, 1959.

Clark, Thomas D. *The Greening of the South.* Lexington: University of Kentucky Press, 1984.

Clary, David A. *Timber and the Forest Service.* Lawrence: University Press of Kansas, 1986.

Cooley, Richard A. *Politics and Conservation: The Decline of the Alaska Salmon.* New York: Harper & Row, 1963.

Cowdrey, Albert E. *This Land, This South: An Environmental History.* Lexington: University Press of Kentucky, 1983.

Cox, Thomas R., Robert S. Maxwell, Phillip Drennon Thomas, and Joseph J. Malone. *This Well-Wooded Land: Americans and Their Forests from Colonial Times to the Present.* Lincoln: University of Nebraska Press, 1985.

317

Bibliography

Craven, Avery O. *Soil Exhaustion as a Factor in the Agricultural History of Virginia and Maryland, 1606–1860.* Urbana: University of Illinois Press, 1925.

Cronon, William. *Changes in the Land: Indians, Colonists, and the Ecology of New England.* New York: Hill & Wang, 1983.

Crosby, Alfred W., Jr. "Virgin Soil Epidemics as a Factor in the Aboriginal Depopulation in America." *William and Mary Quarterly* 33 (1976): 289–99.

Cutright, Paul Russell. *Theodore Roosevelt: The Making of a Conservationist.* Urbana: University of Illinois Press, 1985.

Davis, Richard, ed. *Encyclopedia of American Forest and Conservation History.* 2 vols. New York: Macmillan, 1983.

de Buys, William. *Enchantment and Exploitation: The Life and Hard Times of a New Mexico Mountain Range.* Albuquerque: University of New Mexico Press, 1985.

Denevan, William M., ed. *The Native Population of the Americas in 1492.* Madison: University of Wisconsin Press, 1976.

Dobyns, Henry F. *Their Numbers Became Thinned: Native Population Dynamics in Eastern North America.* Knoxville: University of Tennessee Press, 1983.

Doughty, Robin W. *Wildlife and Man in Texas: Environmental Change and Conservation.* College Station: Texas A & M University Press, 1983.

Duffy, John. *Epidemics in Colonial America.* Baton Rouge: Louisiana State University Press, 1971.

Dunlap, Thomas. *DDT: Scientists, Citizens, and Public Policy.* Princeton, N.J.: Princeton University Press, 1981.

Saving America's Wildlife. Princeton, N.J.; Princeton University Press, 1988.

Earle, Carville V. "Environment, Disease, and Mortality in Early Virginia." In *The Chesapeake in the Seventeenth Century,* edited by Thad Tate and David Ammerman, pp. 96–125. Chapel Hill: University of North Carolina Press, 1979.

Ekirch, Arthur A., Jr. *Man and Nature in America.* New York: Columbia University Press, 1963.

Engel, J. Ronald. *Sacred Sands: The Struggle for Community in the Indiana Dunes.* Middletown, Conn.: Wesleyan University Press, 1983.

Fahl, Ronald J. *North American Forest and Conservation History: A Bibliography.* Santa Barbara, Calif.: ABC-Clio Press, 1977.

Flader, Susan L., ed. *The Great Lakes Forest: An Environmental and Social History.* Minneapolis: University of Minnesota Press, 1983.

Thinking Like a Mountain: Aldo Leopold and the Evolution of an Ecological Attitude toward Deer, Wolves, and Forests. Columbia: University of Missouri Press, 1974.

Fox, Stephen. *John Muir and His Legacy: The American Conservation Movement.* Boston: Little, Brown, 1981.

Gates, Paul. *History of Public Land Law Development.* Washington: Government Printing Office, 1968.

Genovese, Eugene. "Cotton, Slavery, and Soil Exhaustion." Chap. 4 in *The Political Economy of Slavery.* New York: Pantheon Books, 1965.

Greven, Philip. *Four Generations: Population, Land, and Family in Colonial Andover, Massachusetts.* Ithaca, N.Y.: Cornell University Press, 1970.

Hays, Samuel P. *Conservation and the Gospel of Efficiency: The Progressive Conservation Movement, 1890–1920.* Cambridge, Mass.: Harvard University Press, 1959.

Bibliography

Beauty, Health, and Permanence: Environmental Politics in the United States, 1955–1985. New York: Cambridge University Press, 1987.

Hoffman, Abraham. *Vision or Villainy: Origins of the Owens Valley–Los Angeles Water Controversy.* College Station: Texas A & M University Press, 1981.

Hughes, J. Donald. *American Indian Ecology.* El Paso: Texas Western Press, 1983.

Hundley, Norris. *Water and the West: The Colorado River Compact and the Politics of Water in the American West.* Berkeley and Los Angeles: University of California Press, 1975.

Hurst, James Willard. *Law and Economic Growth: The Legal History of the Lumber Industry in Wisconsin, 1836–1915.* Cambridge, Mass.: Harvard University Press, 1964.

Huth, Hans. *Nature and the American: Three Centuries of Changing Attitudes.* Lincoln: University of Nebraska Press, 1972.

Innis, Harold A. *The Fur Trade in Canada.* New Haven, Conn.: Yale University Press, 1962.

The Cod Fisheries: The History of an International Economy. Toronto: Toronto University Press, 1954.

Irland, Lloyd C. *Wildlands and Woodlots: The Story of New England's Forests.* Hanover, N.H.: University Press of New England, 1982.

Jacobs, Wilbur. "The Great Despoliation: Environmental Themes in American Frontier History." *Pacific Historical Review* 47 (1978): 1–26.

Johnson, Hildegard Binder. *Order upon the Land: The U.S. Rectangular Land Survey and the Upper Mississippi Country.* New York: Oxford University Press, 1976.

Kahrl, William L. *Water and Power: The Conflict over Los Angeles' Water Supply in the Owens Valley.* Berkeley and Los Angeles: University of California Press, 1981.

Kline, Marcia B. *Beyond the Land Itself: Views of Nature in Canada and the United States.* Cambridge, Mass.: Harvard University Press, 1970.

Kolodny, Annette. *The Lay of the Land: Metaphor as Experience and History in American Life and Letters.* Chapel Hill: University of North Carolina, 1975. *The Land before Her: Fantasy and Experience of the American Frontier, 1630–1860.* Chapel Hill: University of North Carolina, 1984.

Labaree, Benjamin W. "An Historical Perspective." In *New England Prospect,* edited by Carl H. Reidel, pp. 24–58. Hanover, N.H.: University Press of New England, 1982.

Lemon, James T. *The Best Poor Man's Country: A Geographical Study of Early South Eastern Pennsylvania.* Baltimore: Johns Hopkins University Press, 1972.

Leuchtenburg, William E. *Flood Control Politics: The Connecticut Valley Problem, 1927–1950.* Cambridge, Mass.: Harvard University Press, 1933.

Limerick, Patricia Nelson. *Desert Passages: Encounters with the American Deserts.* Albuquerque: University of New Mexico Press, 1985.

Lockridge, Kenneth. "Land, Population, and the Evolution of New England Society, 1630–1790." *Past and Present* 39 (1968): 62–80.

Lund, Thomas A. *American Wildlife Law.* Berkeley and Los Angeles: University of California Press, 1980.

Malin, James C. *The Grassland of North America: Prolegomena to Its History.* Gloucester, Mass.: Peter Smith, 1967.

Bibliography

History and Ecology: Studies of the Grassland, edited by Robert P. Swierenga. Lincoln: University of Nebraska Press, 1984.

Martin, Calvin. *Keepers of the Game: Indian-Animal Relationships in the Fur Trade.* Berkeley and Los Angeles: University of California Press, 1978.

Marx, Leo. *The Machine in the Garden: Technology and the Pastoral Ideal in America.* New York: Oxford University Press, 1964.

McCarthy, Michael. *Hour of Trial: The Conservation Conflict in Colorado and the West, 1891–1970.* Norman: University of Oklahoma, 1977.

McEvoy, Arthur F. *The Fisherman's Problem: Ecology and Law in the California Fisheries, 1850–1980.* New York: Cambridge University Press, 1986.

Matthiessen, Peter. *Wildlife in America.* New York: Viking, 1959.

Meine, Curt. *Aldo Leopold: His Life and Work.* Madison: University of Wisconsin Press, 1988.

Meinig, D. W. *The Great Columbia Plain: A Historical Geography, 1805–1910.* Seattle: University of Washington Press, 1968.

The Shaping of America: A Geographical Perspective on 500 Years of History. Vol. 1: *Atlantic America: 1492–1800.* New Haven, Conn.: Yale University Press, 1986.

Melosi, Martin V. *Coping with Abundance: Energy and Environment in Industrial America.* Philadelphia, Pa.: Temple University Press, 1985.

Garbage in the Cities: Refuse, Reform, and the Environment, 1880–1980. College Station: Texas A & M University Press, 1981.

ed. *Pollution and Reform in American Cities, 1870–1930.* Austin: University of Texas Press, 1980.

Merrens, H. Roy. *Colonial North Carolina in the Eighteenth Century.* Chapel Hill: University of North Carolina Press, 1964.

Mitchell, Lee Clark. *Witness to a Vanishing America: The Nineteenth Century.* Princeton, N.J.: Princeton University Press, 1981.

Mitchell, Robert D. *Commercialism and Frontier: Perspectives on the Early Shenandoah Valley.* Charlottesville: University of Virginia Press, 1977.

Mitchell, Robert D., and Paul A. Groves, eds. *North America: The Historical Geography of a Changing Continent.* Totowa, N.J.: Rowman & Littlefield, 1987.

Mowatt, Farley. *Sea of Slaughter.* Toronto: McClelland and Stewart, 1984.

Nash, Roderick. *Wilderness and the American Mind.* 3d ed. New Haven, Conn.: Yale University Press, 1982.

Nelson, Richard K. *Hunters of the Northern Forest: Designs for Survival among the Alaskan Kutchin.* Chicago: University of Chicago Press, 1973.

Hunters of the Northern Ice. Chicago: University of Chicago Press, 1969.

Make Prayers to the Raven: A Koyukon View of the Northern Forest. Chicago: University of Chicago Press, 1983.

Novak, Barbara. *Nature and Culture: American Landscape and Painting, 1825–1875.* New York: Oxford University Press, 1980.

Opie, John. "Frontier History in Environmental Perspective." In *The American West: New Perspectives, New Dimensions,* edited by Jerome O. Steffen, pp. 9–34. Norman: University of Oklahoma Press, 1979.

Perkins, John. *Insects, Experts, and the Insecticide Crisis: The Quest for New Pest Management Strategies.* New York: Plenum, 1982.

Petulla, Joseph. *American Environmental History: The Exploitation and Conservation of Natural Resources.* San Francisco: Boyd & Fraser, 1977.

Bibliography

American Environmentalism: Values, Tactics, Priorities. College Station: Texas A & M University Press, 1980.

Pinkett, Harold T. *Gifford Pinchot: Private and Public Forester.* Urbana: University of Illinois Press, 1970.

Pisani, Donald J. "Forests and Conservation, 1865–1890." *Journal of American History* 72 (1985): 340–59.

Preston, William L. *Vanishing Landscapes: Land and Life in the Tulare Lake Basin.* Berkeley and Los Angeles: University of California Press, 1981.

Pyne, Stephen J. *Fire in America: A Cultural History of Wildland and Rural Fire.* Princeton, N.J.: Princeton University Press, 1982.

Reiger, John F. *American Sportsmen and the Origins of Conservation.* New York: Winchester Press, 1975.

Reisner, Marc P. *Cadillac Desert: The American West and Its Disappearing Water.* New York: Viking, 1986.

Richardson, Elmo R. *Dams, Parks, & Politics: Resource Development & Preservation in the Truman-Eisenhower Era.* Lexington: University Press of Kentucky, 1973.

The Politics of Conservation: Crusades and Controversies, 1897–1913. Berkeley and Los Angeles: University of California Press, 1962.

Robbins, Roy M. *Our Landed Heritage: The Public Domain, 1776–1936.* Rev. ed. Lincoln: University of Nebraska Press, 1976.

Robbins, William G. *Lumberjacks and Legislators: Political Economy of the U.S. Lumber Industry, 1890–1941.* College Station: Texas A & M University Press, 1982.

American Forestry: A History of National, State, & Private Cooperation. Lincoln: University of Nebraska Press, 1985.

Rosenberg, Charles. *The Cholera Years: The United States in 1832, 1849 and 1866.* Chicago: University of Chicago Press, 1962.

Rowley, William D. *U.S. Forest Service Grazing and Rangelands: A History.* College Station: Texas A & M University Press, 1985.

Runte, Alfred. *National Parks: The American Experience.* 2d ed. Lincoln: University of Nebraska Press, 1979.

Sauer, Carl O. *Seventeenth-Century North America.* Berkeley: Turtle Island, 1980.

Sixteenth-Century North America: The Land and People as Seen by the Europeans. Berkeley and Los Angeles: University of California Press, 1971.

Scarpino, Philip V. *Great River: An Environmental History of the Upper Mississippi, 1890–1950.* Columbia: University of Missouri Press, 1985.

Schmitt, Peter. *Back to Nature: The Arcadian Myth in Urban America.* New York: Oxford University Press, 1969.

Schrepfer, Susan R. *The Fight to Save the Redwoods: A History of Environmental Reform, 1917–1978.* Madison: University of Wisconsin Press, 1983.

Sherwood, Morgan. *Big Game in Alaska.* New Haven, Conn.: Yale University Press, 1981.

Siry, Joseph V. *Marshes of the Ocean Shore: Development of an Ecological Ethic.* College Station: Texas A & M University Press, 1984.

Smith, Henry Nash. *Virgin Land: The American West as Symbol and Myth.* Cambridge, Mass.: Harvard University Press, 1950.

Stackpole, Edouard A. *The Sea-Hunters: The New England Whalemen during Two Centuries, 1636–1835.* Westport, Conn.: Greenwood Press, 1972.

Steen, Harold K. *The U.S. Forest Service: A History*. Seattle: University of Washington Press, 1976.

Stegner, Wallace. *Beyond the Hundredth Meridian: John Wesley Powell and the Second Opening of the West*. Boston: Houghton Mifflin, 1954.

Stilgoe, John R. *Common Landscape of America, 1580 to 1845*. New Haven, Conn.: Yale University Press, 1982.

Strong, Douglas. *Tahoe: An Environmental History*. Lincoln: University of Nebraska Press, 1984.

Swain, Donald C. *Wilderness Defender: Horace M. Albright and Conservation*. Chicago: University of Chicago Press, 1970.

Tanner, Adrian. *Bringing Home Animals: Religious Ideology and Mode of Production of the Mistassini Cree Hunters*. New York: St. Martin's, 1979.

Tarr, Joel. "Historical Perspectives on Hazardous Wastes in the United States." *Waste Management & Research* 3 (1985): 95–102.

Tarr, Joel, with James McCurley III, Francis C. McMichael, and Terry Yosie. "Water and Wastes: A Retrospective Assessment of Wastewater Technology in the United States, 1800–1932." *Technology and Culture* 28 (1984): 226–63.

Terrie, Philip G. *Forever Wild: Environmental Aesthetics and the Adirondack Forest Preserve*. Philadelphia, Pa.: Temple University Press, 1985.

Tichi, Cecilia. *New World, New Earth: Environmental Reform in American Literature from the Puritans through Whitman*. New Haven, Conn.: Yale University Press, 1979.

Tobey, Ronald C. *Saving the Prairies: The Life Cycle of the Founding School of American Plant Ecology, 1895–1955*. Berkeley and Los Angeles: University of California Press, 1981.

Turner, Frederick Jackson. "The Significance of the Frontier in American History." In *Frontier and Section: Selected Essays of Frederick Jackson Turner*, edited by Ray Allen Billington, pp. 11–27. Englewood Cliffs, N.J.: Prentice-Hall, 1961.

Underhill, Ruth M. *Red Man's America: The History of Indians in the United States*. Chicago: University of Chicago Press, 1971.

Vecsey, Christopher, and Robert W. Venables, eds. *American Indian Environments: Ecological Issues in Native American History*. Syracuse, N.Y.: Syracuse University Press, 1980.

Vietor, Richard H. K. *Environmental Politics and the Coal Coalition*. College Station: Texas A & M University Press, 1980.

Webb, Walter Prescott. *The Great Plains*. Boston: Ginn, 1931.

White, Richard. *Land Use, Environment, and Social Change: The Shaping of Island County, Washington*. Seattle: University of Washington Press, 1980.

"Native Americans and the Environment." In *Scholars and the Indian Experience*, edited by W. R. Swagerty, pp. 179–204. Bloomington: Indiana University Press, 1984.

The Roots of Dependency: Subsistence, Environment, and Social Change among the Choctaws, Pawnees, and Navajos. Lincoln: University of Nebraska Press, 1983.

Williams, Michael. *Americans and Their Forests: A Historical Geography* New York: Cambridge University Press, in press.

Wishart, David. *The Fur Trade of the American West: A Geographical Synthesis*. Lincoln: University of Nebraska Press, 1979.

Bibliography

Wonders, William C., ed. *Canada's Changing North*. Toronto: McClelland and Stewart, 1971.

Worster, Donald. *Dust Bowl: The Southern Plains in the 1930s*. New York: Oxford University Press, 1979.

Nature's Economy: A History of Ecological Ideas. New York: Cambridge University Press, 1977.

Rivers of Empire: Water, Aridity, and the Growth of the American West. New York: Pantheon, 1985.

Wynn, Graeme. *Timber Colony: A Historical Geography of Early Nineteenth-Century New Brunswick*. Toronto: Toronto University Press, 1981.

Contributors

ESTER BOSERUP is a Danish author and consultant on international development problems. She has a master's degree in economics from the University of Copenhagen. Her best-known book is *The Conditions of Agricultural Growth*, published in 1965. Other writings include *Women's Role in Economic Development* (1970) and *Population and Technological Change* (1981).

ALFRED W. CROSBY is professor of American Studies, University of Texas, Austin. He received a doctorate in history from Boston University in 1961. His major writings include *Ecological Imperialism: The Biological Expansion of Europe, 900–1900* (1986), *Epidemic and Peace, 1918* (1976), and *The Columbian Exchange: Biological and Cultural Consequences of 1492* (1971). He is coeditor of Studies in Environment and History, Cambridge University Press.

RAYMOND F. DASMANN is professor of ecology at the University of California at Santa Cruz. He has a doctorate from the University of California at Berkeley and has served as senior ecologist for the International Union for the Conservation of Nature. His book *Environmental Conservation* has gone through four editions; he is also the author of *The Destruction of California* (1965) and *The Last Horizon* (1963).

CARVILLE EARLE is professor and chair of geography at Miami University in Oxford, Ohio. He received his doctorate in geography from the University of Chicago. His writings include *The Evolution of a Tidewater Settlement System: All Hallow's Parish, Maryland* (1975) and *Geographical Inquiry and American Historical Problems* (forthcoming).

CLAYTON R. KOPPES has a doctorate in history from the University of Kansas. He is presently Houck Professor of Humanities and chairman of the history department at Oberlin College in Ohio. He served as president of the American Society for Environmental History, 1985–6. His major writings include *Hollywood Goes to War: How Politics, Profits, and Propaganda Shaped World War Two Movies* (1987) and *JPL and the American Space Program: A History of the Jet Propulsion Laboratory* (1982).

Contributors

ARTHUR F. McEVOY is associate professor of history at Northwestern University, Evanston, Illinois. He has a doctorate in history from the University of California at San Diego and is completing a law degree at Stanford University. His writings include *The Fisherman's Problem: Ecology and Law in the California Fisheries, 1850–1980* (1986).

RICHARD P. TUCKER is professor of history at Oakland University, Rochester, Michigan, and adjunct professor in the School of Natural Resources, University of Michigan, Ann Arbor. He has a doctorate in history from Harvard University. He is the author of *Ranade and the Roots of Indian Nationalism* (1972) and coeditor of *Global Deforestation and the Nineteenth-Century World Economy* (1983).

GUSTAF UTTERSTRÖM is a native of Sweden and holds advanced graduate degrees from the University of Stockholm. His dissertation, published in 1957, dealt with agricultural laborers in Sweden. Subsequent writings, all available in his native language, include studies of Swedish economic and social conditions (1977) and of orphans and orphanages in Stockholm (1978).

DOUGLAS R. WEINER is assistant professor of history at the University of Arizona, Tucson. He holds a doctorate in history from Columbia University, where he studied Russian science and conservation. His writings include *Models of Nature: Conservation, Ecology, and Cultural Revolution* (1988).

TIMOTHY C. WEISKEL has a doctorate from Oxford University, where he was a Rhodes Scholar and a student of social anthropology. He has taught at Yale and Williams; currently he holds a Luce postdoctoral fellowship at Harvard University, Cambridge, Massachusetts. His previous writings include *French Colonial Rule and the Baule Peoples: Resistance and Collaboration, 1889–1911* (1980).

RICHARD G. WILKINSON was educated at the Reading Technical College and the London School of Economics. He also has received a masters degree at the University of Pennsylvania. His major works include *Poverty and Progress: An Ecological Perspective on Economic Development* (1973).

DONALD WORSTER is Jack E. Meyerhoff Professor of American Environmental Studies at Brandeis University, Waltham, Massachusetts. He has a doctorate from Yale University. He served as president of the American Society for Environmental History and is coeditor of Studies in Environment and History, Cambridge University Press. His writings include *Rivers of Empire: Water, Aridity, and the Growth of the American West* (1985), *Dust Bowl: The Southern Plains in the 1930s* (1979), and *Nature's Economy: A History of Ecological Ideas* (1977, 1985).

Index

Abel, Wilhelm, 71–2
Abidjan (village, Ivory Coast), 155–6, 159
aborigines, 106, 107, 110, 111–13, 116–17
Academy of Sciences (Soviet Union), 254,
257–8, 259, 265, 266; Biological
Research Center, 263; I. M. Sechenov
Institute of Evolutionary Physiology, 264;
Institute of Geography, 268
acceleration phase (long waves), 179, 181
acid rain, 281
Adams, Robert, 37
Africa, 29, 37, 142; Europeans in, 104–5;
planter class, 147, 148; see also Ivory
Coast (Africa)
African Environmental Network, 287
agrarian epistemology, 189–90
agrarian reform: and destructive occupance,
198–200; scientific, 178, 189–90, 191,
192, 198–9, 200, 205, 208, 209–10
agricultural experimentation/innovation:
diffusion of, 189–90, 191, 202, 205–6,
208–9; ecologically adaptive (U.S. South),
191, 195–8, 199, 200; and environmental
change, 182–4, 191–2; indigenous (Ivory
Coast), 163, 164, 165, 166–8; local (U.S.
South), 178, 190, 191, 192–3, 201, 205,
209–10; long-wave depression, 184–7,
191; and macrohistorical rhythms,
179–92
agricultural systems, 171n53; Ivory Coast,
143, 151–2; U.S. South, 176, 177–8,
191–3, 204, 205–8
agriculture, 5, 6–7, 97, 106–7, 295, 301;
change in, 12–13; climate and, 40–1;

history, 25–7, 29, 32–3; intensified, 151;
science, 282; settled (India), 118, 119–20,
121, 126, 139–40; technological
innovation in, 29–30
Ahlmann, Hans W., 43, 44
Albright, Horace M., 238
All-Russian Society for Conservation
(VOOP), 254, 256, 257, 262, 264,
269–70; cooptation of, 258–60, 270
Amazon Basin, 33
America, 37; see also United States
American society, critique of, 175–6, 178,
183, 246
Americas (the), discovery of, 3–4
Angola, 105
Angoulvant, Gabriel, 165, 166
Animal Liberation (Singer), 264
animals, 142, 292; domesticated, 109–10,
116; in European expansion overseas,
107–11, 116–17; study of cruel behavior
toward, 263–4
Annales (journal), 291
Arctic Ocean, 41
Argentina, 9, 106, 114, 115; European
immigrants to, 104, 107
Ariyaratna, A. P., 286
Army Corps of Engineers (U.S.), 248, 249
Asia, 15, 28, 29, 37, 104
Assam (India): forest depletion, 118–40;
plantations, immigrants, deforestation,
121–8
Assam Forest Department, 124, 125–6, 127
Astaf'ev, Viktor, 265
atmosphere, 5, 288

Index

Chipko ("Hug-a-Tree") movement, 286–7
Chivilikhin, Vladimir, 265
Christensen, Aksel E., 74–5
cinchona, 134–5
Cincinnati, Ohio, 240
civilization, 17, 33, 277, 288; early, 37, 38
Clean Air Act (U.S.), 225
Cleghorn, Hugh, 137, 139
climate, 5, 38; and economic change, 52–4;
    India, 119, 120
climate theory, 39–40, 41–8, 49, 55–6; in
    Mediterranean, 71–4
climatic fluctuations, 280; and population
    problems, 39–79
*Climatic Variations in Historic and
    Prehistoric Time* (Pettersson), 41–2
climatology, 294
Clow, A., 95
Clozel (governor, Ivory Coast), 165
coal, 86–7, 88–9; substituted for firewood,
    81, 83–5, 91, 92
coal mines, 85–6
Cochin (Princely State, India), 131, 138
cocoa industry (Ivory Coast), 146, 147,
    163–5, 167–8, 169
Cocoyoc Declaration, 283–4
coffee industry: India, 121, 133–7; Ivory
    Coast, 146, 147, 165, 168, 169
Collinson, Peter, 76
Columbus, Christopher, 3–4, 5, 7, 19
commercial centers (Ivory Coast), 155–7
Commission for Zapovedniki, 257–8
Companies Act (England), 135–6
competition, 217, 221, 228
Conklin, Harold, 300
conservation: modern, 219; Progressive Era,
    226, 228, 229, 233–4, 236, 238, 239,
    241, 243, 250, 272; in Soviet Union,
    252–73; U.S., 230–51
Conservation Department (Soviet Union),
    254
conservation movement, 269–70, 281–2;
    politicization of, 285; Soviet Union,
    252–6, 270–1; U.S., 230–1, 233–5, 251,
    271–3
constructive occupance, 178, 208–9
continental climate, 48, 49–50, 54, 64, 72,
    74, 76
contract labor, 134
Coolidge administration, 238
cotton belt (U.S. South), 178, 189;

agricultural practice in, 191–2, 201–8,
    209
cotton gin, 201
cotton industry, 13, 92–4; Ivory Coast,
    163; U.S. South, 178, 190
cotton specialization, eastern cotton belt
    (U.S. South), 205–8, 209
Crane Foundation, 270
"creative destruction," 184
crop diffusion into Africa, 143, 161–9
crop failures, 70, 73, 74, 76, 77; climate
    and, 41, 51–3, 55, 57, 60, 61–6, 67, 68,
    71
crop production, 15; India, 119, 120
crop rotation, 178, 186; cotton belt, U.S.
    South, 192, 201–5, 206, 207, 209
cruelty, phenomenon of, 263–4
cultigens, exogenous, Africa, 152, 161–3
cultivation, 27, 28, 29, 33; continuous,
    199; shifting, 194, 195, 197, 198, 209
cultural core, 300–1
cultural ecology, 300
cultural-esthetic-ethical approach, Soviet
    conservation movement, 253, 255, 258
cultural materialism, 300–1
Cultural Revolution (Soviet Union), 255,
    272
culture(s), 11, 149, 293; created by people,
    298; and development, 284; and
    ecosystems, 298–302, 304–5
cyclones, 54–5, 65, 72

Daly, Herman, 17
dam projects (U.S.), 241–2, 243, 248, 249
Daniels, Joseph, 236
Darby, H. C., 306
Darien (colony), 105
Darwin, Charles, 103, 106, 108, 111,
    114–15, 294
"De l'influence de l'homme sur la terre"
    (Woeikof), 16
Death Valley National Monument (U.S.),
    239
deceleration phase (long wave), 179, 181,
    182, 189, 190
deforestation: Assam (India), 121–8, 139;
    Kerala (India), 128–40
democracy, 285; in environmental use,
    235–7, 242
demographic change, 10; effects of
    technology on, 23–5

329

Index

demographic growth, 4; ecological impact of, 9–10, 14; European, 104–17; and social organization, 36–8

demographic trends, 8–10; as adaptive factor, 23, 24–5; divergent, 38; effects on environment, 27–8; and nonagricultural technology, 34–6

Denmark, 46, 57, 66–7; climate in, 47–8, 60

depression(s), 39, 124, 179, 183, 197; climate and, 37, 51–3, 55–6; see also Great Depression

depression phase (long-wave), 179, 181, 183, 188–9, 190, 191, 192, 198, 200, 205, 208; and reappraisal of agrarian practice, 192–3; as source of agricultural innovation, 184–7

Derby, Abraham, 84

Des epochs de la nature (Buffon), 6–7

Deserts on the March (Sears), 16

"Destructive Exploitation in Modern Colonial Expansion" (Sauer), 16

destructive occupance, 183; agrarian reform and Chesapeake tobacco economy, 198–200; U.S. South, 175–8, 191, 201, 205, 207–8, 210

development: bias toward, 232, 234; approaches to, 283–4; and conservation, 281–2; grass-roots, 286–7; population pressure and, 13; scientific (Soviet Union), 242; see also sustainable development

directional migration, 152

diseases, 38, 143; European, 111–13; see also epidemics

disjunctive migration, 152

diversification, agricultural production, 178, 198, 201–5, 209

division of labor, 34, 149

Domesday Survey, 45

Dorovatovskii, Nikolai Sergeevich, 260

Dorst, Jean, 16

Dougan, Morgan, 165–6, 167

drought, 50, 55, 63, 65, 66, 74, 280

druzhina movement (Soviet Union), 260–4, 265

Dubos, Rene, 5–6

Dutch East India Company, 151

earth: in capitalist ethos, 11; ecological impact of humans on, 17; human transformation of, 6–8; living resources of, 292; understanding of, 5; vulnerable, 3–20; see also nature

East Greenland Current, 41

East India Company, 94, 123, 135

East Pakistan, 126, 127

Echo Park Dam, 250, 251

ecodevelopment (concept), 283, 284

eco-history, 142nl, 145–6

ecological consequences: of agricultural innovation diffusion, 189–90; of separating man from nature, 213, 217, 223, 226

ecological neutrality, 182, 183

ecological school, 299–301

ecological transformation (Ivory Coast), 143, 145–6, 160–71; elements of, 148–71; political form and, 146, 148

Ecological Transition, The (Bennett), 299

Ecologist, The, 279–80

ecology, viii, 149, 216, 229, 294–5; awareness of, 282; and capitalism, 12; and economy, 301–2; and esthetic conservation, 246–7, 248; ideas and, 304–5; market and, 216–17, 222; study of, in Soviet conservation movement, 252, 255, 256, 271

economic change, 14, 15, 17; climate and, 52–6, 59–66, 70–7; and conservation (U.S.), 251; India, 119

economic crises, cyclic, 178

economic growth, 4, 17; and conservation, 248; and environment, 230; long-wave, 187–9; resource depletion and, 217–18; S-shaped/logistic curve, 181, 187

economic system(s): and English industrial revolution, 80, 97–9; India, 120

economy (the), 5; centrally planned, 284; and conservation, 282; and conservation movement in Soviet Union, 253, 255, 265–6, 267; ecology and, 97, 301–2; Ivory Coast, 167–8; U.S., 213; world, 10, 277–8, 279

ecosystem conversion, Ivory Coast, 168–71

ecosystem people, 277, 278, 279

ecosystems, 15, 142, 296–8, 299; humans in harmony with, 304–5

education, Ivory Coast, 158, 159–60

efficiency issues, U.S. conservation, 230–51

Efron, K. M., 260

Egypt, 37

Index

Ehrlich, Paul, 16
Ellen, Roy, 299
Endangered Species Act, 225
Enequist, Gerd, 57–8
energy needs, sources, 281, 282, 300
Engels, Friedrich, 12, 92–3
England, 47–8, 72, 78; climate in, 45–6, 52, 53, 55, 58, 75–6; industrial revolution, 80–99
environment: Americans' approach to, 232; carrying capacity of, 23, 27–8, 29–30, 31–2; degradation of, 5–6, 16–17, 300–1, 305; effects of demographic trends on, 27–8, 38; impact of innovation diffusion on, 183, 184; of the past, 294–8; in primitive societies, 23–38; and social change, 216; understanding of, 216
environmental change, 8, 9–10, 18, 229, 297; agricultural innovation and macrohistorical rhythms in, 179–92; and agricultural innovation/technology, 26–7, 182–4, 191–2; capitalism and, 14–15
environmental history, vii–viii, 5, 289–307; cross-disciplinary cooperation in, 305–7; levels/issues/questions in, 293, 295; material of, 292–3; U.S. South, 208–10
environmental law, 224, 225, 228, 229
Environmental Liaison Centre, 287
environmental management, 246–7
environmental movement, 139, 231, 251, 281–2, 290–1; Soviet Union, 264–8
epidemics, 24, 26, 46, 63–4, 67, 72, 73, 77, 156, 158; caused by European pathogens overseas, 111–13
erosion, 74, 170, 189, 288; India, 137, 138–9; U.S. South, 175, 178, 190, 191, 194, 195, 199, 201, 205, 207, 209
Estonia, 269
Europe: in African trade, 150–1; agriculture in, 40–1; climate in, 41, 44, 46–7, 48–9, 59, 60, 65, 73, 74–5; climatic fluctuations and population problems in, 39–40, 42, 54, 55; population increase in, 23, 25–7, 71–3, 78; subsistence technology in, 25–7
Europeans, 4, 7, 14, 15; effect on Africa, 145–6; overseas migration of, 103–17, 118, 120; population increase of, 8–9, 13
evolution, 18; in agricultural change, 32; human, 300

export economy: Ivory Coast, 146, 148, 165, 169, 171

factories, 11, 13, 97–8
fallow, 151; in land-rotation system, 195, 197; length of, 25–6, 27–8, 29, 30, 31, 33, 35, 36
famine(s), 9, 15, 40n2, 52, 60–2, 65–6, 69, 70, 73, 77, 119, 158
Farewell to Matyora (Rasputin), 265
faunal shifts, Ivory Coast, 141, 142, 161–71
Febvre, Lucien, 291, 306
Fehlsiedlungstheorie, 48
fertilizers, 189, 192; and cotton specialization, 205–8, 209; with tobacco, 193–4, 199
firearms, trade in, 150–1, 152
First Five-Year Plan (Soviet Union), 255, 256
First International Conference for the Protection of Nature, 254
Fish and Wildlife Service (U.S.), 244
fisheries, 215; management of, 219–20; North Sea, 217
Fishery Conservation and Management Act, 225
fishing industry, 95, 153; *see also* California fishing industry
Fitzhugh, George, 200
Flannery, Kent V., 32
Flohn, Hermann, 50–1, 58
floods, 73, 137, 281
floral shifts: Ivory Coast, 141, 142, 161–71
food chains, human in, 293
food gathering, 27, 29, 30, 32
food production: in Africa, 161–3; technology of, and demographic trends, 23, 24
forest conservation, 287
forest fallow, 25–6, 27–8, 29
forest management, 219–20, 241, 244–5, 249
forest reserves, India, 133, 139
Forest Service (U.S.), 234, 239, 245, 247, 248–9
forestry: India, 120; U.S., 233, 236
forests: Assam, 121–8; conservation of (England), 82–3; depletion of Indian, under British imperialism, 118–40; Ivory Coast, 169–71; Kerala (India), 128–40

Index

Index

hunting-gathering communities, 25, 31–2, 36, 301
hunting societies (Soviet Union), 254
Huntington, E., 54
Hurst, James Willard, 232
hydroelectricity projects, 236, 239, 241–2, 243

Iceland, 77; climate in, 40, 41–4; corn growing in, 41, 42, 43, 45, 53–4
Ickes, Harold L., 240, 241, 243, 244, 246, 247, 248, 249, 250
ideas, 302–3; as ecological agents, 304–5
ideology, 200, 229, 302–7
immigrants: Assam (India), 121–8; see also Europeans, overseas migration of
Imperial Russian Geographical Society, 254
Imperial Society for Responsible Hunting, 254
import/export economy, Ivory Coast, 147, 155, 166
India, 15, 104; forest depletion under British imperialism, 118–40; independence, 118, 119, 138, 139
Indian Forest Service, 119
industrial revolution, see England, industrial revolution
industrial societies, 303; culturally maladaptive, 305; new environmental efforts in, 287–8
industrialism, 10, 14, 18, 19, 79
industrialization: England, 81, 98–9; global effects of, 280–1; Soviet Union, 269, 272–3
infrastructure development, 181, 232, 248; Ivory Coast, 147, 155–7, 166
innovation(s): laboursaving, 98; lag between, and installation, 181–2; see also agricultural experimentation/innovation
innovation diffusion, 183, 184, 186–7; lag in, 181–2; S-shaped/logistic curves, 181, 182, 187–8, 191, 198, 209
Inquiry into the Human Prospect, An (Heilbroner), 16
Interagency State Committee for Conservation (Soviet Union), 254
interdependence, 5, 219
Interior, Department of (U.S.), 242, 243, 244, 247, 248, 249, 250; Grazing Service, 245–6
International Biological Program, 270

international coalitions, 287
International Monetary Fund, 284
international power structure, 284–5, 287–8
International Union for the Conservation of Nature and Natural Resources (IUCN), 269–70, 282
Inuit, 287
investment: in long-wave theory, 181, 183; small-scale, continuous, 183
iron industry, 69, 84
irrigation, 36, 235–6, 244
irrigation empires (ancient), 300
Isle Royale National Park (U.S.), 247
Italy, 9
Ivory Coast (Africa): ecological transformation of, 141–71; floral and faunal shifts in, 141, 142, 161–71; political continuity in, 148, 160, 171; political control of, 143–8; political independence of, 148, 159, 168–9; population dynamics in, 158–61

Jacks, Graham, 16
Jackson Hole National Monument (U.S.), 248
Jacobs, Jane, 243
James, Henry, 104
Jamestown, Virginia, 110
Japan, 9
Jarman, L. W., 206–7
Jefferson, Thomas, 109–10, 198
Jevons, William Stanley, 51
Josselyn, John, 113, 115

Kalahari Desert Bushmen, 31
Kashkarov, Daniil Nikolaevich, 256
Kavtaradze, Dmitrii Mikhailovich, 263, 270
kelping industry, 95
Kerala (India), deforestation, 128–40
Kerala Forest Department, 138
Keyes, Ken, 281
Keynes, John Maynard, 78–9
Khimiia i zhizn' (Chemistry and Life) (journal), 266
Khortitsa Society of the Defenders of Nature, 254
Khruschev, Nikita, 258, 260, 261, 264, 269, 272
Kimble, George, 45–6

Index

Index

Marine Mammals Protection Act, 225
maritime climate, 54, 55
market (the), 10–11, 12; and conservation (U.S.), 242; and ecology, 216–17, 224; global, 283; and lawmaking, 221, 223; and management of natural resources, 234–5; and subsistence system, 35
market economy, 12, 14, 119, 140
Marsh, George Perkins, 7–8, 9, 10, 14, 16, 18
Marshall, Robert, 246
Martin, Paul, 278
Martyr, Peter, 3–4
Marx, Karl, 12, 17, 301
Marxists, Marxism, 12, 17, 301
material culture, 298–302
materials substitution and English industrial revolution, 81–5, 90, 91–7
Mather, Stephen, 238
maximum economic yield (MEY), 224
maximum sustainable yield (MSY), 220, 224
Meadows, Dennis, 16
Meadows, Donella, 16
Mediterranean: climate, 76–7; population increase, 69–74
Méditerranée et le monde méditerranéen . . . , La (Braudel), 69
Meggers, Betty, 300
Meinig, Donald, 306
Mellon, Andrew W., 238
mental/intellectual realm: and environment, 293; *see also* consciousness; ideas
Mesoamerica, 32–3, 37
Mesopotamia, 28, 29, 32, 37
Mexico, 104, 111
microorganisms in European expansion overseas, 107, 111–13, 116
Middle Ages, 40n2, 53, 78; agriculture in, 41; climate in, 42–3, 77; climatic fluctuations in, 50–1, 54, 55, 56
migration(s), 27, 74; forced, 38; to Ivory Coast, 151–2, 159; of Western Europeans, 103–17; *see also* frontier migration, U.S. South
military technology, 23, 24
Mill, John Stuart, 13–14
Minhas, Marquis das, 163
Mitterrand, François, 147, 148
modern history, climatic fluctuations and population problems in early, 39–79

Mongoloids, 104
monoculture, 201, 202; cotton (U.S. South), 206–7; India, 133, 134, 137
Monterin, U., 71n95
Moran, Emilio, 299
Morgan, Arthur, 241, 242
mortality and population dynamics (Ivory Coast), 142, 158
mortality rate, primitive societies, 23, 24, 38
Moscow Society of Naturalists (MOIP), 260–2, 263
Moscow State University (MGU), 261, 263
Motovilov, G. P., 259
Muir, John, 16, 237, 238, 252, 273
Müller, K., 51
multicropping, 27, 29
Munro, John Daniel, 135
Murdock, William, 96

Nabokov, Vladimir, 103
Napoleonic Wars, 89, 90, 98, 99
Nash, Roderick, 237, 291
nation-state, 289, 290
national forests (U.S.), 234, 235, 236, 238, 245
National Park Service (U.S.), 237–8, 247
national parks, 214; Soviet Union, 252, 269; U.S., 239, 247–8, 250–1
National Resources Committee (U.S.), 241
nationalism; and conservation, 243; and history, 289; Ivory Coast, 147; Russian, 264, 265–6; U.S., 198–9
Native Americans, 109, 227, 231, 278; epidemics, 111, 112; hunting/fishing rights, 287
native peoples, 4, 5, 9; *see also* aborigines
"Native Princes" (India), 119
natural resource problems, 212–14, 215–29; commons tragedy as model of, 215–19; laissez-faire view of, 216–19
natural resources: control and use of (U.S.), 231–3; depletion of (U.S.), 231, 277–8; destruction of, 285; management of, 219–20, 224, 228, 229, 241, 243, 244–6, 248–9; management of, British, in India, 118–19, 120, 139–40; management of, efficiency, equity, and esthetic schools, 233–8
nature, 5, 8; changeableness of, 39, 77–8; and civilization, 17; as commodity, 237;

335

Index

nature (*cont.*)
    concepts of, 253; destruction of, 5;
    human manipulation of, 219; human
    relation to, 213, 217, 223, 225, 226, 229,
    292–3, 301; as idea, 302–3; as
    instrument of power, 18–19; science and,
    18; understanding of, 293, 303–4
nature–culture relation, 211–29, 300–2,
    305
nature reserves, 287; Soviet Union, 254,
    255, 258, 268–9
nature/society relation in Soviet
    conservation movement, 271
nature-spirit-culture triangle, 279
Naumov, N. P., 261
Near East, 37, 70
Nehru, Jawaharlal, 139
Neolithic Revolution, 32, 116
Neronov, Valerii Mikhailovich, 270
Nesmeianov, A. N., 257–8
Netting, Robert, 299, 300
New Deal, 178, 183, 236, 240–1, 243, 244,
    245, 246, 248
New Economic Policy (NEP) (Soviet Union),
    255
new international economic order, 284
New South Wales, 108
New World, 4, 5, 7, 8; migration to, 9
New Zealand, 111, 112, 115, 278;
    European animals in, 108–9, 110–11;
    European immigrants in, 104, 107, 116
Newell-Weaver agreement, 249
Newlands, Francis G., 235, 244
Ngokro (village, Ivory Coast), 157, 158
Nicaragua, 284
Nigeria, 104
Nikolaev, A. G., 259
Nilgiri Hills (India), 121
Nkrumah, Kwame, 147
Nonet, Philippe, 227–8
North America, 9, 15; European
    immigrants to, 104–5, 106–7; European
    plants in, 113–14, 115
North Temperate Zone, 104
Norway, 62, 66–7; climate, 41, 47–8, 60;
    decline of, 46–8, 53–4, 77
Notes on Virginia (Jefferson), 198
nuclear annihilation: threat of, 18–19,
    279–80
nuclear power, 243, 282

Occupational Health and Safety Act, 225
oceanic circulation, 41
Odum, Eugene, 297
oil industry, 236, 238
Okhrana prirody (Conservation) (journal),
    254–5
Old World, 9
Olympic National Park (U.S.), 247, 248,
    250
Only One Earth (conference report), 5–6
Oppenheimer, J. Robert, 19
optimum yield (OY) standard, 225, 227
Orans, Martin, 35
Osborn, Fairfield, 16
Our Plundered Planet (Osborn), 16
out-migration, 8, 9, 10, 142; Africa, 143,
    158; U.S. South, 192, 194–5
overexploitation, 277–8
ozone layer, 281

Pakistan, 119, 124, 127, 139
paleoecologists, 297
palm oil trade, 143, 144, 147, 152–3, 154,
    164
Panama, 287
papermaking, 95–6
paradigm shifts, 185, 304
Parti Démocratique de la Côte d'Ivoire
    (P.D.C.I.), 147, 148
pathogens, 292; in European expansion
    overseas, 107, 111–13, 116
peasants, 35, 36; and deforestation (India),
    121, 122, 125, 126, 127, 128, 140
Peermade Planters Association, 136
People's Commissariat of Education (Soviet
    Union), 254
People's University for Conservation, 268
perception, 302–7
Person, Yves, 150n11
Persson, Lars, 61
Peru, 104, 111; anchoveta fishery in,
    222n33
Pest og Prisfall i Senmiddalalderen
    (Schreiner), 46–8
pesticides, 5, 282
Petrov, Fedor Nikolaevich, 260
Pettersson, Otto, 41–2
phenology, 48
Philip II, king of Spain, 150

Index

Index

radiative migration, 152
railroads, 15; and English industrial
 revolution, 89, 90–1; Ivory Coast, 155–6
rainfall, 41, 48, 49, 53, 54–5, 62, 65, 73,
 74, 76
range management, 244, 245–6, 249
Rape of the Earth, The (Jacks and Whyte),
 16
Rappaport, Roy, 304–5
Rasputin, Valentin, 265
Reclamation, Bureau of (U.S.), 236, 238,
 239, 242, 248–9, 250; dams, 250
reclamation projects (U.S.), 235–6, 239,
 244
recreation and conservation (Soviet Union),
 252, 268–9, 271
Redwoods National Park (U.S.), 247–8, 250
Reimers, Fedov Eduardovich, 261
religious beliefs, 279, 304–5
research and development, 19
Reserved Forests (India), 139
resource base, 14, 171, 230
resource depletion, 171; and economic
 progress, 217–18; as social problem, 228
resource extraction/allocation, British rule in
 India, 118, 120
resource regulation (U.S.), 233
resource scarcity, 12, 301; and English
 industrial revolution, 80, 81–2, 85, 90,
 92, 93, 96, 97–9
Rich Land, Poor Land (Chase), 241
Richards, John, 15
risk (economic), 188, 191
risk assessment in agricultural innovation,
 188, 189
Road to Survival (Vogt), 16
roads, 34, 88; India, 133, 134; *see also*
 transportation
Rodionenko, G. I., 260
Rogers, Thorold, 40n2
Rolt, L. T. C., 90
Rome, 54
Roosevelt, Franklin D., 239, 242, 248
Roosevelt, Theodore, 16, 219, 233, 237,
 239, 243
Rostow, Walt, 181, 182
rubber industry: India, 137–8; Ivory Coast,
 147, 166
Ruffin, Edmund, 200
Russia, 9, 15, 107; *see also* Soviet Union
Russian Socialist Federated Soviet Republic

(RSFSR) Union of Hunters and
 Fishermen, 267

Sahlins, Marshall, 300
St. Jean de Crèvecoeur, Michel-Guillaume,
 109
salmon industry (U.S.), 227, 244, 249
Sanders, William T., 32–3
sardine fishing, 221–2, 226
Sarvodaya movement, 286
Sauer, Carl, 16, 306
Save-the-Redwoods League, 247
Savery, Thomas, 86
Scandinavia, 60, 78, 79; climate in, 39, 40,
 41, 59, 65
Schell, Jonathan, 18
Schove, D. J., 59
Schreiner, Johan, 40n2, 46–8
Schumpeter, Joseph, 179, 181, 184
Science, 18–19, 304; and management of
 natural resources, 219, 220, 225, 226,
 234; in Soviet conservation movement,
 253, 255
scientific method, 303–4
Scientific Revolution, 19
scientists (Soviet Union), direction of
 conservation movement, 252, 256–7,
 261, 265, 266, 267, 268–9, 271, 272,
 273
Sears, Paul, 16
sedimentation, 170, 190, 199–200, 207
self-reliance, local/national, 284, 285
self-sufficiency, 87, 89, 91
Semenov-tian-shanskii, Andrei Petrovich,
 256
Semenov-tian-shanskii, Veniamin, 256
Semenova, Ksenia, 263–4
settlement patterns, 142, 143; Ivory Coast,
 149–58
Shvarts, Stanislav Semenovich, 271
Sicily, 70
Sierra Club, 238
Silcox, Ferdinand A., 244–5, 249
Silent Spring (Carson), 16
Singer, Peter, 264
slave trade, 37, 143, 150, 151, 152
slavery: Chesapeake tobacco economy, 194,
 195–9, 200, 209; U.S. South, 176, 177,
 204, 210
slaves, 25, 36, 143, 153, 163, 185
smallpox, 111, 112

338

Index

Smith, Adam, 11, 34
Smith, Philip E. L., 32
social anthropologists, 142
social change and conservation movement (Soviet Union), 266–7, 270–1
Social Contract theory, 214, 271
social Darwinism, 214
social ecology, 271
social history, viii, 290
social organization, 35, 303; demographic growth and, 36–8
social policy: conservation and (U.S.), 242; in conservation movement (Soviet Union), 263–4
social relations, 213, 293, 304; in capitalism, 12; and culture, 300; and human/environment relation, 279
social thought and market behavior/ecology relationship, 217, 222
Société Coloniale, 165
society: and nature, 271; science in, 304
Society for the Study of Local Lore (Soviet Union), 255, 256
soil, 151n15, 170–1, 291
soil chemistry, 206, 294
soil conservation, U.S. South, 177, 178
soil depletion, 152, 189, 202; U.S. South, 175, 176, 190, 191, 192, 194, 195, 199, 204, 205
South (U.S.): agricultural practice, 191–2; as archetype of destructive occupance, 175–8; environmental history in macrohistorical context, 208–10
South Africa, 9, 104, 106
South America, 115
South Temperate Zone, 104
Soviet Union, 4; conservation in, 252–73; reform in, 273
Spain, 70, 73, 74
specialization (agriculture), 34, 35; U.S. South, 192, 204, 205–8
species extinction, 17, 142, 278
Sri Lanka, 285–6
Stalin, Joseph, 255, 258, 272
Stanchinskii, Vladimir Vladimirovich, 255
Standard Oil, 236
state: and conservation movement (Soviet Union), 273; see also government(s)
"State of Environmental History, The" (Nash), 291
steam engine (power), 85–7, 90–1

Steward, Julian, 299–300
Stoel, Thomas, 282–3
Straus, Michael, 249
Strong, Maurice, 283
student movement (Soviet Union), 260–4, 267, 270, 271, 272
subsistence, 23, 98, 300, 301; ideas and, 303
subsistence systems, 130, 167, 298; crop rotation and, 202–3, 204; demographic trends and, 25–8, 35, 36, 37; labor productivity and, 30–3; population pressure and, 25–7, 28–30, 31–2, 33
Sukachev, Vladimir Nikolaevich, 257–8, 260
Sundbärg, Gustav, 68
Sundquist, S., 68
surplus(es), agricultural, 30–1, 35, 36
sustainable development, 282–3, 288
sustained-yield model, 220–2, 224, 229, 233
Sweden, 39, 46, 47, 71, 73; agricultural conditions, 68–9; climate, 48, 52, 57–8, 76; crop failures, 60–6; golden age, 56–7; plague, 66–7
swidden farming, 151, 296
Syndicat Agricole Africain, 168
system, defined, 296n2
systems: integrated, 148–9; in nature, 296, 297; self-equilibrating, 296

Tahiti, 111
takeoff phase (long wave), 179, 181, 191
Taliev, Valerii Ivanovich, 254
Taylor, John, 199
Taylor Grazing Act (U.S.), 245
tea, 13
tea industry (India), 121, 122–5, 133, 135, 136, 137, 139
techno-environment(s), 300–1, 303, 304
technological change/innovation, 17, 79; in agriculture, 29–30; effects on population, 23–5; in English industrial revolution, 81, 83, 84, 85–7, 90–1, 94, 97–9; timing of, 84
technology(ies), 5, 15, 298, 300; agricultural, 31–2; demographic trends and, 34–6; and destructive occupance, 278; diffusion of, 30; domination of earth through, 11; faith in, 282; in

Index

Wallace, Henry A., 246
Wallerstein, Immanuel, 10
Ward, Barbara, 5–6
wars, 9, 24, 26, 37, 38, 124, 158, 288; and innovation diffusion, 189n17; Sweden, 68, 69
water resources (U.S.), 233, 237; (India), 137, 138–9
Watt, James, 87
Wealth of Nations, The (Smith), 11
"Weather and Harvest Cycles" (Beveridge), 51
weather fronts, 54, 55
Webb, Walter Prescott, 291
weeds in European expansion overseas, 103, 107, 113–16
Welsh, James, 132–3
"Wesen und geographische Verbreitung der Raubwirtschaft" (Friedrich), 16
Western civilization, 79
Western Ghats (India), 120, 121, 128
Westin, J., 58
White, Richard, 291
Whyte, R. O., 16
Wiebe, Georg, 81
wilderness, 7, 237–8, 247
wildlife depletion, 214, 288
wildlife management (U.S.), 221–3
Willett, H. C., 55–6
William of Malmesbury, 45

Williams, Michael, 306
Wilson, Woodrow, 236
Winthrop, John, 231
Woeikof, Alexander, 16
Woodwell, George, 292
woolen industry, 93–4
work, 293; in English industrial revolution, 97–8
World Conservation Strategy, 282
World War I, 124, 248
World War II, 126–7, 146, 243, 246, 248; effect on conservation movement (Soviet Union), 256–8
Wrigley, E. A., 88
writers (Russian), and conservation movement, 265–6
Wynaad plateau (India), 132–3, 134, 135

Yammoussou (village, Ivory Coast), 157–8
Yosemite National Park (U.S.), 234, 238, 247
Young, Arthur, 88
Young, T. Cuyler, Jr., 32
Yukon National Park (Canada), 287

Zalygin, Sergei, 265
zapovedniki (ecological reserves), 253–4, 256, 257, 258, 264, 268–9, 270, 272
zero population growth, 23, 24, 38

LIBRARY ST. MARY'S COLLEGE